CW01498963

CONTENTS

PART II
THE SOVIET ARMY AND NAVY IN THE COLD WAR AND BEYOND

# The Military History
# of the Soviet Union

Edited by

Robin Higham
and Frederick W. Kagan

palgrave

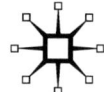
First published 2002 by PALGRAVE™
175 Fifth Avenue, New York, N.Y. 10010 and
Houndmills, Basingstoke, Hampshire, England RG21 6XS.
Companies and representatives throughout the world.

PALGRAVE is the new global publishing imprint of St. Martin's Press LLC
Scholarly and Reference Division and Palgrave Publishers Ltd. (formerly
Macmillan Press Ltd.).

ISBN 0-230-10839-3
ISBN 0-312-29412-3 (two volume set)

**Library of Congress Cataloging-in-Publication Data**
available from the Library of Congress.

A catalogue record for this book is available from the British Library.

Design by Letra Libre, Inc.

First edition: February 2002
10  9  8  7  6  5  4  3  2  1

Printed in the United States of America.

# ABOUT THE CONTRIBUTORS

*Christopher C. Lovett* holds a Ph.D. from Kansas State University and is an associate professor of Modern European History at Emporia State University. He has written articles on Soviet naval aviation, Vietnam, and the Second World War. Currently, Dr. Lovett is completing a history of the Russian and Soviet Naval air arm and of the Army-McCarthy Hearings.

*David R. Stone* received his Ph.D. in Russian history from Yale University in 1997. His dissertation on the origins of the Soviet military-industrial complex has been published as *Hammer and Rifle: The Militarization of the Soviet Union, 1926–1933* (Lawrence, KS, 2000). He has also published several articles on Soviet military and diplomatic history. He currently teaches at Kansas State University.

*Frederick W. Kagan* received his Ph.D. in Russian and Soviet military history from Yale University in 1995. He is the author of *The Military Reforms of Nicholas I: The Origins of the Modern Russian Army* (New York: St. Martin's Press, 1999), and co-author with Donald Kagan of *While America Sleeps: Self-Delusion, Military Weakness, and the Threat to Peace Today* (New York: St. Martin's Press, 2000), as well as numerous scholarly and defense-policy related articles. He is currently an associate professor at the United States Military Academy at West Point.

*John Erickson* is a Fellow, British Academy, Royal Society of Edinburgh, and Professor Emeritus, Honorary Fellow Defence Studies, University of Edinburgh, Scotland. Select publications: *Soviet High Command 1918–41, The Road to Stalingrad, The Road to Berlin, The Soviet Armed Forces 1918–92, A Research Guide, Barbarossa, The Axis and the Allies;* as well as studies in Russian military organization, theory, and doctrine.

*Mark O'Neill* received his Ph.D. in Modern Soviet/Russian History from Florida State University. His doctoral work focused on Soviet Air Force and Air Defense participation in the Korean Air War. O'Neill continues to work on the impact of Soviet air power on the Cold War, particularly technology transfers to the developing world. In addition to his research, he teaches a U.S. foreign policy course at Tallahassee Community College. Despite his professional focus on high performance technology, O'Neill prefers pedaling his bicycle around northwest Florida at something less than mach speeds.

*Mary R. Habeck* is an assistant professor of military history at Yale University. She has written on armor doctrine in the Soviet Union and Germany, technology in the First World War, and is the co-editor of a collection of essays on the Great War. She has recently finished a document collection on the Soviets in the Spanish Civil War, with Ronald Radosh (Yale University Press, 2001).

*Robert M. Ponichtera* received his Ph.D. in Modern East European History from Yale University in November 1995. His dissertation, "The Role of the Army in the Rebuilding of Polish Statehood, 1918–21," investigates the army's attempt to create a national identity among the troops passing through its ranks. His publications include articles on Polish military thought and the contribution of women to the fight for national independence. He also wrote volume six ("1914–17: The Eastern Front") of The Grolier Library of World War I.

*Robin Higham,* professor of Military History emeritus at Kansas State University, was editor of *Military Affairs* for twenty-one years and of *Aerospace Historian* for eighteen. He recently co-edited *Russian Aviation and Air Power* with John T. Greenwood and Von Hardesty.

*Scott McMichael* retired from the U.S. Army in 1996 as a Lieutenant Colonel. He has published widely on military history and Soviet military affairs in professional journals on both sides of the Atlantic. His books include *A Historical Perspective on Light Infantry,* published by the Combat Studies Institute (Leavenworth, KS, 1986) and *Stumbling Bear: Soviet Military Performance* in Afghanistan, published by Brassey's (UK) in 1991. He is currently employed by the Illinois Institute of Technology Research as a defense contractor developing future concepts for the U.S. Army.

*Stephen Blank* is Professor of Russian National Security Studies at the Strategic Studies Institute of the U.S. Army War College. Dr. Blank has been an Associate Professor of National Security Affairs at the Strategic Studies Institute since 1989. Dr. Blank's M.A. and Ph.D. are in Russian History from the University of Chicago. He has published over 170 articles and monographs on Soviet/Russian military and foreign policies. His most recent book is *Imperial Decline: Russia's Changing Role in Asia* (Duke University Press, 1997), which he co-edited with Professor Alvin Rubinstein of the University of Pennsylvania. Dr. Blank is also the author of a study of the Soviet Commissariat of Nationalities, *The Sorcerer as Apprentice: Stalin's Commissariat of Nationalities* (Greenwood Publishing Group, 1994), and the co-editor of *The Soviet Military and the Future* (Greenwood Publishing Group, 1992).

*Steven J. Zaloga* is a senior analyst with the aerospace consulting firm, Teal Group Corp., where he covers missile technology and international arms transfers for clients in the aerospace industry and government. He also serves as an adjunct staff member with the Institute for Defense Analyses, a federal think-tank. Mr. Zaloga is an author of over fifty books on military technology and military history including *Target America: The Soviet Union and the Nuclear Arms Race, 1945–64* from Presidio Press and *Soviet Air Defense Missiles: Design, Development and Tactics* from Jane's Information Group. He writes extensively on military subjects for defense journals, and is a special correspondent for *Jane's Intelligence Review.* He serves on the executive board of the *Journal of Slavic Military Studies* and the New York Military Affairs Symposium.

*William E. Odom,* Lt Gen, USA, Retired, is a professor (adjunct) at Yale University and a senior fellow at the Hudson Institute. He is the author of *The Collapse of the Soviet Military,* among many other works.

# LIST OF MAPS

CHAPTER 1

# INTRODUCTION

*Robin Higham and Frederick W. Kagan*

THERE ARE THEMES RUNNING THROUGHOUT THE MILITARY HISTORY of Russia and the Soviet Union that go back to the days when Mongols in the thirteenth century threatened Mother Russia. The first of these has been geography. From the late nineteenth century to the advent of the Commonwealth of Independent States (the CIS), Russia has stretched from Europe and the Baltic Sea in the west to the Bering Strait in the east. From north to south it extends from the Arctic tundra and forests to the Muslim mountain barrier all along the borderlands from the Black Sea to China. The country has also suffered from multiple coastlines on various seas that permanently divided naval forces and never let them become paramount in Russian policymaking. The vast country even under the Soviets contained a daunting mixture of nationalities, languages, and cultures. Conquest and control were made easier by the development of communications in the twentieth century, though even these were handicapped by vast distances, climatic changes, thin population and tiny markets, limited industrialization, and lack of capital before 1921.

The drive to rectify these disadvantages and to make use of plentiful natural resources was started by Peter the Great (1690–1725). His efforts to westernize the country introduced tensions between modernizers (or westernizers) and slavophiles, which have lasted into the twenty-first century. Parallel to this struggle was that between the autocrat of all the Russias and the nobles, merchants and entrepreneurs, and the peasants. Then, too, there was also the conflict between local entities and St. Petersburg.

From the military point of view, the size of the country and the tenuous-ness of communications meant that control of operations was difficult to im-possible. Moreover, the xenophobia and fear of the unknown made the Russians very suspicious of outsiders, whether German entrepreneurs within the capital or outside imperialists. Not only were there internal threats, but out-side powers such as Sweden, Poland, Ukraine, Austria, Prussia, Germany, and even France, not to mention the British in India playing "the great game," were perceived threats. All of these dangers led Russia to maintain immense armed forces—the largest army in Europe, for many decades—and multiple fleets. Such armaments were a constant threat to the state's fiscal health and accounted for many of the frictions between the nobility and the tsar, as well as those later between the bourgeoisie and the government over managerial efficiency.

What ultimately caused the medieval monarchical system to creak to the breaking point was the rapid rise of technology in the latter nineteenth century. Costs rose sharply, accompanied as they were not only by the need for technical skills from finances to manufacturing, but also by the require-ment for more educated military personnel from officers to privates and sailors. Merely the costs of re-equipping the million-man army was so nearly impossible that it called for a total rethinking of the foundations of the Russ-ian military. Not until the establishment of the Soviet Union were these dilemmas solved by the Communist autocracy, which imposed the Indus-trial Revolution upon the country with ruthless and bloody efficiency.

Russian relations with the West went back to the days of the Hansa in the sixteenth century and continued in the Teutonic-Slav wars of the seven-teenth through the nineteenth and twentieth centuries. If the Soviets loathed imperialism, the Romanovs had abhorred the French Revolution, even as they professed some interest in liberalism. Fear of the French Revo-lution was impressed upon the Russians by Napoleon's invasion and the burning of Moscow in 1812, followed by the Russian occupation of Paris with the victorious allies. A consequence of this was that the troops brought back unsettling ideas and had to be purged for the safety of the state. So an-other friction in the nineteenth century was between the slavophile suspi-cion of anything new and the need for technology transfer to enable Russian armies to face their potential and actual foes, as in the Crimean War of 1853–56. That at last made St. Petersburg realize that fundamental changes had to be made, leading War Minister D. A. Miliutin (1) to import for-eigners to run the Baltic Locomotive Works, which was to build a railway to Europe to avoid a Baltic blockade, (2) to modernize all arms, (3) to reform fiscal policy, and (4) to emancipate the serfs. At the same time, Russians moved both eastward and to the cities.

These migrations led to two conflicts that came to a head in 1905—the Russo-Japanese War and defeat, and the Revolution of that year—which brought glimmerings of both democracy and the Bolshevik Party.

In the nine years that elapsed before the outbreak of the fateful Great War, the government tried to reform doctrine and remake the Russian armed forces, but the guidance was not clear enough nor the finances strong enough to do what war plainly showed had been required. The general backwardness of the state could not be overcome in a mere nine years. The Russian Bear no longer had the power to hold enemies at leg's length.

All of the above has been described in detail by the authors in the companion volume, *The Military History of Tsarist Russia*. The road to Soviet Moscow had already begun under the Imperial Romanovs.

The Revolution of 1905 had boded ill for Russia and the world's largest army if the Motherland came under the strains of war under a weak Romanov. The year 1914 again brought those stresses. The effects on the battlefield from Tannenberg onward offended the middle class's sense of decent management and, together with the enormous economic disruptions occasioned by the prolonged war, led to the first of the 1917 revolutions. The weakness of the new regime, combined with its unfortunate determination to continue to fight the war against Germany, doomed it. The Bolsheviks, under V. I. Lenin's leadership, seized their chance in November to unseat this regime, kill the tsar and his family, and proclaim the new Soviet Socialist state.

Despite the Bolsheviks' determination to end the civil war, they found themselves fighting for five more years against defenders of the old regime, the Whites, who were supported by supplies and the armed forces of England, France, the United States, and Japan. The newly recreated state of Poland, what is more, took advantage of Russia's apparent weakness to attack in 1920. The new Soviet state was able to withstand all of these challenges, however, and by 1922 was able to settle down, continued rebellions in Central Asia notwithstanding, to the business of building communism and governing the transformed empire.

Once the wars of 1917–22 ended, Russo-German cooperation started. As the two major states that had lost the last war and remained outside the League of Nations and the society of "decent" states, Germany and Russia sought to combine their efforts to develop and field modern forces. The Soviets made available to the Germans facilities for air and ground studies at Fili and elsewhere, where both sides experimented with the new technologies of aircraft and tanks, as well as with chemical weapons. These joint activities did surprisingly little to bring the military operational techniques of Germany and Russia into accord, for the Germans began developing the concepts that would underlie *blitzkrieg,* while the Soviets developed the far more sophisticated theories of "deep battle."

The November 1917 Revolution occurred during that fleeting technological moment in Russian history when seizure of the railway stations and telegraph offices could paralyze the country. The 1917 Revolutions that truly did alter the political, economic, social, and ideological milieu, were another case of continuity and change. The old wars ended, but the new imperialist enemy arose and was fought by the armed services still officered by many tsarists and still manned by the peoples of Russia, now united in the Union of Soviet Socialist Republics. Under state direction and control, resources were mobilized for the predicted showdown with the capitalists. In particular, Soviet military industries received a great deal of emphasis in the early "Five Year Plans" that aimed, above all, to provide the military-industrial basis for large-scale conflict. Although the armament and re-armament of the Soviet armed forces was far from complete by the beginning of the war in 1941, the basis for its wartime mobilization had been laid.

So conscious were the Bolsheviks under Lenin and Trotskii of the need to be able to defeat enemies real or imagined, that they created a fortress state that Stalin inherited and managed as his sacred trust. The USSR needed external enemies such as Poland up to 1920 and internal ones, as in the Civil War of the 1920s, and in the purges of the armed forces beginning in 1937. Some of these cleansings were required for the safety of the state and some because it was necessary to retire the ineffective. But the conspirators of the Russian and Soviet state once in power always knew that others could follow in their footsteps—and were determined to use whatever methods, however brutal, to prevent that.

The setting up of the Frunze Academy and other higher military educational institutes, however, did show that the Russians understood better, perhaps, than anyone but the Germans of the interwar years, the need to shift from Victorian concepts of progress to modern ones of management. This could clearly be seen in Stalin's much-maligned Five-Year Plans, a proper grand-strategic tool. Both Stalin and his predecessors obscured their leadership talents with their ruthless violation of human rights for raison d'état. So in reality, while other states stumbled through the post-1918 depression, Russia began to set her house in order and was a decade ahead of Hitler's Germany and Roosevelt's United States, and contemporary with Mussolini's Italy. Soviet armor, air, and naval forces were on the road, in spite of setbacks in Spain (1938) and Finland (1940), to go successfully on the offensive against the Third Reich in 1942.

Stalin in the new capital of Moscow well remembered that the imperialists had defeated Russia in 1917 in large part because the lack of preparation by and the mismanagement by the tsarist government of the war had left the troops ill-armed and ill-supplied. Determined not to allow that and the subsequent invasions of the Motherland to be repeated, Stalin sped up the industrialization so incomplete in 1914–17 and at the same time encouraged the military to seek a solution to the problems that had led to failure in the Great War. The result was seen in 1943–45 when a plentiful supply of the sinews of war was coupled to the concept of deep battle supported by a genderless air arm. In spite of the purges of the 1930s and Stalin's refusal to be warned of Barbarossa, he was no fool. The Red Army and Air Force proved a most formidable adversary by the end of World War II.

Of the three armed services, the navy had developed modern weapons, but lacked unity of operational theaters so that during the Great Patriotic War its only visible area was the Black Sea and there its surface and air work was mainly in a secondary role and under the command of junior officers, all of which gave it little political clout postwar until Admiral Gorshkov became its head in 1956.

In spite of purges and imprisonments, the air forces had developed both doctrine and machines by 1941. True the Spanish Civil War had eventually lowered its reputation once the new German types of the Condor Legion appeared and the failures in Finland had raised doubts, but the air forces knew their purpose. They were not a grand-strategic bombing force, for there were too few targets within range. The air forces had learnt the lessons of 1918 on the Western Front, which they had garnered during the years of Soviet-German collaboration down to 1933. Their purpose was tactical support of the surface arms.

Moreover, in a land of limited skills, it was important to mobilize manpower so as to make the most of what was available. Thus infantry weapons, artillery, rocket forces, tanks and trucks for the army, and attack aircraft, notably the IL-2 Shturmovik, for the air forces, were all rugged, maintainable, or replaceable in the field. This allowed for simplified training of the average soldier, male or female, and massively effective combat use.

In the Great Patriotic War of 1941–45, traditional themes of Russian military history continued. Space was traded for time and for the arrival of winter for which the Soviets were prepared and the invader was not. The vast movement of the aircraft and armaments industries to east of the Urals was a major case in point, while German failure to attempt to strike the power plants on which industry depended, or the withdrawing of industries themselves, was a blessing. Moreover, the Caucasus and its oil-fields proved as tough for the Germans to take as the area had earlier for the Russians themselves. And this time Turkey remained neutral. Man- and woman-power was fully employed. Nevertheless the war washed to the gates of Leningrad, Moscow, Stalingrad, and the Caucasus and it had taken massive frontal armies to defeat the Germans. Soviet casualties in the Great Patriotic War were more than 27 million.

The victory in the Great Patriotic War thrust the Soviet Union onto the global stage. In the first two decades after the war the need to recoup from the devastation of European Russia and its accompanying fear of the imperialist enemy together with the Motherland's defenselessness against a NATO/U.S. urban bombing campaign conditioned the Kremlin's actions. The government acted as a fortress state's would, subordinating everything to its fear of outsiders. This trend continued into the new era. In contrast, the United States, which had not suffered an enemy invasion, Europe, and Japan all were stimulated not so much by Cold War defense spending as by consumer demand and the great availability of credit as well as American advertising and culture. The Western economies rapidly recovered and expanded, while the Soviet economy languished.

The war had brought U.S. aid to Russia, intentional in Lend-Lease and unintentional in the A-bomb-capable B-29s interned in the Far East. It had also, ironically, seen the clear emergence of the epitome of capitalism, the United States of America, as the only other superpower. This meant that the postwar settlement was not similar to the balance emerging from Vienna in 1815, but was a confrontation of two giants lacking finesse in international relations since both had been isolationist in the interwar years.

The Soviets were impressed in 1941–45 not by the Allied ground operations, which were quite small when compared with their victorious combined armed forces, but with the bombing of German and Japanese cities and especially with the danger posed by the atomic bomb. The fact that not only had European Russia been devastated heavily by the imperialist Germans in their invasion, but that a single B-29 could destroy a Russian city, reinforced Soviet fear of an imperialist attack. Against this new threat the USSR was defenseless. There had been so few Nazi grand-strategic air attacks that the Soviet fighter force had been fully deployed to the battlefields. American shuttle bombing using Russian airfields had also reinforced the anxiety about foreigners on the Motherland's soil.

And, while the Soviets had partly been involved in the aviation revolutions of the 1934–45 period, they were woefully behind in such things as electronics and radar. Against a naval carrier power, such as the U.S. Navy of 1945, the Soviet navy was impotent not merely physically, but also politically. Thus while on the one hand the USSR sought to continue western-ization through technology, importing German and British jet engines, on the other it had the myopic concentration of the slavophile peasant, an atti-tude encouraged by the secret police establishments even after Stalin's death in 1953. And that suspicion was evident not only in the new United Na-tions, but in the development, again in the Russian tradition, of a giant spy organization while closely guarding secrets at home. Yet another element was the disinformation technique as visible in the May Day parades in Red Square in Moscow, which were designed not only to reassure the people, but also to mislead foreign attachés and intelligence agencies. As a result, the North Atlantic Treaty Organization (NATO) partners and the uncommitted world saw the USSR as having powerful, if crude, forces.

The formation of NATO in 1948 led the USSR to establish the War-saw Pact in response. In this organization the Soviets took the lead both as the senior partner and as the ideological leader. The advantage was that Moscow could supply arms to its satellites and thus keep production flow-ing at the factories and people employed. At the same time, in addition to its Eastern bloc role, the USSR once again began to roam overseas, dis-patching missions, instructors, and intelligence units to help make recipients of its arms comfortable in their use. Thus in the post-colonial world of the former British, French, Belgian, and Portuguese empires revolutions and rebels were supported. While small arms such as the AK-47 assault rifle were much in demand, the larger and more complex Russian weapons did less well in the former imperial lands than they did in the satellites and in China, where the infrastructure and the know-how of the inhabitants was more suited to maintaining modern military equipment.

While in the West the strain of conflicting fiscal, social, military, and diplomatic priorities tended to see compromises and cuts in the various mil-itary programs over the long term for the period from the start of the Cold War in 1947 to the beginnings of détente and arms-limitation talks in the 1970s, the military got a major share of the budget. In the USSR, of course, what that meant was unclear as budgets were not published and the indus-trial and military machines just rolled along.

By 1945 aviation had become a very well-established part of the Soviet economy. Unlike in the West after the early 1920s, however, in Russia design bureaus were separate from the factories, a state of affairs that remained in being until after 1995 when consolidations on a capitalist basis occurred. Given a boost by the German scientists and engineers seized in 1945, the air-craft industry made rapid leaps forward thanks to the excellent training and hands-on experience of its talented designers. By the Korean War (1950–53) it was already producing challenging jet fighters and long-range bombers. These trends continued with, however, the insistence that all be able to operate off of natural airfields. The weakness of the Red Air Force was an old one—the command system stifled initiative. While there were no occasions when there officially was combat between Soviet and Western air forces, the proxy wars, especially in Korea and in the Arab-Israeli wars, suggested that this was so.

On the other hand the navy developed effective long-range cruisers, powerful destroyers, and an ocean-going submarine fleet in sharp contrast to the fleet of the Great Patriotic War. Moreover, not only did the submarines go nuclear, they also carried ballistic missiles. And starting in the 1960s there was a ping-pong development of aircraft carriers to challenge the dominance of the United States in that category. This slow evolution from helicopter ships to full-scale supercarriers was terminated by the collapse of the USSR before any one of the giant new vessels had become operational. In the aftermath of that collapse, the navy, as the other armed forces, was split among those CIS members including Russia that had ports accessible to the world's oceans, sold or scrapped.

Complicating the post-1945 military history of Russia was the necessity to develop anti-aircraft defenses, civil defense, and ballistic missiles. Concern—fear—of the imperialists and xenophobia had long been ingrained in the Russians just as suspicion of strangers was a normal component of the peasant mindset. Devastated by the Great Patriotic War following within living memory of the turmoil and foreign interference of 1918–22, it is small wonder that the Soviet leadership was concerned with defense. The plain lessons in Germany were the need for a well-organized home defense against air attack in the *Luftwaffe* style. This meant fighters and flak guns controlled by one command coupled with shelters for the population. At the same time the massive, victorious ground forces had to play a deterrent role against potential anti-Bolshevik aggressors as Trotskii had had to organize them in the early Soviet days. Ironically, of course, neither side saw what its own moves did to its opponent's thinking. The American and British response, already in train by mid–World War II, was the development of both long-range jet bombers with one obvious target and of ballistic missiles as airpower had become a dominant, and supposedly economical, force in their arsenals. The creation and expansion of the United States Air Force and, after 1950, the new nuclear-strike role for the United States Navy, gave the Russians backing for their fears. Rhetoric reinforced the defense demands of both sides and culminated in the proliferation of nuclear weapons after the Soviets exploded their first A-bomb in 1949. This shattered U.S. and NATO illusions about a nuclear monopoly and led swiftly to the perfection also of the H-bomb. It took a long time for each side to realize that nuclear weapons were unusable, whether land-based beginning in the 1950s or sea-based from the next decade. The successful Soviet launch of the satellite Sputnik in 1957 stimulated not only theoretical imaginations, but also vast defense spending. This economic boom boosted the imperialist (capitalist) fortunes and busted those of the socialist economies. The spinoffs were significant.

Yet, interestingly, in the Cold War days of doom and deterrence, of containment, and of overseas adventures, the Soviet armed forces gained very little useful experience. The stifling of the 1956 Hungarian uprising and the 1968 invasion of Czechoslovakia were only traditional uses of the army. Operations in the decade-long attempt to pacify Afghanistan (1979–88) failed. And the defeat of Iraq in 1991 was a loss also for Russian arms and advice.

By the age of glasnost and Gorbachev, the Soviet armed forces had had little if any combat experience; their deep battle doctrine, modified in the 1970s in light of the experience of the Arab-Israeli wars, had not been tested; and morale and infrastructure were declining due to the debilitating effects of peace and the power struggle with the West. The armed services' leadership was corrupted by its association with the Politburo.

The realities of the Yeltsin 1990s saw the armed forces facing not only the breakup of the USSR and the creation of the fractured CIS, itself a reversion to the nationalities held together by the USSR, but also the drastic demobilization and base closures that should have taken place from 1945 on. The realities of peace, of a world in which the United States of America would perforce take on the role of world policeman, culture model, and economic stimulant, saw the Russians not only forced to dismantle their nuclear and other arsenals, to learn how a free-market economy even in arms worked, but also to learn how to share peacekeeping duties in the former south Slav enclave of Bosnia.

The story of the armed forces very much reflects the national character, the history, and the themes of both Russian and global history. The military, broadly speaking, history of Russia is, as are all such histories, an interweaving of a number of themes. There is, of course, pure campaign and battle history, there is the institutional story, and there is the development of the invisible infrastructure, all of which have to be set against ends and means as displayed in grand strategy and the doctrine by which they have to be carried out.

The contributors have been asked to consider the themes suggested above and at the same time in each of their chapters to look at strategy and structure, means and ends, the international milieu, the armed forces and society, recruiting and training of officers and men, and finally at procurement and the invisible infrastructure. That was a lot to compress into 25 double-spaced pages, but those parameters were essential to provide a single volume of readable length and reasonable (in these days) price.

We desired to fill the void in the literature with a volume that has never existed in English. To get involved scholars to do this required short chapters in which their knowledge could be summarized in short order. Unfortunately this short history cannot be as comprehensive as we would like because there are many areas, particularly in the spheres of economic and social history, where studies have not yet been undertaken. We hope, however, that this volume will provide a coherent analytical history of the development of the USSR's armed forces, that it will spark interest in this important topic, and that it will provide, at least, a brief roadmap to the critical areas, charted and as yet uncharted, in this field.

PART I

# THE FORMATION OF
# THE SOVIET ARMY AND NAVY

CHAPTER 2

# THE RUSSIAN CIVIL WAR, 1917–1921

*David R. Stone*

THE RUSSIAN CIVIL WAR WAS A VICIOUS AND EPIC STRUGGLE between the Reds—Bolsheviks and their sympathizers—and all those who attempted to stop them from cementing their control over Russia. These included separatists from the non-Russian territories around the fringes of the old Russian empire, peasant anarchists who wanted little but to be left alone, and (most prominently) the Whites. The Whites were the last remnants of Russia's old regime, especially military officers, government officials, and the leaders of pre-revolutionary Russia's political parties.

The war between the Reds and Whites and all the other warring factions was fiendishly complex, and defies any attempts to force it into a neatly coherent narrative. In the Bolsheviks' campaign to retain and expand their newly won power after October 1917, they confronted internal and external opposition from their non-Bolshevik fellow socialists, two exceedingly dangerous right-wing competitors from Siberia and southern Russia, along with other White armies, a host of nationalist movements aimed at splitting parts of the tsarist patrimony away from Soviet Russia, intervention by a host of foreign states, and not least massive and violent opposition from the peasantry under Soviet rule. Fronts moved with dizzying rapidity back and forth across Russia, accompanied by near-total social breakdown, epidemic disease, and mass hunger. The Civil War is thus far more complex than can be portrayed in a short summary; the best this chapter can hope to do is indicate the most important developments.

Despite this complexity, we can simplify matters somewhat by concentrating on the two groups that had a serious potential for overturning Bolshevik rule, rather than simply denying the Bolsheviks control of imperial Russia's peripheries or hindering Bolshevik attempts to consolidate power. Looked at in that sense, the two theaters worthy of sustained attention are the south and the east, both of which were marked by large and relatively effective White movements.

## The First Shots of Civil War

When did the Civil War begin? Some historians have pointed to the clash of major armies in the summer of 1918. Should we move further back to the Bolsheviks' forcible dissolution of the Constituent Assembly, which marked Lenin's refusal to cooperate with other socialists in governing the new Russia? Did the Civil War begin from the Bolsheviks' seizure of power in October 1917? Should we go back even further to the Kornilov Affair of August 1917, in which General Lavr Kornilov attempted to seize power from Aleksandr Kerenskii's Provisional Government?

Simply raising the question shows that there is no clear answer. This essay, however, picks up the story with the Bolshevik coup in October 1917. It is from that point that the essential thread of the Civil War began: the Bolshevik party attempted to hold the state power it had seized against desperate effort to deny it this authority. In the immediate aftermath of the October coup, the Bolsheviks faced in microcosm the foes they would eventually confront in much larger numbers. In contrast to the ease with which the Bolsheviks seized power in Petrograd, the capital, they were forced into several days of bloody street fighting in Moscow against military cadets. Within days after the coup, an improvised group of Red Guards (revolutionary workers and sailors formed into a militia), fought a battle on the Pulkovo Heights just west of Petrograd to repel a half-hearted attempt by Kerensky and the Cossack General Petr Krasnov to crush the Revolution.

Soon thereafter, Bolshevik leader Vladimir Lenin acted against the sentiments of the Russian proletariat; the Mensheviks, his fellow Marxists but political rivals; the Socialist Revolutionaries or SRs, a pro-peasant socialist party; and even a substantial portion of his own party by decisively rejecting any Bolshevik cooperation in government with a broad coalition of socialists. He chose to rely instead solely on his own Bolsheviks and his temporary allies, the Left SRs, a breakaway faction. This became quite clear with the first and only session, on 5 January 1918, of the Constituent Assembly, a constitutional convention elected by the Russian people. The Assembly was dominated by the SRs, who had won a clear plurality of 40 percent of the popular vote. The Bolsheviks, on the other hand, noted that their 25 percent of the vote represented a clear preponderance in major urban centers and military units, and concluded from that fact that the vanguard of the proletariat endorsed them, not the SRs. The urban-oriented Bolsheviks refused to accept majority rule when that majority was made up of peasants, and shut down the Constituent Assembly after one session.

In the months following the October Revolution in Petrograd, Soviet power rapidly spread. Bolshevik organizations across Russia seized power upon word of the events in Petrograd. The nature of Bolshevik support, concentrated among urban workers, gave them a network of activists across Russia. In non-Russian regions like Central Asia, Bolsheviks were also able to tap into Russian-dominated cities' fears of the alien countryside to broaden their support. Where Bolsheviks were too weak or opposition too strong, a railway war brought recalcitrant areas under control. In the power vacuum of the winter of 1917–18, it was quite simple for small numbers of Red Guards, traveling by train, to impose Soviet rule against disorganized local opposition.

These earliest victories were won with loosely organized forces, for the Bolsheviks had made little effort to salvage the tsar's army, which began disintegrating after the February 1917 revolution. Three weeks after the October Revolution, a delegation of Red Guards under Nikolai Krylenko arrived in Mogilev to take command of the remnants of the tsarist army from General N. Dukhonin, who was lynched for his troubles. Krylenko's duty was to preside over the dissolution of this force, which was demobilizing at great speed in any case. While the imperial military bureaucracy would pass largely intact to Bolshevik control, individual line units would not. Only a handful of formations entered the Red Army directly.

The sole real center of resistance to this improvised railway war was the Cossack territory on the Don River in southern Russia. Here, Cossack ataman Aleksei Kaledin attempted to establish an independent Cossack territory, with at best mixed success. Local non-Cossack peasants and particularly industrial workers and miners had no affection for a Cossack state, and many younger Cossacks had been radicalized by their experiences at the front during World War I. Beginning in December 1917, Vladimir Antonov-Ovseenko marshalled a force of Red Guards for a drive on the Don. Remarkably successful, considering the ad hoc nature of his troops, Antonov-Ovseenko rapidly succeeded in taking the Cossack capital of Novocherkassk and the major city of Rostov-on-Don in January and February 1918. Kaledin killed himself.

The Cossack collapse also threatened another nascent center of White resistance: the Volunteer Army. After the October Revolution, many tsarist officers and anti-Bolshevik political figures had fled south to the Don, where a
Volunteer Army grew under the command of Kornilov, leader of the earlier
abortive military coup against the provisional government, and the civil administration of General Mikhail Alekseev, formerly Nicholas II's chief of staff.
Despite the tension between the Volunteer Army, committed to a unified and
indivisible Russia, and the Cossacks, dedicated only to separatism, the Cossack
host had provided a measure of protection to the tiny Volunteer Army. When
the Red Guards took Rostov-on-Don and Novocherkassk, the few thousand
men of the Volunteer Army were forced to flee south into the steppe to seek
another base. This "frozen march" brought them to Ekaterinodar (now
Krasnodar), where Kornilov was killed by a Red shell. Leadership of the Volunteer Army fell upon General Anton Denikin, a tsarist officer who had risen
high from humble beginnings. Failing to take Ekaterinodar, Denikin's Volunteer Army finally returned to the Don and found refuge not far from Rostov.

## Bolshevik Victory Evaporates

By early 1918, the Bolsheviks appeared to have their situation well in-hand.
They had established their authority through central Russia, Siberia, and
Ukraine. Denikin's forces were exceedingly small and cut off from any industry or outside assistance. Two key events forced the Bolsheviks to alter
their approach to the Civil War by creating an army worthy of the name and
organizing their new state for total war.

The first was the draconian peace imposed by imperial Germany on the
new Soviet state. When Lenin seized power in October 1917, World War I
still raged. A quick cease-fire ended the fighting on the Eastern Front, and
German and Soviet delegations began peace talks in Brest-Litovsk. The Germans presented extensive territorial demands in western Russia, so extensive
that the Bolsheviks initially refused to accept them. Lenin urged capitulation
on the grounds that Russia was incapable of organizing serious resistance.
He could not convince his own party, however, and Lev Trotskii, commissar
of foreign affairs, attempted (with the support of the majority of his party's
leadership) to simply declare Russia out of the war with the formula of "no
war, no peace." The German army, puzzled by this diplomatic innovation,
simply reopened hostilities on 17 February 1918, and marched east to seize
territory as fast as railroad cars full of German soldiers could move to the
next station. Once it was clear that "no war, no peace" would soon mean no

Bolsheviks, Lenin cajoled his reluctant party into accepting the new peace of Brest-Litovsk, worse than the original terms the Germans had offered. Signed on 3 March 1918, Brest-Litovsk forced Russia to surrender Finland, the Baltics, Poland, and Ukraine. Ukraine in particular was rapidly occupied by German troops and became a German puppet state under the conservative Hetmanate of Pavlo Skoropadskyi.

The effects of Brest-Litovsk were staggering. Not least, the lost territories rendered Petrograd exceedingly vulnerable and forced the Bolsheviks to shift their capital southeast to Moscow. It also substantially boosted Allied interest in intervening in Russia. The Provisional Government had already revealed that Lenin had accepted German aid, and now his party had surrendered staggering amounts of human and material resources to imperial Germany, freeing large numbers of troops for a final attempt to win the war in the west. The Allies began moving troops to Russian ports to prevent war materiel from falling into German hands, maintain a potential second front against Germany, and if possible replace the Bolsheviks with a Russian government more willing to carry on the war. In the immediate aftermath of Brest-Litovsk, British troops landed in Murmansk and then Archangel in Russia's far north. Japanese and British troops moved into Vladivostok in April, and shortly thereafter the American government decided to add American troops to the mix in the north and the Far East.

The peace with Germany also poisoned Bolshevik relations with their erstwhile allies, the Left SRs. They shared with many Bolsheviks a passion for maintaining a revolutionary war against Germany, however impractical. The capitulation of Brest-Litovsk drove the Left SRs to a revolt intended to seize power and restart the war with Germany. On 6 July 1918, Left SRs launched an armed uprising in Moscow and assassinated the German ambassador. The same day, in what may have been a coincidence, the SR Boris Savinkov began his own anti-Bolshevik uprising in Yaroslavl. The Moscow coup was crushed immediately; it took two weeks for the Reds to end Savinkov's uprising. The Bolsheviks' last ally was gone; from this point forward they would be opposed by the entire spectrum of Russian politics.

In the south, German occupation strengthened White forces on the Don. Petr Krasnov, elected ataman of the Don Cossack Host after fleeing south from the Pulkovo debacle, traded Cossack grain for German weapons. Denikin was much more fastidious in his choice of partners, but also benefited greatly from German arms after they had been suitably laundered by passing through Cossack hands.

It was also the German threat before anything else that forced the Bolsheviks into imposing a regular Red army. The official decree creating the Red

Army dated from January 1918, but the effort did not gain momentum and serious attention until March with Trotskii's takeover as People's Commissar for Military Affairs. He began the herculean task of building a regular army essentially out of nothing. Well before the revolt of the Czech Legion or the opening of the Turkish Straits to supplies for the White armies in the south, the Reds were already taking steps to convert their ill-trained Red Guards into a regular army by imposing greater discipline, ending the election of military officers by their units, and, in a particularly telling decision on 29 April 1918, abolishing the right of individuals to form units of the Red Army on their own initiative. Lack of officers and organization, however, limited the size of the Red Army as of late spring to just under 200,000 men, with 300,000 by May, and 550,000 by September. In an attempt to improve this situation, the Bolsheviks established Vsevobuch, General Military Training of Laborers, to deliver basic military skills to the population.

The German threat also made it much simpler for Trotskii to employ the services of former tsarist officers, the "military specialists," in building the Red Army. Defending the Fatherland against Germany motivated several thousand to volunteer for service. Having procured their aid, it was simple for Trotskii to turn them against the Reds' internal enemies. By July 1918, Trotskii began conscripting tsarist officers into service. To ensure their loyalty, for they were absolutely necessary for the Red Army to effectively wage war but could never be fully trusted, the Reds introduced the institution of political commissars—men trusted by the party but not necessarily expert in military affairs. Their duty was to keep watch over military specialists, countersigning their orders when they appeared to be in keeping with the goals of the Revolution, and preventing treason at gunpoint. Precise figures are difficult to determine, but 50,000–75,000 officers served the Reds over the course of the Civil War, along with hundreds of thousands of former non-commissioned officers.

While the German occupation of Ukraine enabled the growth of the White movement there, the other event that dramatically increased the scope and intensity of the Civil War came in May 1918 in the Urals and Siberia with the revolt of the Czech Legion. The Legion had been created during World War I from Czechs and Slovaks resident in Russia, later supplemented with Czech and Slovak prisoners-of-war in Russian hands. Once the Bolsheviks took Russia out of the war, the Czech Legion negotiated passage east across Siberia to return by sea to the Western Front to continue the war. The Bolsheviks were quite anxious about the passage of such an army across Russia, and tensions ran high. After a riot in Cheliabinsk and an ill-considered order by Trotskii to shoot any Czech found with a weapon, the

Legion broke into open revolt on 25 May 1918. The 40,000 soldiers in the Legion rapidly seized control of thousands of miles of Trans-Siberian railroad, instantly wresting Siberia from Red control.

This revolt in the east created an opening for Russian socialists and military officers to establish anti-Bolshevik governments and make a serious attempt at resistance. It also boosted Allied sentiment in favor of intervention against the Reds, for now there was a formidable anti-Bolshevik force-in-being controlling Siberia. Sadly for the Whites, Siberia's sheer size (combined with the inherently fractious nature of White politics) made any united front impossible to achieve. The front line against the Bolsheviks was the Komuch (Committee of Members of the Constituent Assembly) government, based in Samara and largely composed of SRs. Komuch introduced radical land policies that were too radical for the military officers who would have to wage war against the Bolsheviks, but insufficient to win peasant loyalty.

Despite its political handicaps, this government did manage to field a small but effective military force and seize control of Simbirsk, Ufa, and Kazan by the end of the summer. Its authority was only local, for another center, the Provisional Siberian Government, had established itself 1000 miles past the Urals in Omsk. Other local power centers flourished temporarily in Siberia's spaces. The Allies and the Czechs alike realized this division was folly, and pushed the Siberian factions toward unity. A September State Conference in Ufa with representatives of Komuch, the Provisional Siberian Government, and other movements endorsed a new Provisional All-Russian Government under a five-man Directory that would eventually make its headquarters at Omsk.

The Directory was short-lived. Established in late September, it found itself assailed by enemies from the left and the right. Its enemies to the right, however, were better organized, had more force at their disposal, and enjoyed greater sympathy from the Allies. As a result, an Omsk coup on the night of 17–18 November 1918 installed Admiral Aleksandr Kolchak as supreme commander in the east. Kolchak began the difficult task (a task for which he was entirely ill-prepared) of consolidating the fractious forces of Komuch, the Provisional Siberian Government, and the army officers gathering in the east into an effective fighting force.

The Czech Legion's break with the Soviets forced the Reds to make the Eastern Front a priority, which it had not been before. The situation grew even more complicated when Mikhail Murav'ev, first commander of the Reds' Eastern Front, mutinied and was killed in July. The Bolshevik defenses in the east were near collapse, but Murav'ev was replaced by I. I. Vatsetis, who first halted the initial offensives of the Komuch government and then began an offensive of his own to retake the Volga region and prepare for a drive on the Urals. With improvised forces in many cases still little better than partisans, and enjoying a small numerical edge over the White forces in the east, the Reds retook the Volga city of Kazan in early September, and immediately thereafter the talented young Red commander Mikhail Tukhachevskii crossed the Volga at Simbirsk to the south. The Red offensive maintained its momentum through early October, when the Komuch capital of Samara fell, forcing the Komuch to flee further east to Ufa.

## The Nature of Warfare

This early campaign from the Volga River to the Urals displays many of the characteristic features of combat during the Civil War that are worth noting. The campaigns of the Civil War were unique, for the particular social and geographical realities of the Civil War produced a peculiar kind of warfare. First of all, the nearly total breakdown of all political and social institutions with the February and October Revolutions of 1917 meant that all sides in the Civil War faced great difficulties assembling and supplying effective armies. For one, the dual revolutions of February and October 1917 had been so successful at destroying morale and discipline in the Imperial Army that it was wholly useless. The earliest campaigns of the Civil War were, therefore, fought with tiny, improvised forces that could achieve results far out of proportion to their actual combat power.

Even when Red and White armies began to grow dramatically in late 1918 and in the climactic campaigns of 1919, the Red Army had (according to a Soviet history) 1,800,000 men, but only 382,000 on the war's various fronts. This included an eastern front stretching 1500 kilometers north from the Caspian Sea, a southern front reaching from the Caspian Sea to the Crimean Peninsula, and subsidiary but still significant fronts defending central Russia against Whites in the Baltics and the Russian far north. The Reds at least had the benefit of controlling Russia's populous heartland and urban centers. The Whites had even greater difficulty assembling sufficient forces.

As a result of this low troop density and Russia's vast geographic expanse devoid of major natural barriers, the fronts of the Civil War were exceedingly fluid and mobile. This was exacerbated by the horrible morale of inadequately trained and led peasant conscripts on both sides. As a result, once an offensive broke through the defender's front, there were astonishingly few reserves to plug any gaps and no natural stopping points to check its momentum. Advances could continue for months and hundreds of kilometers before grinding to a halt from sheer exhaustion. Quite typically, then, Reds and Whites alike could launch attacks that would easily break through sparsely manned front lines, advance quickly and decisively through essentially empty rear areas, only to be brought up short once the enemy could muster enough units to counterattack and send the initial attackers back as fast as they had come.

In this atmosphere, cavalry came into its own. Russia's empty spaces were the perfect venue for highly mobile cavalry forces that both the Reds and Whites employed as a decisive branch. The Whites were the first to take advantage of this historically aristocratic arm, but the Reds eventually realized cavalry's usefulness. The First Cavalry Army (the Konarmiia) under the command of Semyon Budennyi would eventually play a central role in the defeat of Denikin's White armies in the south in 1919, and its veterans would take a disproportionate share of the military leadership under Stalin. One unintended consequence of this, however, was that many in the Red Army's high command saw the role of cavalry as a signal of its importance in future wars, not as a result of the particular peculiarities of the Civil War.

The mobile and fluid fronts of the Civil War did not come from the widespread use of technology, for the Russian Civil War used the same weapons that had produced stalemate on the Western Front during World War I. As an example of just how starved the Reds were, according to a Soviet source, the Red Army's armor as of end of 1918 consisted of 150 armored cars and 23 armored trains. The Red air force had 435 aircraft, but only around 300 pilots. The Whites did have some tanks provided by the Allies, but they were largely of only psychological impact, with the exception of some 1919 battles around Tsaritsyn.

As the armies of the Reds and Whites grew in size in late 1918 and 1919, their organization and discipline increased, but at the same time both sides were forced to resort to conscription to supplement the meager numbers of ideologically committed volunteers. As a result, the need for discipline to keep reluctant peasant soldiers in line grew at the same time. The Whites were rarely able to establish an effective mechanism for conscription, so their numbers remained far smaller than the Reds on almost all the key fronts for most of the Civil War. The Reds' chief problem was an epidemic of desertion. Their forces peaked at 5 million men by the end of the Civil War, but in 1919 alone the Red Army had over 1.5 million deserters. The Reds resorted to draconian discipline to keep soldiers in their units and fighting: at one point, Trotskii had to resort to the ancient Roman technique of decimation, executing a proportion of the soldiers of a unit retreating in disarray, along with the unit's political commissar. The Reds also relied heavily on infusions of Communist volunteers to strengthen wavering Red units; the terrible need for Communists to bolster flagging morale at the front led to shortages of Communists for administrative tasks in the Bolshevik rear.

The late spring and summer of 1918 and the steadily escalating Civil War also marked the conversion of Lenin's government to a philosophy of total war through the introduction of "war communism." Though the term "war communism" was not coined until the Civil War was over, it effectively describes a whole host of measures by which the Bolsheviks took advantage of military necessity to institute a vast series of measures that were philosophically attractive in any case. In September, the Reds created a Military-Revolutionary Council, or Revvoensovet, to coordinate the war effort. Declaring the Soviet state to be a single armed camp, the Bolsheviks engaged in wholesale nationalization of commercial enterprises (including petty trade), centralization of economic planning, universal service obligations, and mass conscription. The most pernicious aspect of war communism, however, was the Bolshevik attempt to extract grain forcibly from Russia's peasantry to feed the hungry cities. Beginning in late spring, the Bolsheviks began using armed detachments to confiscate grain, supplemented by attempts to ignite class war within Russian villages. These efforts turned the countryside against Soviet power and made many peasants as fearful of Red rule as of the restoration of White rule. This would have frightful later consequences.

## Resistance Grows in the South

While Bolshevik attention was focused on the crises of the Eastern Front in the summer of 1918, White resistance in the south was growing in strength and intensity, led by reorganized Cossack separatism and a reinvigorated Volunteer Army. By the spring of 1918, Cossack uprisings had shaken the control over the Don territory that the Reds had established in January and February, while German troops had occupied the city of Rostov-on-Don and began providing the Cossacks with arms. Over the summer, the Volunteer Army embarked on a campaign south into the Kuban, securing its rear and recruiting new soldiers for an anti-Bolshevik crusade.

Among the Don Cossacks, Ataman Krasnov attempted to secure the frontiers of Don Cossack territory through an assault on the Red-controlled city of Tsaritsyn (later Stalingrad, then Volgograd) on the northeastern edge of the Don region. These efforts to take the city over the autumn and winter of 1918–19 failed, but did succeed in igniting a leadership controversy in September within Bolshevik ranks that would have great significance later. Joseph Stalin had been caught in Tsaritsyn over the summer of 1918 by the Cossack attack en route to the Caucasus. He established a firm working relationship with Kliment Voroshilov, commander of the defense of Tsaritsyn, and both were particularly outraged by the thought of military specialists usurping their private war. As part of his ongoing attempts to professionalize the Red Army in the autumn of 1918, Trotskii attempted to install General Pavel Sytin, a tsarist veteran. Voroshilov and Stalin's opposition to this reached the point of insubordination, permanently wrecked their relationship with Trotskii, and led to their eventual recall.

Germany's defeat on 11 November 1918 immediately changed the balance of forces in the East. The Bolsheviks were brought out from under the horrific burden of Brest-Litovsk, but it was quite another matter to reassert their control over the territories rapidly evacuated by German armies. In Ukraine, Skoropadsky's regime quickly collapsed without German support, plunging the entire area into utter chaos, and making it an anarchic melange of Red detachments, White sympathizers, local warlords, peasant anarchists, and Ukrainian nationalists. The Baltics were only marginally less complex, as local nationalists struggled against Reds for supremacy.

The defeat of the Central Powers also took the Ottoman Empire out of the war, and opened the Black Sea to British and French intervention. The British took the Black Sea's eastern littoral as their sphere of influence, and began a substantial stream of supplies to Denikin to enable him to equip his rapidly growing forces. Denikin also benefited from Krasnov's relative decline, since his strategy of seeking German patronage had failed along with his patron.

## 1919: Year of Decision

1919 would prove to be the decisive year of the Civil War. In a stroke of luck for the Bolsheviks, their moments of crisis in the east, in the south, and in the northwest were sequential—the White Armies proved incapable of coordinating their offensives. In addition to permitting some transfer of troops among the Red Army's fronts, this also prevented Lenin's government from facing multiple crises at once. By the time things looked especially dark in the south against Denikin or in Petrograd against Iudenich, for example, Kolchak's forces were in headlong retreat.

The first crisis for the Bolsheviks came on the Eastern Front, where fighting at the end of 1918 had been inconclusive. The Reds and Whites had traded cities: at the very end of the year the Whites had driven the Soviet Third Army out of the city of Perm, while the Reds shortly thereafter captured Ufa, 400 kilometers to the south. After consolidating control over Siberia, and rallying such supplies as the Allies could deliver him through the bandit Cossack atamans of Siberia, Kolchak prepared a spring offensive to push the Bolsheviks back toward Moscow. Should it succeed, Kolchak had at least some chance of linking up through Viatka to the northwest with the Whites around Murmansk and Archangel, or by pushing southwest through Samara to connect with Denikin in the south. To be sure, the huge distances involved made that extremely unlikely, but the fronts of the Civil War were exceptionally fluid, and made even the unlikely seem possible.

Kolchak had a choice: he could push directly toward Moscow or move toward one or the other of the White strongholds, but not all three. His chronic indecisiveness and lack of experience with land warfare meant that his spring offensive, launched in March, was doomed to failure from the start. Kolchak simply lacked the human and material reserves to carry out the vague goals he set.

Kolchak's troops faced six Bolshevik armies, under the command of S. S. Kamenev, a former colonel in the tsar's army, on a front stretching over 600 kilometers south from Perm. Despite Kamenev's generally competent leadership, the brittle morale of Civil War armies and the lack of sufficient troops to cover the Eastern Front meant that the Reds would have little success in halting the initial White onslaught. The spring offensive easily broke through the center of the Reds' Eastern Front. Kolchak's troops recaptured Ufa in mid-March, and broke the fragile link connecting Bolshevik-controlled central Russia with Red Central Asia. By the end of April, Kolchak had advanced nearly 500 kilometers from his jumping-off points, and was within 60 to 80 kilometers of the Volga, endangering the cities of Kazan to the north and Samara to the south. Kolchak's successes produced panic in Moscow, where Lenin promised additional rations for the families of those volunteering for the Red Army, and the party organized a stream of Communists to stiffen wavering Reds in the East.

Even Kolchak's string of successes was not enough to convince all Bolsheviks that the Red Army desperately needed harsh discipline and the widespread employment of military specialists to emerge victorious. Trotskii's use of tsarist officers had been controversial from the beginning, and a few high-profile defections reinforced the party rank-and-file's distrust of this group. Numerous party activists who had formed half-wild guerrilla bands in the earliest days of the Civil War resented the Red Army's increasing reliance on class enemies and Trotskii's insistence on order and discipline. This resentment would break into open opposition and crisis at the Eighth Party Congress, meeting from 18 to 23 March 1919 just after the fall of Ufa. A substantial insurrection from the rank-and-file "military opposition" opposed bourgeois methods and personnel in a socialist army. Lenin's personal and emphatic endorsement of anti-revolutionary methods to win a revolutionary war was required to keep the Congress in line. The Congress underlined the requirements of strict discipline by replacing the old All-Russian Bureau of Military Commissars with a Political Section within the Red Army. Controversy over the role of ideology and professionalism would last into the interwar period.

Despite his initial successes, Kolchak was not able either to penetrate the Bolshevik heartland, nor to establish a defensible position to withstand the inevitable counterattack. He was hindered by the eternal problems of the White armies—lengthy supply lines that grew longer with every victory, staggering levels of indiscipline and corruption, and peasant fears of the return of the old regime, a prospect even worse than continued Bolshevik rule. Kolchak faced the additional problem of ruling large amounts of empty territory. His control over Siberia gave him a tiny population base from which to draw, whereas Red rule in central Russia enabled them to to pull more and more soldiers, however unwilling, into their armies.

The Reds reorganized their forces, putting the southern four of their six armies on the Eastern Front (the First, Fourth, Fifth, and Turkestan) under the general command of Mikhail Frunze, professional revolutionary turned soldier. He organized a counterattack to throw Kolchak's slowing advance away from the Volga and back toward the Urals. Concentrating the bulk of his forces on the right (southern) wing of the Soviet front, Frunze launched a highly successful offensive on 28 April. A White counterattack in the north toward Viatka failed.

Initial successes in pushing Kolchak's forces back from the cities of the Volga did not head off political controversy within Bolshevik ranks. Once the danger in the east was past, Commander-in-Chief Vatsetis (with Trotskii's support) advocated postponing pursuit of Kolchak's defeated forces to transfer sorely needed troops south to counter Denikin, only now beginning his own drive on Moscow. Vatsetis and Trotskii continued to advocate such a move through June, until Vatsetis was finally sacked as supreme commander and replaced with his nemesis Kamenev. Frunze was then promoted to fill the new vacancy as commander of the Eastern Front. With Lenin's endorsement, the pursuit of Kolchak would continue.

By the end of May, the Reds were back at the city of Ufa on the Belaia River, the city they had captured at the end of 1918 and lost in March.

Frunze's main forces failed to cross the Belaia south of the city, but a secondary attack to the north forced a crossing, which Frunze quickly reinforced. The Reds entered Ufa on 9 June.

White resistance was collapsing. The Urals and Siberia rapidly slipped out of White control, as the region's major cities fell like dominoes into Bolshevik hands. The Reds followed the fall of Ufa with a further offensive in the north against Perm, which was taken by the beginning of July. The next cities east, Ekaterinburg and Cheliabinsk, were both under Red control by the end of July. Those two cities established the Reds beyond the Ural Mountains, not a particularly imposing barrier in any case, leaving little that could stop the Reds on their march toward Kolchak's capital, Omsk, which fell in November. Kolchak and the rest of the Whites saw their situation clearly, and fled east. Kolchak's progress was halted at every opportunity by Red-sympathizing railroad workers and slowed further by the rapid disintegration of White rule. He was finally stopped in Irkutsk, where soldiers of the Czech legion arrested him in January 1920 and handed him over to the local socialists. They in turn handed over power and Kolchak to local Bolsheviks, who shot him on the night of 6–7 February 1920.

The disintegration of Kolchak's regime ended any possibility of a direct threat from Siberia to Soviet power, but it was quite another matter for the Soviets to reassert control over the immense territories from the Urals to the Pacific, a process that would take years. Vladivostok in the Far East was not free of Japanese troops and back in Soviet hands until October 1922. Clearing Kolchak's troops from the Urals did, however, enable the Reds to reopen communications with Bolshevik-controlled cities in Central Asia.

As the decisive battles to seize the line of the Ural Mountains were taking place on the Eastern Front, the major struggles in the south were only beginning. Aided by recruiting among the Cossacks of the North Caucasus and supplies from the British through Novorossiisk, Denikin managed to assemble a substantial force of upwards of 100,000 men, though still far smaller than the forces the Reds could put in the field. Over the winter of 1918 and 1919, his Volunteer Army had consolidated its control in southern Russia. At the same time, the Don Cossack Host, which had blocked the Volunteer Army's path north just as it had provided some protection, was falling apart. In January and February 1919 Krasnov's Don Cossacks had made further failed attempts to seize Tsaritsyn, after which a successful Red counterattack into the Don wrecked Krasnov's authority as ataman and left much Cossack territory in Red hands. Denikin then brought what remained of the Don Cossacks under his command.

After the Red drive south ground to a halt in late spring, Denikin began his own move north in May 1919, assisted by Cossack uprisings and general Red exhaustion. Denikin's forces managed to capture Kharkov, on the road to Moscow, in late June, and General Petr Wrangel's troops to the east finally managed to capture Tsaritsyn on the 30th. Despite an ever-widening front line that thinned White armies as they pushed north and northwest, momentum was on Denikin's side. On 3 July, he declared that the Whites' goal was to capture Moscow by autumn. This was a terrific gamble; any attempt to reach the Bolshevik capital would stretch the Whites' supply lines and scant reserves of manpower to the absolute limit. To achieve any mass for a final assault on Moscow, the White flanks would essentially be hanging on thin air. Denikin had, however, little choice. The only alternative to gambling on victory was certain defeat as the Reds pulled experienced troops from the Eastern Front and tapped their greater population base.

The same day that Denikin ordered a drive on Moscow, the Reds shook up their command structure. As mentioned above, Denikin's unexpected success in the south, together with disputes over the proper course of action on the Eastern Front, finally pushed Vatsetis out of office as commander-in-chief. He was replaced by S. S. Kamenev. Trotskii attempted to resign, seeing this as an attack on his authority as commissar of Military Affairs, but had his request denied.

Denikin's new offensive began in July. Wrangel's troops were to move north to Saratov and then swing west toward Moscow, while the main body of White troops would push more directly north through Kharkov to Kursk, Orel, and then on to Moscow. The Reds attempted an August counterattack through Tsaritsyn on Denikin's right flank, but initial successes were not followed through. A major raid by White cavalry under Konstantin Mamontov disrupted all Red attempts to break the White offensive.

The White move north continued to gain ground. The city of Kursk fell in late September, and Voronezh, just to the east, at the end of the month. With the capture of Orel on 14 October, the Whites were just 300 kilometers from Moscow, with the major arms-producing center of Tula as a tempting target halfway there. The worsening crisis pushed the Reds to throw any available reinforcements to the Southern Front to hold Denikin back from Moscow. Poland, seeing little benefit from a White victory, eased its pressure on Soviet Russia's western frontier to enable the Reds to transfer much needed troops south.

To make matters worse for the Reds, the moment of Denikin's closest approach to Moscow with the seizure of Orel coincided with an unexpected crisis in Petrograd, where a small White force under General Nikolai Iudenich made a desperate attempt to seize the city. The north and northwest had previously been a quiet theater. There was a substantial British and American presence in the far north, but the distance and empty terrain between Archangel and Murmansk and the centers of Soviet power to the south meant there was little real threat from that direction. Finland showed no interest in joining the crusade against Bolshevism, and the governments of the newly independent Baltic states were more interested in maintaining their precarious freedom than reopening hostilities with the Reds.

Still, a small White army had managed to sustain itself on the Estonian-Russian borderlands. Hostilities had briefly flared in May 1919 but accomplished little, for the number of troops the Whites were able to muster was exceedingly small—around 15,000. In late September 1919, with Denikin making his closest approach to Moscow, N. N. Iudenich made his own final gamble in an attack on Petrograd. With the advantage of surprise and Red preoccupation with greater threats on other fronts, Iudenich's campaign was surprisingly successful. By mid-October, his forces had taken the palace towns of Gatchina, Pavlovsk, and Tsarskoe Selo, and reached the Pulkovo Heights outside Petrograd. Iudenich, however, suffered even more severely than the rest of the Whites from his crippling lack of manpower. His 15,000 troops could not conceivably expect to take and hold Petrograd without substantial and direct assistance from Britain or Finland, assistance that was simply not coming. In late October, Trotskii regained the initiative and drove Iudenich in a headlong retreat back to Estonia, where its government disarmed his demoralized and freezing troops before permitting them into the country. The threat to Petrograd was gone.

In the south, Denikin reached his own high-water mark and that of the entire White movement with the capture of Orel. Denikin's advance stalled in the face of increasing resistance, and his lack of reserves and terribly dispersed troops had little chance of halting the inevitable Soviet counterattack. Ukrainian peasant uprisings in Denikin's rear drew off desperately needed troops. Unfortunately for the Whites, the Reds had also finally mastered the use of mass cavalry. Budennyi's First Cavalry Corps smashed Denikin's cavalry around Voronezh and tore open his right flank in a series of battles in late October and early November; after its triumph, the unit was upgraded to the First Cavalry Army. Denikin was forced to retreat, and his withdrawal was exceedingly rapid. Kharkov, through which the main White offensive had run, fell to the Reds on 12 December, and Kiev on Denikin's far left flank on 16 December.

The failure of Denikin's drive on Moscow, coming as it did in the wake of Kolchak's collapse, convinced the Allies that the Whites were a lost cause.

Though the fighting would go on, the Whites would have less and less material support. Confirming the Allies' verdict, the early months of 1920 saw mopping-up operations that cleared further centers of White activity. The pursuit of Kolchak's defeated forces continued in Siberia, and in northern Russia the White enclave around Murmansk and Archangel rapidly collapsed. With Britain and the United States no longer interested in propping up the Whites, the Reds made short work of the far north in February and March 1920.

Denikin's retreat from Moscow toward the North Caucasus ended in chaos. The Reds took city after city, with Tsaritsyn falling on 3 January 1920 and Rostov-on-Don a week later, forcing Denikin to abandon the Don River line and retreat still further south. Disgruntled White officers' failed attempt to replace Denikin led to the dismissal of Wrangel, the Whites' best remaining field general, in February 1920. Denikin's troops were pushed into the Black Sea at Novorossiisk on 27 March 1920. Over 30,000 managed to escape to the Whites' last stronghold, the Crimean peninsula, but another 20,000 were left behind and taken prisoner. Once in the Crimea, Denikin's authority was exhausted and he was replaced in April by Wrangel, who would command the Whites until their final defeat.

The Crimea provided a temporary respite. The Perekop, the narrow isthmus linking the peninsula to the mainland, was a natural defense of great power. In addition, the outbreak of the Russo-Polish War in the summer of 1920 gave Wrangel much needed time to organize his demoralized forces and try to make the best he could of an impossible situation. He was presented with a terrible strategic conundrum. The Crimea itself could not feed the population under his rule, but expansion to the fertile lands on the north shore of the Black Sea would lose the natural defenses that protected the Whites in the Crimea. Southern Ukraine offered no geographic features other than the Perekop, which could provide a defensible stopping point.

In a desperate move, Wrangel began a last offensive in June 1920, taking advantage of the distraction provided by Soviet Russia's war with Poland. His attack quickly lost momentum, and the Reds prepared for the Crimea's final reduction. Frunze arrived in September 1920 to command the Southern Army Group in its assault. Initial campaigns brought the Reds to the neck of the Perekop, where they massed at least four times as many troops as the 30–35,000 that Wrangel could muster. On the night of 7–8 November, Red troops began their assault on the Perekop along with enveloping moves through the frozen flats of the Crimea's north coast. Once the Reds had achieved their breakthrough on the Perekop, Wrangel realized his position's hopelessness and ordered an evacuation. Nearly 150,000 fled across the Black Sea to Turkey by 16 November 1920.

With Wrangel defeated, the reduction of all remaining centers of re-sistance was merely a matter of time. The independent states of Transcau-casia, Azerbaijan, Armenia, and Georgia were returned to Moscow's control during 1920 and 1921. In Central Asia, Kolchak's collapse enabled the Reds to reestablish contact with Soviet Turkestan, though continuing resistance by the bandit-rebels known as the Basmachi would continue well into the 1920s.

The Reds were also faced with continuing peasant resistance to Bolshe-vik rule. As soon as Ukraine had been cleared of Denikin's troops, for ex-ample, the Reds began liquidating the bands of peasant anarchists and Ukrainian nationalists who had fought against both sides. This aspect of the Russian Civil War was until recently very little known; recent research has told us much more about the anarchic "Green" peasant opposition to the Reds and the Whites, but it is still far less understood than other issues of the Civil War. Often illiterate, peasants left little record of their desperate struggle, and the Soviet regime had little interest in publicizing its struggles against its own people. This war was even more brutal than the Red-White struggle. In the particular case of the Tambov uprising, southeast of Moscow, peasants under the leadership of Aleksandr Antonov occupied as many as 40,000 Red troops during 1920 and 1921. Tukhachevskii ultimately smashed these peasant formations, employing poison gas in the process. Antonov himself was killed in a fight with Soviet internal troops in 1922.

Why did the Whites fail, given their advantages in terms of trained leadership, international backing, and the undoubted disaster of Bolshevik rule? Perhaps the most crippling handicap was the lack of clarity on what a White Russia would look like. The leadership of the White movement, es-pecially after Kolchak's coup in Siberia, was made up of the tsar's military of-ficers, often of noble background. The Russian peasantry, who quickly lost any illusions about the Bolsheviks, mistrusted the Whites and the Old Regime they came from even more. This lack of a clear program was exac-erbated by disunity. Nicholas II had managed to thoroughly discredit the Romanov dynasty through his complete mismanagement of the First World War, leaving the Whites with no symbol to unify them, even before the tsar's death at the hands of the Bolsheviks in July 1918.

Geography worked against the Whites as well. The Bolsheviks' con-stituency in the urban working class gave them solid control over Russia's in-dustrial heartland. This left the Whites to rally their forces on Russia's periphery: Kolchak in Siberia, the Volunteer Army in the south, and Iu-denich in the Baltic. While this made it much simpler for the Whites to re-ceive supplies by sea from the Western allies, it kept them far away from

Russia's population centers and geographically isolated from one another. The Red Army had the great advantage of interior lines and a railroad network centered on Moscow to enable the relatively rapid transfer of troops from front to front. To make matters worse, the Whites, especially Denikin, were fighting for a Russia, one and indivisible, while trying to rally support from peripheral territories inhabited by national minorities and rife with separatist tendencies.

Additionally, the Whites suffered from poor leadership, particularly in comparison to the Bolsheviks. Lenin's ruthless nature notwithstanding, he had clear notions of what had to be done to win the war and was able to use the Bolshevik Party to control Red territory effectively. On the White side, neither civilians nor military officers proved to be up to the most fundamental tasks of extracting taxation or conscripts. The Whites' inability to rally Russia's peasant mass to their cause also crippled their attempts to sustain armies in the field. White armies were top-heavy with officers, making them quite well led and trained but short on mass. Whites would often impress peasants or even captured Red prisoners en masse into their armies with predictable results for morale. White civil administration also suffered from a lack of capable and honest bureaucrats, and corruption became endemic, bleeding away much of the aid provided by the Allies.

The Civil War's impact was first and foremost its human cost. In the wake of revolution, Russia was visited by war, famine, disease, and death. Russia's cities were depopulated as urban residents fled to their roots in the countryside in search of food. There they found epidemics of typhus and a terrible famine in 1921–22. Trying to put exact figures on the loss of life is nearly impossible, but the number of soldiers dead likely approaches one million, and civilian deaths from disease, starvation, or violence could easily total seven or eight million.

While the number of lives lost to terror does not approach deaths from disease and famine, it marked the regime that survived. All sides in the Civil War, Reds, Whites, and peasant bands, fought with utter viciousness. Atrocities of all sorts were commonplace: murder and torture of prisoners, mass executions, hostage-taking, mass reprisals. The extent and scale of horrific crimes on all sides makes taking stock of the terror very difficult. Some tentative conclusions are, however, possible. Red terror generally tended to be more systematic than White terror, and more a matter of policy. White terror tended more toward terror as a result of indiscipline or reprisal rather than cold calculation, though there were certainly exceptions. The Whites were also far more likely to engage in pogroms against Russia's Jewish population. The hands on all sides were soaked in blood.

The staggering loss of life and suffering induced by the Civil War and the methods the Bolsheviks used to fight it, including forcible grain requisitions and terror, eventually forced Lenin into a tactical political retreat. The massive peasant uprisings against Red rule in the last year of the Civil War, together with the March 1921 mutiny of the sailors of the Kronstadt naval base in the Gulf of Finland, left Lenin no choice but to moderate his policies. The Kronstadt mutiny, like the peasant uprisings, was crushed with utter ferocity, but at the Tenth Party Congress in March 1921 Lenin conceded that war communism had to end. With the New Economic Policy, he permitted the reintroduction of private enterprise into the Soviet economy, and replaced forcible grain requisitions with a tax-in-kind on the peasantry.

While this restored a kind of peace to Soviet society, and allowed economic recovery from the horrible depths of the Civil War, it did not heal the hatreds the war left. The Bolshevik party had only 24,000 members in February 1917, 300,000 in October 1917, and 730,000 in March 1921. Taking into account the loss of life during the Civil War, well over half of the membership of the ruling party had as their formative experience a brutal and bitter war. The regime would never fully trust its own peasantry, a mistrust that would produce the devastation of collectivization in the late 1920s when Stalin and the Soviet leadership decided to settle accounts with the peasants once and for all.

## Further Research

The military history of the Civil War offers many promising lines of inquiry. The opening of the Russian archives has produced a flowering of research on Russian society during the Civil War, but much less on the war's military aspects. For example, the literature has long emphasized problems with White administration. More recent scholarship has started to undermine this picture, at least in the limited area of White attempts to set up effective intelligence and propaganda organs. Peter Holquist, Viktor Bortnevski, and Christopher Lazarski have all suggested that White attempts to gauge popular attitudes and manipulate them through agitation and propaganda were far more effective than historians had heretofore understood. White administration in general is quite understudied, and further archivally based research might in fact change our picture of this side of the Civil War.

The war against the peasantry also cries out for further study. Much initial work has been carried out by Viktor Danilov, Orlando Figes, and Andrea Graziosi, among others, but much still remains to be done.

## Sources and Further Reading

The literature on the Civil War is vast, so all that this section can offer is the most general introduction. Luckily, the English-speaking reader has two readily accessible and thoroughly readable starting points for further investigation. Both Evan Mawdsley's *The Russian Civil War* (Boston and London, 1987) and W. Bruce Lincoln's *Red Victory: A History of the Russian Civil War* (New York, 1989) provide excellent introductions. Of the two, Mawdsley's is more scholarly and complete, Lincoln's more readable and anecdotal, but both would serve well as a further introduction. Among older works, the second volume of William Henry Chamberlin's *The Russian Revolution* (New York, 1935) holds up remarkably well, considering its age, as a survey of the Civil War's campaigns, and is written with remarkable skill by an eyewitness. E. H. Carr's three-volume *The Bolshevik Revolution* (New York, 1950–53) has aged even better as a survey of the Civil War's non-military aspects.

In more recent years, the amount of more specialized literature has become truly staggering. Rather than attempting to survey it here, this essay instead directs the reader to the excellent volume edited by Edward Acton, Vladimir Cherniaev, and William Rosenberg: *Critical Companion to the Russian Revolution, 1914–1921* (Bloomington, IN, 1997). See also Murray Frame's *The Russian Revolution, 1905–1921: A Bibliographic Guide to Works in English* (Westport, CT, 1995).

In terms of strictly military issues, interested readers can turn as always to John Erickson's *The Soviet High Command* (New York, 1962) and Dmitri Fedotoff-White's *The Growth of the Red Army* (Princeton, 1944).

As for primary sources, Lenin and Stalin's works are available in English in any good university library. Trotskii's classic *How the Revolution Armed* has also been translated and published (London, 1981). Wrangel and Denikin also published their memoirs in English.

# CHAPTER 3

# THE RUSSO-POLISH WAR

## Robert M. Ponichtera and David R. Stone

NO DEFINITIVE ARMED CLASH MARKED THE BEGINNING of the Russo-Polish War. Rather, the forward probings of opposing forces resulted in repeated skirmishes that led to a full-blown conflict. The underlying causes of this struggle, however, were the new social forces and political configurations of Eastern Europe in the aftermath of World War I. The successive collapses of the Russian and then the Austro-Hungarian and German Empires made possible the resurrection of a Polish state. Absent from the map of Europe for 123 years, a reconstructed Poland was immediately set on a collision course with Soviet Russia. Both countries laid claim to a broad swath of territory extending from the lands around Vilnius (Lithuania) in the north through the Pripet Marshes (southern Belarus/northwest Ukraine) to the Romanian border in the south. Russia maintained direct political control over this territory throughout the nineteenth century, and since it made up a portion of the lands of ninth to thirteenth century Kievan Rus, the Russian tsars considered it to be an integral part of their patrimony. On the other hand, this same territory was under Polish control for the intervening centuries, and only fell into Russian hands after the partition of the Polish-Lithuanian Commonwealth by Russia, Prussia, and Austria between 1772 and 1795.

To complicate matters, there was simply no precise way of determining where Poland stopped and Soviet Russia began except by the direct exertion of political control. Between territories that were indisputably Russian and indisputably Polish lay hundreds of miles of land populated by a confusing mixture of Belorussians, Lithuanians, Jews, Poles, and Russians, along with a large number of inhabitants not entirely clear on, and rather ambivalent about, their ethnic identity. In short, there was no neat geographic or ethnographic frontier to divide Poland from Russia, and no legal precedent acceptable to both sides. The result from the end of 1918 was a scramble to assemble military formations and exert control of the anarchy in the marchlands of Eastern Europe.

The Polish army's ability to impose the political will of the state anywhere in 1918–19 is a marvel. Cobbled together from a medley of volunteers and soldiers who had served in various formations during the World War, the army entered 1919 lacking administrative structures, and facing acute supply problems, a chronic shortage of weapons, and serious rivalries among soldiers who had fought in those different formations (and sometimes against each other) during the war. The best armed and equipped unit, formed in France from Poles held in Italian POW camps and recruited from the United States, was the "blue army" of General Jozef Haller. Nearly 70,000 strong, its transport to Poland was held up by Great Power negotiations and domestic political intrigues, and would begin only in April 1919. Meanwhile, military planners at home worked hard to augment the number of troops in the ranks. In a moment of fluid borders and conflicting claims, Poland found itself facing Ukrainian, German, Czech, Lithuanian, and Russian opponents. Of the 170,000 troops in the Polish army in March 1919, 47 percent were already fighting on Poland's various fronts.

The commander of the Polish armed forces and, for many Poles, "the figure symbolizing independent Poland," was Jozef Pilsudski. Even though he rose to the rank of brigadier in the World War (in the command of a Polish brigade in the Austrian army), Pilsudski had no formal military training—he had undertaken a serious study of warfare on his own. Yet even many of his enemies acknowledged his reputation as an implacable fighter for Polish independence. He spent his adult life conspiring against Imperial Russian authority and then, during the World War, opposed the efforts of the Central Powers to make use of Polish troops without corresponding political concessions, defying authority until he was imprisoned by the Germans in 1918. Of Poland's traditional opponents, however, Imperial Russia was the power that he considered the greatest threat to Polish political and national aspirations. Russia's weakened state in the wake of revolution and civil war presented Pilsudski with the supreme opportunity to implement his eastern strategy: to build a federation of states among Poland, Lithuania, Belarus, and Ukraine, thus creating a bloc of countries strong enough to resist a future resurgent Russia. In the opening days of independence, Pilsudski sought to insure the security of the Polish state by pushing Russian power back as far eastward as possible.

Thus, at the turn of 1918–19, conflict between Soviet and Polish forces flared up on a local level, as the two sides groped about in Belarus and Lithuania, seeking to fill the vacuum left behind by the defeated and evacuating German army. Throughout 1919, confused diplomatic maneuverings between Poland and Soviet Russia coincided with quick military campaigns to seize key cities. In February, Polish forces took Brest-Litovsk, and the Polish government followed that with a proposal to determine the Polish-Soviet frontier via plebiscite of the local population. Vladimir Lenin, head of the Bolshevik government, countered by suggesting a plebiscite limited to the "laboring" population. Talks in Moscow proved fruitless, and the Poles struck to the northeast. Concerned about the attitude of the Entente Powers at the Versailles Peace Conference regarding Polish claims to the area around Vilnius, Pilsudski, a native of the region, occupied the city in a lightning campaign, proclaiming it liberated on 22 April 1919.

After the Polish seizure of Vilnius, the Russo-Polish front quieted temporarily, but unofficial diplomatic conversations between Poland and Soviet Russia proved ineffective at reaching a permanent settlement. The situation was complicated further by the improving fortunes of the anti-Bolshevik White armies, which had their greatest successes over the summer and early fall of 1919. A White victory would only exacerbate Poland's situation, since it was clear that the anti-Bolshevik leadership were not friendly toward Polish independence. This concern did not, however, halt Polish expansion at Bolshevik expense. Throughout the summer, Polish forces took the initiative, aiming to establish control over the lands of what is today central Belarus. After capturing the city of Minsk in early August 1919, Pilsudski decided that it was not in Poland's best interests to continue offensive operations against Soviet forces, and he reopened negotiations with the Bolsheviks.

Peace talks from October through December of 1919 progressed quite well, at least from the Bolshevik point of view, and Lenin and the members of his Politburo expected a relatively easy settlement with Poland and an end to at least one of the ongoing campaigns of the Civil War. These negotiations broke down, however, ostensibly over the Bolshevik refusal to refrain from aggressive actions directed against Ukrainian nationalist leader Semyon Petliura, at this point under Polish protection. Mutual distrust was the real reason for the collapse of the talks. The Soviet side had no use for Polish machinations in Ukraine, and the Poles were no more enthusiastic about Bolshevik plans to spread the workers' revolution westward through Europe. As negotiations ran hot and cold, both sides planned for a military solution.

As 1919 drew to a close, outside forces contributed to unfolding events. Great Britain and France made a key change in strategy in dealing with the

Soviet Union. Their backing for the White armies of Kolchak and Denikin had clearly failed, as the campaigns of fall 1919 had wrecked White strength and demonstrated that ultimate Soviet victory was only a matter of time. On 12 December, British Prime Minister David Lloyd George and French Premier Georges Clemenceau abandoned their previous support for intervention in Soviet Russia and shifted instead to a strategy of fencing in the Bolsheviks behind a *cordon sanitaire* of reliably anti-Communist East European governments. This accordingly implied increased military and financial aid to those states bordering Soviet Russia, although, as the Poles would come to find out, there would be a great difference between "implied" assistance and real support for "reliable" governments.

The threat of all-out war was clear in early 1920. The Soviet government continued to call for further negotiations, while some leading Bolsheviks simultaneously appealed directly to the workers and peasants of Poland to overthrow their oppressors, trumping foreign war with foreign revolution. The Bolshevik proposal of 29 January was particularly tempting, recognizing Polish sovereignty and independence, guaranteeing that the Red Army would not cross the then-current front line, and stating that it had come to no agreement with Germany or any other power at Poland's expense. Both the Entente Powers and Pilsudski's political opposition in Poland argued that the government should accept these terms, but Pilsudski was of another mind. Distrustful of Russian intentions, he believed that the Bolsheviks were biding their time, planning a decisive attack on Poland as soon as they could gather enough strength. Perhaps as a self-fulfilling prophecy, Polish military intelligence noted a Soviet buildup of forces on the Lithuanian-Belarussian Front. Thus, in March, the Polish government responded to a Bolshevik overture by agreeing to peace talks, but only if a temporary truce could be reached on this front, a condition that the Soviets refused. After all, the Bolsheviks knew that the Poles were readying for a clash as well.

In keeping with his plans for a federation of anti-Bolshevik states, Pilsudski solidified his ties with Petliura, signing a political and military alliance with the Ukrainian National Republic (UNR) on 21 and 24 April. The political agreement acknowledged the independence of the UNR and recognized Petliura's government. The military pact stipulated that Poland would help organize the elements of the Ukrainian national army on Polish territory, and also arranged for mutual assistance in military operations (although under the operational command of the Polish commander-in-chief). The alliance was unacceptable to the Bolsheviks, as Pilsudski knew it would be. Both sides expected the final decision at any time; only the opening shots remained.

They were not long in coming. Even before signing the agreement with Petliura, Pilsudski gave the order (on 17 April) for a major offensive against Soviet Ukraine to begin on 25 April. According to plan, Poland's forces would first seize western Ukraine and then Belarus in a second offensive.

Much controversy has surrounded Pilsudski's decision to invade Ukraine. Soviet historians insist that the Poles embarked on a reckless plan of conquest that would simply attach as much of the borderlands as possible to Poland. Although the Polish political right supported the reinstatement of the borders of pre-partition Poland, which would put a good portion of Ukraine and cities to the north like Vitebsk and Polotsk in Polish territory, this scheme ran counter to Pilsudski's federalist plans. Supporters of the marshal argue that his drive deep into Ukrainian territory was a well-planned diversion, designed to draw Bolshevik forces southward while Polish forces could deal a knockout blow on the Lithuanian-Belorussian front. The Polish high command did in fact believe that the largest portion of the Red Army was concentrated in Ukraine. Even before Polish forces struck eastward toward Kiev, the latest intelligence reports warned that Bolshevik troop strength was at its heaviest in Belarus, not to the south. Yet it was too late to change the plan, and it is not clear that Pilsudski would have wanted to do so. Operationally, if the Polish high command attempted to switch fronts, it would give the Red Army the opportunity to strike against Polish forces vulnerable in transport. Politically, the greatest gain in the east was a Ukrainian entity detached from Russian control and allied with Poland. Pilsudski anticipated a Soviet counterstrike from Belarus, but hoped he could dispatch Bolshevik forces in Ukraine and turn to the north while his defenses on the Lithuanian-Belorussian front still held up. The best the Poles could hope for was that the Bolsheviks would act rashly and divert their strength to the south.

At the outbreak of hostilities, Poland had more than 700,000 men under arms; only a fraction of them, however, were on the Russo-Polish front. The Bolshevik side had perhaps three million men, though any figures on the Red Army's strength are terribly unreliable. Soviet Russia could devote only an even smaller fraction than Poland of its available manpower for service in the armies of the Western Front (in Belarus, north of the Pripet Marshes) and the Southwestern Front (in Ukraine, south of the Marshes). The precise number of effective Soviet troops is especially difficult to determine. Typically, the number of soldiers actually organized and capable of combat was far smaller than the number of men formally enrolled in the Red Army. At the outbreak of hostilities, the Western Front (the Fifteenth and Sixteenth Armies) had perhaps 50,000 troops ready, while the Southwestern Front had somewhere between 28,000 (Polish accounts) and 12–15,000

(Russian accounts) ready for duty in the Twelfth and Fourteenth Armies. The Southwestern Front had an additional army, the Thirteenth, under its command, but it was directed against Wrangel's White forces in the Crimea.

The Red Army was utterly unprepared for the Polish attack. In the run-up to Polish offensive, Galician brigades of the Southwestern Front mutinied in sympathy with Petliura's Ukrainian forces on the Polish side, substantially disrupting Soviet dispositions. When the attack came, the Twelfth and Fourteenth Armies were quickly separated and lacked reserves to halt the attack. Their very unreadiness, however, gave them no alternative to rapid withdrawal, saving their soldiers to fight another day. The Soviet retreat was quick and complete. By 6 May, the Soviets had evacuated the city of Kiev, which the Poles occupied the next day.

Yet, instead of blindly stumbling southward to meet Pilsudski's excursion, the Red Army's commanders and leading Bolsheviks saw the Polish invasion for what it was—an opportunity for a decisive counterattack. Just as Pilsudski had anticipated and feared, the Polish offensive in the south left the door open for a Soviet strike on the Western Front north of the Pripet Marshes. The Soviet government dispatched reinforcements to its troops on the western frontier, and pulled Semyon Budennyi's First Cavalry Army, the dreaded Konarmiia, from the North Caucasus for use in the west against either Wrangel or Poland. Bolshevik propaganda made use of both revolutionary and Russian nationalist rhetoric to inspire a war that would tap into both political and ethnic hostility.

Mikhail Tukhachevskii, a young, brilliant, and ambitious commander who had jumped easily from the Russian Imperial Army to the Red Army, was given command of the Soviet Western Front at the end of April. The troops under his command, now including the Fourth, Fifteenth, and Sixteenth Armies, totaled perhaps 90,000 soldiers, giving him a degree of numerical supremacy over the Polish armies facing him. In mid-May, Tukhachevskii launched a general offensive. Its initial results were unimpressive, particularly because Tukhachevskii had few troops to spare for reserves to exploit breakthroughs, but his attack did preempt a Polish offensive planned for 17 May, which aimed to break up the growing concentration of Red Army forces.

By the end of May, fighting had shifted south again. The Konarmiia had arrived on the Southwestern Front on 25 May, and a counteroffensive by the replenished front began the next day. The Konarmiia broke through Polish lines to inflict a devastating raid on the city of Zhitomir at the beginning of June. Although this sudden stroke failed to trap the Polish Third Army, it did force a rapid Polish withdrawal to avoid encirclement. As a re sult, the Poles evacuated Kiev on 10 June and the city was occupied by the Red Army two days later.

With the Poles in retreat south of the Pripet Marshes, it was again Tukhachevskii's turn to drive forward in the north. On 2 July, with his forces bolstered by the addition of the Third Army and the III Cavalry Corps, Tukhachevskii proclaimed that the war with Poland would be a war for world revolution. The war, he told his troops, was "a war of the Russian nation with the Polish aggressors," and that "over the corpse of White Poland lies the path to world conflagration. On our bayonets we will carry happiness and peace to laboring mankind." Tukhachevskii saw the next stop after Warsaw as Berlin, and German revolution would mean an end to Soviet isolation and the beginning of world revolution. His offensive that followed was highly successful, pushing the Poles back still further and capturing Minsk on 11 July and Vilnius (with Lithuanian aid) on 14 July. This success, combined with Tukhachevskii's ambition, created the strategic confusion that would lead to ultimate Soviet defeat: the Soviet war aim was never clear. Was the goal to seize and defend an acceptable frontier, destroy the Polish armies in the field, capture Warsaw, or spread revolution to Western Europe? Lack of clarity was no hindrance when the Red Army was making easy gains, but would prove dangerous when success was not so simple.

In Warsaw, concern increased daily over the inability of the units on the Lithuanian-Belorussian front to halt the Bolshevik advance. Casualties were tremendous. For example, the Polish First Army, on the northernmost wing of the front, lost 40 percent of its strength in a week (4–11 July). Writing in 1924, Pilsudski laid the lion's share of the blame for the demoralizing and panicked withdrawal on his army commanders. These generals, he argued, were accustomed to the trenches of the Great War and could not counter a campaign of rapid movement. Even though Tukhachevskii's opponents sought in vain to establish a set line of defense against him, Pilsudski's characterization is unfair. Given the preponderance of strength and lightning execution of the Red Army, a Soviet breakthrough could not have been prevented.

The series of Soviet offensives that continued to drive Polish troops back toward Warsaw was equally alarming to the Entente Powers, who feared the specter of Communist revolution. On 11 July 1920, Lloyd George drafted and issued the Curzon ultimatum, which went out under the name of Lord George Nathaniel Curzon, British foreign minister. This demanded that the Soviets halt their offensive east of the Bug River at the so-called Curzon Line, which purported to represent a reasonable ethnographic frontier between Poland and Soviet Russia. The Soviet response was a scornful rejection of the Entente's interference, though the Bolshevik leadership did not rule out the possibility of further negotiation with the Poles.

Despite Polish arguments that Poland was the only thing standing between the rest of Europe and Communist onslaught, the Entente Powers did little to support Warsaw. France extended credits in 1919, although it was not terribly generous, given its interest in Eastern Europe. In fact, the French credit of 375 million francs "would not have covered one day's expenditure on the French army during the World War." In lieu of materiel, the French contributed a military mission, which did not sit well with Pilsudski, who was desperate for French equipment, weaponry, and financial assistance. Yet despite a certain amount of friction between Polish and French officers, the mission turned out to be a valuable asset to the Poles, especially for its work in instruction and training. Among the French instructors was Charles de Gaulle, who as a young captain lectured Polish soldiers on infantry tactics. Otherwise, the Poles received a modest amount of support from the United States and Great Britain, although the British government made it clear that it had no sympathy for Pilsudski's plans for a federation of states in the east. Exacerbating the supply situation were workers in England, Germany, and other members of the "international working class," who held up equipment and munitions transports to Poland in order to demonstrate their solidarity with Soviet Russia.

As the summer wore on, Soviet forces had advanced into ethnically Polish territory, forcing an evacuation of Bialystok at the end of July. The campaign had left the Red Army pushed to its limits in terms of supplies and replacements. The Soviet leadership was faced with a dilemma. Continuing to advance was dangerous—in one month, Red Army forces had rolled the Polish army back almost 400 miles. Nonetheless, an opportunity to end the chance of a Polish grab at Ukraine once and for all was quite enticing. The Second Comintern Congress (meeting in July–August 1920) resolved that "if Soviet Russia gives the Polish White Guards a breathing space today," another war would surely come. The Red Army would continue its pursuit.

In keeping with this resolution not to permit the survival of bourgeois Poland, at the end of July the Bolsheviks, working through the Central Committee of the Polish Communist Party, created and proclaimed a Polish Provisional Revolutionary Committee, led by loyal Polish Bolsheviks such as Feliks Dzierzynski, Jozef Unszlicht, and Julian Marchlewski. The Committee announced the nationalization of property and the formation of soviets in the territory under Bolshevik control, but it rode in on the coattails of a Red Army that was not especially generous in its treatment of the local population—Soviet forces made a particularly bad impression on the local peasantry with a series of forced requisitions. As a result, the Revolutionary Committee succeeded only in giving Polish propaganda a great deal of material with which to work.

Even as the Bolshevik leadership was preparing for the sovietization of Poland, the military factors that would end the Soviet advance in disaster were developing. On 22 July, Soviet commander-in-chief S. S. Kamenev gave the order to Tukhachevskii's Western Front to seize Warsaw by 12 August. Tukhachevskii began plans not for a frontal assault on the city but for an envelopment from the north, stretching his dangerously depleted forces along an even greater front. At the same time, the Southwestern Front began preparing an attack to the southwest toward Lvov, chief city of Galicia. The two Soviet fronts were therefore moving steadily further apart as they progressed west.

At the same time, the Bolshevik leadership was plagued by increasing indecision over its choice of objectives. Was the chief objective of operations in the west to conquer border territory, crush bourgeois Poland entirely, or eliminate Wrangel's White forces from the Crimea? Should efforts against Poland focus entirely on Warsaw or incorporate a drive on Lvov as well? Lenin saw all these objectives as within the Red Army's powers and so split the Red Army's efforts among a number of objectives. On 2 August, the Politburo decided to divide the Southwestern Front, sending its Twelfth Army and the Konarmiia to the Western Front for the struggle against Poland, while its commissar Joseph Stalin and the remainder of the Southwestern Front's forces would form a new Southern Front for the fight against Wrangel. This decision was confirmed by orders from the Red Army's high command the next day. Unfortunately, the reorganization left the date of execution and the precise mission of the transferred forces unclear; were they to aid Tukhachevskii's drive on Warsaw or instead focus their efforts on Lvov? Instead of moving quickly to protect Tukhachevskii's vulnerable flank and disrupt the assembly of Polish forces for a counteroffensive, the Konarmiia became bogged down in ineffectual fighting around Lvov. Precisely what halted the transfer of necessary reinforcements to Tukhachevskii and led to the humiliating defeat of Soviet forces before Warsaw is still a matter of considerable dispute.

Despite the fact that the 2 August decision to transfer additional forces to Tukhachevskii remained unfulfilled, the plan for the final drive on Warsaw was set on 10 August. Four Soviet armies would sweep right around the north of Warsaw. Given the incredible attrition Tukhachevskii's armies had suffered from combat, sickness, and simple desertion and straggling, Tukhachevskii had only perhaps a few thousand troops left to defend his center and his left against Polish counterattacks.

The danger of the situation provoked increasing concern in Moscow and calls for the Konarmiia and the Twelfth Army to move north to protect Tukhachevskii's vulnerable left flank. On 11 August, Kamenev gave additional and increasingly frantic orders to speed the transfer of those two armies to bolster Tukhachevskii's forces. It took time for the Southwestern Front to receive and decipher these orders, and even longer to issue its own orders. This process was further delayed by Stalin, who had been political commissar of the Southwestern Front since May 1920 and now refused to approve the transfer of its units to the Western Front. Southwestern Front commander Aleksandr Yegorov issued the requisite transfer orders, but Stalin refused to give the necessary countersignature as the Front's commissar. The time required to find another political commissar to sign the order further delayed Tukhachevskii's reinforcements. By the time the orders were issued and signed, the Konarmiia was already engaged around Lvov, and could not extricate itself until 20 August, long after the battles around Warsaw had already been decided. Stalin himself was recalled to Moscow as a result of his insubordination.

These delays in reinforcing Tukhachevskii were a prelude to disaster. Pilsudski had hurriedly been organizing troops for a counteroffensive from south of Warsaw against Tukhachevskii's vulnerable left flank, which was hanging unprotected southwest of Brest. By 12 August, Soviet forces were already locked in battle around Warsaw, and even here the Polish line wavered. On 13 August, Red Army units captured Radzymin, a town just 20 miles to the northeast of Warsaw that was one of the key points in the capital's defense. Yet over the next few days, and through ferocious fighting, the tide turned. The Polish Fifth Army, still not entirely organized and facing superior numbers, launched a daring attack to the north against the Soviet Fifteenth and Third Armies, despite having the Soviet Fourth Army on its flank and, with a little bit of maneuver, at its rear. A Polish cavalry raid on the Fourth Army command post, however, sent it into panicked flight. In the midst of the attack, the Soviets destroyed their own field communications center, the invading armies' sole contact with the Western Front command in Minsk. To Tukhachevskii's amazement, the Fourth Army was incapacitated and the Poles, unhindered, had time to beat back—one after the other—the Soviet Fifteenth and Third Armies.

The Polish successes to the north of Warsaw seriously weakened Tukhachevskii's forces, making Pilsudski's monumental counterattack, launched on 16 August, all the more effective. His strike-force easily tore through the Western Front's left flank and threatened to isolate the Soviet armies hundreds of miles from home. The day after the start of the Polish counteroffensive, Tukhachevskii's forces began a full-speed retreat to escape the threat of Polish encirclement from the south. Many Soviet soldiers did not avoid the trap. At least 100,000 became Polish prisoners of war, and the Fourth Army and elements of the Fifteenth Army retreated into East Prussia and were interned there.

There is little question that the delayed reinforcements could have had a considerable impact on the outcome of the campaign. At the time of the dispute between Stalin and the high command in Moscow, there were only 60–80 miles between the formations intended for transfer to Tukhachevskii and the staging areas for the Polish counteroffensive. Had Tukhachevskii gained control over those units at the beginning of August when the Politburo resolved to split the Southwestern Front, or even as late as 11 August when Kamenev repeated his orders, it is difficult to imagine the Polish counteroffensive being nearly as devastatingly successful. Tukhachevskii naturally blamed his defeat (with some justice) on delays in reinforcing his troops. "Had we succeeded," he wrote, "in concentrating the units of the Cavalry Army soon enough in the direction of Lublin, those forces . . . might have proved a threat to the [Poles]. In that case the Poles could not have thought of developing an attack from the Deblin-Lublin region . . . they themselves would have been placed in a very critical position."

Though the Bolsheviks' ability to seize Warsaw is open to serious question given Tukhachevskii's exhausted troops and extended supply lines, a less successful Polish counteroffensive would have left large swathes of border territory in Soviet hands and interwar Poland significantly smaller and weaker.

Stalin was at least in part the victim of mixed signals, for Lenin gave the fight against Wrangel in the Crimea at least as much importance as the fight against Poland. Stalin's enormous sense of his own importance combined with Lenin's priorities to make Stalin's missions, whatever they might be, seem overwhelmingly vital. The fact that Lenin gave such weight to Stalin's new assignment, the Southern Front's campaign against Wrangel, made the diversion of any forces from Stalin's jurisdiction to some other front seem both a personal affront to Stalin and a criminally negligent siphoning of valuable resources from a vital task. Stalin could point to the military command's own priorities in defense of his insubordination. Commander-in-Chief Kamenev had as recently as 23 July indicated that the Konarmiia's chief target was to be Lvov. Soviet strategy during the summer of 1920 was clearly torn among the seizure of Warsaw, a second anti-Polish offensive on Lvov, and the campaign against Wrangel in the Crimea. Stalin was able to take advantage of real confusion in the Red Army to forward his own agenda.

Stalin also consistently emphasized the importance of fighting Wrangel before attempting to conquer Poland, long before the dispute over the transfer of the Konarmiia and the Fourteenth Army. Throughout the late spring and early summer Stalin stressed the difficulty of attempting to conquer Poland, and emphasized instead the struggle against Wrangel. In July he proclaimed that the Soviets could repel any potential Polish attack, but "only with the liquidation of Wrangel shall we be able to consider our victory over the Polish gentry secure. Therefore, the new slogan which the party must now inscribe on its banners is: 'Remember Wrangel! Death to Wrangel!'" To be sure, miscommunication and strategic disagreement does not entirely explain Stalin's actions; Trotskii's later accusation that Stalin's ego demanded the gratification of a heroic seizure of Lvov certainly has some justice to it.

Peace talks in Minsk began almost simultaneously with the Polish counteroffensive, but quickly changed their tone when the extent of Polish victory became clear. Tukhachevskii and his commissar Ivan Smilga, still smarting from their defeat, proclaimed to their troops in the midst of negotiations that "entirely composed of spies and counterintelligence agents, the Polish delegation is attempting to exploit its position to gather intelligence." The Poles questioned such a statement in the midst of peace talks, and the Politburo was forced to officially repudiate Tukhachevskii's ill-considered words. Soviet peace proposals were positively insulting—they called for dividing Poland from Soviet territory roughly along the Curzon Line, but demanded that the Polish army be limited to 50,000 troops, with the remainder of its weapons to be distributed to a workers' militia. Upon receiving word of Pilsudski's victory, the Polish delegation broke off talks but agreed to restart them in neutral territory.

In the meantime, Polish forces, flushed from their astounding success after having been pushed to the brink of disaster, drove eastward once more. The victory at Warsaw gave Pilsudski the opportunity to reckon with S. M. Budennyi, who remained a potent threat on the Soviet Southwestern Front. An engagement at the turn of July-August was inconclusive, but on 25 August, the Konarmiia joined units of the Soviet Twelfth Army in a belated offensive action along the upper Bug River, which aimed to storm through Lublin and attack Pilsudski's formations from the rear. Yet with Tukhachevskii's armies in flight, the Poles could muster the forces to counter Budennyi's movements and chip away at his strength. Days of pouring rain hampered operations on both sides. In the waning days of August, Polish forces closed in on the Konarmiia outside of Zamosc. Attacked from all sides, Budennyi broke out to the east just before the circle closed. Units of the Polish Third Army let him go. The Poles could not deliver a knockout punch, but they forced the Konarmiia to retire from combat. A general offensive by the Polish Third and Sixth Armies on the Southwestern Front followed (12–21 September), clearing the Soviet armies from Volhynia and Eastern Galicia.

To the north, the remainder of Tukhachevskii's armies regrouped along the Niemen River. Pilsudski aimed to strike before the Soviet forces could resupply, reorganize, and take to the offensive. He planned to encircle Tukhachevskii's armies from the north, attack from the rear, and push the Red Army into the Pripet Marshes. Pilsudski's strike-group moved forward on 23 September, and fierce fighting left the outcome in doubt for the first few days. Then the Poles descended from the Lithuanian border on the rear of the Soviet Third Army. At the same time, the northern group of the Polish Third Army moved on Pinsk, threatening to swing behind the luckless Soviet Fourth Army. Tukhachevskii again sounded the retreat. Tattered and torn, the Red Army abandoned eastern Belarus to the Poles. Pilsudski was unable to score a resounding victory, but with winter setting in and the season for military campaigns drawing to a close, the victory remained with Poland nevertheless.

Peace talks began again in Riga on 21 September. Both sides reached an agreement in principle on 5 October; the provisional deal was signed a week later with a cease-fire to follow on 18 October. In the time remaining, Polish forces managed to seize Vilnius on 9 October, but failed in an attempt to seize Minsk on 16 October. The final Treaty of Riga was signed on 18 March 1921.

This peace deal did not, however, end the hostility between Poland and the new Soviet state. The lack of a clear geographic or ethnographic divide, along with ideological enmity and a history of strife, made another Russo-Polish conflict almost inevitable. Incidents along the Polish eastern border flared up throughout the interwar period, so much so that the Polish government invested heavily in a frontier defense corps to protect against "marauding bands." In addition, most internal enemies, real or imagined, were perceived as tools of the Communist menace to the east. The Polish-Soviet War shaped the strategic and tactical thinking of the Polish high command. Even into the late 1930s, as the German threat became more and more obvious, the military leadership spent most of its time planning for a war of maneuver against the Soviet Union.

For its part, the leadership of the Soviet Union thought of Poland as a hostile neighbor. Through the 1920s, the Soviet military assumed as a matter of course that the most likely war it would fight would be against a coalition of Poland and Rumania, possibly with the addition of the Baltic States and Finland. It always measured its military strength against the forces those enemies could put in the field. At the end of the 1920s, when Soviet rearmament had clearly outstripped Polish ability to compete, the standards of measurement changed. The heritage of enmity and mutual distrust never ended, however, making it that much more difficult to forge an anti-Nazi coalition in Eastern Europe at the end of the 1930s.

The dispute over the failure of the Soviet drive on Warsaw also poisoned relations between Stalin and Tukhachevskii for years to come. In Tukhachevskii's later account of the campaign, he wrote that he, "the Western Front Commander, counting from day to day on having the Twelfth Army and the First Cavalry Army placed at his disposal, instructed them in advance to proceed to the left flank of the main armies on that front, but the arrangements dragged out, and the execution of instructions was delayed." To those in the Red Army and Soviet leadership, Tukhachevskii's finger of blame pointing at Stalin was clear. Stalin naturally saw matters quite differently. While this dispute over the fate of the 1920 Polish campaign was not the sole cause for Tukhachevskii's later arrest and execution, Stalin's renowned touchiness and willingness to hold a grudge made a bad end to Tukhachevskii's career all the more likely.

The opening of Russian archives with the collapse of the Soviet Union has not produced a great deal of additional research on the Russo-Polish War. Some of what has been produced appears at making a Russian nationalist political point, as with a recent article emphasizing the travails of Russian prisoners in Polish hands. One document collection in the *Military-Historical Journal* (# 12, 1993) was entitled "Long before Katyn: Red Army Soldiers in the Hell of Polish Concentration Camps." The sufferings of Red Army soldiers in Polish prisons was certainly horrific, and thousands died of hunger and disease. Soviet commissions investigating the camps found terrible death rates: at one camp, Polish officials told Soviet representatives that 540 of 1,500 prisoners had died of disease, while prisoners reported that deaths had been still higher. Soviet investigations found widespread reports of beatings of prisoners, who were worked beyond the limits of Geneva Convention restrictions and were left without adequate clothing. In August 1921, 75,000 prisoners were returned to the Soviets, but the Poles had earlier claimed to have 100,000 in custody. Soviet Foreign Minister Chicherin accused the Poles of letting 60,000 of 130,000 prisoners die in their custody.

Polish historians have countered these claims with documents that suggest that camp administrators treated Soviet prisoners as appropriately as conditions allowed and in accordance with international conventions. They argue that sickness and poor conditions were the real culprits in accounting for the Soviet death rate. Polish historians also contend that a large share of the prisoners who did not return to the Soviet Union from Polish camps either joined anti-Bolshevik formations or emigrated to the West. Finally, they note that Polish POWs in Soviet camps received no better treatment from their captors.

In the end, it seems prudent to conclude that high death rates among Soviet prisoners were more a function of the disease and near-famine rampant throughout Eastern Europe at the end of World War I than they were of Polish misconduct. Furthermore, the comparison with the massacre of Polish prisoners in the Katyn Forest in World War II implicit in the title of the article in the *Military-Historical Journal* is misplaced. Polish abuses as they existed, even taking Soviet descriptions at full value, never aimed at the deliberate extermination of Soviet prisoners; they were crimes of neglect rather than deliberate homicide. Scholars still await a balanced history that will take full advantage of newly available sources.

## Further Research

Polish scholars of the interwar period and again after 1989 have done their best to cover every aspect of the Polish-Soviet War, and much of this work is detailed and thorough. The great exception, however, is an examination of the war through the eyes of the Jewish population of Poland, Soviet Russia, and the borderlands. A thorough investigation of Polish, Russian, Ukrainian, and Yiddish sources—admittedly a tall order—nonetheless would be a major contribution to our understanding of the social forces in the region, replacing the fragmented and contentious literature currently available.

## Sources and Further Reading

See Norman Davies, *White Eagle, Red Star* (New York, 1972) and Piotr Wandycz, *Soviet-Polish Relations, 1917–1921* (Cambridge, 1969). Adam Zamoyski, *The Battle for the Marchlands* (Boulder, CO, 1981) is also useful, although somewhat uneven in its treatment. Volume 3 of *The Military Writings and Speeches of Leon Trotsky: How the Revolution Armed* (London, 1974) presents an English version of *Kak vooruzhalas revoliutsiia*. On the controversy over Stalin's role in the Russo-Polish War, see Robert Tucker, *Stalin as Revolutionary* (New York, 1973), chap. 6, and Dmitri Volkogonov, *Stalin: Triumph and Tragedy* (New York, 1988), chap. 6. Tukhachevskii's account of the campaign is included as "March Beyond the Vistula" in Pilsudski's *Year 1920* (New York, 1972). Stalin and Lenin's collected works are instructive on these events, and, helpfully, have been translated into English.

Thomas Fiddick has suggested the controversial thesis that Lenin deliberately sabotaged the Soviet campaign against Poland out of fear of Western retribution. See "The Miracle of the Vistula: Soviet Policy vs. Red Army Strategy," *Journal of Modern History* 45 (1973), 626–643, and *Russia's Retreat from Poland* (London, 1990). In our opinion, Stephen Brown presents a more convincing interpretation in "Lenin, Stalin, and the Failure of the Red Army in the Soviet-Polish War of 1920," *War & Society* 14.2 (1996), 35–47.

CHAPTER 4

# IDEOLOGY AND THE
# RISE OF THE RED ARMY,
# 1921–1929

*David R. Stone*

THE END OF THE CIVIL WAR (1918–21) DID NOT MARK AN END to the Bolsheviks' continuing struggle over how best to construct the proper army for a proletarian state. Only the forms of that debate changed. The same disputes over how best to organize the Red Army, what role Communism and Communists should play within it, and the extent to which Marxism and the experience of the revolution should alter military thought all began during the Civil War and persisted through the first years of the Soviet state.

Despite the definite strains of authoritarianism present in Lenin and in Bolshevism long before the Civil War, the virtues necessary to organize an army and win a war made many Bolsheviks uneasy. The Bolsheviks who had come of age in pre–World War I Europe saw a standing army as anathema to socialist ideals, and the sudden need to fight a war made them no more comfortable with the demands of military discipline. The "military opposition" within the party during the Civil War never quite reconciled itself to the need to tap the expertise of military specialists (officers from the tsar's army and often of noble background), to lead the Red Army. Other leaders of pro-Bolshevik partisan bands, often little better than bandits, saw their unconventional brand of warfare as best suited to a revolutionary state, far better than the uniforms, discipline, drill, and hierarchy of a more conventional army.

Lev Trotskii, whose revolutionary credentials and intellect were second to none, had little patience in his management of the Red Army during the

Civil War for those who protested against the need to employ military specialists or maintain unit cohesion through brutal discipline. He was quite willing to punish those who failed to obey orders on the grounds of their supposed superior knowledge of local conditions. In the summer and fall of 1918, for example, Joseph Stalin and Kliment Voroshilov insisted on their right to participate in the command of Red forces fighting around Tsaritsyn, and refused to defer to Pavel Sytin, the tsarist staff officer dispatched by the Revolutionary-Military Council in Moscow to take over the Southern Front. For his pains, Stalin was pulled out of Tsaritsyn and kicked upstairs to Moscow with a seat on the Revolutionary-Military Council to assuage his humiliation. Trotskii was also willing to countenance the execution of party members for dereliction of duty at the front, something else that stuck in the craw of many Bolsheviks.

Victory was in sight by the spring of 1920, though the war with Poland that summer temporarily interrupted the Bolsheviks' triumphant turn to peacetime development. With the end of the Civil War near, the question of what an ideal Red Army might look like was reopened. Even those who had accepted a standing army characterized by hierarchy and strict discipline as the price of victory could now consider new alternatives. Fighting and winning the Civil War had clearly required methods and institutions alien to the pre-revolutionary socialist tradition: conscription, capital punishment, and the widespread employment of tsarist officers. Even in the desperate struggle for victory against the Whites, however, numerous figures in the party continued to call for a radically different approach to organizing the Red Army. Trotskii himself, the spokesman for military professionalism and chief defender of the employment of military specialists, regarded a militia as clearly preferable to a regular army under ideal circumstances. Though he held no illusions about the practical merits of conversion to a militia, and continued to insist on the importance of technical knowledge and training, he did advocate a mixed system of regular units and militia formations as early as the Ninth Party Congress in April 1920. By this time, victory was sufficiently predictable that the party leadership could reasonably consider what to do with the Red Army when peace finally arrived.

By comparison with Trotskii's defense of competence and professionalism, a substantial section of the party called for a wholly new approach to military science. Dizzy from the successes they had won on the fronts of the Civil War, revolutionary officers argued for a very different kind of Red Army than that which Trotskii envisioned. Their ideological fervor for a more radical path of military development was, of course, fortified by their purely parochial concerns. In the rapid demobilization of the Red Army at the end of the Civil War, military specialists with professional training and extensive experience had a much better chance at maintaining their positions. By contrast, party members who had become commanders during the Civil War out of desperate necessity, not previous qualifications, had little hope of staying on after demobilization. Those who had found military life to their taste could improve their chances of a military career to the degree that the Red Army emphasized revolutionary ideology and partisan warfare over professionalism and training. The unconventional nature of the Civil War created new criteria for military merit in a manner much like other revolutionary states: if Marxism-Leninism had utterly changed the nature of warfare, revolutionary experience and ideological rectitude would far outweigh experience in the tsar's General Staff.

One of the first puzzles the Bolsheviks faced was the sort of Red Army the Bolsheviks needed: a militia or a regular army. In military policy as in many other areas, the Bolsheviks were stymied by Marx's assumption that the proletarian revolution would necessarily be worldwide in its scope. Marx and Engels had not systematically considered the implications of a revolution in one state unaccompanied by revolutions in other states, and as a result the Bolsheviks were left adrift in their debates over what kind of military a socialist government should have. Residual distaste for standing armies' traditional role as guarantors of social stability created widespread affection for a militia system—some sort of citizens' army to defend the new Soviet state.

On the other hand, some Bolsheviks, most notably Trotskii, had grown enamored of the effectiveness of military organization as a tool for crisis management despite its conflicts with traditional socialist virtues. As the end of the Civil War approached, at the Ninth Party Congress Trotskii proposed the introduction of "labor armies," demobilized soldiers set to civilian tasks but retaining their military organization and command, to repair the devastated Soviet economy. The "militarization of labor" would maintain the discipline that had won the Civil War but apply it to the needs of postwar reconstruction. In an address shortly after he endorsed the militarization of labor at the Ninth Party Congress, he told a trade union conference that the Bolsheviks needed "to learn something from militarism, especially from German militarism." His advocacy of a militia as the ideal form for the Soviet military was thus as much a proposal to make the civilian economy military as it was to make the military more civilian.

This proposal, like Trotskii's consistent endorsement of discipline, hierarchy, and the employment of military specialists, drew immediate attack from those elements within the Bolshevik party still dedicated to the rights and independence of the working class. Trade union leaders and the Democratic Centralists, concerned over the erosion of democracy within the Bolshevik party, saw Trotskii's labor armies as removing workers' autonomy by placing them under state control, so his proposals never went far.

Deliberations over how best to demobilize the Red Army were interrupted by Poland's invasion of Ukraine in April 1920. That development made an immediate transition to a militia system seem unwise and potentially dangerous, attractive as the prospect might seem in principle. Early on in the debate, however, commanders and party members suggested a possible compromise: a hybrid of militia and regular formations that would assuage the socialist consciences of idealistic party members and provide a core of regular units to maintain Soviet defenses. Sergei Kamenev, military specialist and commander-in-chief of the Red Army, proposed in January 1920 that the Red Army consist of regular units and cadre formations intended to train militia. His suggestion resolved nothing, for bitter debates over the future of the Red Army persisted, but it did suggest the compromise that would ultimately resolve the dispute.

In March 1921, with the Civil War against the Whites truly over, the Tenth Party Congress met to determine the future direction the Bolsheviks would go in running their new state. Civil war of a kind, against internal enemies, continued and dominated the Congress' deliberations. Massive peasant revolts against the Bolsheviks' brutal grain requisitioning policies, combined with the mutiny of the garrison of the Kronstadt naval base in the Gulf of Finland, forced Lenin and his party into the recognition that the worst excesses of war communism would only lead to the collapse of everything that they hoped to build. Merciless suppression of the Kronstadt mutiny and the use of poison gas against the peasant uprising in Tambov were accompanied by the New Economic Policy, which replaced forced grain requisition by a more tolerable tax-in-kind on peasant grain and restored private small enterprise to the economy.

In terms of military planning, unrest among both peasants and revolutionary sailors proved that a system based entirely around militia would be unworkable, though a minority of delegates still advocated such a step. Only regular troops, the majority of the party's leadership reasoned, could guarantee political reliability. At the same time, the devastated Soviet economy could only support a tiny army of 562,000 men. A mixed system of part-time soldiers given a modicum of training and sent to the reserves would provide a larger pool of manpower in wartime without excessive expense. The creation of these mixed units began in 1923, but progressed extremely slowly.

On the thorny issue of discipline and party democracy, various opposition groups urged a relatively independent and bottom-up network of Communists within the military, both as a means of checking any counterrevolutionary efforts by military specialists and combating the Bolshevik party's own tendencies to ossification and authoritarianism. On this issue, however, supporters of the idea of a powerful and hierarchical Political Directorate permeating the Red Army had a strong argument in the form of the ongoing Kronstadt mutiny. If sailors with a gloriously revolutionary history could turn against the Bolsheviks, what might peasant conscripts and ex-noble officers do? The practical solution was a strong and tightly controlled Political Directorate.

Mikhail Frunze, a long-time Bolshevik who had discovered a talent for soldiering during the Civil War, and Sergei Gusev distributed a list of theses to the delegates of the Tenth Congress on the reorganization of the Red Army to present a coherent vision of what that army should be. As veteran party organizers, they presented the successes of the Civil War as a direct result of the organizational work of the Political Directorate, without which the greater training and professionalism of the Whites would certainly have destroyed the Reds. In future wars, however, the Red Army would have to face well-equipped and technologically sophisticated imperialist armies, against which a militia would be helpless.

Despite this argument in favor of a professional military, the fiscal weakness of the Soviet state provided no alternative to at least a partial transition to a territorial militia. The crippled state of the Soviet economy, hyperinflation, and the state's inability to extract sufficient taxes from the population without triggering dangerous political repercussions insured that the state budget as a whole and the Red Army's funding in particular would be cut to an absolute minimum. Territorial militia were thus the sole alternative to no military at all, but presented an immense political danger. The vast majority of the Soviet population was still rural, and peasant memories of Bolshevik brutality during the Civil War were still strong. Soviet demographics gave the Bolsheviks no choice but to rely on peasant conscripts, but territorial militiamen would be away from the watchful eyes of their commanders and political officers for most of the year. In partial compensation for the problems of political reliability that a militia would present, the Red Army began forming such units initially only in industrial centers with a large working-class population.

The Tenth Congress also acted to stem the bleeding of Communists from the Red Army's officer corps. The most urgent need was rapid expansion of the educational opportunities available to Red commanders, as

Communists who had become officers were known, to ensure them a chance to make their qualifications match those of the military specialists who dominated the Red Army. Official efforts at preferences for the Red commanders were reasonably effective in increasing the political reliability of the Soviet officer corps. As the Red Army shrank, the number of Red commanders grew as a percentage of the officer corps, from 22.5 percent in 1921 to 29.5 percent in 1923 and 31.8 percent in 1924.

The more abstruse issue of doctrine was just as central to the debates on the future of the Red Army as arguments over the merits of a militia or the need to maintain a Communist officer corps. One might question the merits of arguing theory while trying to demobilize nine-tenths of a five-million-man army, but this misses the point of Bolshevik politics. As George Kennan has aptly remarked, the Bolsheviks could tolerate innumerable inconsistencies in practice, but never in theory. Mikhail Frunze, the Red Army's rising star, accordingly carried on calls he had made at the Tenth Party Congress (March 1921) for a "unified military doctrine." As Frunze saw it, the fact that modern war had become so great in its demands and in its destructive potential meant that society had to be unified in its efforts to wage and win such a war. The unified military doctrine Frunze had in mind would "indicate the character of those military clashes that await us," whether defenses should be active or passive, "the entire character of the construction of our armed forces, [and] the character and system of training individual troops and large formations. . . ." These questions had to be closely coordinated. This unified doctrine was "the accepted teaching in the army of a given state establishing the character of the construction of the country's armed forces, the methods of troop training, [and] their leadership on the basis of prevailing views in the state on the character of the military tasks lying before it and their methods of resolution, proceeding from the state's class essence and the development level of the country's productive forces."

As mentioned above, Frunze's military doctrine made an argument that the Russian Revolution and the scientific nature of Marxism had altered military science. Since military establishments inevitably grew out of the class nature of the states they defended, the new Soviet state and its ruling working class must have an army that represented that working class. In particular, "People with an ideology opposed to that of labor must be removed from [the Red Army]." While Frunze stopped short of urging the wholesale purge of non-Communists from the officer corps, the principle of preferring those of sound ideology was clear.

Frunze went further to stress the influence the class nature of the Bolshevik state would have on its tactics and strategy. As a revolutionary state, its doctrine would have to be fundamentally offensive, as the Civil War had demonstrated. The Red Army could compensate for its relative technical weakness by maneuverability, including the widespread application of cavalry, and by the use of partisan warfare. Within the ranks of the Red Army, though discipline and hierarchy were important, Frunze argued that rank and its attendant privileges should be kept to an absolute minimum.

It should be emphasized at this point, however, that personal background did not universally determine positions in the military debates of the early 1920s. Mikhail Tukhachevskii, one of the chief spokesmen for a fundamentally offensive and maneuver-based approach to modern warfare, was a Russian noble by background, brought up in the pre-revolutionary tsarist officer corps. On the other hand, the best protector that tsarist officers had in their appeals for military professionalism was Trotskii, professional revolutionary. It is equally worth stressing, however, that Trotskii's stand in defense of class aliens, the former officers of the tsar, did him terrible political damage among the Bolshevik rank-and-file.

Frunze's call for a new doctrine met with scant enthusiasm on the part of either the bulk of the military specialists inherited from the old regime or Trotskii himself. Military professionals feared the intrusion of Bolshevik ideology into their sphere of competence, while Trotskii possessed an intellect too supple to accept Frunze's rather doctrinaire and determinist attitude toward class, ideology and doctrine. Trotskii declared that a doctrine that neglected the essentials of training and technical competency by proclaiming, "We will crush our enemies beneath a barrage of Red caps," was ludicrous. Maneuver had come from the Civil War's lengthy fronts and small armies, not from Bolshevik ideology, since the Whites had used the same tactics against the Reds. Trotskii remained firmly pragmatist on questions of doctrine: it made no sense to determine in advance whether the Red Army would be on the offensive or defensive in the next war. Circumstances would answer that question.

While Frunze and Trotskii argued doctrine, the most pressing task facing the Red Army after the end of the Civil War was demobilizing its five million soldiers while still maintaining some semblance of combat readiness and avoiding flooding the devastated economy with additional unemployed. By March 1921 the Red Army had dropped to 4.4 million, by December 1921 to 1.4 million, and finally by 1923 to its final target of 562,000.

The inevitable dislocations produced by crash demobilization neatly coincided with the political struggle to control the Bolshevik party and the Soviet Union. After Lenin's first stroke in May 1922, it was clear to Stalin and the rest of the Bolshevik elite that the time had come to begin settling who would be the new master. Lenin's feeble attempts to urge his successors to adopt collective leadership as a means of compensating for their individual shortcomings proved ineffective. Stalin correctly perceived Trotskii as his most dangerous rival, a perception that he shared with Lev Kamenev and Grigorii Zinov'ev. Together this triumvirate steadily worked from 1922 onward to undermine Trotskii's authority and remove his supporters from positions of power.

Stalin, Kamenev, and Zinov'ev could not allow Trotskii to remain as head of the Red Army. They found ready support among some Red commanders who saw Trotskii's continuing insistence on professionalism as both a hindrance to their careers and a misunderstanding of the new class-nature of warfare. The very professionalism that Trotskii supported linked him to a useless and actively damaging constituency: the non-Communist veterans of the tsarist officer corps. In addition, the chaos produced by demobilization and Trotskii's relative neglect of his responsibilities as head of the Red Army left him open to politically motivated but nevertheless factually substantiated accusations of mismanagement.

A series of investigations of the Red Army began in 1923, but Trotskii remained curiously passive in the face of this assault on his authority. His supporters were not quite as resigned. Vladimir Antonov-Ovseenko, Trotskii's ally and head of the Red Army's Political Directorate, acted on his own initiative to unleash the pro-Trotskii sentiment he believed lay within the Red Army. He permitted army publications and party groups to declare their sympathies for opposition to the party line, and announced that the Red Army's political officers were "like one man" behind Trotskii. This was something the ruling triumvirate could not tolerate: both the public statement that the army was solidly behind their political rival, and the very real pro-Trotskii sentiment it represented. Antonov-Ovseenko was unceremoniously removed in January 1924 and replaced by Andrei Bubnov. Though Bubnov had been among the 46 prominent Bolsheviks to sign a manifesto in October 1923 criticizing the party leadership's policies, his appointment to this sensitive position clearly indicated a meeting of the minds between him and the Triumvirate. Bubnov quickly ended the relative democracy in the Red Army's party cells that Antonov-Ovseenko had permitted and eradicated the Trotskii sympathizers within the Political Directorate.

Immediately after Lenin's death in January 1924, a new and authoritative commission began a thorough examination of the state of the Red Army. Perhaps worst were the abysmal conditions that it found in Soviet supply, which left soldiers poorly fed, housed, and clothed. It further found desultory planning for war, poor morale, abysmal living conditions for officers and soldiers, and a resulting critical shortage of reliable officers, 5 percent of whom had actually fought on the White side in the Civil War.

One can easily question whether these findings objectively show incompetent leadership or merely the astoundingly difficult circumstances of life in the Soviet Union in the early 1920s. The ruling Triumvirate, however, had little interest in objectivity, and the investigation was turned into a wholesale condemnation of Trotskii. As a result of the chaos and mismanagement the investigation turned up, Frunze took E. M. Sklianskii's place as Trotskii's deputy at the Red Army in March 1924 and immediately thereafter added the post of chief of staff. Trotskii's authority within the military was broken. A series of appointments to key commands cemented the Triumvirate's, and ultimately Stalin's, domination of the Soviet military. Stalin's old comrade Kliment Voroshilov took over the Moscow Military District, and Frunze presided over a revised Military-Revolutionary Council, the collective body running the Red Army and now devoid of Trotskii sympathizers. On 15 January 1925, Trotskii realized the impossibility of the situation and formally requested to leave his post as head of the Red Army (he was expelled from the Soviet Union in 1929). Frunze was immediately appointed to replace him and assume formally the job he, as chief of staff, had in fact been doing for months.

Without waiting for final appointment to the office of People's Commissar of Military and Naval Affairs, even before he became Trotskii's deputy, Frunze had begun and continued a series of reforms of the Red Army. In February 1924 Frunze was put in charge of a special commission to put the Red Army's affairs in order, with subcommissions responsible for organization, supply, political agitation and control, the officer corps, and living conditions. The reforms Frunze introduced before his death in 1925 gave final form to the Red Army's mixed system of regular formations and territorial militia, regularized the process of conscription, reaffirmed the Red Army's commitment to hierarchy and discipline, and returned power from the political commissars to officers by endorsing "one-man command."

Soviet historiography, intent on lauding Frunze and demonizing Trotskii, has generally found these reforms solidly successful. There is some reason to be skeptical. Frunze split the Red Army's staff into three separate bodies, with the core of the staff itself continuing its responsibilities for war planning. He also set up an Inspectorate to handle training as well as more traditional inspection and verification of readiness, and a Main Administration to handle day-to-day administrative work. Frunze's arrangement turned out to be quite unstable, and the Red Army's high command would continue to shuffle functions among its component parts for the rest of the interwar period. The new accessibility of documentary evidence should make further research possible into the true successes and failures of military reform. As a result, the following remarks are necessarily provisional.

In terms of supply, the Frunze reforms strengthened the Red Army's central Supply Directorate, while increasing the attention paid to logistical issues. The supply system was standardized and the number of intermediate links between the center and individual units was reduced, with the military districts assuming the key role in disbursing supplies. Military districts received more autonomy to make their own local arrangements for supplies. Rank-and-file soldiers appear to have enjoyed a significant increase in their material support, while pay for commanders and political officers also grew substantially. The savings to permit this were created in part by sharp cuts to the Red Army's bloated central bureaucracy.

Frunze also instituted a partially militia-based system. This process had begun well before Frunze, but from the end of 1923 to the end of 1924, the proportion of territorial militia rifle divisions rose from 17.2 to 52.4 percent, a level that the Red Army would sustain through the 1920s. By 1925, the Red Army consisted of 77 infantry divisions, of which 31 were cadre divisions, kept constantly at or near their full complement of troops. An additional 46 divisions were territorial-militia divisions, with a standing complement ranging from a quarter to a substantially lower proportion of their statutory personnel. The militia form of organization was clearly unsuitable for more specialized branches of the armed forces, but this proved little difficulty. Though supplied with cavalry, the Red Army had little air force or armor worthy of the name. Eventually industrialization would create the problem of how best to organize and staff technically sophisticated forces, but that was not a major worry under Frunze. Frunze also began the gradual expansion of the role of national formations—military units manned entirely with members of a particular ethnic group. Such units had existed during the Civil War, but gained new importance with official approval under Frunze.

Military specialists on the whole suffered from the Frunze reforms, though some exceptions did manage to prosper under his new regime. Many were discharged from the Red Army, or shunted to positions of little influence and responsibility. Those who did remain in the Red Army gradually lost the restrictions placed on their independence by political commissars. In a slow process, the dual command instituted during the Civil War, requiring commissars to countersign orders by commanding officers, was eventually phased out. The political commissar moved toward a supportive and ancillary role in charge of agitation and indoctrination, not guarding against counter-revolution by the line commander. This transition was a painstaking one. Where the commanding officer was a Communist, he often combined the role of commander and commissar. In other cases, increased authority went to the line commander, who still had a political commissar assigned to his unit. By 1925 party authorities had decreed that one-man command was the new principle, however long actual application might take.

It was this return to preeminence for the line commander at the expense of the political commissar that would produce probably the last major ideologically based fissure within the Red Army's high command. While there were certainly numerous later disputes within the Soviet military over issues of personality and policy, it was the so-called Tolmachev-Belorussian opposition that last turned the ideological issue of the relative influence of line and political officers into a major dispute.

In 1928, senior political officers led by Ia. L. Berman, an instructor at the Tolmachev Main Military-Political Academy in Leningrad, expressed their collective displeasure at what they saw as the excessively rapid pace at which officers were being freed from the authority of their political commissars. In a speech to the academy on 15 March 1928, Berman decried what he perceived as "a tendency to belittle the role of party organs and a muddying of the functions of party-political work in the Army." These political officers' criticism focused on implementation, not principle, for they continued to endorse one-man command as a worthy goal.

The affair grew even more serious when the political officers of the Belorussian Military District endorsed the same view. This confronted the Red Army's high command and its Political Directorate with more than just a few heterodox voices: now they had a potential opposition movement to deal with. Ironically, the policy that the Tolmachev-Belorussian opposition was attacking was a policy historically most closely associated with Trotskii. Neither for the first nor for the last time, Stalin's military and political elites were defending a Trotskiite policy. But who precisely originated the idea of defending the prerogatives of commanders against political interference was rather beside the point; a decision had been made and its implementation was not open to question. The result was Berman's dismissal and a comprehensive purge of political officers to ensure complete loyalty.

Frunze would not carry his own military reforms to fruition. He died during surgery in October 1925. Trotskii and others subsequently accused Stalin of engineering a medical murder to rid himself of Frunze and install his subservient ally Voroshilov as head of the Red Army. The accusation is certainly possible, though as yet there is no conclusive evidence to prove it. All deaths among the Soviet elite of Stalin's time are open to suspicion, and one can construct a motive on Stalin's part. Frunze's revolutionary and anti-Trotskii credentials were certainly impeccable, but his personal loyalty to Stalin was doubtful. Voroshilov, who took over in November after Frunze's death, was Frunze's clear inferior in terms of his administrative and intellectual gifts, but obviously outranked him in subservient loyalty to Stalin. Voroshilov would serve as Stalin's trustworthy implement for modernizing the Red Army while keeping it under the party's complete political domination.

## Further Research

No major research has yet taken advantage of newly available Russian archives to explore this period of the development of the Soviet army. When scholars finally do examine the archival record, we should expect major revisions of our understanding of the interwar Soviet army. For example, our picture of the Frunze reforms, and to a lesser degree the entire development of the Red Army from the end of the Civil War to Stalin's revolution-from-above, is based on party publications and Il'ia Berkhin's monograph *Voennaia reforma v SSSR, 1924–1925* [*Military Reform in the USSR, 1924–1925*] (Moscow, 1958). While Berkhin's book is remarkably good, as a Soviet work it necessarily paints Trotskii's management in the blackest of terms, a judgment that Western scholars have had little alternative but to accept.

In addition to the Red Army under Trotskii and the Frunze reforms, the role of the Red Army in the Soviet Union's post–Civil War internal conflicts has barely been touched. The place of national formations, units made up of a single non-Russian ethnic group, deserves further attention. A study of popular attitudes toward soldiers and service in the Red Army could also be quite intriguing.

Lastly, all studies of the Red Army that predate the opening of ex-Soviet archives will have to be revised to a greater or lesser degree. Relatively few scholars have thus far tackled this project.

## Sources and Further Reading

For a general introduction to Soviet politics and history in this period, see Robert Tucker, *Stalin as Revolutionary* (New York, 1972) and Isaac Deutscher, *Trotsky: The Prophet Unarmed, 1921–1929* (London, 1959). Lewis Siegelbaum, *Soviet State and Society Between Revolutions, 1918–1929* (Cambridge, 1992) is an able synthesis of more recent scholarship, but devotes little attention to political, military, and diplomatic issues.

Until historians tap the rich archival sources available on the Soviet military, readers should consult the classic and still immensely valuable Dmitri Fedotoff-White, *The Growth of the Red Army* (Princeton, 1944) and John Erickson, *The Soviet High*

*Command* (London, 1962). Among more recent work, see Francesco Benvenuti, *The Bolsheviks and the Red Army, 1918–1922* (Cambridge, 1988) and Mark von Hagen, *Soldiers in the Proletarian Dictatorship: The Red Army and the Soviet Socialist State, 1917–1930* (Ithaca, NY, 1990). Roger Reese's *Stalin's Reluctant Soldiers: A Social History of the Red Army, 1925–1941* (Lawrence, KS, 1996) includes some archivally based research on this period. David R. Stone, *Hammer and Rifle* (Lawrence, KS: 2000) is also useful.

Frunze's thought is best expressed in "Front i tyl v voine budushchego," ["Front and Rear in Future War"] and especially "Edinaia voennaia doktrina i Krasnaia Armiia," [Unified Military Doctrine and the Red Army] both available in *Izbrannye Proizvedeniia* [*Collected Works*] (Moscow, 1940). Trotskii's response, "Unified Military Doctrine," can be found in Leon Trotsky, *Military Writings* (New York, 1971).

Political scientists have debated the nature of civil-military relations in the Soviet state, basing their analyses largely on this period. The major theorists are Roman Kolkowicz, William Odom, and Timothy Colton. For a concise guide to this literature, see Dale Herspring, *Russian Civil-Military Relations* (Bloomington, IN, 1996).

For the political conflicts of the post-Frunze Red Army, see Steven J. Main, "The Red Army and the Soviet Military and Political Leadership in the Late 1920s: The Case of the 'Inner-Army Opposition of 1928,'" *Europe-Asia Studies* 47 (1995): 337–355; David R. Stone, "Tukhachevskii in Leningrad: Military Politics and Exile, 1928–31," *Europe-Asia Studies* 48 (1996): 1368–1371; and Philip Bayer, *The Evolution of the Soviet General Staff, 1917–1941* (New York, 1987).

CHAPTER 5

# INDUSTRY AND THE SOVIET ARMY, 1928–1941

*David R. Stone*

FROM 1928 TO 1941 THE RED ARMY WAS SIMULTANEOUSLY a victim, a beneficiary, and an instigator of Joseph Stalin's revolution-from-above, the violent and sudden transformation of the Soviet Union's economy and society in the name of defending socialism and maximizing Stalin's personal power. In a Faustian bargain, the Red Army became a modern, powerful, mechanized force, but tied itself irretrievably to Stalin. This choice would have fateful consequences for both the Red Army's high command personally and for the Soviet people.

In terms of its human consequences, the collectivization of Soviet agriculture—the forcible conversion of the Soviet countryside from largely independent villages into state-dominated collective and state farms from 1929 to 1931—was by far the most costly of all of Stalin's policies. Millions of peasants starved during the 1933–34 famine resulting from the devastation collectivization inflicted on Soviet agriculture, or were murdered during the "liquidation of the kulaks as a class," the elimination of better-off (and hence more politically dangerous) peasants from the villages.

The Red Army played relatively little role in the process of collectivization, but suffered from the morale problems it created among mostly peasant conscripts. Some doctrinaire Marxists might have believed that turning peasants from private proprietors into good proletarians by forcing them into state or collective farms would make them more loyal, but experience rapidly proved otherwise. Mikhail Tukhachevskii, the Red Army's leading theoretician, had argued in early 1930 that "annihilation of the kulaks as a class and the collectivization of means of production in areas of complete collectivization undoubtedly puts our use of the peasant mass in war on a different basis, and in particular allows a broader approach to territorial militia methods of construction." Those with a firmer grasp of the realities of collectivization, however, realized that the Soviet state's assault on the countryside would inevitably produce great resentment among the vast majority of peasants who made up the Red Army's conscripts and had families in the countryside.

During 1929, soldiers were employed for *khlebozagotovka,* the forcible requisitioning of stocks of grain from recalcitrant peasants. The Red Army's Political Directorate, charged with organizing military participation, reported widespread discontent with such an unsoldierly task. As one soldier was brave enough to tell his political officer, "Grain requisitioning rakes the peasants! Under the tsar life was better."

Once collectivization proper began, with peasants cajoled, intimidated, or forced into signing over their property to collective farms, and the more-prosperous kulaks murdered or deported, soldier discontent increased. The Soviet government knew better than to employ soldiers in large numbers for such a distasteful job, but even so, over 10,000 soldiers were expelled from the Red Army in 1929–30 for excessive sympathy with the peasantry. The dirty work of collectivization and especially dekulakization was typically done by the USSR's internal troops, not the regular army. Some soldiers were temporarily and voluntarily organized by special sections of the OGPU political police to force peasants to collectivize, but this was evidently not a general practice.

The Red Army's chief task was instead to prepare its soldiers for their discharge and return home to the countryside. The Red Army veteran, having been educated and politically indoctrinated in the basics of Marxism and Soviet ideology, was seen as the natural source for leadership in the new collective farms. The Red Army's Political Directorate thus devoted its resources to training soldiers in agricultural trades and the basics of organizing. This effort had, however, only mixed success. Peasant resistance to collectivization was strong and lasting, and there was little the Red Army could do to change that.

Persistent rumors circulating in the USSR and in contemporary diplomatic reports suggest that the Red Army's high command took a stand against Stalin as the horrors of mass collectivization became clear, forcing him into the tactical retreat and temporary halt to his campaign announced in his "Dizzy from Success" article on 2 March 1930. Though no direct evidence has emerged to confirm this, it is not impossible. The peasants who made up the overwhelming majority of the Red Army were horrified by collectivization, a sentiment dutifully noted and reported by the Political Directorate. What is problematic, then, is explaining why the military high command never wavered from supporting Stalin in his struggle with the Bolshevik Right at the end of 1928 and the beginning of 1929. This group, led by Nikolai Bukharin, Aleksei Rykov, and Mikhail Tomskii, was committed to a non-confrontational policy toward the peasantry and maintaining the peaceful equilibrium that NEP, the New Economic Policy, had established in the Soviet economy. Since the Red Army depended on reliable peasant conscripts, why didn't its leadership support Bukharin in his showdown with Stalin?

Part of the answer lies with the man at the head of the Red Army. After Mikhail Frunze's mysterious death on the operating table in 1925, Kliment Voroshilov took over the leadership of the Red Army as People's Commissar of Military and Naval Affairs (the Soviet war minister) and as chairman of the Revolutionary-Military Council (the Red Army's collective decision-making and leadership body). Voroshilov had no formal military training, only his experience as an amateur soldier fighting in the Civil War. Not especially bright, he won his job running the Red Army thanks chiefly to his close relationship with Stalin, dating back to their service together on the fronts of the Civil War. For Stalin, Voroshilov's failings as an administrator and thinker were more than outweighed by his unquestioning loyalty and commitment to keeping the Red Army under tight political control.

The other half of the answer to the question of why the Soviet high command sided with Stalin against those who spoke for the peasants who made up the bulk of the army seems to lie in the chief way the Red Army benefited from Stalin's revolutions: industrialization. In the wake of the Civil War, the Red Army lacked all the newer technologies of war. It was still the same sort of army that had fought the First World War, based around infantry, cavalry, and artillery. Industrialization offered the Red Army's high command an opportunity to increase radically the USSR's military potential through the mass employment of tanks, aircraft, and mechanization. The Bolshevik Right, in keeping with its soft line on questions of agricultural policy, emphasized the importance of moderate, balanced industrial growth. Stalin's version of industrialization, by comparison, offered the Red Army immediate gratification. This, combined with Aleksei Rykov's record of opposing high military budgets, convinced Voroshilov to maintain absolute loyalty in this factional fight.

After the Right had been completely defeated, the way was clear for the formal approval in April 1929 of the First Five-Year Plan, a staggeringly ambitious blueprint for the transformation of the Soviet economy into a modern industrial powerhouse. The plan called for more than doubling the Soviet Union's output of steel and coal in five years, while quadrupling its output of electricity. A whole series of motivations coincided here in driving the Soviet leadership to undertake such an ambitious plan: the Plan would provide the industrial might necessary to make the Soviet Union a military power, while expanding the industrial working class that the Bolsheviks saw as their key base of support. Finally, Bolsheviks in this period saw all problems as soluble by force of will; commitment and struggle could overcome the laws of economics, aided of course by the unceasing toil and suffering of the Soviet population.

The First Five-Year Plan did not include specific provisions for defense. Until the time the Plan was declared complete at the end of 1932, Soviet defense industry worked largely on an ad hoc basis, striving each year to meet the steadily growing demands of the Red Army. Stalin's Politburo did try to establish some shape for the growth of the Red Army and military industry with two key decisions on 15 July 1929. "On the state of defense" and "On military industry" sought to do for Soviet security what the First Five-Year Plan had done for the economy as a whole: to set goals for wholesale overhaul. These decisions committed the USSR to limit the size of its military while focusing on technical improvements to boost the relative weight of armor and aviation. The overall goal was to match potential opponents (generally thought of as the states along the USSR's western border) in numbers of troops while maintaining superiority in at least two of three key technologies: aircraft, artillery, and tanks. The Politburo boosted the size of the fully mobilized Red Army from 2.6 to 3 million men, and made a commitment to creating by the end of the Five-Year Plan "a modern military-technical base for defense." Within four years the Politburo wanted 3,500 aircraft and 4,500–5,500 tanks ready in the event of war.

These projections would prove remarkably conservative. In the meantime, however, the Red Army altered its own organization to cope with the Politburo's new commitment to technical rearmament. By the end of 1929 it had replaced its antiquated Supply Directorate with a new, streamlined Armaments Directorate, headed by Ieronim Uborevich and dedicated to providing the Red Army with the most advanced weaponry possible. It created a new Motorization and Mechanization Directorate under Innokent Khalepskii to develop tanks; Khalepskii soon traveled abroad to purchase designs for production under license in the USSR.

The Red Army's appetite for the military power that modern industry could provide only grew in the eating. For example, Tukhachevskii, who had served as the Red Army's chief of staff from 1925 to 1928, drafted a proposal in January 1930 calling for the even more radical militarization of the Soviet economy to enable it to produce yearly 122,500 aircraft and 100,000 tanks. (For comparison's sake, over the *four* years it fought in World War II, the Soviet Union produced a total of approximately 100,000 tanks.) Stalin and Voroshilov saw this as so outlandish and dangerous that Tukhachevskii was banned from discussing economic issues. Within a year and a half, however, both Stalin's inner circle and the Red Army's high command had been so radicalized by mesmerizing thoughts of how much Soviet industry could provide that Tukhachevskii was brought back to Moscow from commanding the Leningrad Military District to replace Uborevich as head of the Armaments Directorate. Tukhachevskii was thus placed in charge of operations he had been forbidden to discuss only the year before.

With the Red Army's peacetime procurement and wartime mobilization plans growing steadily, the final trigger for all-out military production was the Manchurian Crisis of September 1931. Soviet intelligence had already intercepted Japanese cables advocating a preventive war against the Soviet Union when Japan's Kwantung Army quickly moved to occupy all of Manchuria in late 1931. Faced by the possibility of a far away war against a major power, Stalin and his Politburo quickly moved the economy to a war footing. They set a production program for 1932 of 10,000 tanks. Even though only 4,000 tanks were actually produced in 1932, this was still a stunning achievement and nearly matched in a single year what the Politburo had expected to produce in four years as recently as 1929. To add to the achievement, though the designs were purchased abroad, the tanks themselves were quite sophisticated for their time. At great human and economic cost, the Soviet economy made the transition to mass production of sophisticated tanks and aircraft.

The First Five-Year Plan was declared complete at the end of 1932. The Second Five-Year Plan moderated the dizzying speed of its predecessor, but the Soviet economy continued to churn out tanks, fighter aircraft, artillery pieces, and ammunition throughout the 1930s. Stalin also began ratcheting up military production in areas that had previously been deliberately neglected in the name of economy. For most of the 1920s and 1930s, the Soviet navy had a been a distinctly low priority. Whatever resources had been scraped up for naval construction had gone strictly to surface vessels and submarines intended solely for coastal defense. At some point in 1935 or 1936, however, Stalin moved toward the construction of a major capital ship fleet. The logic behind this decision is difficult to puzzle out, for it predated the Soviet difficulties with Italian naval power during the Spanish Civil War. Though the Second World War interrupted this construction program, as factories and workers were turned over to the urgent needs of the army, the end to tight budgets in naval policy was evident.

The Red Army's air arm benefited during the USSR's industrial expansion from the guidance of a pair of competent, effective administrators who presided over a substantial expansion in the size and technological sophistication of Soviet air assets. Pyotr Baranov, who had joined the Bolshevik Party well before the October Revolution and became a soldier only out of necessity, ran the Soviet air force from 1924 to 1931. He then managed the Soviet aviation industry before dying in a plane crash in 1933. Iakov Alksnis, like Baranov a revolutionary before a soldier, took over the Red air force in 1931, learning to fly while serving, before being purged and killed in 1938. Despite their non-military backgrounds, both men became strong advocates for the needs of their service.

The Soviet Air Force was torn between the talent of its designers and the dangers of the terror-state. The USSR was lucky enough to draw on a tradition of aircraft design and a number of talented designers who produced a series of innovative and serviceable aircraft. At the same time, those designers suffered from the institutional paranoia of the Stalinist state, which interpreted any failure of a new design as deliberate sabotage. Despite this handicap, Soviet designers managed to produce numerous advanced designs, including arguably the most potent heavy bomber force in the world in the early 1930s. The experience of the Spanish Civil War also pushed Soviet designers to focus their efforts on effective ground-attack aircraft.

A large portion of the credit for Soviet successes in weapons design and manufacture in the interwar period belongs to the widespread foreign technical assistance the USSR employed. Most notoriously, the Soviet Union relied in part for its rearmament on a program of collaboration with Weimar Germany. Both states were outcasts in the post-Versailles international system, feared a war with Poland, and naturally saw great advantages in military and economic collaboration. Germany, barred from possessing tanks by the terms of the Treaty of Versailles, could use the Soviet Union's vast spaces to hide its experiments with prohibited technologies. The Soviet Union could benefit from the German Reichswehr's experience and expertise in technology and organization.

Starting as early as 1921, the collaboration involved the training of Soviet officers in German military courses or by German instructors in the Soviet Union. German industrial giants also participated: Junkers manufactured aircraft in the early 1920s in Fili, a Moscow suburb, until that partnership withered and died, and the Soviet government later established industrial partnerships with Krupp and Rheinmetall. Special schools to explore technical advancements in military science existed for tank warfare at Kazan, air warfare at Lipetsk, and gas weapons at Saratov. Though this collaboration benefited both sides, its scale should not be overestimated. The tank school at Kazan, for example, though it may have inspired some fertile exchanges of information on the theory of tank warfare, could do little to develop actual practice. An inventory in January 1929 found only one tank, six automobiles, three trucks, and three tractors in the school's possession.

To some degree, historians have exaggerated the relative importance of the German connection. The 1939 Molotov-Ribbentrop Pact, which gave Hitler a free hand to attack Poland and launch the Second World War without fears of fighting a two-front war, has focused historians' attention retrospectively on the German-Soviet collaboration, giving it an immense weight after the fact that it did not enjoy at the time. The fact that Germany lost World War II also made this process much simpler. The records of German collaboration with Stalin were open and relatively available; the record of the Soviet Union's successful purchases of military technology from other sources was much harder to get at, and therefore under-researched.

These other contacts were quite significant. Despite ideological differences, the Soviet Union enjoyed solid trade relations with fascist Italy throughout much of the interwar period, and obtained the designs for numerous naval vessels along with seaplanes from Italian sources. France provided aviation technology. Perhaps the greatest importance of foreign technical assistance came in establishing the mass production of tanks. The Soviets' first serious attempt at modern tank production (the MS-1 / T-18) was based around a World War I–vintage Renault design. When that tank proved to be inadequate, the Soviets were forced to look abroad for more suitable designs. Germany could be of little assistance. As a result, when the Soviets first moved to truly mass production of tanks, the three designs they used were all of foreign origin and purchased by Khalepskii in late 1929 and early 1930. The T-27 tankette was a British Carden-Lloyd design, the T-26 light tank came from Vickers, and the BT medium tank was sold to the Soviets by the American designer Walter Christie.

While the Red Army gained immensely from Stalin's industrialization, it suffered as the rest of Soviet society did from the final aspect of Stalin's revolution: his unceasing and paranoid drive to centralize all power in his own hands. One important aspect of this was the increasingly hierarchical nature of society under Stalin. During the NEP period, the Soviet Union had been characterized by cultural pluralism, at least by comparison with what would come later, and in the early years of Stalin's rule this even shifted toward radical egalitarianism, iconoclasm, and a celebration of breaks from established culture. By the early 1930s, however, Stalin began to reimpose social hierarchy and respect for authority. He reinstituted higher pay differentials between skilled and unskilled workers, and reasserted the importance of traditional gender roles.

The Red Army was no exception to this pattern. For most of its existence it had been run on the collegial principle. That is, the true authority in the Red Army had come from collective leadership. Though Trotskii, Frunze, and Voroshilov undoubtedly had a great deal of individual authority within the Red Army, many of the most important policy decisions were made by the dozen or so officers in the collective Revolutionary-Military Council. That began to change in 1934. As part of Stalin's general defense of order and authority, he returned to the Red Army much of the independence and status it craved. In March 1934 the last vestiges of political commissars' control over line officers went out. The Revolutionary-Military Council was abolished as well on 20 June 1934 and replaced by a larger and wholly advisory body, giving Voroshilov a much freer hand in implementing policy. Stalin reestablished traditional military ranks as well in September 1935, bringing back "captains," "majors," and "colonels" to the Soviet army. The rank of "general" was the only one still politically unacceptable. Simultaneously Stalin created the rank of "Marshal of the Soviet Union" as a further mark of status and prestige. The first five marshals were Voroshilov, Tukhachevskii, Semyon Budënnyi, Aleksandr Egorov, and Vasilii Bliukher. Three of those five would not survive the honor.

Military officers appreciated their new marks of status, but this return to order had a darker side. Stalin's particularly pathological brand of paranoia only grew and strengthened over time. His propensity to nurse grudges and search out conspiracies strengthened the already-poisonous atmosphere of Soviet politics, in which any mishap was seen as deliberate sabotage and any disagreement as a deadly schism. Starting from the still mysterious 1934 assassination of Sergei Kirov, the party boss of Leningrad, Stalin carefully laid the groundwork for settling scores with all those who had challenged him in the past, regardless of their current weakness. His old foes Lev Kamenev and Grigorii Zinov'ev, falsely implicated in the Kirov murder, fell victim to a show trial and were executed in August 1936. Stalin soon cast his net wider, hunting down all who had been part of opposition to him in the 1920s, ignoring their now-complete submission to his rule.

Nor did Stalin ignore the Red Army, which despite its network of political controllers could still pose a serious potential threat to his rule. Evidence suggests that German intelligence prepared forged documents implicating Tukhachevskii in treason, documents subsequently relayed to Stalin by Czechoslovak president Eduard Benes. The influence of these forgeries, in all probability, was minor. Stalin needed few justifications for purging anyone who could pose an actual or potential threat to his power. Tukhachevskii's evident ambition and arrogance, together with his strained relations with Voroshilov, made him the natural target of a purge directed at the army.

Early signs of danger for the Red Army's leadership had come in January 1937, when Karl Radek, starring in another show trial, had mentioned Tukhachevskii's name. On 4 May, Tukhachevskii's trip to London for the coronation of King George VI was abruptly cancelled, and then on 10 May Stalin restored full power to the Red Army's political commissars. These guardians of political orthodoxy were intended to maintain iron control over military officers, even as they were under attack by the state they were sworn to serve. The same day Tukhachevskii was removed from his position as deputy commissar for defense and appointed to the command of the backwater Volga Military District. Two weeks later, on 25 May, Voroshilov further prepared the ground for massive purges by decrying a series of mishaps in the Soviet Air Force that he attributed to deliberate sabotage by foreign agents.

At the time of Tukhachevskii's transfer to the Volga, several high-ranking military officers were already under arrest. He was taken into custody at the end of May with seven fellow officers, including Ieronim Uborevich, commander of the Belorussian Military District, and Iona Iakir, commander of the Ukrainian Military District. They were quickly tried, found guilty of treasonous conduct as members of a "fascist-Trotskiite band" who had aimed "at any cost and by any means to liquidate Soviet order and annihilate Soviet power," and immediately shot in June 1937. Voroshilov was careful to emphasize in his announcement of their crimes that they had neither confessed all their evil deeds nor named all their confederates, so many more spies and saboteurs must remain in the ranks of the Red Army. He went further and declared that those in the Red Army who voluntarily came forward to confess their crimes and name their co-conspirators would not be arrested or prosecuted. This triggered a steadily widening circle of denunciations and counter-denunciations. In a process very similar to the cycle of arrests, denunciations, and further arrests in broader Soviet society, those officers falsely accused of treason could try to save themselves by fabricating a long list of fictional crimes and denouncing their fellow officers as foreign agents.

Accounts vary on the precise number of officers discharged from service, imprisoned, or executed over the next two horrible years. One newly available 1940 account, prepared after the worst of the purges were over, puts the number of officers (not enlisted men) expelled from the armed forces or arrested by the NKVD at just over 34,000. The number of those arrested and subsequently executed after their discharge is still unknown, but at least 8,000 were subsequently rehabilitated and returned to duty in 1938–39 as the purges slowly ground to a halt and the need for competent officers grew more apparent.

The purges went so far and killed so many of the Red Army's desperately needed officers that the terror eventually burned itself out. By November 1939 Voroshilov was reprimanding officers for being too zealous in rooting out enemy agents and saboteurs, something impossible to imagine two years before. The approach of war even meant that some military officers were rehabilitated, brought out of prison camps, and returned to active duty. Boris Vannikov was pulled from prison to run the Soviet Union's ammunition industry during World War II; Konstantin Rokossovskii returned from arrest to command a Soviet corps, an army, and finally numerous fronts before becoming Poland's minister of defense after the war.

The purges appear to have been disproportionately aimed at the highest ranks of the Red Army. Enlisted men escaped relatively unscathed, while around 20 percent of the officer corps, which grew from around 150,000 in 1937 to nearly 180,000 in 1938, suffered some sort of repression. By comparison, 3 of the USSR's 5 marshals were executed along with 14 of 16 army commanders who were purged, 60 of 67 corps commanders, 136 of 199 division commanders, and 221 of 397 brigade commanders. Finding a pattern to who survived and who did not is exceedingly difficult. The purges slaughtered many veterans of the tsar's officer corps while leaving others untouched. Serving alongside Stalin during the Civil War, especially in the First Cavalry Army (Konarmiia), seems to have afforded some degree of protection. The two marshals who survived the purges, Voroshilov and Budënnyi, had been closely associated with Stalin. Other prominent survivors—including Georgii Zhukov and Semyon Timoshenko—were veterans of the First Cavalry. Even this pattern does not always hold true; Marshal Egorov had served with Stalin, yet perished.

The Red Army's development in the interwar period has to be judged at least to some degree by its dismal performance in 1941. The summer of 1941 was so disastrous that in some ways the entire interwar history of the Soviet military has been read backwards from it. The great majority of Russian and Soviet historians have attempted to place the blame for the staggering losses of the first several months of the war against Nazi Germany squarely on Stalin, who had purged the Red Army of its most talented commanders and had refused to believe ample warnings of Hitler's intentions to invade the USSR. This is certainly true, though some correctives must be introduced. Not all of the Red Army's failures can be attributed to Stalin.

The most obvious explanation for the Red Army's disasters has been one of the most popular. Stalin's Great Purges removed the Red Army's most talented officers, leaving behind either inexperienced commanders asked to fulfill responsibilities they had never been prepared for, or long-serving mediocrities distinguished only by their sycophancy toward Stalin. Though talented commanders like Timoshenko, Zhukov, and Rokossovskii did survive the purges, the loss of so many experienced officers made the Red Army at the outbreak of World War II, in David Glantz's words, a "stumbling colossus."

Despite the inherent plausibility and popularity of this interpretation of the Red Army's failures, historians have recently advanced other explanations for the Red Army's terrible showing. Roger Reese has turned away from the purges to look at the Red Army's excessively rapid expansion in the late 1930s. Industrial expansion gave the Soviet Union the potential to field a modern, technologically sophisticated army but did not create either the educated population needed to man a mechanized army nor the large cohort of well-trained officers and bureaucrats to coordinate it. It was this excessively rapid expansion, Reese argues, that led to disaster in 1941.

My own work suggests still a third explanation for the Red Army's disastrous performance. After the Manchurian Crisis of 1931 triggered a huge Soviet military buildup in response to fears of war with Japan, Soviet procurement never slowed back down. Soviet factories continued to devote scarce resources to churning out ever more tanks, aircraft, and artillery pieces, while neglecting the importance of keeping abreast of technological developments. As a result, the USSR entered World War II in June 1941 with an immense tank force of almost entirely obsolescent vehicles. Of the over 20,000 tanks in the Red Army, only 1,800 were modern, highly effective KV-1 heavy and T-34 medium tanks. The rest were mostly light tanks and tankettes built from the designs Khalepskii had purchased over a decade before. Soviet pilots were likewise only just beginning to receive new advanced aircraft like the Il–2 (Shturmovik) ground attack plane; the bulk of Soviet aircraft was of outdated design and not capable of meeting Hitler's Luftwaffe on even terms. Obsolete tanks and aircraft could only consume scarce supplies of fuel, ammunition, and trained crews.

Cynthia Roberts has explored yet another problem: the Red Army's continuing and unquestioning commitment to a strategy of forward defense and immediate counterattack, without considering the comparative merits of defense-in-depth against the German army. All of these explanations should be seen as complementary. The problems of disorganization and lack of discipline that Reese outlined were only worsened by stretching skilled personnel thinly over a vast array of obsolete tanks and aircraft. The slaughter of the Red Army's best thinkers and most experienced administrators made dealing with the challenges of changing strategy and technology that much more difficult.

The Russo-Finnish War of 1939–40, and the humiliating initial defeats the Red Army suffered at the hands of outnumbered and outgunned Finns, brought home many of the problems that would prove so costly in 1941. For one, it became immediately apparent that most of the Soviet Union's tanks were far too lightly armed and armored to survive on a modern battlefield, even against the armorless Finnish army, and that the multi-turreted T-28 medium and T-35 heavy tanks were a dead-end design. The Red Army's high command accordingly accelerated the introduction of the vastly superior KV-1 heavy and T-34 medium tanks.

Another positive result of the debacle of the Russo-Finnish War for the Red Army's combat effectiveness was the replacement of the poor leadership at the very top of the Soviet Army. On 7 May 1940 Stalin removed Voroshilov and Boris Shaposhnikov as people's commissar for defense and chief of staff, respectively. They were replaced by Timoshenko, who had successfully reorganized the Red Army finally to defeat the Finns, and Kirill Meretskov. Timoshenko quickly moved to overhaul the Red Army's training methods to make them more realistic and effective.

As a sop to the Red Army's beleaguered officer corps, high military ranks were reinstated to boost Timoshenko's standing and salve the wounds of great purges. The rank of "general" was restored, so Soviet officers could now become major-generals, lieutenant-generals, colonel-generals, and generals of the army on their way to the ultimate rank of Marshal of the Soviet Union. Shortly thereafter, Stalin formally eliminated the hated institution of political commissar, converting them en masse from commissars into deputy officers for political affairs and thereby significantly reducing their influence and prestige.

These last-minute efforts to restore competence and professionalism to a devastated Red Army did not have nearly enough time to succeed. In the final run-up to the 22 June 1941 Nazi invasion of the Soviet Union, the Red Army's leadership took increasingly frantic measures to prepare for the German onslaught. Despite Stalin's bizarre refusal to believe that Hitler's attack was imminent, Timoshenko and Zhukov issued urgent orders over the week preceding *Barbarossa* to camouflage airfields and other military installations. Stalin's inability to recognize the Soviet Union's imminent disaster forced Timoshenko and Zhukov to soften their warnings of surprise attack by mentioning the possibility of German bluffing or provocation. On 21 June they warned their western military districts "to be in complete combat readiness to meet a possible surprise attack by the Germans or their allies," but cautioned their troops "not to give in to any kind of provocations." On 22 June, Stalin and the Red Army alike realized that they were not dealing with a provocation.

## Further Research

Since the opening of former Soviet archives, unfortunately, relatively little research has been done on the Red Army. The exceptions are welcome, but sparse compared to the work done on other aspects of Soviet history. Almost all facets of the interwar Red Army still await serious, archivally based research.

Perhaps the most crying need for research is a more in-depth look at the purges of the Red Army officer corps. Soviet technical and economic cooperation with countries other than Germany is terribly understudied, as are the Soviet Union's military relations with governments and political parties in the developing world, particularly China and Turkey. Lastly, while there is a great deal of scholarship on the Soviet military economy, it tends to be much richer for the late 1920s and early 1930s, but thinner on the early 1920s and the immediate prewar years. In general terms, source materials tend to be much more chaotic and difficult to find for the early years of the Soviet Union and for the period of the purges. In addition, the lack of any political opposition and pervasive fear common by the late 1930s renders the sources that did survive much less insightful than those for previous years.

## Sources and Further Reading

All research on the interwar Red Army starts from two classic studies: D. Fedotoff White's *The Growth of the Red Army* (Princeton, 1944) and John Erickson's *The Soviet High Command* (London, 1962). Those two books took the study of the Red Army about as far as it was possible to go in the absence of archival sources.

Since the opening of the archives, the area that has received the most study is the growth and development of the Soviet military economy in the interwar period. This boomlet in research includes R. W. Davies, "Soviet Military Expenditure and the Armaments Industry, 1929–33: A Reconsideration," *Europe-Asia Studies* 45 (1993): 577–608; Davies and Mark Harrison, "The Soviet Military-economic Effort during the Second Five-Year Plan (1933–1937), *Europe-Asia Studies* 49 (1997): 369–406;

Lennart Samuelson, *Plans for Stalin's War Machine: Tukhachevskii and Military Economic Planning, 1925–1941* (London, 1999); Nikolai Simonov, *Voenno-promyshlennyi kompleks SSSR* (Moscow, 1996); Sally Stoecker, *Forging Stalin's Army: Marshal Tukhachevsky and the Politics of Military Innovation* (Boulder, 1998); and my own *Hammer and Rifle: The Militarization of the Soviet Union, 1926–1933* (Lawrence, KS, 2000) and "Tukhachevskii in Leningrad: Military Politics and Exile, 1928–31," *Europe-Asia Studies* 48 (1996): 1365–1386.

Archival documents on the Soviet side of the collaboration with Germany are available in Yuri Dyakov and Tatyana Bushueva, *The Red Army and the Wehrmacht: How the Soviets Militarized Germany, 1922–1933* (Amherst, NY, 1995).

For new information on the Soviet Navy, see Jurgen Rohwer and Mikhail Monakov, "The Soviet Union's Ocean-Going Fleet, 1935–1956," *International History Review* 18 (1996): 837–868.

David Glantz' *Stumbling Colossus* (Lawrence, KS, 1998) explores the parlous state of the Red Army on the eve of World War II. See also Cynthia Roberts, "Planning for War: The Red Army and the Catastrophe of 1941," *Europe-Asia Studies* 47 (1995): 1293–1326. The disastrous Finnish campaign is covered in Carl Van Dyke, *The Soviet Invasion of Finland, 1939–1940* (London, 1997).

Other scholars have examined the social history of the Red Army. Written before archives became available, Mark Von Hagen's *Soldiers in the Proletarian Dictatorship: The Red Army and the Soviet Socialist State, 1917–1930* (Ithaca, NY, 1990) looks at the Soviet state's changing view of the place of the military in its new order. Roger Reese, *Stalin's Reluctant Soldiers: A Social History of the Red Army, 1925–1941* (Lawrence, KS, 1996) delivers exactly what its title promises. See also his "Red Army Opposition to Forced Collectivization, 1929–1930: The Army Wavers," *Slavic Review* 55 (1996): 24–45.

New scholarship, especially in Russia, on the purges of the military has tended to celebrate those purged without exploring the purges themselves. Until large-scale new research is carried out, see the chapter in Reese, *Stalin's Reluctant Soldiers,* and Robert Conquest, *The Great Terror* (London, 1968).

# CHAPTER 6

# THE RISE AND FALL OF SOVIET OPERATIONAL ART, 1917–1941

*Frederick W. Kagan*

THE OPERATIONAL LEVEL OF WAR, THE LEVEL BETWEEN TACTICS and strategy, links tactical missions together to accomplish strategic aims. Before the nineteenth century it was not generally recognized that there was such a level. During the nineteenth century military theorists sometimes referred to "grand tactics" in an effort to get at this concept, if only vaguely. But by the end of that century and the beginning of the next the concept came into being both in Germany, where the term *operativ* came into parlance in the General Staff, and in Russia. This chapter will explore the development and refinement of this important concept by Soviet military theorists in the years between World Wars I and II. The sophisticated theories they developed based on the notion that there was an "operational art" that would lead to success at this level laid the basis for Soviet success in World War II, and for the theories of armored maneuver warfare in practice both in the Soviet Union and in the West in the latter half of the twentieth century.

Soviet operational doctrine came into being in the early 1920s as a tentative answer to the fundamental problem of war at that time: how to return maneuver to a battlefield dominated by the firepower revolution. As tanks and aircraft increased in performance and reliability, Soviet doctrine changed to meet the new warfare brought about by the maneuver revolution in military affairs (RMA). This process continued, although interrupted by the purge of the army in 1937 and the consequent triumph of ideological stupidity through 1941, when the Germans struck. Once the initial cata-strophes of 1941 and 1942 were over, the Red Army returned to the theo-retical basis developed in the interwar years, improving upon it using the lessons learned during the war. The operational art created in the 1920s and 1930s, therefore, was the basis for eventual Soviet victory in World War II.

Soviet operational art was a highly sophisticated set of theories, reflect-ing both the extreme difficulty of the task the Soviet theoreticians set them-selves and the surprising number of thinkers involved in its development. Its significance has been widely discounted in the West for a number of reasons. First, Stalin executed M. N. Tukhachevskii, chief of the General Staff in the 1930s and the principal proponent of the most advanced element of these theories, in 1937. He even forbade use of the term "deep battle," which had been coined to describe one of the key elements of Soviet operational art. As a result, the Soviets entered World War II with an almost completely wrong-headed understanding of armored warfare—and it showed. When the Sovi-ets resurrected the theoretical concepts of the 1920s and 1930s and perfected them after the debacles of 1941 and 1942 (a process that will be explored in a later chapter), most Western observers chalked their successes up to the "limitless Russian hordes" and dismissed the importance of the So-viet doctrine of 1943–45, let alone that of the apparently irrelevant back-ground to that doctrine in the interwar years.

Second, to the extent that the West has acknowledged the quality of So-viet interwar thinking, it is still common to dismiss that thought as deriva-tive of either the Germans (notably Heinz Guderian) or of the English (notably B. H. Liddell Hart and J. F. C. Fuller). There are a number of rea-sons to reject this notion. The most obvious is a chronological one—the the-ories of Liddell Hart and Fuller were not widely publicized until the late 1920s and early 1930s (Guderian's work was even later), whereas the most critical portion of Soviet thinking on this subject was published in the 1920s. It was not until the mid-1930s, however, that Soviet official doctrine changed dramatically to encompass the most sophisticated aspects of Soviet theory, a change brought about during Tukhachevskii's reign as chief of the General Staff. The myth of the derivative nature of Soviet thinking, there-fore, is largely based on the myth of Tukhachevskii's preeminence in that thinking, whereas it is now clear that Tukhachevskii's thought, itself, was more synthetic than original, relying on the efforts of numerous Soviet the-orists who had gone before him.

But the most important reason for rejecting the notion that the Soviets merely aped and adapted Western theories is that Soviet operational art be-tween 1919 and 1937 was fundamentally different from anything being developed in the West at that time. It was similar only in that, like German notions of warfare or Liddell Hart's and Fuller's imaginings, it relied upon armored vehicles operating in conjunction with strike aircraft at high speed over great distances. It differed, however, in almost every particular after those agreed-upon fundamentals and was, in the end, not merely different, but more sophisticated and better than Western concepts, as the Germans learned to their dismay.

Soviet doctrine in the interwar years was developed specifically to solve the fundamental problem in war at the time: how to restore maneuver to a battlefield that had become static. A number of technological developments had combined to create the static and deadly conditions of the Western Front in World War I. The widespread use of machine guns and barbed wire made it suicide for soldiers to attempt to cross the no-man's land between the opposing trench systems. This problem preoccupied the attention of soldiers and their leaders then, and has held the attention of readers and writers of military history since, but it was not, in fact, the worst problem. In almost every major offensive operation on the Western Front, soldiers did manage to make it across no-man's land in sufficient numbers actually to enter and overrun most, if not all, of the enemy trench system. The real problem only began then.

It was the railroad, much more than the machine gun, that rendered combat on the Western Front so deadly and static. For the soldiers who had managed to penetrate and seize the enemy trench system found, to their dismay, that whereas their supplies and reinforcements had to walk slowly over a cratered and devastated wasteland to get to them, the enemy's supplies and reinforcements moved easily and speedily along the rail system in his rear. As a result, it was invariably the case that the defender was able to shift reinforcements rapidly and restore a crumbling front faster than the attacker could take advantage of his temporary success. In this way every initially successful attack, bought at so high a price in casualties, was rendered irrelevant as the defender set up new defense lines just out of the reach of the attacker, which could halt the attack and allow the defender to counterattack.

It is worth noting that the Soviet perception of the fundamental problem in war and its solutions differed profoundly from the German, French, and British perceptions during the First World War, and from the British and French perceptions even into the 1930s. Whereas in the 1920s and 1930s the Soviets focused their attention on the problem of transforming a breakthrough into an exploitation—the tactical success into the operational—the French, British, and Germans all focused their efforts during the war almost exclusively on attaining a breakthrough at a lower cost in lives. All of the major doctrinal innovations of the war were aimed at solving the tactical problem and did not in any way assist in the operational problem. The introduction of gas at Ypres in 1915 helped attain a breakthrough there—but it could not be followed up. The first mass use of tanks at Cambrai in 1917 was spectacularly successful tactically—and of no operational significance whatsoever because success and the means required to exploit it had not been clearly envisioned beforehand. German infiltration tactics, although they attained unprecedented tactical successes during the Ludendorff offensives in 1918, seem as though they were designed to preclude the possibility of transforming those tactical successes into operational successes. This failure may be due to the fact that the Germans and their enemies foresaw that operational success was impossible at the current level of technology, or it may have been simple shortsightedness. It did show, however, that the solution of tactical problems does not necessarily lead to the solution of operational problems, and that the introduction of new technology is not significant if it is not accompanied by appropriate changes in doctrine. For the Soviets and the Germans turned their attention after the war to designing a doctrine to solve the operational dilemma, and did solve it, whereas French and British armor doctrine, aimed at solving only the tactical problem, did not.

In any case, despite the Soviets' excellent understanding of the problem, they could propose no solution to it initially, aside from the wish that technology would solve the dilemma that technology had created. What they could and did do, however, was to identify the key characteristics that the new technology would require in order to solve the principal problem in war. They recognized that they were in a period of rapid technological change and that a revolution in military affairs was imminent, but they did not simply wait to see what that RMA would bring. On the contrary, even in 1921, when the performance of tanks was hopelessly inadequate to solve the operational problem, they began to outline what characteristics tanks would have to have in order to do so. The conditions of warfare at the time, rather than the changing technology, took precedence. The Soviet military leaders were determined to guide the RMA by driving technological change in a direction determined by doctrine rather than to allow unfettered technological development to guide the doctrine.

Thus, Deputy Chief of Staff of the Red Army V. K. Triandafillov wrote in 1929 that tank development since the end of the World War had been a series of "continuous attempts to convert the tank from a tactical resource to a resource of great operational significance." During the war, tanks had been designed solely to assist the infantry in the deadly dash across no-man's land—a purely tactical mission. Triandafillov argued that tank development since then had aimed at creating a weapon that could solve the more fundamental problem of transforming a tactical breakthrough into a successful operational exploitation. He noted that in order to accomplish that task, great efforts had been made to "provide new, more mobile, faster tanks with a greater radius of actions to replace the former barely mobile, barely maneuverable, short-range . . . tanks."

The tanks Triandafillov imagined faced a series of daunting challenges. The new tank "must participate not only in a relatively fast-moving attack as it accompanies the infantry into combat, but in all phases of pursuit beyond the field of battle as well." It must be "powerful enough to be able to pave the way for smaller tanks without being afraid of artillery fire," fast enough to penetrate into the enemy's rear before his railroad-mounted troops could establish secondary defensive positions, and have long enough range to make the penetration and exploitation meaningful operationally and strategically. It must accomplish those tasks, moreover, as "part of new vehicle-mounted (motorized) units" including infantry and artillery.

This vision of future war differed from Fuller's and Liddell Hart's contemporary visions in several important ways. First, in contrast with Fuller's vision, in which armies equipped only with tanks would fight one another in fluid maneuver war, the Soviet thinkers from the outset assumed that tanks would fight in combined-arms units, and that infantry and artillery would have to be motorized in order to keep up. Unlike Fuller, Liddell Hart had already accepted the notion that tanks could only function as part of a combined-arms team (relying on naval analogies for armored warfare, he called motorized infantry "tank marines"). Liddell Hart, however, held with Fuller a vision of future war that was mobile and fluid from the outset— neither one envisioned a painful penetration battle of the sort that haunted the English psyche in the aftermath of World War I.

But the Soviets from the beginning imagined that their armored forces would face a coherent defensive position at the outset and that a penetration battle was unavoidable. Thus, whereas Liddell Hart and Fuller worked almost exclusively on the problem of maneuvering armored forces in the depths of the enemy defenses, the Soviets concerned themselves first with penetrating the enemy defensive positions, transitioning from that breakthrough into an exploitation phase, and only then with maneuvering the exploitation forces deep in the enemy's rear. This focus on all aspects of the problem was one of the greatest advantages of Soviet theory over Western developments in the interwar years.

It is not that the Soviets were smarter than the British—on the contrary, Liddell Hart and Fuller were as well-educated, creative, and intelligent as any of the Soviet theorists (indeed, as any military thinkers of any time). But the Soviets had not experienced the horrors of the Western Front trench warfare and both Liddell Hart and Fuller had done so directly. The Soviets, therefore, were able to consider the possibility of fighting a penetration battle with equanimity, whereas for Fuller and Liddell Hart, and almost any Englishmen in the 1920s or 1930s, for that matter, such a prospect was horrific and unacceptable. Western conceptions of future war, thus, assumed scenarios in which penetration battles would not be necessary, focusing on the more congenial aspects of their visions, while the Soviets were able to take a grimmer and more realistic view of the problem as a whole.

It is important to note here that the difference in perspective did not result from the different experiences of the Russian army on the Eastern Front or the Bolshevik armies in the Russian Civil War, except indirectly. Very little of Soviet interwar doctrine was based on careful examinations of those experiences. Soviet theorists, instead, relied on the close study of the Allies' experiences on the Western Front to draw their conclusions, informed to a relatively minor degree by their own experiences in the Civil War. The main significance of the difference, as mentioned above, lies in the fact that since the Soviets did not participate in the horrific struggles on the Western Front, their analyses could be more dispassionate and objective.

The Soviets benefited as well from the fact that Marxist-Leninist dogma emphasizes human and social developments over technological changes. They thus came to believe that the particular technological developments that had occurred before and during the World War were far less important than a more profound social, economic, and political change that resulted from the aggregate of the technological advances: the advent of truly mass armies. The Soviets believed that the development of mass armies and the complete mobilization of societies for war, even more than particular pieces of technology, had fundamentally transformed war. Specifically, they believed that the age of decisive battles was over and that strategy had to change at the deepest level as a result.

S. S. Kamenev, commander-in-chief of the Soviet Union's Armed Forces (1919–24), wrote in 1922, "The general engagement, that is, one in which one of the belligerents wins the entire campaign, has been transformed in the struggle of mass armies into an entire period of battles . . ." He asserted that the destruction of any one sector of a front would not end the campaign; indeed, it would hardly be noticed in other sectors of the front. The defender would merely rush reserves and reinforcements to the destroyed sector and resurrect it. He concluded that in contemporary war, victory in a campaign can only result from an uninterrupted series of successive victories. Napoleon's age had passed: the search for a single decisive battle in the modern age would be fruitless.

The reason for this development was that modern armies had become vast, multi-million-man organizations, spread out across tens of thousands of square miles. An attack on one sector of a front necessarily engaged only a small portion of the enemy's overall strength, because the vast bulk of the enemy's army was dispersed over such a large area. When the Germans destroyed two Russian armies at Tannenberg in 1914, for instance, they found their victory most incomplete not through any fault of the commanders, but because the bulk of the Russian army had not even arrived in the theater of war yet. Likewise when the Germans attacked a large concentration of French forces at Verdun in 1916, not only were the French able to shift great numbers of reserves from other parts of the front, but their British allies were even able to launch a major attack of their own along the Somme. By contrast, when Napoleon's forces engaged the main Prussian army at Jena-Auerstädt in 1806, or the main Austrian army at Wagram in 1809, the forces they defeated were the overwhelming majority of the forces Prussia and Austria could mobilize to fight at the time. The Soviets studied that contrast and concluded that Napoleonic-style decisive battles were no longer attainable, that the essence of strategy had fundamentally changed.

They came to believe, therefore, that victory in modern warfare could only be attained through a series of operations executed consecutively. In this way, each concentration of enemy forces could be destroyed in rapid sequence and if decisive battles were no longer possible, then perhaps decisive campaigns could still be contemplated. The question then arose, how quickly should each operation follow the last? The Soviets answered unequivocally: "the uninterruptedness of the conduct of operations is the main condition of victory." Operations can not and should not alternate with pauses, they argued, and commanders must act creatively to maintain constant pressure on the enemy. This belief in the critical importance of successive operations conducted without pauses between them became a cardinal tenet of Soviet operational art that had no parallel anywhere in the world at the time.

The need for immediately successive operations arose, for the Soviets, primarily from the fear that pauses would allow the enemy time to regroup and restore a coherent defensive position—precisely the problem that had bedeviled World War I commanders. M. N. Tukhachevskii, chief of the General Staff of the Red Army in the 1930s, wrote in 1924 that operations must follow one another seamlessly—they must flow together as though they were simply "separate extensions of a single operation." If the enemy can once be brought to battle, Tukhachevskii reasoned, and his defensive position then be broken, then the "new destructive operation must follow straight from the advance, without any loss of time whatever. . . ."

The key to victory in operations, Tukhachevskii believed, was maintaining the initiative at all times. He noted, "One must remember that, even if he has only routed the enemy in the initial operation rather than destroyed him, the attacker is in an extremely favorable position vis-à-vis the defeated side. He has control of the situation, provided only that he denies the enemy freedom of action by continuous pursuit and that he maintains unrelenting pressure in striving for the final destruction of all the forces opposing him."

Tukhachevskii placed special emphasis on the absolute necessity for exploitation to follow immediately on penetration. German armored doctrine, like the doctrine embodied in the Schlieffen Plan in 1914, relied on the *kesselschlacht,* or battle of encirclement, in which the point of an operation was the reduction of encircled enemy pockets. Tukhachevskii felt that the importance of an operation was in turning the penetration of the line immediately into an exploitation, and then into a pursuit of the defeated enemy forces, without pausing to mop up enemy forces remaining in their initial defensive positions. He warned, "Abstaining from follow-on operations until the enemy army is completely destroyed deprives the victor of continued control of the situation. A pause faces him with the need to fight a new battle, in which the chances of success are more or less equal for both sides, just as they are in the initial operation."

This belief in the danger of pauses was one of the fundamental principles of Soviet operational art. Kamenev asserted that, in the conditions of mass warfare armed with railroads, "during the smallest respite the defeated side, having in its dispositions a rear with working railroads, was fully able to put its forces in order, strengthen them, and become stronger than we, the victors." Precisely this, he said, had occurred during the Russian Civil War.

This element of Soviet operational art has received little attention in the studies of Soviet doctrine, although the Soviet authors themselves—including the oft-cited Tukhachevskii—laid great stress on it. Noting that "1918, with its grandiose deadly battles, did not resolve the problem of overcoming the front on an operational scale and was the apotheosis of the dead-end which military art in the epoch of imperialism attained," G. S. Isserson, the chief of the Department of Operational Art at the Frunze General Staff Academy in the 1930s, saw the uninterruptedness of operations as critical. He argued that in the conditions of contemporary warfare, "future deep operations will appear not as single links of a series of interrupted engagements, but as an unbroken chain extending for the entire depth of military activities." Isserson went on to redefine the very concept of the "operation": in modern war any "operation" must be seen as a series of operations merging into one another to form a unified whole. He regarded this development as introducing a new dimension, the dimension of depth, into warfare, and concluded that "we find ourselves on the border of a new epoch of military art and must transition from linear strategy to deep strategy."

Isserson noted that the mere appearance of new technology does not solve a problem that is really one of conceptualizing the nature of modern war. He believed that the development of technological tools was necessary to make possible the deep operations he foresaw, but that by themselves they did not solve the problem. Throughout history, he argued, "one may point to many circumstances when new means of battle did not provide the necessary effect" because they were used in "antiquated forms of deployment and methods of action that were not appropriate." He concluded, "New weapons demand new forms of implementation in combat."

Isserson was witnessing, we must remember, a profound revolution in military technology. The development of bombers had led many in the West to believe that all other forms of war were irrelevant, and that this new technology would alone dominate all future battles, while Fuller, at times, argued that tanks—flying tanks, swimming tanks, and rolling tanks—would be the only weapons on the future battlefield of any importance.

Nevertheless, the real solution to the problem, Isserson argued, lay not in technology or even in the development of appropriate doctrine for using the technology, but in the proper understanding of the nature of war. In the period of mass armies and defenses deployed in great depth, Isserson believed that "one wave of operational efforts employing a linear strategy will not be able to resolve anything at all . . . and must smash itself helplessly in the depths of contemporary opposition." Army doctrine must be changed fundamentally, he argued, because an army simply cannot deploy for maneuver in depth in the same fashion in which it would deploy to fight linear war.

For Isserson recognized, as any proponent of consecutive, uninterrupted operations must, that the critical problem remained: at some point any given group of attacking forces must reach a limit beyond which it can attack no more. At that point, that group of forces must go over to the defensive, thereby providing the enemy the respite the Soviets so feared. His solution was to realize that, "The exhaustion of the offensive has its true cause not so much in the self-exhaustion of the strength of the attacker as in the growth of the opposition of the defender." For the defender, pushed back on his reserves and his logistical bases, may well end up stronger at the culminating point of the attack then he had been at the beginning. Isserson believed that the greatest danger for the attacker lay in preparing himself most thoroughly for the initial attack and penetration, and failing to prepare adequately for the final, climactic battle deep in the enemy's rear, thinking that "the final moment of the operation would be the easiest."

He argued that, on the contrary, the initial attack, "always secured by the timely concentration of forces and well-planned preparation," will be by far the easiest, but that "the greatest tension and crisis must be expected at the end. The art and firmness of the operational commander consists in approaching this decisive moment with full providence, with a new wave of operational efforts and fully armed with the necessary forces and means for the final completion of the destruction operation. . . ." He concluded that "the contemporary operation is an operation of depth; it must be calculated for the entire depth and must be prepared to conquer the entire depth."

Such a general statement of the "solution," Isserson recognized, provided no solution at all. He saw, rather, that doctrine had to include concrete suggestions for the solution of known problems. Isserson was not willing to accept a doctrine that foresaw that attacks would culminate prematurely and go over to the defensive while they prepared new strikes. He believed instead that the deployment and maneuver of the attacking forces had to be changed to avoid such premature culmination: "The deep echelonment of the opposition calls forth just as deep a deployment of the offensive. This offensive must be like a whole series of waves flowing toward the shore with growing strength in order to wash away and destroy it with their uninterrupted blows from the depths." Thus, in a poetic turn of phrase, Isserson introduced the notion that is at the heart of Soviet operational art: the echelonment of the attack to match the structure of the defense, and the principle of strategic dispersion of forces prior to their massing for the final decisive blow.

Since the defense would be deployed in a layered series of belts separated one from the next by several kilometers, any attacking force would face a wearying series of penetration battles before it found its way into the open spaces of the operational rear. The linear formations that had dominated war for two centuries could not cope with this situation: their strength would inevitably wear away long before the last defensive belt had been breached. The solution that Isserson foresaw was the equivalent echelonment of the attack: waves advanced upon the defensive belts, and when the first wave had crested, so to speak, the second wave would overtake it and carry on the attack anew.

One may argue that Napoleon also practiced strategic dispersal of his forces prior to massing them for the main blow—the development of the corps/division system was aimed precisely at making this possible and thereby easing the burden on his logistics administration. Napoleon, however, aimed to keep his forces dispersed until he had maneuvered the enemy into position for a single decisive battle in which the campaign would be decided. His aim was always to concentrate his entire force on the field of that battle. The objective of Soviet echelonment was quite different. Rather than seeking to cut short the campaign in a single climactic battle, the "layering" of Soviet offensive forces was designed to prolong the campaign by ensuring that the attack did not exhaust itself prematurely. The Soviets recognized that there would, of course, be a "decisive battle" in which the campaign was won or lost—it would be the last battle. They were determined to mass their forces for that battle, for they believed that it would be the hardest to win. In contrast with Napoleon, however, who scrupulously kept his forces from battle until the "decisive" battle was at hand, the Soviets knew that their "decisive" battle would come only after a long string of lesser battles—after they had "fought for every kilometer." Isserson's dispersal-concentration plan was designed to ensure that the attack would not culminate before the decisive final battle had been won. It was a plan designed to ensure the uninterrupted conduct of operations from the moment that breakthrough had been achieved to the final defeat of the enemy.

The outgrowth of the echelonment of the offensive was the "operational-maneuver group" (OMG). The concept is obvious in light of the experience of the First World War: the forces that make the breakthrough cannot then exploit it in the face of strong resistance, for they will already have exhausted themselves, whereas arriving defending reserves will be fresh. A special "exploitation echelon" must, therefore, be maintained that can penetrate the breach opened by the assault forces and move for decisive victory into the operational depths. The failure to maintain such an echelon, Isserson argued, would be "to continue the system of mindless, exhausting frontal assaults in which the linear strategy of 1918 was born."

What Western scholarship does not emphasize, despite the stress on it in Isserson and others, is that the Soviets conceived of the OMG not simply as a force to develop the attack into the operational depths, but as a second echelon force that, itself tactically echeloned, would be capable of carrying on a series of uninterrupted consecutive operations culminating in "the destruction of the opposition of the defense throughout the entire operational depth." Isserson believed his principal enemy to be positional warfare, and sought to defeat it with the true implementation of the operational art: the pursuit of dominating maneuver in the form of a planned series of consecutive operations conducted without pause from the moment when a breakthrough was achieved to the complete destruction of the enemy's defense throughout its entire depth.

The various threads of Soviet interwar thought came together in the 1936 edition of the *Field Regulations of the Red Army* (PU-36). The doctrine outlined in that document emphasized using surprise and deception to seize and hold the initiative, attacking the enemy throughout the entire depth of his *operational* defense, echeloning the attacking forces, and moving from breakthrough to exploitation and pursuit immediately and without delay.

The Soviet emphasis on surprise and deception is well known. It sprang from a truth that all participants in and analysts of the war on the Western Front perceived: the repeated inability of attackers to conceal the preparations for the attack from the defenders allowed the latter to mass reserves behind the threatened sector even before the attack itself began—always before the defensive lines had been breached. What made this possible was the fact that the defender could use the rail network in his rear to transport troops, but the attacker had to walk across no-man's land and fight through the trenches. The advent of long-distance, fast-moving tanks changed this equation and made the Soviet emphasis on surprise and deception feasible. Now the attack could penetrate the initial defensive lines in a matter of hours, certainly within a day or so—the attackers could win the race. What is more, the speed of the tanks would allow them to disperse prior to the attack, thus rendering more difficult the defender's task of discerning the location and timing of the attack.

But the Soviets were not content to rely on surprise to facilitate the breakthrough, for they realized that the defender could still respond rapidly and seal off the breaches in his line. They thus developed a concept called "deep battle," which relied upon strike aircraft, long-range artillery, and rapidly penetrating tank thrusts to penetrate and disrupt the entire operational depth of the defender. Aircraft would strike reserve concentrations, forcing them to disperse or die. They would attack rail junctions and bridges, slowing the movement of reserves toward the threatened sectors to a crawl—if not isolating the battlefield altogether. They would attack supply depots and command and control centers, seeking to disrupt the defense on a large scale.

While the defending commanders were busy dealing with all that, special "shock" groups, heavy in artillery and infantry-support tanks, would crush selected sectors of the front with overwhelming force. When the breakthrough had been accomplished, the second echelon exploitation forces would race through the breach and into the enemy's rear. In this way, the enemy would be faced with the destruction of the infrastructure and command and control nets he needed to move his forces around *at the same time as* powerful armored forces thrust deep into his rear. It was a combination that, when executed properly (as it was toward the end of World War II), no defender could hope to stand up against.

The emphasis throughout PU-36 was on speed, audacity, seizing the initiative at all levels, and the aggressive use of their own initiative by subordinate commanders at all levels. At the same time, it required careful coordination not only of all branches within the Red Army, but of the ground forces with the air forces as well. Similarly, the Soviets' own command nets would be placed under maximum strain in the effort not only to coordinate this incredibly complicated movement of hundreds of thousands of troops, but also to find out what was going on, since it was expected that subordinate commanders at all levels would deviate from the plan when they saw opportunities or dangers. Finally, it would be necessary to keep these fast-moving forces supplied at all times, and the strain on the logistics system seemed likely to be overwhelming.

And therein lay the problem: none of the technological systems or organizational structures were in place in the interwar years to give any hope of success in these endeavors. In the interwar years Soviet theory far outstripped Soviet practice and Soviet capabilities. In fact, no army in the world in 1945, let alone 1935, could have implemented the Soviet theory of operational art developed in the 1920s and 1930s. The demands for high-speed tanks with rapid-firing, highly accurate main guns firing effective armor-piercing rounds on the move could not be met by military technology until the 1970s. Nor could the Soviets produce the armored personnel carriers, or even trucks, necessary for the infantry and artillery to keep up this fast-paced armored strike—despite the fact that Soviet doctrine explicitly called for continuous combined arms operations. The characteristics that the doctrine demanded for aircraft were similarly unattainable until the most recent generation of high-performance aircraft went into production.

Similar problems existed with the support services. The radio-poor Red Army was not up to the communications and command and control challenge posed by the complexity of these operations. Worst of all, however, was the situation in the logistics services. As the Soviets set about creating the military might they felt they needed, priority had to go to the production of tanks, without which armored doctrine is not armored. But what the logistics administration desperately needed was trucks—and those were in short supply. The problem of supplying these lightning-strike attacks as they expanded over hundreds of kilometers of devastated territory would prove to be almost insurmountable for much of the Second World War.

Still, by 1945 the Soviets had solved, or at least found acceptable "fixes" for, all of these problems, and were able to implement something that looked very much like the doctrine described in PU-36. By looking at the problem from the bottom up, objectively, and with all its complexities, the Soviets evolved the most sophisticated and accurate concept of modern armored war. From this standpoint, the purges of 1937 that swept these developments aside were among the most tragic events in Russian history.

## Further Research

For all that has been written about it, this topic is far from exhausted. Much work remains to be done both on individual thinkers and writers and on the development of the theory as a whole. If the Soviet-era archives open fully enough to permit their use, then a careful study of the interrelationship between the doctrinal debate and the organization, training, and general preparation of the Red Army in this period would be invaluable, as would an examination of the relationship between doctrine, threat assessment, and war planning.

## Sources and Further Reading

There are a number of very good studies on the development of Soviet operational art. The most recent is Shimon Naveh, *In Pursuit of Military Excellence: The Evolution of Operational Theory* (Portland, OR: Frank Cass, 1997), which contains the most up-to-date and complete bibliography of works on the topic in both English and Russian. David Glantz has produced a number of solid works, including *Soviet Military Operational Art: In Pursuit of Deep Battle* (Portland, OR: Frank Cass, 1991) and *Soviet Conduct of Tactical Maneuver, Spearhead of the Offensive* (Portland, OR: Frank Cass, 1991). Richard Simpkin, *Deep Battle: The Brainchild of Marshal Tukhachevskii* (London, 1987) is somewhat dated, but its collection of translated Soviet articles and manuals is invaluable for those approaching this topic without a reading knowledge of Russian.

The most easily accessible collection of key writings for those who do read Russian is A. B. Kadisnev, Ed., *Voprosy Strategii i Operativnogo Iskusstva v Sovetskikh Voennykh Trudakh (1917–1940)* (Moscow: Voennoe Izdatel'stvo, 1965).

CHAPTER 7

# DRESS REHEARSALS, 1937–1941

*Mary R. Habeck*

BY THE MID-1930S, THE SOVIET ARMY SHOULD HAVE felt confident that it was prepared to meet the challenges posed by the enemies that encircled the country. Once devastated by civil war, famine, and economic collapse, the socialist homeland now possessed a thriving military industry, a large, modern army, and a people who seemed united behind their charismatic leader. Stalin's ideology and ambitions had apparently transformed his country's economy, society, and army into an efficient machine dedicated to national defense.

The new Stalinist nation, however, had not yet faced war, the ultimate test of its preparations for the inevitable clash with the imperialists. Fifteen years would pass between the last retreat of the Red cavalry from Warsaw and the first combat employing the rebuilt and modernized Soviet Army. Then, in battlefields as far flung as in Spain, Finland, Poland, and the Far-Eastern borderlands, the Soviets finally tried out their armed forces and learned how well their new army, weaponry, and ideas about warfare suited modern combat. Although none of these five conflicts were protracted affairs, and the Red Army did not deploy its full strength in any of them, the Soviets took their "small" wars very seriously. The high command argued that the conflicts provided a picture in miniature of the coming larger conflict and used them to make broad generalizations about how to fight modern battles.

The result was that the wars took on a significance for the Soviet army far beyond their modest size. Red Army officers endlessly analyzed the performance of their fighting forces, while the high command ordered extensive

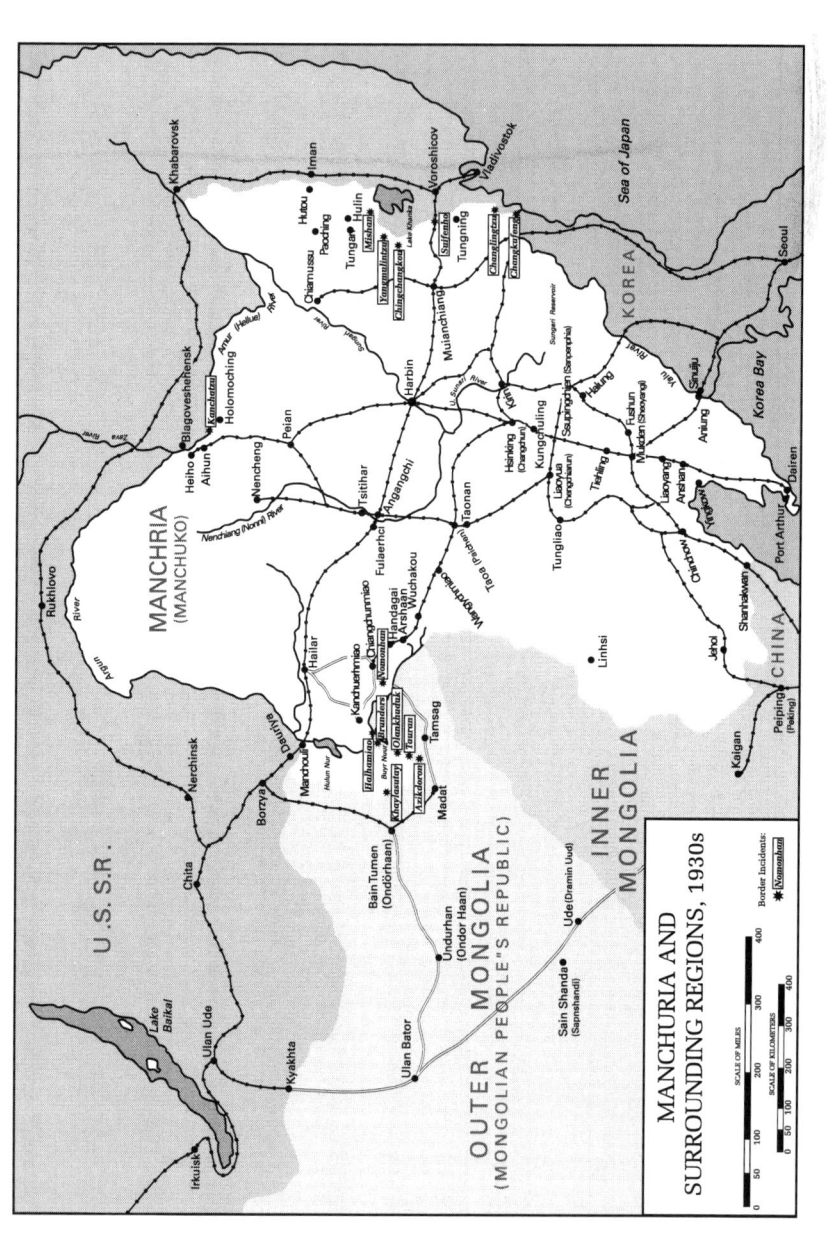

MANCHURIA AND
SURROUNDING REGIONS, 1930s

changes in technology and tactics to reflect the lessons that battle had taught. Stalin would also exploit the weaknesses exposed by combat to rid himself of troublesome officers and to promote men who would support him more whole-heartedly. The army that emerged from these wars was ideologically unified but also younger, less willing to take chances, and saddled with outmoded ideas about warfare that the Second World War would soon prove wrong.

The one factor ignored by every Soviet analysis of these wars was the debilitating effect of the purges that had decimated the Red Army officer corps. Soviet observers duly noted the terrible command and control of their forces, and complained about the inexperience of the thousands of young men thrust into positions of authority. They never dared, however, to criticize or even mention publicly Stalin's decision to decapitate the army at the moment of greatest danger for the Soviet Union. Neither the enemies nor potential allies of the Soviet Union were so delicate. Japan and Nazi Germany in particular took notice of the generally poor performance of the Red Army in their "small" wars and believed that the conflicts showed the effects of the purges. Their consequent conclusion that Stalin had fatally weakened his defensive forces persuaded them to take chances that a strong and experienced Soviet officer corps might have discouraged.

## The Spanish Civil War, 1936–39

The first test of the new Soviet military took place during Spain's civil war. Although the initial rebellion of July 1936 was a purely Spanish affair, foreigners soon became involved in the battle between Franco's Nationalists and the radical Republican government. Hitler and Mussolini shipped weapons to Franco almost immediately and would provide the largest totals of men and equipment. In an attempt to keep the war from spreading, the British government persuaded the French not to send aid to Spain. The French reluctantly agreed and instead proposed a Non-Intervention Committee (NIC) to make certain that none of the Great Powers interfered in the civil conflict. At first Stalin agreed to support the NIC, but when it became plain that Nazi and fascist technology had given the Nationalists an overwhelming advantage, he decided to intervene covertly. Within a few weeks, Soviet tanks, airplanes, and technical specialists poured into the Spanish arena. Soviet envoys to the NIC would protest that they knew nothing about shipments of war material to Spain, but found it difficult to explain away the presence of Russian-speaking commanders and the capture of Soviet-made armaments by the Nationalists.

Meanwhile, the war in Spain gripped the popular imagination in the Soviet Union as it did throughout Europe and the United States. The press painted the war as a struggle between the isolated workers of Spain, abandoned by the Western powers, and the ruthless fascists, who were aided by their ideological allies from around the world. In massive public demonstrations orchestrated by Stalin's regime, Soviet citizens marched to show their solidarity with the "Spanish people" and pledged to help the beleaguered Republic. Just a few weeks after the war began, donations by factories and private individuals raised over two million dollars for the Republican cause. There were, however, no ordinary Soviets among the thousands of foreigners who spontaneously gathered to fight on the Spanish government's behalf. Stalin's paranoia about foreign contamination meant that he allowed only trusted military and intelligence officers to "volunteer" for action in Spain.

At first Stalin warned the men sent to Spain to keep out of harm's way, perhaps so that there would be less opportunity for the outside world to discover how deeply the Soviet Union was involved. In keeping with these instructions, the Soviets confined their activities early in the conflict to advising the Spanish high command and to leading intelligence operations. As the war began to go badly for the Republicans, however, they were encouraged to take a more hands-on approach to the fighting. Soviet commanders were soon giving orders in battles while Soviet armor officers and pilots went beyond training Spanish personnel to taking part in combat operations. Among other accomplishments, Soviet officers organized partisans in the Nationalist rear, aided in the creation of the regular Republican Army and, as commanders of the international brigades, helped to stop Franco's drive on Madrid in late 1936. In the meantime, the Republican decision to ship most of the Spanish gold reserves to Moscow for safekeeping encouraged Stalin to intervene even more deeply. From 1936 through 1938, the Soviet government would contribute over two thousand Red Army officers to the Republican cause, along with hundreds of tanks and airplanes and thousands of tons of other military material, all paid for by the Spanish government.

As the Republicans continued to lose ground to Franco's Nationalists, however, the Soviets extricated themselves from the Civil War as quietly as they had become involved. At some point in 1938, perhaps after Munich made it clear that the Western powers would never intervene in Spain, Stalin decided that the conflict was no longer worthwhile. The fact that the Republicans had used the last of their gold credit may have encouraged his change of heart. Whatever the reason, arms shipments declined throughout the year. By December, as Franco was preparing his last push on Catalonia, the Spanish government would vainly beg the Soviets for assistance. Without the backing of their only consistent supporters, the Republic was doomed and Madrid fell soon afterward to the Nationalists.

Despite repeated assurances to their Spanish comrades that they were only interested in helping to put down the uprising, the Soviet high command never lost sight of how they could profit from their participation in this conflict. Not long after the war began, Defense Commissar Kliment Voroshilov issued orders detailing the specific tactics and technology that his men were to study. His directives focused in particular on those areas, such as the coordination of combined-arms battle, where the Soviet army was experiencing difficulties. The men in the field responded with weekly situation reports and analyses of the air forces, tank units, artillery, infantry, and navy. At several points during the conflict commanders also submitted lengthy reports that evaluated the overall performance of Soviet and Spanish forces. The most important repercussion of these studies was to elicit a reconsideration of armored and air doctrines. The fighting in Spain, commanders wrote, had shown that it was useless to create mechanized corps that would fight far from infantry support. Instead, tanks performed best when split up into smaller units and distributed to the foot soldiers. Likewise, strategic bombing had failed to produce any significant results in the conflict while direct tactical air support for the infantry had been extremely successful. These conclusions, together with the purge of Tukhachevskii and his supporters, would eventually lead the Soviet military to discard deep battle/deep operations as the official doctrine of the Red Army.

The lessons learned in Spain affected other areas of the Soviet military as well. After carefully studying the technology used by both sides, the high command decided that their tanks, even the formidable T-26, were too small and too lightly armed and armored. They also thought that Soviet airplanes were much slower than those of the fascists, and not as maneuverable as they needed to be. These conclusions informed the decisions to produce the T-34 tank and the superb ground support bombers and fighters that the Soviets used in the Second World War. The Spanish war was a boon as well for military intelligence and the NKVD (People's Commissariat of Internal Affairs). The international brigades proved to be fertile grounds for recruiting agents from both Europe and the United States, and the GRU (Main Intelligence Administration) took advantage of the capture of enemy hardware to "borrow" technology for Soviet exploitation.

Finally, Stalin used the mistakes of commanders in Spain, or their supposed ties to Trotskiist plots, to order the liquidation of a disproportionate number of those high-ranking officers who fought in the Spanish Civil War. Among the commanders recalled from Madrid and shot were General

Vladimir Gorev (the military attaché), General Ian Berzin (in charge of the GRU) and three prominent generals in the international brigades. Service in Spain was not, however, inevitably a black mark. A few Spanish veterans went on to have successful careers in the Soviet military, including the future head of the navy, Nikolai Kuznetsov, and five marshals of the Soviet Union (Konstantin Rokossovskii, Kirill Meretskov, Ivan Konev, Rodion Malinovskii, and Nikolai Voronov). All of these men were lower-ranking commanders during the Spanish war who learned early on to avoid politics and to shun the company of suspected "enemies of the people."

## Lake Khasan, July-August 1938

Events on the Far-Eastern borders would reinforce the lessons that the Red Army believed it had learned in Spain. Just at the moment when Stalin was reconsidering his support for the Republicans, tensions with Japan heated up, culminating in a month-long war on the border between China and the Soviet Union. Japanese army forces, including the Korea and Sixth Armies, had been fighting in Manchuria for a year in a vain attempt to bring order (and Japanese domination) to China. By the summer of 1938 there were several thousand Japanese troops stationed near the border with the Soviet Union. The Soviets, not unnaturally, found this build-up threatening and had reinforced both NKVD border troops and regular Red Army units on their entire frontier. To complicate matters, the Japanese and the Soviets disputed the precise location of the border on the small strip of land, containing a lake called Khasan, that separated the Soviet Union, China, and Korea.

Before 1938 both sides had taken care not to station troops near the disputed area. This changed when the Soviets became vitally concerned about border security after the defection to Japan of an NKVD general intimately familiar with Soviet defenses in the region. A decision was made to fortify the heights around Lake Khasan, definitively claiming these strategic points for the Soviet Union. At first the Japanese reacted tentatively. It was only after a second foray by the Red Army that went even further into Manchuria that the Korea Army attacked, taking the hills from the small Soviet detachments that had occupied them. In a telegram to Stalin, the commander in charge of the Soviet Far-Eastern Military District, Vasilii Bliukher, agreed with the Japanese version of events. He wrote that troops from the NKVD border guards had provoked the Japanese by firing across the border and seizing land in Manchuria. Bliukher's attitude infuriated Stalin, who chose to believe the NKVD story that it was the Japanese who had crossed into Soviet territory. This was either because it was he who had ordered the original incursion by Soviet forces, or because he did not trust Bliukher, whose army had until then escaped the purges.

Since he thought that the hills were part of Manchuria, Bliukher did not counterattack promptly. Only after Stalin contacted him by direct line from Moscow and personally ordered him to retake the territory did the doomed general at last realize the seriousness of the situation. He immediately gathered the forces available to him, including large numbers of aircraft, tanks, and infantry, and led several assaults on the heights. The Soviets had far superior forces compared to those of the Korea Army (at least three to one), yet the Japanese managed to beat back every attack by the Soviets, inflicting heavy casualties. Before there could be a further escalation in the fighting, Japanese and Soviet negotiators reached a diplomatic solution. The Japanese retreated from Khasan in early August, having made their point that they could take and hold any land they wanted.

The fall-out from this small war was profound. Unlike the distant conflict in Spain, this clash occurred on Soviet soil, involved what the Soviet leadership perceived as an attempt to invade the Motherland, and led to far greater loss of life (approximately 5,000 casualties). It had also seriously damaged the prestige of the Red Army, which was supposed to be able to fight two full-scale wars on both ends of the Soviet Union. Newspapers in the West reported extensively on the war and observers commented on the clumsiness of the Soviet response to this probing of its defenses. The army too saw Khasan as an even more realistic test of their military readiness than Spain, one that they had failed miserably. Tactical and operational studies of the war concluded that the army had been inexcusably incompetent in its handling of the crisis. Commanders had thrown artillery, tanks, aircraft, and infantry into combat without any regard for terrain or coordination with the other arms. Ordinary soldiers had shown their complete lack of training, failing to fight energetically and throwing away their weapons at the first sign of resistance. The analyses of Khasan confirmed, however, that the new thinking about armor and air doctrine was correct. Yet another trial of war had shown that the old ideas about mechanized warfare were erroneous and had to be discarded. One result of the war, therefore, was a further undermining of support for gathering armored units into large mechanized corps and a strengthening of the infantry's power at the expense of the other branches. Another repercussion came shortly after the war ended. For refusing to defend the Motherland and carry out direct orders, Stalin relieved Bliukher of his command and ordered him imprisoned and shot for treason. Not long afterward, in one of the most vicious chapters of the great purges, the NKVD eliminated Bliukher's supporters in the Far-Eastern army as "enemies of the people." Yet, because the Soviet army had achieved what it had set out to do—take and fortify the heights—there was little pressure for other, more serious reforms of the army.

## Khalkhin-gol, May-September 1939

Convinced by their easy victory at Khasan that the weakened Red Army was unable to prevent them from doing as they wished, the Japanese became more willing to take chances on the Manchurian borderlands. Just one year after that small conflict, the Japanese and Soviet armies would once again probe the borders and each other's weaknesses, this time in Mongolia. As at Khasan, the initial clash erupted over the exact location of the frontier. The Japanese recognized the Khalkhin-gol River as the border between Manchuria and Outer Mongolia, while the Soviets and Mongolians argued that the line extended some 15 miles to the east of the river. Throughout the spring of 1939 both sides charged the other with border violations and there were several bloody engagements with no clear winner. Then, in late May, the Soviets decided to stake a clear claim to the eastern side of the Khalkhin-gol. Significant Red Army forces moved across the river and, despite repeated attempts by the Japanese to dislodge them, managed to hold a bridgehead. In June and July the Japanese Sixth Army, convinced that they could easily throw back the "invading" troops, mounted a larger assault. To their surprise, they were again unsuccessful in pushing the Soviets across the river. During this offensive, some Japanese units crossed the Khalkhin-gol, causing the Soviets to fear that the clash was actually the start of a serious bid to invade Mongolia and thus the Soviet Union. Voroshilov had already brought in Georgii Zhukov, then a commander in Byelorussia, to oversee operations, but now he promised the general any quantities of men and equipment necessary to stop the Japanese.

Zhukov decided that it was useless simply to defend the areas already held by the Soviets. Instead he would carry out a decisive offensive that would destroy the Sixth Army and lay permanent claim to the disputed territory. He began a massive build-up of tanks, aircraft, artillery, and men, eventually gathering about 500 tanks, an equal number of airplanes, and perhaps as many as 20 rifle divisions. In late August he employed the old deep-battle tactics to attack the 75,000 Japanese troops facing him. Achieving total surprise, he assaulted the Japanese simultaneously in the front and on both flanks using the combined fire power of all of his forces. The encirclement maneuver had almost surrounded the enemy when the Japanese, low on ammunition and supplies and completely demoralized, withdrew at the very last moment. Diplomats in Moscow arranged a cease-fire as the Japanese were planning a counterattack and the Soviets were left in possession of the field. Losses for both sides were quite high. The enemy Sixth Army suffered close to 20,000 men killed and wounded, with one division destroyed completely. Although the Soviets once admitted to fewer than 10,000 casualties for Zhukov's forces, new archival evidence puts their losses at over 23,000.

In some ways, the contrast between the larger battle near Khalkhin-gol and the clash at Khasan could not be more striking. Just one year before, the Red Army had displayed an amazing incompetence against a much smaller invading force. Yet Zhukov, facing essentially the same enemy, had organized and carried out an operation involving much larger mechanized forces, hundreds of airplanes, and tens of thousands of men. The logistical feat of gathering the necessary men and equipment on the Mongolian border was impressive enough. The skill and creativity he showed in using them seemed to argue that Soviet war-fighting capabilities had improved beyond measure. If Khasan made the Japanese disdainful of the Soviets as warriors, Khalkhin-gol showed them how bloody a protracted war with the Red Army might be. Some scholars have argued that this small war may, in fact, have convinced the Japanese to turn their attention away from a drive northward and to consider in its place an invasion of southeast Asia. If so, it was because the Japanese did not see the many problems that again plagued the Soviets in this test of their preparedness. As at Khasan, soldiers had thrown their weapons away and fled the battlefield, supplies and equipment had been lacking, and Zhukov had been willing to accept losses that would have doomed the career of an officer in any other army. But he had achieved victory, and that was what impressed both the Japanese and the Soviet high command.

It is important to note that not everyone grasped the significance of the conflict in Mongolia. While the Soviets did not suppress the news of events at Khalkhin-gol, developments in Europe soon overshadowed them. The Great Powers, most significantly the Germans, ignored the signs of Soviet military prowess and the Red Army's willingness to fight on after taking great losses. The Soviet high command did little better. Internal army analyses of the war concluded that the deep battle idea was badly flawed despite the evidence of Zhukov's huge encirclement. The conflict at Khalkhin-gol, commanders wrote, had affirmed that the correct way to win a modern battle was through a slow, methodical advance by masses of foot soldiers, closely supported by artillery, aircraft, and tanks that would act as little more than moving shields. In addition, two factors meant that the Soviet high command did not take the necessary steps to correct the many other problems that their army had uncovered in the conflict. The military purges, then at their height, meant that there was little continuity in the command staff for lessons learned by officers in one conflict to be passed on to other officers. And, as at Khasan, while reports noted the inefficiencies, low morale, and poor leadership that were endemic throughout the Red Army, the fact of victory, however achieved, meant that there was little resolve for major reforms.

## Poland, September-October 1939

Much the same was true of the Polish campaign, where the Red Army stumbled badly in combat on its own borders. The background to the invasion of Poland (or the Liberation of Western Ukraine and Byelorussia, as the Soviets called it) is plain enough. After Munich, Stalin's enthusiasm for collective security with Britain and France waned. The withdrawal from the Spanish conflict signaled an end to direct Soviet confrontation with Hitler, and after May 1939 Stalin began looking for a way to cooperate with his erstwhile enemy. At the same time, Hitler was hoping to prevent a two-front war by making a temporary peace with the Soviets. The result was the Molotov-Ribbentrop Pact, ostensibly a non-aggression treaty, but with secret protocols that divided Poland between the dictators and gave the Baltic states to the Soviet Union.

It is very likely that Stalin timed Soviet intervention in Poland for mid-September to allow Zhukov to finish off the Japanese before fighting in the West would commence. On 23 August, three days after Zhukov began his offensive at Khalkhin-gol, Germany and the Soviet Union signed the Pact. The peace with Japan took effect on 16 September, and the Soviet Union invaded Poland the next day. The time between the signing of the Pact and the actual beginning of offensive operations was an anxious period for the Soviet leadership. Not only were there problems with the mobilization of the necessary forces and supplies, but many Soviets feared that Hitler would not stop at the agreed-upon line in Poland. The high command, amazed at how quickly the Wehrmacht defeated the Polish army and sped toward the east, realized that they could not have their own troops in place if the Germans chose not to hold up their end of the bargain. Fortunately for the Red Army, Hitler planned to destroy the Western powers before he turned on his supposed ally. The call-up of the Soviet army proceeded with as much speed as possible, and by 17 September, at least half a million soldiers were ready to take part in the offensive. Not every piece of equipment was in place by the deadline, however. The forces that entered Poland should have included about 4,000 tanks, but the army managed to mobilize less than half of these in time for the attack. This may explain why Japanese forces at Khalkhin-gol described Soviet tanks in Mongolia speeding away toward the northwest as soon as the peace there took effect. But it would take them many days by rail to reach the western Soviet front.

On the surface, the partition of Poland proceeded without any serious complications. Within one month after entering the country, the Red Army had subdued the Polish defenders and the fighting ended. A closer look showed that while the Soviet forces were vastly superior to their opponent, who numbered only about 150,000 men, they had still experienced difficulties in defeating the Poles. Some of the problems were self-inflicted (troubles with logistics and supplies plagued the Soviet units), but the Polish army had caused others. It had managed, for instance, to put more than 330 Soviet tanks out of commission, despite an acute shortage of anti-armor weaponry. This reflected poorly on the tactics used by the Soviet army in Poland, and also on the terrible command and control of the tank units, many of which had lagged behind even the horse cavalry. Foreign observers were also struck by the incompetence and general military weakness shown by the Soviets. The entire course of the Polish campaign thus confirmed their poor opinions about the Red Army that Khasan had established the year before.

There was one facet of the invasion of Poland that the Soviets managed, at least at first, to hide from foreign eyes. Soon after his army had suppressed the last of the Polish armed resistance, Stalin sent in the NKVD. The secret police rounded up anyone who would not fit into the Communist regime that the Soviets hoped to create on Polish soil. A group of 14,000 officers and policemen were among those taken away and never seen again. After the Germans broke their treaty with Stalin and conquered the Soviet side of Poland, they discovered a mass grave in the Katyn Forest containing thousands of hastily buried bodies. In one of his few propaganda coups of the war, Hitler announced that he had found the missing Poles and exposed this Soviet atrocity to the rest of the world. During the Second World War, Britain and the United States chose to believe Stalin's explanation that the Germans had killed the officers themselves, but doubts about Stalin's innocence emerged even before the Cold War began. The recent opening of the former Soviet archives has confirmed Polish (and German) claims that it was indeed the NKVD who shot these potential troublemakers.

As in past conflicts, the Red Army learned some wrong lessons from their experiences in Poland. Unlike the rest of the world, which saw the new "lightning war" of the Germans as the obvious future of combat, the Soviet high command ignored the success of blitzkrieg. They decided that it was simple Polish incompetence that had allowed the Wehrmacht to brush aside Polish defenses so easily. A well-prepared, better-armed, and modern military, such as the Red Army, would be able to stop the Germans and then counterattack in force. Soviet reports on battle effectiveness in the Polish campaign focused instead on their own problems with combat. These concluded that all of the rethinking about mechanized warfare from the previous few years was entirely correct. In November the Main Military Council met and decided to disband the tank corps, replacing them with small armored detachments distributed to individual rifle units. There were few other reforms proposed or carried out, however. The Soviet military leaders, blinded again by the fact of their success, chose to believe that the difficulties experienced during the invasion were minor inefficiencies that they could easily overcome.

Yet one good thing did come out of this war and the small conflicts in the Far East: they showed the high command that the army needed the best tanks and aircraft that their country could produce. After Poland, Stalin's regime put more energy into fulfilling production plans that had stalled in the mid-thirties. The result was the creation of the largest mechanized and motorized army in the world (including about 17,000 tanks) just in time to meet Hitler's invasion.

## Finland, November 1939–March 1940

Not long afterward, the Soviets became involved in the last of their small wars. Relations between Finland and the Soviet Union had always been tense. The Soviets thought that their Finnish neighbors were too favorable to the Nazis, and that they probably had secret plans to ally themselves with Hitler in case of war. The Finns viewed the Soviet Union as their primary enemy, suspecting that Stalin had designs on at least some of their territory. They were right. As tensions in Europe exploded into war, Stalin became convinced that his northern border could not be held without a buffer zone much like the new Polish territory. The Soviet leadership viewed certain islands around Leningrad and a strip of land on the Karelian Isthmus as particularly desirable. When negotiations between the two countries failed to achieve any results, Stalin determined that he would have to resort to war, and called on the Red Army to defeat the Finns. To his own people and the outside world he would defend this "Winter War" as absolutely necessary for the security of the Soviet Union and as a way to liberate the Finnish people from their oppressive capitalist system.

The war that followed showed the Soviet military at its worst. Although outnumbered about four to one in manpower, the Finnish army had trained well for a defensive war in winter conditions. Among other preparations, they had equipped their soldiers with skis and white camouflage suits, and planned to employ guerrilla tactics if attacked by the much larger Soviet army. They also had good, deep defenses in the form of the Mannerheim Line. The Soviets chose to assault the Line with massed infantry attacks supported by tanks using tactics that were not suited for the terrain or weather. The result was a literal massacre, as the Finns decimated the poorly trained and badly led Red Army soldiers. After an entire month of frontal assaults, the high command finally realized that they would be unable to take the Line with their current tactics. Meanwhile, attacks on other parts of the Finnish frontier stalled because of a lack of equipment for fighting in deep snow, the infantry's poor training for winter warfare, and a spirited defense by Finnish regular and guerrilla forces. A month of relative silence followed as the Soviets gathered more men, tanks, and artillery. The second offensive, led by Semyon Timoshenko, lasted from February to March 1940. It succeeded in breaking through the Line and encircling the Finnish defenders, but only after massive losses for the Red Army. The final toll was almost unbelievably high: 400,000 Soviet casualties, more than 120,000 of these killed outright in battle.

The reasons for the catastrophe were not hard to find: poor command and control; a willingness to use tactics that wasted soldiers' lives, a disregard very much like that of the Tsars; an inefficient employment of technology; inadequate coordination of the various units that took part in the war; and the lack of preparation for winter combat. Although the earlier conflicts in the Far East should have warned the high command about most of these problems, "victory disease" had led them to focus on the fact of success rather than on the high costs their men and material had suffered. After the Finnish War, the Soviets could no longer afford to ignore the difficulties experienced by the army and everyone was now willing to admit that the military needed major reforms. In a move to show his determination to transform the army, Stalin removed his old friend Voroshilov from his position as defense commissar and demoted Chief of Staff Boris Shaposhnikov. The army also undertook extensive studies to understand and correct the other failings that had caused the debacle. The catalog of mistakes made and problems that still existed filled a lengthy report given by Voroshilov later that spring.

Most of these shortcomings, however, could not be dealt with before the Germans used their blitzkrieg tactics to defeat the French and British armies. Unlike the invasion of Poland the year before, this stunning victory, in conjunction with the events in Finland, convinced the Red Army leadership to rethink its rejection of deep battle. In December 1940 a major conference brought together all of the decision-makers in the military to discuss what the army's fundamental battle doctrine should be. Zhukov argued persuasively for the adoption of the tactics that the Wehrmacht had used in France and Poland. Other officers at the meeting tried to convince the high command that choosing this course, basically a return to deep battle, would be disastrous for the army, but they went unheard. Events had convinced most Soviet military leaders that they had erred in their evaluation of Tukhachevskii's vision of future war.

Over the next six months the Soviet high command would attempt to remedy the problem areas that their small wars had exposed. In some cases they would succeed in preparing their army and country for the coming conflict. The military industrial complex, for instance, turned out incredible numbers of high quality, modern tanks, airplanes, and artillery. In almost every category of weapon, Soviet-made arms equaled or were better than those manufactured in the West. The army tried to redress other shortcomings through intensive retraining of commanders and soldiers and the construction of a series of defensive fortifications on the western borders. Unfortunately, these reforms took much longer to complete than the high command had expected. The German general staff was not unaware of this salient fact. While racist and expansionist ideology motivated Hitler to order the invasion of the Soviet Union in June 1941, the Wehrmacht agreed to his plans in part because of their conviction, supported by Khasan, the Polish invasion, and the Finnish War, that the Soviets were not ready for a full-scale war. They concluded that Stalin's purges of the Red Army had weakened the Soviet Union's defenses and that the experience of war had proven that the Soviets had not been able to remedy this fatal flaw. The history of the first three years of the Great Patriotic War would be one of the Soviet military playing catch-up to the Germans, as they attempted to compensate for the purges and to learn the right lessons from their dress rehearsals for the Second World War. Fortunately for the rest of the world, it was a game at which they would show themselves to be extraordinarily adept.

## References

The primary sources used to write this essay are in the Russian State Military Archive (RGVA), fond 33987, opis 3, dela 832, 1015; fond 31811, opis 4, dela 20, 22, 28, 36; fond 31811, opis 2, dela 640, 646; fond 35082, opis 1, delo 483; fond 4, opis 18, dela 46, 56; and fond 4, opis 14, delo 2737. In addition, many secondary works were consulted and used in writing the essay, including Alvin D. Coox, *The Anatomy of a Small War. The Soviet-Japanese Struggle for Changkufeng/Khasan, 1938* (Westport, CT: Greenwood Press, 1977) and *Nomonhan. Japan Against Russia, 1939* (Stanford, CA: Stanford University Press, 1985); Keith Sword, ed., *The Soviet Takeover of the Polish Eastern Provinces, 1939–41* (London: Macmillan, 1991); and Carl Van Dyke, *The Soviet Invasion of Finland, 1939–40* (London: Frank Cass, 1997).

## Further Research

There is much work to be done in the realm of comparative studies of other states' reactions to small or colonial wars as they affected doctrine, technology, logistics, and manpower. The impact of these smaller conflicts on Soviet industry and procurement would also repay study, and medical issues raised in these conflicts are worth a look.

## Sources and Further Reading

The literature on the Spanish Civil War is extensive, however, many fewer books explore the Soviet experience in the conflict. The most important single work on the war, and still the best treatment of Soviet involvement, is Hugh Thomas, *The Spanish Civil War* (New York: Simon and Schuster, 1986). E.H. Carr's *The Comintern and the Spanish Civil War* (New York: Pantheon Books, 1984) primarily looks at the participation of international communism, but also contains some good information on the Soviet intervention. Two other sources useful for understanding this aspect of the conflict are David Cattell's *Communism and the Spanish Civil War* (Berkeley, CA: University of California Press, 1955), and *Soviet Diplomacy and the Spanish Civil War* (Berkeley, CA: University of California Press, 1957). The other small wars have many fewer sources, but these are generally of high quality. Alvin Coox has produced two very good works on Khalkhin-gol and Lake Khasan, *The Anatomy of a Small War. The Soviet-Japanese Struggle for Changkufeng/Khasan, 1938* (Westport, CT: Greenwood Press, 1977) and the multi-volume *Nomonhan. Japan Against Russia, 1939* (Stanford, CA: Stanford University Press, 1985). Carl Van Dyke's examination of the Winter War in *The Soviet Invasion of Finland, 1939–40* (London: Frank Cass, 1997) is similarly excellent. The invasion of Poland still awaits thorough treatment. One of the best sources now available is the collection of essays in Keith Sword, ed., *The Soviet Takeover of the Polish Eastern Provinces, 1939–41* (London: Macmillan, 1991).

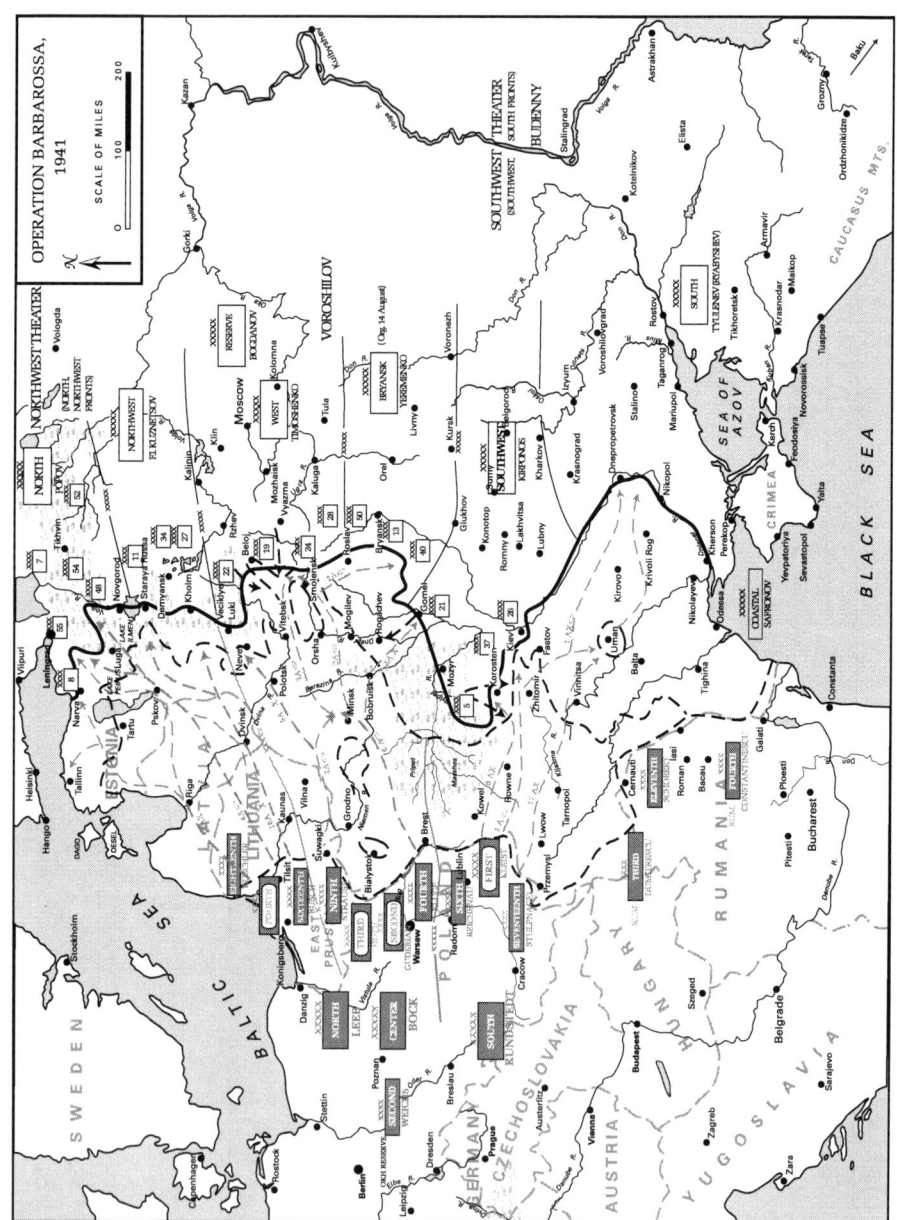

OPERATION BARBAROSSA, 1941

SCALE OF MILES

0    100    200

CHAPTER 8

# THE GREAT PATRIOTIC WAR
## Barbarossa to Stalingrad

*John Erickson*

*On Sunday [22 June 1941] about 0400, the bombardment started: the at-*
*tack was at 0500.*
At first we thought it was the usual kind of exercises, with artillery and
aircraft, including mock air attacks. So we went back to sleep. Ten days
earlier there had been exercises with live firing. We never thought it
could be the Germans this time. When daylight came I grabbed some
binoculars and realised I was looking at a group of German planes returning from bombing our rear. . . . We ran half dressed to our unfinished defense positions.

*—personal communication,*
*recollection of Red Army soldier, 345ᵗʰ Rifle Regiment*

THE PLIGHT OF ONE SOVIET SOLDIER WAS AN INSTANCE of the condition
into which the Red Army had been plunged, in June 1941, unable either
to attack or defend. The ensuing haplessness laid bare a warfare state without a functioning war machine, lacking a high command, bereft of operational plans. Not that the road to the catastrophe of 1941 was without its
warning signs. They were strewn from east to west, beginning in Spain in
1936, moving from Lake Khasan in 1938 to Khalkin-gol and Zhukov's declared "victory" in 1939, the "liberation march" into eastern Poland in
1939, and the humiliating disasters of the 1939–40 "Winter War" with
Finland. What they conveyed were shortcomings in Red Army organization

and performance disregarded or uncorrected, poor training, questionable morale, indifferent leadership, outmoded equipment, grave deficiencies in supply. What the war with Finland also demonstrated was dangerously defective strategy.

In this predestination of near-fatal destruction visited upon the Soviet Union by the Wehrmacht, the system, the army, and society were inextricably linked and equally vulnerable. The roots of impending disaster ran deep. From its earliest days the Soviet political leadership, engaged in an "uncompromising ideological struggle," was unable to dispense with the military, yet, out of residual fear, was never averse to undermining or demeaning it. Stalin's murderous military purge of 1937–38 was itself an extreme paranoid instance of that disposition. Damaging though that was, graver injury had been done to the Soviet military, the Red Army in particular, by the social and economic consequences of Stalinist collectivization and industrialization. Change and upheaval in civil society inevitably impinged on the military. Collectivization alienated the peasant recruit; industrialization overwhelmed an officer corps with technology for which they had neither appropriate education, adequate training, nor great personal aptitude. Building "a new material and technical base for war" could not be managed overnight, "the general cultural level" precluded "the training of skilled military cadres" as well as the development of "modern-day military theory." Military matters were "administered through propaganda slogans," party-directed military doctrine responsible for the cult of the offensive was more expressive of a political imperative than of military rationale.

"Cadres decide everything!" To its misfortune and ultimate undoing, in 1941 the Red Army showed the Stalinist slogan to be cruelly accurate. Difficulties in officer manning, education, training, retention, and performance had plagued the Red Army from the first days of its existence, but chronic problems assumed a dangerously acute form as Red Army numerical and technological expansion increasingly moved into high, hectic gear. For the failure to meet the requirements of a modern mass army, both the system and the military were culpable. The political premises and coercive practices imposed by the regime in pursuit of a "class-based army" not merely contradicted but actually obstructed and inhibited moves to a modern mass army. The military leadership understood mass largely in brute terms, whether men or machines, dismissive of the individual soldier, incapable of training and retaining officers minimally proficient in handling even a relatively undifferentiated mass. As a result Soviet soldiers became countless victims of a system combining numbing incompetence with ferocious ruthlessness.

## Meeting the Threat

The fall of France in June 1940 severely agitated Stalin. He predicted gloomily, "now the Germans will come for us, eat us alive." Hitler's success in the West provoked little short of a panic reaction in Moscow. Within hours, Stalin ordered the Red Army into the Baltic States, into Bessarabia and the northern Bukovina. Designed to increase the Soviet "buffer zone" to the north and south, these deployments made existing mobilization plans obsolete at a stroke. On the home front, industry was placed on a virtual war footing. Workers were now subject to an eight-hour working day and a six-day working week. Absenteeism was punishable, labor migration practically forbidden. This *frisson de terreur* seized the military, prompting an urgent review of the current Soviet war plan formulated by B. M. Shaposhnikov as far back as March 1938.

Hurriedly revised in July 1940 by Major General Vasilevskii, the new version simply revamped the old: the Soviet Union faced the threat of a two-front war from Germany and Japan. Any German attack would develop its main thrust *north* of the river San rather than from southern Poland aimed at Kiev. Marshal Timoshenko, Voroshilov's replacement as *defense* commissar, questioned the focus on "north of Warsaw." Convinced of Hitler's need for Ukrainian grain and Donbas coal to sustain a protracted war, Stalin intervened in the debate. At his insistence the final draft of the war plan confirmed the primacy of the *southwestern theater*. It was here that the main German attack would develop, the immediate objective being Kiev and the Ukraine.

Accordingly the Red Army would deploy its own main strength south of Brest. Having first repelled enemy attacks, Red Army strategy involved unleashing a powerful "retaliatory blow" (*otvetnyi udar*) in the direction of Lublin, Cracow, and Breslau designed primarily to isolate Germany from its Balkan allies. A surprise attack was not considered. On the contrary, it was assumed that both sides would initiate operations with their forces only partly concentrated: some two weeks would be needed to complete full deployment. Both of these assumptions, the presumed location of the main German thrust and the nature of the "initial period" of war, proved eventually to be ruinously at odds with reality.

Timoshenko discovered on succeeding Voroshilov an army not fit to fight. While the civilian labor force needed discipline and greater regulation, the Red Army was in greater need of retraining and refurbishing. What afflicted civilian society also affected the military. The army was saddled with over-bureaucratized administration in a commissar-ridden system. At troop level, training was aimless and unrealistic. Training for senior commanders and for staffs was only in the planning stage. The fitting out of potential theaters of operations was "extremely weak." The immediate answer was intensive training in the field, supported by iron discipline and the imposition of unconditional obedience. Military formality reminiscent of the Imperial Army was reintroduced in the form of the obligatory salute and officer "honor courts." The excesses of the military commissars were momentarily curbed by the abolition of "dual command." In the wake of the striking German success of the Panzer corps and divisions in the West, a frantic effort was made to rectify the glaring error committed in 1939, the decision to disband the Red Army's large tank and mechanized corps, the armor distributed among the rifle divisions. In June 1940 Stalin approved the reestablishment of mechanized corps, a month later the General Staff authorized eight mechanized corps and two tank divisions.

The rush to rebuild the armored forces was but one instance of the Red Army caught up in a disparate process of reorganization and rearmament. The confusion was made worse as operational plans and mobilization timetables slipped increasingly out of alignment. What none of the planners could overcome was a situation in which the "economic potential" of the country failed to correspond to the demands imposed by the planned deployments and systematic reequipping of the Soviet armed forces in their entirety. Fully five years were needed to meet mobilization needs at the prescribed level. Meanwhile tactical performance had to be improved, command competence and understanding of modern war increased.

The "generals and admirals of 1940," newly promoted by Stalin, were sent briefly back to school. The navy had already convened its own command conference in October. The Red Army conference on modern offensive and defensive operations opened in late December 1940, followed in early January by a secret two-part strategic war game. The army conference proved to be strangely, even predictably, inconclusive. The critical "initial period" of hostilities was ignored, as was "the surprise factor." Static or mobile defensive tactics elicited a schizoid response: greater reliance on fixed *defense*s, alternatively more mechanized corps. The strategic "Red vs. Blue" war games then supposedly "tested" the revised Soviet war plan. Stalin was not impressed. He accepted the likelihood of frontier battles, but criticized the lack of clarity and execution of the "retaliatory blow," asking bluntly: Who won? Clearly the counterstrike needed reinforcement. The games had "confirmed" the primacy of the "southwestern axis" so, not surprisingly, that is where reinforcement, especially armor, was directed: into the Kiev Special Military District.

Obsession with a German strike into the Ukraine, belief in initial extended frontier battles, confidence in a 10 to 15 day delay between Wehrmacht concentration and full deployment ran like triple red threads through the whole of Soviet operational thinking and planning. As one senior Soviet officer observed, it was as if the Soviet Union was preparing for 1914, not 1941. General Zhukov's updated war plan submitted in March 1941 was a further restatement of these ideas, at a time when intelligence was reporting greatly increased German traffic eastward. The seriousness of the situation was underlined by Stalin in his 5 May 1941 speech to military academy graduates, warning of a danger period lasting to mid-summer yet hinting at the possibility of deferring war until 1942 or even later.

The effect was zigzag propaganda, partly reassuring, partly unnerving the populace, and confusing the army. But Stalin's strategy of avoiding war and the military's approach of "creeping up on war" suffered a shattering blow that same day, 5 May. A Soviet intelligence report identified powerful German concentrations in the east, no less than 112 divisions. The General Staff had to face the fundamental error of its "war concept," the product of military myopia and military illiteracy. The Wehrmacht was fully mobilized, rear services organized, positioned to preempt Red Army deployment, and poised for surprise attack.

The "threat" was now manifest, its execution seemingly imminent. The only course was either to forestall (*predupredit*) the Germans, deny them the initiative, or preempt *(upredit')* their deployment, prevent the formation of a coherent front. To this end on 15 May 1941 Zhukov submitted a "pre-emptive plan," proposing a two-stage Soviet strategic offensive employing 152 Soviet divisions to destroy 100 German divisions. The first strategic objective envisaged the destruction of German forces south of Demblin, the second a thrust in the center and northwest to invest Poland and East Prussia. Mobilization would be concealed by an ostensible troop recall for reserve training.

Stalin clearly saw this as a recipe for disaster. It ran counter to his "war avoidance" strategy. Present Soviet deployments were insufficient to mount the operation. Only 102 divisions were at hand, second-echelon and reserve forces were as yet on the move, due to arrive later. Sixty days were needed to generate the requisite "correlation of forces" by which time German strength would have increased. Finally, in spite of his boasting on 5 May, Stalin had learned in January that the Red Army was in no fit state to launch a major strategic offensive. The moment of truth had arrived for the General Staff: either launch a Soviet version of "blitzkrieg" or implement full mobilization. Stalin forbade both. So hobbled, the Red Army could neither attack nor defend.

Mobilization planning, MP-41, proceeded in fits and starts. By June 1941 the fully revised plan had not yet been completed. Timetables slipped remorselessly, some projected into July. Plans at military district level were unfinished. No plan existed to bring *all* forces to full readiness. The General Staff "Plan for the *defense* of the state frontiers" outlined deployments but lacked operational orders. Many divisions were undermanned, badly deployed, or were yet to be deployed. Stalin had categorically ruled out general mobilization, conscious that in 1914 it had acted to trigger war. He even withheld authorization to increase unit readiness. Worse, the TASS statement of 14 June 1941 acted as a self-disarming mechanism, discounting the imminence of war, dismissing such rumours as deliberate *provokatsiia* spread by "false friends." Recent German troop movements had no bearing on the state of Soviet-German relations.

The whole ramshackle system in which few, Stalin least of all, had any confidence and that most mistrusted, simply accelerated its own near-destruction.

## Post-Attack Catastrophe

The war Stalin had hoped to escape, or at least postpone into the future, became inescapable reality in the early hours of Sunday, 22 June. Not until noon was the Soviet populace informed of a state of war. Red Army forward elements, belatedly advised of a possible German attack, were ordered by Moscow's initial directives to hold enemy attacks and then unleash a "powerful counter-blow." The immediate and widespread havoc wreaked by German air and ground attacks made this wildly unrealistic. In Moscow, a preliminary wartime command system was hastily organized, the *Stavka* of the High Command, "General Headquarters," still lacking a specific commander-in-chief. Administrative decree placed the Soviet Union on a war footing, the first of a flood of decrees engulfing the population presently mobilizing under fire. One early decision proved to be critically important, the establishment of an industrial evacuation group (*Sovet po evakuatsii*). Here was the first step toward transferring industrial facilities plus their workers eastward, prelude to the greatest industrial migration in history.

It took a week and horrified awareness of the scale of the catastrophe on the western and northwestern frontiers to energize government, party, and nation. On 30 June the State Defense Committee (*Gosudarstvennyi komitet oborony:* GKO) was formed under Stalin's chairmanship, a body small in size but endowed with massive authority. The GKO and the *Stavka* were quickly and closely fused by virtue of interchangeable membership, an act of super-centralization that unified the military and political direction of the war effort. Effective control of military action had yet to be established. Stalin failed to grasp the scale of operations at the front or the vastness of war into which the Soviet Union had been plunged. He demanded the destruction of the enemy in the shortest possible time and no surrender of territory. False slogan-ridden ideas of how to wage war were fused with military incompetence and illiteracy.

The Red Army had been caught disastrously in strategic maldeployment, its strength mustered in the southwest while powerful Panzer groups attacked in the northwest and at the center, closing on Leningrad, striking along "the Moscow axis." The simple structure of the initial *Stavka* was sagging. Stalin now interposed an additional "high command" echelon (*Glavkom*) between the *Stavka* and the several fronts, assigning three *Glavkom*, "theater commanders" to the northwestern, western and southwestern axes. The "*Stavka* of the High Command" was abolished, replaced by the "Stavka of the Supreme Command" (*Stavka verkhovnogo komandovaniia*). As yet the position of supreme commander lay vacant. "By authority of the *GKO*," Stalin quickly assumed it.

It was a system at Stalin's command that was criminally profligate with soldiers' lives and that brutally coerced or callously abandoned the civilian population. Wartime mobilization had proceeded relatively smoothly, bringing 5.3 million men (ages 23–36) to the colors by the end of June, but from the first days of war, losses had begun to mount in terrifying fashion. Newly mobilized men were sent into disorganized units, creating more confusion, or were thrown into "human wave" attacks, advancing in ranks 12 deep or riding in trucks side-by-side with tanks on to the German guns. "Young Communists" were mobilized for the front, filling gaps in the line at horrendous cost. Civilians in front line areas were conscripted to dig trenches and build rudimentary fortifications. Poorly trained, badly armed "militia divisions," literally recruited off the streets or from factory benches, marched to nearby front lines. "Revolutionary will" had to substitute for weapons. In Civil War style, "cowards and traitors" were subject to "the discipline of the revolver." For the early "loss of control" and the disintegration of the Western Front, the commander General Pavlov and his staff were put before a firing squad.

The wreckage of the Western Front lay strewn over 200 miles. The German haul of prisoners was staggering: three million by the end of the year. Huge masses of men drifted across the battlefield, marooned or encircled. On 16 July Stalin signaled that he had lost confidence in his commanders, re-imposing "dual command" and commissar control. To stem the military hemorrhage he issued punitive orders demanding a purge of "unreliable elements." His draconian 16 August Order No. 270, following Civil War practice, held the families accountable for officers and political workers abandoning the battlefield. Unit commanders who cowered in slit trenches or failed to "lead from the front" could be demoted or shot out of hand. In front of the Soviet soldier were the German guns, behind him NKVD machinegunners of the "holding detachments" (*zagradotriady*), beside him the military commissar brandishing his revolver and using it on "panic mongers." Spies and "alien elements" were hunted down amid counterintelligence reports of drunkenness, panic, desertion, self-mutilation.

Vast military wreckage littered the battlefields, Soviet tanks and aircraft in their thousands were destroyed, lost, or abandoned. In June 1941 the Soviet tank park stood at 23,485 machines, 8,000 assessed as operational with a sprinkling of the newest KV-1s and the agile T-34s. Losses were on a stupefying scale: 20,000 tanks and 18,000 aircraft by the end of the year. As industrial evacuation gained momentum, output of weapons fell off and replacements dwindled. The German army now occupied great swathes of Soviet territory, driving ever deeper. It seemed to many, Germans and Russians alike, that the Red Army was on the verge of disintegrating and Soviet society teetering on the edge of destruction. The massive, near-fatal crisis deepened in the late autumn. Leningrad was besieged. Kiev fell on 18 September, due to Stalin's insensate obduracy forbidding timely withdrawal, costing a huge encirclement that robbed the Red Army of 600,000 men. The Ukraine was lost. Yet complete collapse at the front and in the rear failed to materialize.

In the Soviet Far East, Japan did not attack. Any hope of survival would have ended with a two-front war. Long semi-militarized, accustomed to collective action, hardened to privation, Soviet society showed an unexpected capacity to absorb immense damage and an ability to improvize amid wild disorder. Drastic emergency mobilizations were brutal. Moscow incessantly demanded recourse to "local resources," yet drained them with its own priorities. As an administrative agent, the party operated indifferently, inflexibly at lower levels. Popular response was uneven, depending on local pride and local circumstances, following a tacit "contract of obedience." If minimum security vanished, the "contract" was void. The front line was no exception. The Soviet soldier could and did fight tenaciously given firm leadership, but was otherwise subject to sudden, even inexplicable defeatism. *Neorganizovanost',* disorder and uncontrollable shambles, speeded the collapse of discipline, the onset of panic, and flight. The Moscow "panic" of October 1941 was a prime example, when Stalin's nerve reportedly wavered.

Yet in spite of years of repression and intimidation, basic moral resilience had survived, intensified now by the theme of "patriotic war" and impassioned reaction to German barbarism.

The Germans failed to destroy the Red Army. The Soviet response to save the mangled remains was realistic and ruthless. Pretensions of mass vanished. The 15 July *Stavka* Directive 01 ordered a transition to "small armies with five and a maximum of six divisions." Corps administration was abolished. Remnants of the mechanized corps were disbanded, available tanks acting as infantry support. A huge expansion in cavalry was to furnish a mobile force. The Red Air Force was similarly pruned, its long-range bomber aviation (ADD) abolished. With immediate effect Colonel-General Voronov ordered guns stripped from divisions to form a High Command Artillery Reserve, insisting also on direct fire, putting "the guns up front where gunners could see and hit the enemy." In the rear the chaos had quickly become unmanageable. To remedy this the GKO centralized "rear services," food, ammunition, weapons, transport under one Chief of Rear Services, Lieutenant-General Khrulev.

To the surprise and consternation of the German high command, fresh Soviet divisions and armies appeared in the Red Army order of battle. After the first general mobilization in June, no less than 13 new field armies appeared on the list in mid-July, a further five by October. Stalin grasped the importance of reserves. He rushed through the establishment of a Main Directorate to Raise and Recruit Forces (*Glavuproform KA*), the source of fresh reserves. He disciplined officers for complaining about assignments to the rear to organize new divisions. In the field, available reserves and the reductions in the existing armies facilitated the creation of new armies, though a truly desperate need remained for "trained forces in adequate strength" and, above all, for tanks. Replacements were largely insufficiently trained; illshod, short of rifles if liberally supplied with vodka, crowded out with military commissars.

November 1941 was the cruellest month. Red Army strength dropped to its lowest level ever. Factories relocated in the deep rear had barely started production. Between August and October, 80 percent of Russian industry was "on wheels" (*na kolesakh*): ammunition plants, tank-engine plants, armor plate mills. The loss of 300 sites producing ammunition was calamitous as the Red Army exhausted its prewar stocks. The railroads were jammed with the movement of two and a half million men westward to the front and fifteen hundred industrial plants trundling east.

The German army closed in on Moscow. But small straws were blowing in an icy winter wind. Promised only meagre reinforcement, Meretskov in the north undertook to recapture Tikhvin, prevent a fatal junction of German and Finnish forces, and secure the "ice-road" over Lake Ladoga, besieged Leningrad's vital life-line. In the south Timoshenko planned to recapture Rostov and bar the way to the Caucasus. On 17 November German and Soviet forces moved simultaneously to attack and counterattack. Twelve days later Soviet troops cleared Rostov, the first significant reverse for the Wehrmacht after 161 days of war in the East.

The skilful use of reserves and replacements had allowed the *Stavka* to stabilize the front line early in November and to grind down the "final" German offensive driving on Moscow after mid-November. A Soviet counterblow was being prepared in the greatest secrecy. At the beginning of December 1941 Red Army front line strength had recovered to almost 4,200,000 men. Total strength topped five million, plus half a million men each in the navy and air force. The *Stavka* could reckon on 7,400 aircraft and 4,490 tanks. From July to December the Soviet mobilization-replacement system had performed prodigiously. To replace losses, 227 rifle divisions had been raised, 84 divisions had been reformed, and 143 created anew. From 22 June to 1 December the *Stavka* had directed 181 rifle divisions, 35 "militia divisions," 43 cavalry, tank and motorized divisions, plus 94 brigades to the front. In the last desperate encounters to hold off the German encirclement of Moscow, Stalin only dribbled reinforcements to the defenders, morsels of tanks, packets of men to shredded Soviet divisions. The *Stavka* hoarded its reserves, 44 rifle and 14 cavalry divisions, 13 brigades, sufficient to field eight armies. Zhukov's staff scraped together its own reserve, cannibalizing three armies by taking one rifle section from every division in each army.

Decimated Soviet units and exhausted German soldiers grappled as temperatures plunged. Improvised Soviet "composite groups" fought to hold off the German pincers curling round the capital, itself a bristling hedgehog of hastily erected defenses, barricades, and anti-tank traps. On 4 December 1941, the last German thrust due east along the Minsk-Moscow highway had been fought to a standstill, but powerful German armored wedges were nevertheless jammed deep into Soviet defences covering Moscow.

The Wehrmacht had been seriously weakened. German forces were greatly extended, deployed in exposed positions, ill equipped for a savage winter. German intelligence presumed that now Soviet reserves were totally exhausted. The Red Army had fought down to the last battalion. Several months must pass before fresh armies could be built, during which time the Red Army might turn to positional warfare, withdrawing units for training and reinforcement. "Attacks could be reckoned on," but as of 1 December 1941 the Red Army lacked "large reserve formations on any significant scale."

## Counterattack, Counteroffensive

On 30 November 1941, General Zhukov submitted his plans for a counterstroke at Moscow to Stalin and the *Stavka*. For Stalin, timing was of the essence: to wait but not to wait too long. A premature blow meant attacking when the Red Army lacked a minimum favorable force level, without any margin of advantage. Waiting too long would leave a formidable German force wedged immovably within Moscow's inner defences. The fate of the key central industrial region had also to be considered.

Presently German offensive operations had literally frozen in their tracks. No provision appeared to have been made to turn to the defensive, no sign of redeployment. German troops were strung out along a few roads without defense lines and without reserves. The moment had come to strike in an operation as desperate as any undertaken during the autumn crises, though since the German army had dangerously overreached itself and its resources, there was a real prospect of the Soviet command imposing its will on the situation.

Throughout late November and early December the *Stavka* had carefully fed reinforcement "packages," some substantial, to the three Soviet fronts, Kalinin, Western and Southwestern, assigned to the counteroffensive. A force of 1,100,000 men, 15 field armies, 774 tanks, and 1,000 aircraft was assembled for the attack. The defensive battle for Moscow had seen the climax of the *Stavka's methods* that had been developed since the beginning of the war. Operational forces at whatever cost were committed to counter German offensive thrusts. Reserves were then used either to stabilize fronts or to create new ones.

While German strength inevitably declined and operational reserves dwindled, the *Stavka* continued to assemble an impressive reserve force, which it now deployed to power the Soviet counteroffensive. The strength of refurbished Red Army divisions just about equalled that of the decimated formations of the Germans' Army Group Center, but there was little if nothing to spare. The 325th Rifle Division (Tenth Reserve Army) had not received winter clothing. Men deserted, 16 were apprehended and tried. Zhukov lacked the large tank formations needed for the planned breakthroughs. The six tank and motorized divisions attached to the Western Front had virtually no armor: the 108th Tank Division had 15 tanks; the 38th, 1 medium tank and 30 obsolete machines. Artillery was in short supply. Ammunition was issued only to assault units. Time was at a premium: too short to train fresh troops or to undertake special preparations. The Soviet plan was coherent and realistic, needing only a minimum of operational skill. Zhukov was relying on speed and surprise to offset the lack of fully trained troops, missing weapons, and equipment, and the absence of large mobile forces.

The Red Army attacked at 0300 hours on 5 December 1941. For eight days the country heard little or nothing. Only on 13 December did Radio Moscow announce "the failure of the German plan to encircle and capture Moscow." The first stage of the Soviet counteroffensive had deflected the German armored "wedges;" Soviet troops had advanced 60 kilometers to the north and 120 kilometers to the south. The first stage of the operation had been successfully accomplished. On 16 December the Red Army turned to pursuit. Stalin and Shaposhnikov were already scanning wider horizons. In the north, Tikhvin had finally fallen on 9 December. In the south the *Stavka* in mid-December ordered the risky Kerch-Feodosiia amphibious operation, an extremely bold stroke designed to assist the defense of Sevastopol and prepare for the eventual recovery of the Crimea. Fired by the recapture of Rostov, Timoshenko was already proposing hugely ambitious plans for a "broad offensive" in the southwestern theater, aiming at nothing less than the recovery of the Donbas and an advance to the Dnieper.

In spite of the initial successes, the Red Army overrated itself. The Soviet counteroffensive exposed continuing problems with tactical performance and the organization of the higher direction of the war. On the ground, Soviet strength was frequently dissipated by faulty dispositions. Failure to concentrate provided only inadequate force at necessary points, resulting in costly frontal attacks and heavy casualties. The profligate attitude to human life finally became too much. Letters of protest to the *Stavka* and to Stalin piled up, denouncing the "criminally negligent attitude" (*prestupno-khalatnoe otnoshenie*) of all officers who squandered the lives of Soviet infantrymen.

Zhukov was finally compelled to issue orders that required "abnormal losses" to be reported, together with the identities of those responsible and the measures taken to prevent any repetition. Infantry attacks must be properly planned and prepared. Commanders simply throwing infantry against unsuppressed defenses faced demotion. To speed the Soviet offensive on its way, Stalin issued special tactical instructions, some derived from the ideas circulated in the 1930s. For the first time Soviet artillerymen heard the term "artillery offensive." Stalin demanded more "shock groups," but shortage of time did not permit commanders to reorganise to form these groups. Even if assembled, lack of weapons and equipment forced the dispersal of these "shock groups" to stiffen other formations. Worse, no second echelon existed to exploit a breakthrough that had been achieved, albeit at huge cost in casualties.

Stalin imposed himself directly on the higher direction of Soviet operations. The Moscow operation had been conducted by Stalin, Zhukov, and Shaposhnikov acting in close concert, using the *Stavka* apparatus and increasingly that of the General Staff. "Decentralized" high command, the *Glavkom* system, had failed. Formal front command arrangements meant little or nothing to Stalin. He simply connected himself to the front commander in order to advise or chastize, personally directing the pursuit of the Germans westward. The effect was either to enforce decisions or to confuse those already taken. Stalin obtained information from a variety of sources: his midnight interrogations, General Staff liaison officers, front reports, his "watchdogs," the likes of Mekhlis, Malenkov, Bulganin, and, as ever, Beria of the secret police.

Persuading Stalin of the front line reality, of stiffening German resistance and decimated Soviet divisions, of overextended fronts, was fraught not only with difficulty but also danger. Commanders summoned to face him were cautiously advised "not to make trouble." An increasing feature of the operational scene was the creation of smaller fronts, whereby a particular front operation was now cast as a constituent of a larger strategic operation. The effectiveness of the centralized control exercized by the *Stavka,* particularly over reserves, derived from the fact that presently only one undifferentiated "strategic front" existed, facilitating "concrete direction" of the preparation and conduct of operations.

Subsequent changes in that situation would demand greater sophistication in the organization of the higher direction of the war, but as yet Stalin believed in simply hurling his armies simultaneously across a single Soviet-German "front" running from the Baltic to the Black Sea. Inevitably this stretched the capabilities of the Red Army to the breaking point as it painfully transformed itself from "a horde of riflemen." But signs of greater competence at front and army level were already discernible. "Purge by battle" slowly eliminated Civil War relics. A small but expanding group of able younger officers was emerging: field commanders Zhukov, Vasilevskii, Rokossovskii, Koniev, Vatutin, specialists such as Voronov, Katukhov with armor, Novikov at the air force, all men who knew their jobs and were learning more with each passing day.

## The First Winter Offensive, 1942

The Moscow counteroffensive ended officially on 7 January 1942. Stalin had already presented the *Stavka* with his proposals for the further conduct of the war, nothing less than offensive operations launched across the entire front along three strategic axes. Decisive offensives, outlined by the General Staff in mid-December, would destroy the basic German force concentrations, "drive them westwards without pause," exhaust their reserves. Come spring, the Red Army would again have powerful reserves, the Germans few. The way would be open for "the complete destruction of the Hitlerite forces in 1942." Army Group Center was the prime target, though Leningrad was to be relieved, Army Group North destroyed, and in the south two Soviet fronts would attack Army Group South and liberate the Donbas and the Crimea.

Being overly grandiose and wildly incommensurate with available resources were not the only faults in Stalin's plan. Zhukov objected to the "strategic inversion," expanding outward to every other front, rather than "going for the kill" at the center. Chief economic planner Voznesenskii supported Zhukov. Supplies of weapons, munitions, and other necessities essential to sustain simultaneous offensives on all fronts, would not be forthcoming. All to no avail; Stalin had decided. Even before the *Stavka* meeting, attack directives had already gone out to front commanders.

In spite of Voznesenskii's realistic warning, Soviet war industry had begun to recover from the massive chaos brought on by German occupation and relocation to the east. Economic planners now struggled to bring the economy into greater balance and organize it for protracted war. Industrial managers worked furiously to increase output. Once unloaded and reassembled at evacuation sites, factory machines started up, many on the bare earth, in primitive or half-finished buildings, in sub-zero temperatures relying on emergency power and lighting. The work force, relying heavily on pensioners and juveniles, found shelter difficult, often improvising crude earthen bunkers. Heavy tank production was transferred to Chelyabinsk, known as "Tankograd"; Nizhny-Tagil Factory No. 183 produced medium tanks. Demand for aircraft was insatiable, particularly for the ground attack Il–2 *Shturmovik* produced in Moscow and Kuibyshev.

At the price of great hardship and personal suffering, Soviet workers brought about a real increase in output, despatching 4,648 tanks and 3,301 aircraft to the front in the first quarter of 1942. By the end of the year, aircraft production had doubled. Stalin and the *Stavka* were fully aware of the insufficient resources available for the planned strategic offensive and what strain this would place on men and machines. To compensate for shortages *Stavka*'s 10 January 1942 directive No. 03 stressed: "incisive troop performance," the role of "shock groups," narrow frontages to achieve local superiority, resort to the "artillery offensive." None of this took any account of the inexperience, even ignorance, of Soviet commanders or most immediately of an acute shortage of artillery ammunition.

By the end of February Stalin's attempt to seize the strategic initiative had failed. Uninterrupted offensive operations were designed to prevent the German army from establishing a firm defensive line, but Hitler's "Stand fast" order brought German troops to a halt, bitterly contesting every yard of ground. The Soviet offensive was dashed against these rocks and ultimately wrecked. The attempt in the north to isolate the Eighteenth German Army throttling Leningrad ended in failure and culminated in disaster: the martyrdom of the Soviet Second Shock Army.

At the center Zhukov aimed to destroy four German armies. Deep and dangerous thrusts into the German flanks north and south placed German forces in great peril. The Red Army smashed its way into the junction of Army Group Center and North but the Soviet tide rolled past rather than into the German positions barricaded around major and minor "hedgehogs." Toward the end of February the Soviet offensive began to exhaust itself, forcing Zhukov to throw in every last resource including parachute troops to energize flagging operations at Viazma. Parachute troops alone were no substitute for the lack of brute strength, mobility, and fire support. In March 1942 Zhukov's offensive halted 45 miles east of Smolensk, stalled before Viazma, Orel, and Rzhev.

Far to the south, in two months of terrible fighting Timoshenko's armies hacked their way into German Army Group South, battling to expand penetrations into a major strategic breakout designed to destroy German forces in the Donbas and at Kharkov. But Soviet attempts to break out west and south from their bridgeheads on the Northern Donets, the "Izium bulge," failed. The attacks designed to pin German forces against the Sea of Azov failed, as did the push to burst into the Crimea from the Kerch bridgehead.

On Red Army Day, 23 February 1942, Stalin revealed what he considered to be the five "permanently operating factors" determining the course and the outcome of the war. Heading the list was "stability of the rear," followed by "the morale of the army," conscious statements of Stalin's view of the major vulnerabilities of the system. Both had shown dangerous deficiencies in the aftermath of the German invasion. The last three factors were "quantitative," the number and quality of divisions, armament, and bringing up the rear, "the organizing ability of command personnel." The sole "transient factor" deemed worthy of mention was surprise. The only amendment to what were and would continue to be Stalinist tablets cast immutably in stone came guardedly from Voroshilov, emphasising adequacy of reserves.

The obsession with the political reliability of Soviet society at large, "the rear" and the moral sturdiness of the army never abated. The gates of the wartime Gulag were ever open for those convicted of "counter-revolutionary and other especially dangerous crimes," while within the camps anti-Soviet activity increased. In January 1942 Vorkuta witnessed the first ever armed uprising in the camps, denounced by the authorities as a "Fascist conspiracy." It was nevertheless fear of Soviet defeat and its consequences for the prisoners, hanging like some dread contagion over the camps in the winter of 1941–42, that provoked this desperate action.

Late in March the Soviet winter offensive, while still capable of dangerous lunges imperiling German positions, shuddered to a halt. Stalin once again assembled his commanders to determine the strategy of the coming summer campaign. After reviewing current Red Army strength and resources, emphasizing the lack of substantial, trained reserves, Shaposhnikov and Vasilevskii recommended a turn to the "provisional strategic defensive." Stalin agreed. But behind the back of the *Stavka*, by personal agreement with select commanders, Stalin was planning "partially offensive operations." Timoshenko was a party to one such "deal." In mid-March he proposed a huge three-front offensive, discreetly reduced to an "internal matter" that involved attacking from the "Izium bulge" to recover Kharkov. On Stalin's express instruction the General Staff was not to involve itself. Duly decided, the "Kharkov operation" was timed for May. Other "partial offensives" were spawned in the guise of integral operations reaching from Leningrad to Kerch. In effect Stalin quite incongruously proposed "to attack and defend simultaneously."

Stalin's optimism, if such it was, was not entirely without foundation. The "correlation of forces" was not wholly unfavorable. From June 1941 to the spring of 1942 the Red Army had suffered 6,836,400 casualties, of whom 4,090,900 were "irrecoverable": killed in action, missing, or prisoners. The Wehrmacht had lost almost one-third of its initial strength. The Red Army order of battle presently consisted of 400 divisions, a manpower pool of 11 million, supported by 11,000 aircraft and 10,000 tanks. However, much of this strength was illusory. More than half of the reinforcements were untrained, the divisions and units moving up lacked men, weapons, and ammunition. Favorable "correlation of forces" was also a fiction, based on inflated intelligence estimates of German losses and an unfounded assumption that the German army would be unable to take the offensive.

Slowly, agonizingly, the Red Army struggled to become a modern, viable fighting machine, but too often the steps were precipitate and ill conceived. Increased tank production prompted a move in the late spring of 1942 to begin reconstituting large armored formations. Tank corps reappeared on 31 March 1942; their composition modified in May to one heavy tank brigade and two medium tank brigades. At the same time, tank armies were being formed, designed to penetrate German defenses and act as an "exploitation echelon" in any breakthrough. Large armored formations, hastily reconstituted, were now about to undergo a fresh baptism of fire, handicapped by inadequate training, unsatisfactory organization command deficiencies, and poor tactics.

## Disaster in the South: 1942

In the late spring of 1942, Hitler's attention was fixed on the flanks, the south in particular. Directive No. 41, dated 5 April, stipulated that all available forces would be concentrated on the "*main operations in the Southern sector*" to destroy the enemy west of the Don, secure the Caucasian oilfields and the mountain passes. The *Stavka,* the Soviet General Staff, the majority of front commanders, and Stalin himself, took a wholly different view of the German intentions. They concluded that Moscow and the "central region" would be the main German target, though Soviet military intelligence reported otherwise. Stalin dismissed and denounced intelligence "disinformation." Even with incontrovertible captured documentary proof in his hands in June, Stalin persisted in denying its validity. Moscow would be secured against any repetition of the near disaster of 1941.

Otherwise Stalin intended to hold his advanced lines in the center, push forward where he might, de-blockade Leningrad, and liberate Kharkov and the Crimea. Assessing Soviet intentions on 1 May, German military intelligence (*Fremde Heere Ost*) reported that the Soviet command was organizing "several *Schwerpunkte.*" No major breakthrough was likely to materialize, though a "Kharkov offensive" was very possible from the "Izium bulge."

What German intelligence judged a possibility became a reality. Timoshenko launched the "Kharkov offensive" on 12 May, attacking north and south of the city. German forces had already concentrated at Kharkov and, unnoticed by the Red Army, also to the south. Soviet troops scored some initial success, but within five days, once the German counterattack opened, they were in a perilous situation. Timoshenko's forces continued to advance, straight into a trap, into encirclement and ruinous defeat. Reassured about the situation by Timoshenko, Stalin and the *Stavka* refused to abandon the Soviet offensive. The German army closed in; the Red Army lost more than a quarter of a million men. Only 27,000 escaped encirclement. The entire Soviet "south-western axis" was on the verge of ruins. Stalin's fury knew no bounds. For the first time he used the word "catastrophe." He compared this defeat in the south to the catastrophic defeat of Samsonov and Rennenkampf in East Prussia in 1914. Rounding on General Bagramian, chief of staff of the Southwestern Front, he warned him that "if we gave the country the full details of what the front has gone through and continues to experience I fear they would deal very harshly with you."

Disaster piled on disaster. Criminally incompetent command of operations designed to clear the Crimea not only led to further huge losses but also to Soviet forces being driven off the Kerch peninsula. In the north Vlasov's Second Shock Army fighting in the Liuban operation, long immured in encirclement, was deprived of rescue and perished in June. Great gaps had been torn in the Soviet lines. To plug these "black holes" and to replace a mass of dead, missing, and prisoners, Stalin turned to the Far East. Finally convinced that Japan was inextricably engaged in the Pacific, he ordered the transfer of 10 to 12 divisions to European Russia for assignment to the Supreme Command Reserve. He doggedly persisted in believing that Moscow was the German objective, hence more armor and reserves were directed to the Western and Briansk Fronts. A German deception operation *Kreml* (Kremlin) duly "confirmed" this impression, leaked "top secret" directives indicating a resumption of the November 1941 drive on Moscow. Soviet armor and reserves piled up on the Western and Briansk Fronts.

The Wehrmacht launched Operation *BLAU* (*Blue*) on 28 June 1942. German forces had unmistakably turned southeast, forcing Stalin to consider redeploying the reserves clustered in defense of Moscow. All too soon there was desperate need of them. On 12 July the Soviet Southwestern Front, already badly weakened by the May disasters, had been virtually ripped to pieces and its rear threatened. That of Malinovskii's Southern Front was also in danger. The *Stavka* wound up the Southwestern Front, replacing it with a new Stalingrad Front stiffened with three reserve armies, which had yet to arrive. They were presently on the move, their echelons stretching back northward for many miles. Infantry nearer to hand faced brutal forced marches to a "front" whose exact location was a mystery.

A sense of disaster was beginning to spread at a time when a small but significant sea-change was coming over the high command. Timely authorization for withdrawal was issued to both Timoshenko and Malinovskii, avoiding the "hold at any cost" orders that inflicted colossal damage on the Red Army at Kiev and Viazma in 1941. Grim resistance at Voronezh was fully justified in order to pin German forces, which might otherwise turn south, and to cover a section of Moscow's communication with the east. Resistance at Voronezh gave Timoshenko time to pull his divisions back over the rivers Oskol, Donets, and finally the Don. This large-scale orderly withdrawal was covered by rear-guard actions fought in almost classic Russian style. Battered, dispirited, the Red Army had nevertheless escaped east and south. As Stalin redirected his reserves, in order to tie up German reserves at the center and on the northern flank, he ordered four armies of the Western and Kalinin Fronts to attack the bulging Rzhev salient at the end of July. Offensive operations would be resumed in the Leningrad area, where for the past two months armored and artillery reinforcements had been moving up.

On 10 July Hitler reformed Army Group South into two separate elements: Group A and B. Three days later he abandoned the idea of a rapid advance on Stalingrad, choosing instead to fight an encirclement battle on the lower Don with Rostov as its focus. This would deliver the coup de grace to the Red Army, which was in his opinion already "finished." The German Sixth Army commanded by General von Paulus would now advance on Stalingrad alone: 40 Panzer Corps had already been detached, streaking off to join the battle for Rostov. After 50 hours of ferocious fighting Rostov fell on 23–24 July. The great bridge over the Don was in German hands, whereupon Hitler ordered Army Group A to drive for Maikop-Grozny, and Group B to prepare a defensive line on the Don and "thrust forward" to Stalingrad.

Stalin portrayed the fall of Rostov as the final crack of doom. NKVD machine-gunners had turned the city into a death-trap, but Stalin calculatedly misrepresented the loss of the city as an unauthorized withdrawal. As a great shudder ran through Russia, the propaganda line was changing. Hatred of the Germans was intensified, but after the disasters in May and the looming crisis at Stalingrad and in the Caucasus, it was the Red Army itself which was singled out for mounting, stinging criticism. The army had failed the country. This was the burden of the draconian Order No. 227, personally edited by Stalin, issued on 28 July 1942 and read out to all companies, squadrons, and batteries. "Not a step back" literally meant what it said; no space existed for further retreat, citing the great swathes of territory lost to the Germans. "The very idea of retreating without orders is impossible," the very act of retreat, even authorized retreat, was shameful. "Iron discipline" was demanded, the penalty for cowardice and treachery the bullet. The result was indiscriminate shooting; wanton enough to raise protests at excesses largely committed by military commissars early in August. The publicity accorded this concealed a hidden agenda, preparing the way for the abolition of the present role of the military commissar.

Conversely Stalin was persuaded to improve the status of officers and institute new decorations limited to officers only: the Orders of Alexander Nevskii, Suvorov, Kutuzov, named after Russian heroes. Stalin pursued his own version of the attractive carrot and the brutal stick. On 1 August he sent the Moscow, Volga, and Stalingrad district commanders and Lavrenti Beria orders to assemble "command staff" from officer-prisoners in NKVD special camps for "assault rifle battalions," each with 929 men. These penal battalions would be assigned to the "most active" sectors of the front line, the ex-prisoners allowed to "purge their guilt" to the Motherland with "arms in their hands." Most knew this to be a death-sentence, but saw in it the means to absolve their families of disgrace and free them from further retribution.

The situation was perilous in the extreme. German forces were in the great bend of the Don, the threat to the Caucasus great and growing daily. Three reserve armies were rushed to the Stalingrad Front. Their nominal strength was 38 divisions, though many "divisions" could muster only 300–1,000 men. Order No. 227 failed to halt withdrawals. Almost immediately Stalin and Vasilevskii had to order "holding detachments" of 200 men to be formed from the best elements of newly arrived Far Eastern divisions and be positioned in the rear of the Sixty-second and Sixty-fourth Army. In Stalingrad itself the military cupboard was depressingly bare. On 19 July Stalin had ordered the city on to a war footing, but turning an industrial center into a fortress was a nightmare. "Local resources" mobilized the civilian population to dig trenches and build rudimentary fortifications, industrial evacuation halted earlier was now resumed, livestock and stores transferred to the eastern bank of the Volga. The situation in the Don bend deteriorated, the danger magnified, as the German Fourth Panzer Army was suddenly detached from operations in the Caucasus. Stalingrad was doubly threatened, from the northwest and now the southeast.

The German Sixth Army attacked on 15 August. One week later *Fliegerkorps* VIII inflicted terrible damage on Stalingrad with a massive air attack. The same day, 23 August, striking from a bridgehead east of the Don, 16th Panzer Division drove 25 miles across the steppe, ramming an armored fist into the northern suburb of Stalingrad at 1600 hours. At 2310 hours German tanks reached the Volga. Stalin raged and cursed. He refused to discuss the evacuation of civilians and industry or the mining of factories. "It should be understood" that such moves would be "taken as a decision to surrender Stalingrad." The GKO forbade any preparation for evacuation or demolition. The Red Army was thus committed to one of the most terrible battles in the history of warfare.

## Post-Rostov Reform

Order No. 227 had a limited shock effect. German officers noted a certain rally in Soviet performance, but the real transformation was taking place behind the scenes. After the Kerch disaster Stalin had noted on the *Stavka* summary that the Red Army did not understand modern war. Not only must it be made to understand it; it must also be equipped to fight it. But first the Red Army had to be unshackled, allowing the professionalism, which Stalin demanded, to be exercized. From the Stalingrad Front Colonel-General Voronov wrote to the Central Committee recommending a return to "unitary command" as "the only path to follow." Inefficient and incompetent commissar control had no place in a modern fighting machine. On 9 October the matter was finally resolved: "dual command" was abolished and the institution of military commissars wound up. The next step in the emancipation of the Soviet officer followed in a few days, the subordination of heads of counterintelligence "Special Sections" (OO) to the formation or unit commander.

In the summer of 1942 the last of the *Glavkom* disappeared. High command organization reverted to a formal two-echelon structure: Supreme Commander (*Stavka*) and Front, within which Stalin continued to run his own arbitrary, personalized system. A telephonic "visitation" from Stalin was the Damocletian sword hanging over the heads of all commanders. No man, whether marshal or ordinary *krasnoarmeets*, remained unaffected by the rigors of the Stalinist system. Certain decentralization, however, was introduced into the system with the emergence of *Stavka* "representatives" (*predstaviteli*) to Front commands, senior officers invested with considerable authority. The first of these "representatives" were assigned to the Stalingrad Front. Late in August the GKO, namely Stalin, appointed Zhukov to the post of deputy supreme commander, a move signaling that Stalin would now swim with the tide of younger, experienced commanders. At the General Staff, Colonel-General Vasilevskii demonstrated a high degree of professionalism, sufficient to restore the reputation of the General Staff as the "brain of the army" (*mozg armii*) and to foster Stalin's growing confidence in it.

Stalin also understood that as yet the Red Army lacked power equivalent to its mass. With the workers in his Urals industrial fortresses producing more and improved weapons, the Red Army was slowly changing, no longer simply a "horde of riflemen" so disparaged by the Germans. Rifle divisions reduced manpower in favor of increased firepower, automatic weapons, mortars, anti-tank weapons, and divisional artillery. The corps level, abolished in 1941, reappeared. By the autumn of 1942, 27 corps had been established with the field armies. Artillery expanded with the creation of artillery brigades, artillery divisions, and Supreme Command Reserve anti-aircraft divisions. Badly bludgeoned in the summer battles, the tank corps were rebuilt once more, but suffered again from poor tactics and lack of proper handling. The tank armies raised in 1942 proved less than effective, a primary cause being the inclusion of rifle divisions within them. Infantry was unable to keep pace with the armor, consequently tank spearheads unsupported by infantry and anti-tank guns were an easy prey to German counterattacks. In September 1942 the new mechanized corps replaced the rifle division in "homogeneous" tank armies, balanced formations organized around two tank and one mechanized corps. Reorganization swept through the Soviet air force under Novikov. The first air armies appeared. Now the *Stavka* could amass reserves, improve the maneuvrability of its air assets, and employ them on a mass scale.

## The Counteroffensive Constellation, November 1942

On 3 September the situation at Stalingrad deteriorated. Demanding urgent counterattacks Stalin gloomily asserted that "they [the Germans] can take Stalingrad today or tomorrow." The city had become a giant funnel of destruction, relentlessly sucking in men. German tanks and infantry attacked Stalingrad from all sides, but contrary to German expectations Stalingrad did not fall quickly. Nor did Soviet forces fall back to the eastern bank of the Volga.

Further north, in August the Western Front under Koniev launched heavy attacks in the direction of Rzhev, enough to endanger the German Ninth Army. Prone to describe the Russians as all but finished, Hitler dismissed these operations as inevitable "diversionary attacks" given the situation at Stalingrad. German intelligence was more sanguine. Soviet reserves existed, 70-plus rifle divisions, more than 80 armored formations. Soviet factories were producing large numbers of KV and T-34 tanks. German armies were becoming increasingly dispersed, their flanks exposed, whereas the Red Army was concentrating.

Amid appalling carnage at Stalingrad, Zhukov and Vasilevskii outlined a counteroffensive plan to Stalin on 12 September. The situation of German troops operating on the "Stalingrad axis" looked increasingly unfavorable, some 50 divisions forming a huge salient with its point embedded in Stalingrad. The initial Soviet plan envisaged two "operational tasks," encirclement and isolation to be followed by annihilation of the main German force within Stalingrad. Meanwhile, the Soviet Sixty-second and Sixty-fourth Armies had to hold the Stalingrad bridgeheads whatever the cost. Planning for the 1942–43 Soviet winter campaign embracing huge strategic perspectives had also begun, but the immediate attention of the General Staff and the *Stavka* was fixed on the basic operation, Stalingrad, and a supporting operation at Mozdok in the northern Caucasus.

Hitler terminated the German summer offensive on 14 October, halting all offensive operations save for Stalingrad and the Caucasus. The forthcoming winter campaign was to lay the foundations for the "final destruction" of the Red Army in 1943, but the Red Army was too weak to field any great force during the coming winter. One day earlier Stalin had just reviewed the outline of the Stalingrad counteroffensive plan. Possibly mindful of what havoc had ensued from his peremptory demands at the January *Stavka* meeting, Stalin on this occasion looked and listened, finally scrawling one word, "Agreed" (*soglashen*) on the "decision map" of *Uranus,* code name for the Stalingrad counteroffensive. What distinguished the planning for 1942–43 from that of the first ill-fated winter offensive was the abandonment of simultaneous offensive operations across every strategic axis. Sequential attacks would aim to destroy the most powerful German concentrations in turn.

German intelligence argued in early November that if the Red Army needed "decisive success," it must seek it at the center. The situation in the south was "unclear," but two major operations were out of the question. This conformed precisely to Zhukov's own opinion that the prime target was Army Group Center. But it was wholly confounded since he was convinced, and was able to convince Stalin, that the Red Army could launch *two* major, mutually supporting counteroffensives at the center and in the south. The offensive aimed at the Rzhev salient, and ultimately Army Group Center, code named *Mars,* was timed for late October, but poor weather conditions forced a postponement. On 13 November, without any great argument, Stalin approved 24–25 November as the new start-date for *Mars* and confirmed 19 November for *Uranus* at Stalingrad.

Which way would the strategic scales tip? At Stalingrad the *Stavka* was virtually gambling that the German offensive would fail, that the enemy could not move on to the defensive and that his deployments remained unchanged. Even as late as 11 November *Uranus* appeared to be at grave risk. The strength of Chuikov's Sixty-second Army was fast failing, Stalingrad defenders at their last gasp: *my poistrepalis.* Higher hopes were held out for *Mars,* invested with greater strength than *Uranus,* 700,000 more men, more than twice as many tanks (3,375:1,463), more artillery and aircraft. *Mars* stood to gain whatever the outcome. If *Uranus* succeeded, German armor must move south as reinforcement, easing the path for the Western and Kalinin Fronts. Should *Uranus* falter, with available reinforcements delivered at the center, *Mars* would not be seriously jeopardized.

During the first week in November Soviet units moved to their start positions. Manpower in the Soviet armed forces now topped 10 million men deployed on 12 fronts in 75 field armies, 2 tank and 15 air armies. The Red Army fielded 6.6 million men in 370 rifle and motor-rifle divisions, 156 brigades, 10 out of 12 tank corps, 5 out of 8 mechanized corps, 62 aviation divisions, supported by more than 7,000 tanks and 4,500 combat aircraft. The *Stavka* had at least learned a bitter lesson from the spring of 1942. Already in September the *Stavka* held two tank armies, Third and Fifth, in reserve, and was raising five reserve armies (First, Second, Third, Fourth and Tenth). When *Uranus* opened on 19 November the *Stavka* held five field armies and one tank army in reserve.

In the event, *Uranus* succeeded. *Mars* plunged on to disaster. After 100 hours of offensive operations at Stalingrad the Soviet outer encirclement was complete. By the end of the month an inner encirclement had trapped more than 20 German divisions, elements of two Rumanian divisions, specialist support groups, and over 300,000 men. On 24 November Hitler transformed the massive trap into *Festung Stalingrad,* effectively entombing the German Sixth Army. Zhukov's two-stage strategic operation *Mars* opened on 25 November but after five days Soviet attacks faltered, "grinding attacks" achieving little. In mid-December calamitous losses in men and machines mounted. *Mars* had spent itself and was formally abandoned on 20 December, having cost the Red Army half a million men and 1,700 tanks.

Justifiably acclaimed a triumph, *Uranus* temporarily shifted the strategic center of gravity to the southeast. The counteroffensive had demonstrated advances in strategic planning and a discreet revival of the principles of "deep battle," a posthumous tribute to Tukhachevskii. Recourse to double encirclement was a bold move, though precarious enough not to tempt the Soviet command to repeat it. Soviet planners had not anticipated the difficulties in reducing the encircled German divisions nor the scale of German operations to relieve them. No preparation had been made to forestall German withdrawal from the Northern Caucasus. On the northwestern and central axes, too often old-style stereotyped offensive operations were planned, seriously underestimating the capabilities of German troops secured in strong defensive positions.

Old habits died hard and with them the "old" Red Army, cumbersome, overly rigid, inefficient, ill-fitted to the complexities of modern war. Reduced to skeletal form by December 1941, the Red Army had to be fleshed out and fitted out anew in 1942. Organizational change helped it adapt to the battlefield. The "speedy, utterly ruthless" replacement system kept it on the battlefield, in spite of huge losses. The unexpectedly rapid recovery of Soviet industrial output had already begun to affect the overall balance of strength in Soviet favor. Soviet technological inferiority was quickly waning. Improved technology, increased "armament norms," and tactical doctrine were slowly becoming better aligned. The Soviet tank arm was a prime example, beginning its extraordinary evolution from "an apathetic and ignorant crowd," lacking training or aptitude, into "crews endowed with brain and nerves."

The Red Army and Soviet society had survived the panic of 1941 and the defeatism of 1942. At fearful cost both had outlived the terrible damage inflicted by Stalinist unpreparedness, the brutal anachronisms of supposed "revolutionary will," and the early mismanagement of economic mobilization. Under conditions of maximum stress this war-waging system worked indifferently, badly, disconcertingly, surprisingly, callously, and wastefully, but it worked finally. In the Red Army the ill-prepared *krasnoarmeets* of 1941 was giving way to the hardened *frontovik* of 1942. His fate and that of his successors throughout the Great Patriotic War was inextricably linked with the continuous struggle to produce effective commanders, suitable organization, superior weapons and appropriate tactics.

## Further Research

The congruence of Russian and non-Russian research has illuminated many "blank spots" in Red Army history and that of the Soviet-German war, but "systematic clarification" is still required of Soviet war plans from 1928 to 1941, the 15 drafts, reviews, revisions, and important associated memoranda, such as those disclosed by Lennart Samuelson. Equally, analysis of Soviet strategic war games, particularly the January 1941 series, for which archive material is available, would be an important complement. The social conditions of the Soviet Union at war, the front, the rear, and the Gulag, constitutes a huge field of research as yet wide open, as does the highly controversial and emotive subject of war losses.

## Sources and Further Reading

Following the demise of the Soviet Union, the historiography of the Soviet-German War of 1941–45 has undergone a transformation little short of a revolution. Much is owed to access to former Soviet archives and to declassified documentation.

## Russian Historiography

The 4-volume revised "official history" of the "Great Patriotic War," *Velikaia Otech-estvennaia voina 1941–1945. Voenno-istoricheskii ocherk* (Moscow: Nauka, 1998–99), jointly compiled by the Institute of Military History and the Historical Section of the Russian Academy of Sciences, wholly supersedes the 1960–65 6-volume "official history" and the 1973–85 12-volume history. Essentially, "de-politicized" military history, it utilizes a combination of archive materials, declassified documents, and secondary sources. Both predecessor of and complement to this history are the declassified documentary collections in *Russkii arkhiv* Series *Velikaia Otechestvennaia* beginning with the December 1940 command conference proceedings (Vol. 12.1 Moscow: Terra, 1993), Defense Commissariat Orders 1937–1941 (1994), Soviet-Polish relations 1941–45 (1994), Berlin 1945 (1995), *Stavka VGK 1941–45* (1996–99), 1940 Naval command conference proceedings (1997), Rear Services (1998), and General Staff 1941–42 (1997–99). Separate documentary collections are exemplified by *Bitva za Stolitsu* Vols. 1–2 (Moscow, 1994) and more recently the collection of military, diplomatic, and military-economic documents, *1941 god* Vols. 1–2 (Moscow, 1998) in the series *Rossiia XX vek. Dokumenty.* Arguably the definitive account of the prewar military purge has been furnished by O. F. Suverinov, *Tragediia RKKA 1937–1938* (Moscow: Terra 1998) with extensive recourse to archives. Yet another significant element in post-Soviet historiography is the protracted and intensive debate on Stalin's pre-June 1941 intentions, largely positive and negative responses to Viktor Suvorov's *Icebreaker* thesis. The diverse arguments presented in *Gotovil li Stalin nastupatel'nuiu voinu protiv Gitlera? Nezaplanirovannaia diskussiia* edited by G. A. Bordiugov, published in 1995 are one example. The debate is by no means foreclosed, nor is the controversy on Soviet wartime losses triggered by *Grif sekretnosti sniat* (Moscow: Voenizdat, 1993) edited by Colonel-General G. F. Krivosheev; in translation *Soviet Casualties and Combat Losses in the Twentieth Century* (London: Greenhill, 1997).

## International Historiography

Soviet military history, the development of the Red Army, the Soviet-German war of 1941–45, and the Soviet war economy, have all been reexamined in the light of archival disclosures. The prewar Red Army has been investigated in depth by Mark von Hagen, *Soldiers in the Proletarian Dictatorship* (Ithaca, NY: Cornell University Press, 1990) and Roger R. Reese, *Stalin's Reluctant Soldiers* (Lawrence, KS: University Press of Kansas, 1996), the prelude to disaster analyzed by Carl Van Dyke in *The Soviet Invasion of Finland 1939–40* (London: Cass, 1997), the actual condition of the Red Army in 1941 laid bare by David M. Glantz in *Stumbling Colossus* (Lawrence, KS: University Press of Kansas, 1998). *The Attack on the Soviet Union* Volume IV in the Research Institute for Military History, Potsdam series *Germany and the Second World War,* drawing on German archives and Soviet sources, a translation from the German published by Oxford University Press in 1998, is the most authoritative account of Operation Barbarossa, its planning, preparation, and military operations. Making extensive use of Soviet archives, Gabriel Gorodetsky reexamines "the other side of the hill," the well-springs of Stalin's policy and behavior in 1941 in *Grand Delusion. Stalin and the German Invasion of Russia* (New Haven, CT: Yale University Press,1999).

David M. Glantz has provided a series of major in-depth studies of Soviet military operations, as editor of *The Initial Period of War on the Eastern Front* (London: Frank Cass, 1993), author of *Kharkov 1942* (London: Ian Allan Publishing, 1998), *Zhukov's Greatest Defeat* (Lawrence, KS: University Press of Kansas, 1999) on Operation *Mars,* with Jonathan M. House, *The Battle of Kursk* (Lawrence, KS: University Press of Kansas, 1999). Archives have again facilitated fundamental studies in Soviet prewar military-economic planning and the performance of the Soviet war economy; Sally W. Stoecker, *Forging Stalin's Army* (Boulder, CO: Westview Press,1998), Lennart Samuelson, *Plans for Stalin's War Machine* (London: Macmillan Press, 2000) and Mark Harrison, *Accounting for War* (New York: Cambridge University Press, 1996) on the Soviet wartime defense burden, employment, production.

Soviet wartime operational studies, derived from the declassified multi-volume Soviet General Staff *Collection of Materials for the Study of War Experience,* are represented by *The Battle for Moscow* (London: Pergamon-Brassey's, 1989) edited by Michael Parrish, *Battle for Stalingrad* (London: Pergamon-Brassey's, 1989) edited by Louis Rotundo, latterly *The Battle for Kursk 1943* (London: Cass, 1999) translated, edited by David M. Glantz and Harold S. Orenstein.

## Military Journals

*The Journal of Soviet Military Studies,* retitled *The Journal of Slavic Military Studies,* published by Frank Cass, London and *Voenno-istoricheskii Zhurnal,* published in Moscow under the auspices of the General Staff of the Russian Federation Armed Forces, are prime sources for Red Army history, operational studies, combat documents, and archive materials.

BATTLE OF STALINGRAD

# CHAPTER 9

# THE GREAT PATRIOTIC WAR
## Rediscovering Operational Art

*Frederick W. Kagan*

THE CHALLENGE FACING THE SOVIET UNION REMAINED DAUNTING in the spring of 1943. The Germans had been halted at Moscow in 1941 and defeated decisively at Stalingrad in 1942, but the front line remained deep in Soviet territory and the residual combat power of the Wehrmacht forces there promised a long and bitter struggle to free the USSR. Nor did Soviet operations in the first two years of the war bode well for their ability to expel the invaders rapidly. The winter counteroffensive of 1941, considered as a large-scale offensive operation, had been a disaster, although it had achieved its main purpose. It was the failure of another Soviet offensive in early 1942 that had facilitated the German advance across Ukraine. And even as Soviet forces were trapping and then destroying the German Sixth Army at Stalingrad in Operation *Uranus,* another massive concentration of Red Army units was suffering an embarrassing defeat to the north in Operation *Mars.* Before the Soviets could confidently expect to drive the Germans out, they would have to learn how to conduct modern large-scale armored offensive operations.

The timing of the Red Army purges in the late 1930s could not have been worse from the standpoint of the development of Soviet military theory and practice. The Red Army had held a commanding lead in developing a framework within which to understand and conduct armored war before that time, and the theory of deep battle and successive operations was light-years ahead of the armored warfare doctrine of any other state in the

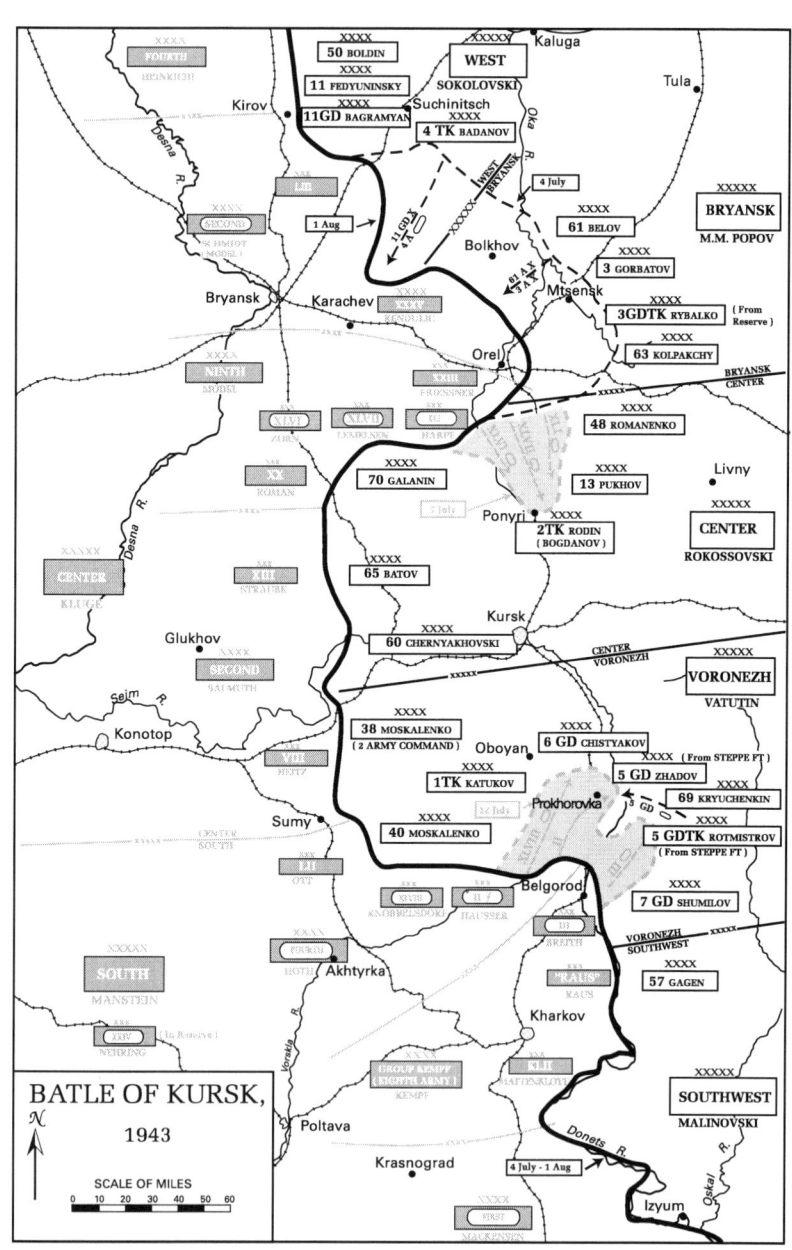

XXXX
**50** BOLDIN
XXXX
**11** FEDYUNINSKY
XXXX
**11GD** BAGRAMYAN

XXXXX
**WEST**
SOKOLOVSKI
Suchinitsch
XXXX
**4 TK** BADANOV

XXXXX Kaluga

Tula

FOURTH
BRENRICH

Kirov

LII

XXXXX
SECOND
SCHMIDT
(MODEL)

1 Aug

Bryansk

Karachev

NINTH
MODEL

Glukhov

Konotop

Sumy

Akhtyrka

Poltava

Krasnograd

Bolkhov

Orel

XXXX
FROESSNER

XLVI
ZUR

XLVII
LEMKENEN

XX
ROMAN

XIII
STRAUBK

XXXX
BALMUTH
SECOND

CENTER
KLUGE

VIII
HEITZ

LII
OTT

XXXX
KNOBBELSDORR

BR903
HOTH

XXV
XX
XXV
HARPE

XXXX
**70** GALANIN

XXXX
**65** BATOV

XXXX
**60** CHERNYAKHOVSKI

XXXX
**38** MOSKALENKO
( 2 ARMY COMMAND )

XXX
**1TK** KATUKOV

XXXX
**40** MOSKALENKO

XLVIII
HAUSSER

II

Belgorod

XXXXX
SOUTH
MANSTEIN

XXV
NEHRING

4 July

WEST
BRYANSK

XXXX
**61** BELOV

XXXX
**3** GORBATOV

Mtsensk

XXXX
**3GDTK** RYBALKO

XXXX
**63** KOLPAKCHY

XXXXX
**BRYANSK**
M.M. POPOV

( From
Reserve )

BRYANSK
CENTER

XXXX
**48** ROMANENKO

XXXX
**13** PUKHOV

Ponyri

XXXX
**2TK** RODIN
( BOGDANOV )

Livny

XXXXX
**CENTER**
ROKOSSOVSKI

Kursk

CENTER
VORONEZH

Oboyan

XXXX
**6 GD** CHISTYAKOV

XXXX
**5 GD** ZHADOV

Prokhorovka

XXXXX
**VORONEZH**
VATUTIN

( From STEPPE FT )

XXXX
**69** KRYUCHENKIN

XXXX
**5 GDTK** ROTMISTROV
( From STEPPE FT )

XXXX
**7 GD** SHUMILOV

B3
BREITH

"RAUS"
RAUS

Kharkov

KB.II
RATTENRUDT

VORONEZH
SOUTHWEST

XXXX
**57** GAGEN

XXXXX
**SOUTHWEST**
MALINOVSKI

## BATLE OF KURSK,

N

1943

SCALE OF MILES
0  10  20  30  40  50  60

XXXX
GROUP KEMPY
( EIGHTH ARMY )
KEMPE

4 July - 1 Aug

XXXX
FIRST
MACKENSEN

Izyum

world at the time. What was needed to perfect that doctrine was the careful study of the armored operations conducted in Europe from the Spanish Civil War to the fall of France. If the Soviets had carefully and critically evaluated the lessons of those campaigns, fitting those lessons into their already well-conceived understanding of modern war, the results should have been most positive. Unfortunately, the triumph of ideological stupidity in 1937 not only missed that opportunity, but set Soviet thinking back 20 years. As a result, the German invasion forced the Soviets hurriedly to dust off their old doctrines, update them, and figure out how to implement them—doing in weeks and months what should have been going on for five years. That they were able, in the end, to do so is a testimony to the surprising professionalism and flexibility of the senior Red Army command, and even of Stalin himself.

## Stalingrad and its Lessons

For all its success and decisive significance, Operation *Uranus* was far from a perfect operation. The outer ring of the encirclement snapped shut within 100 hours of the beginning of the operation, but not before a number of German units had slipped out of the closing trap. The reason for the delay was that the shock groups designated to achieve breakthroughs in the critical sectors had only partially succeeded. The Fifth Tank Army, deployed behind the lines to the northwest of Stalingrad, was to await the achievement of a breakthrough and then drive through the German rear, bypassing centers of resistance, until it met with other Soviet forces coming up from the southeast, closing the trap.

For all the success this unit had, it failed in a number of important ways. First, the units on the line before it did not complete the breakthrough in time. Rather than awaiting the accomplishment of that mission or reordering its plans, the Fifth Tank Army instead found itself committed to the breakthrough battle. As a result, its strength was prematurely exhausted and its advance held up. In the course of its exploitation, further, its subordinate units frequently failed to bypass German defenders, or to do so rapidly enough. Where speed was all, the Soviet exploitation echelon allowed itself to be drawn into a number of unimportant, but time-consuming, fights in the German rear.

The flaws were relatively minor blemishes on an outstandingly successful operation; what was important was the Soviet effort at understanding and addressing them. Beginning in early 1942, the Soviet General Staff began the systematic study of its combat experiences with an eye to improving the organization, doctrine, and technique of the Red Army. The observations recorded above were drawn from the General Staff study of the Battle of Stalingrad. This study, however, was only number 6 of 26 studies of operations and major battles of the Red Army. As a result of the conclusions drawn by these studies, Soviet operational planning repeatedly changed, and Soviet doctrinal manuals were twice updated. The professionalism of the Soviet General Staff and its ability to learn from its mistakes, even in successful operations, were essential elements in the ultimate victory of the Red Army over Germany.

The importance of this constant self-study lay in the fact that, for all the brilliance of Soviet interwar military thinkers, deep battle doctrine at its most sophisticated required adaptation for use in war. The emphasis in that theory had been at the operational and strategic levels: that special exploitation forces should be maintained separately from the breakthrough forces; that successive operations should follow each other without pause; the way air forces should be employed to prevent the movement of enemy reserves, etc. What interwar thinkers had not worked out were precisely the problems that had plagued the Fifth Tank Army: when to commit the exploitation echelon; how it should conduct its operations; how to supply it and maintain command and control of it, and so forth. In a sense, the development of Soviet operational art during the war, which was as important as that of the interwar period, was focused on finding the solutions to the practical problems that emerged when attempting to implement the theory. It is not surprising that there should have been mistakes along the way far worse than the relatively minor failings of Operation *Uranus*.

## *Saturn* and Beyond

The planning and execution of the initial operations immediately following Stalingrad, for example, left much to be desired. From the outset, Stalin had seen Operation *Uranus* as only the first step in the rapid destruction of Army Group South, and Operation *Saturn*, which was to follow straight from the completion of *Uranus*, was being planned even as the battle for Stalingrad raged. *Saturn* at first was supposed to strike toward Rostov-on-Don, cutting Army Group A off in the Caucasus even as the troops encircled near Stalingrad were destroyed. The reconquest of Ukraine and the Caucasus would naturally and speedily follow.

Three factors forced Stalin to revise this plan. First, it emerged that the Soviets had trapped not 70,000, but 330,000 Germans in the Stalingrad pocket, and it would take much longer to reduce that garrison than previously estimated. Second, the Germans were much quicker to recover from the shock of *Uranus* and launch an offensive of their own—Operation *Wintergewitter* (Winter Storm). Under the command of Fieldmarshal Erich von Manstein, *Wintergewitter* aimed to relieve the beleaguered German forces by a rapid armored thrust from the southwest in the vicinity of Kotelnikovo. The battle to stop this attack would prove difficult, and would draw off combat power originally earmarked for Operation *Saturn*. Third, and perhaps most important, Stalin continually overestimated the offensive capabilities of the Red Army. This factor alone would not have prompted the abandonment of *Saturn*, but it would likely have led to disaster in the south in 1943 for the Soviets had the other two factors not forced Stalin to see reason.

The revised plan of 1943, renamed *Little Saturn*, aimed more modestly to break into the German rear, isolate some German and Italian units, and push the Germans further away from the Stalingrad pocket, still resisting destruction. Specifically, the Soviets hoped to seize and hold the airfield at Tatsinskaya, which was being used by the Luftwaffe as a forward base from which to supply the trapped German forces.

The operation was, in many respects, successful. German *Armeeabteilung* Hollidt and the Italian Eighth were largely destroyed following a reasonably successful breakthrough and exploitation by Soviet forces, and the Soviet Twenty-fourth Tank Corps, commanded by Major General V. M. Badanov, took Tatsinskaya, although it could hold it for only four days. But many of the same problems that had plagued Operation *Uranus* resurfaced here with more baleful consequences.

Once again, the breakthrough was achieved too late and imperfectly, and forces designated for exploitation found themselves committed to the fighting too early. Worse still, the Soviet mobile forces exploiting the breach operated along diverging axes of advance and without any overall coordination of their efforts. The result was that although Badanov's Twenty-fourth Tank Corps took Tatsinskaya, it immediately found itself surrounded and besieged there with no help available. Although Badanov and some of his men managed to escape, the corps itself, for all intents and purposes, was destroyed. The Soviets also found that the infantry walking behind the rapid armored thrusts could not even keep to their assigned timetable, let alone keep up with the tanks, while the logistical support of the operation was woefully inadequate. For all its successes, Operation *Little Saturn* remained an example of how not to conduct large-scale armored offensive operations.

The Soviets had done the German forces in Ukraine considerable damage at Stalingrad and in *Little Saturn,* and with the remainder of the German line in considerable disarray, *Stavka* was dazzled by the possibility of completely clearing Ukraine in short order. In late January, therefore, *Stavka* ordered F. I. Golikov's Voronezh Front and N. F. Vatutin's Southwestern Front to prepare two simultaneous offensive operations, code-named *Star* and *Gallop* respectively. *Stavka* conceived of these operations as part of the general pursuit of the battered German forces in the south, and was not, therefore, concerned with the overextension and near-exhaustion of the Soviet forces earmarked for them. On the contrary, Stalin ordered Vatutin and Golikov to launch their offensives without permitting any significant operational pause, for he was more fearful that such a pause would give the Germans time to regroup than that the Soviet offensive would suffer for lack of preparation.

The closing of *Little Saturn* had left Army Group A in considerable danger of being trapped in the Caucasus, while von Manstein's Army Group Don lay battered and overextended along the north coast of the Sea of Azov. Operation *Gallop,* which began on 29 January, aimed not merely at cutting off Army Group A, but also at encircling and destroying Army Group Don by attacking from the area of Starobelsk southward, reaching the coast at Mariupol and trapping von Manstein. Operation *Star,* launched a few days later, was a broader and even more ambitious attack aimed at securing Kursk, Belgorod, and Kharkov.

Both attacks largely failed to achieve their objectives. Von Manstein was able to block Soviet mobile forces north of the critical rail line that ran from Dnepropetrovsk to Stalino, averting the danger that the Soviets might surround Army Group Don. The timely arrival of reserves in the Kharkov sector and to the south not only allowed the Germans to retake Kharkov, which had fallen on 15 February, but to launch a counteroffensive that drove all the way to Belgorod and the Donets River line. As before at Stalingrad and during *Little Saturn,* the Germans sustained fearful losses in these battles—losses they could ill afford—but the Soviets also suffered heavily and the final objectives of these operations remained dauntingly out of reach.

The Soviet conduct of Operations *Star* and *Gallop* reflected a number of lessons learned in *Little Saturn.* Above all, the destruction and near-destruction of the isolated tank and mechanized corps that had conducted the exploitation during the earlier attack had convinced the Soviets that it was essential to concentrate control of the exploitation echelon in a single command. Thus Lieutenant General M. M. Popov was placed in charge of the Front Mobile Group of Southwestern Front, designated to exploit the initial breakthrough and charge all the way to the Sea of Azov.

Although this organizational change was salutary, the general weakness of Soviet mobile forces committed to this operation rendered it nearly irrelevant. Worse still, the Soviet high command consistently ignored clear evidence that the Germans were not bent on withdrawing, but on counterattacking and stabilizing their lines. Repeatedly, reconnaissance information on the *arrival* of armored units in the area of operations was taken as proof of the continued *departure* of German forces. Vatutin and Golikov both continued to believe that the appearance of German armored reserves indicated a determination to cover the withdrawal they believed was ongoing. This overconfidence and misinterpretation of intelligence would cost them dearly.

By mid-February, the Soviet offensives had taken Belgorod and Kharkov, temporarily cut the rail line from Dnepropetrovsk to Stalino (one of two that fed von Manstein's forces), and were advancing on the Dniepr River itself in several places. To accomplish these gains, however, the Soviets had been forced to commit all available reserves, and even so their combat forces had been whittled down to pitiful remnants—by the time of the German counterattack, Popov's "mobile group" was down to fewer than 53 tanks in its four tank corps (it had started with 212). The arrival of the German SS Panzer Corps, and several other armored divisions, as well as the reserves freed up by von Manstein's retreat from the Don to the Mius River line, gave the Germans more than enough power with which to counterattack.

Had Vatutin and Golikov recognized and responded rapidly to the signs of the impending German attack, the situation could well have been stabilized. As it was, reports of German concentrations, taken to be covering forces for further withdrawal, only spurred Vatutin on—he ordered accelerated advances for all of his mobile forces. As a result, Mobile Group Popov, like Badanov's Twenty-Fourth Tank Corps during *Little Saturn,* was cut off by the German counterattack and largely destroyed. Soviet lead forces along the front were badly mauled and driven back. The price of overconfidence was high.

*Little Saturn, Star,* and *Gallop* finally convinced the *Stavka* and Stalin that they must set more reasonable objectives and expectations for their offensive operations. Although *Star* and *Gallop* had recalled one basic tenet of interwar Soviet operational doctrine—the need to maintain constant pressure and avoid operational pauses—they had forgotten another: that the enemy will always be stronger at the end of an operation than at the beginning, and that it is the last battle, not the first, that is the most difficult and dangerous. Henceforth planning for Soviet offensive operations would concentrate much more on seeing them through all the way to their planned conclusions, and Stalin and his commanders would be much less easily be-guiled by fleeting visions of rapid and decisive victories.

## Kursk and the Destruction of Army Group South

The end of *Star* and *Gallop* left the Eastern Front relatively quiet for almost four months as both sides awaited the coming and departure of the spring thaw and prepared their forces for further operations. The evacuation of large salients around Demyansk and Rzhev in the center and north of the front provided the Germans with sufficient reserves to contemplate another large offensive operation. Characteristically, Hitler determined to make it grandiose, hoping to retrieve the Third Reich's battlefield reputation. The obvious target was the bulge in the Soviet line created by the disastrous con-clusion of *Star* and *Gallop*, centered around the city of Kursk. After much vacillation, Hitler settled on a massive offensive operation designed to cut off and destroy that salient—Operation *Citadel.*

The problem with this operation was that it was obvious not only to the Germans, but to the Russians as well. When it was originally conceived in March, the Soviets were still recovering from their disastrous setbacks, and a German attack in the nature of a counteroffensive stood some chance of suc-cess. But the German forces that had been beating off and then beating back the Soviet advances were exhausted and could not immediately carry out the plan. As *Citadel* was delayed time and again, however, the Soviets also re-covered and, as the Kursk salient was so obviously an inviting target, they fortified and reinforced it heavily.

*Citadel* opened on 5 July with two massive attacks led by enormous ar-mored forces from the vicinity of Orel south through Ponyri to Kursk, and from the vicinity of Belgorod north through Prokhorovka to Kursk. With over 2,700 tanks and assault guns, the German attack was the largest ar-mored attack in history. It found Soviet defenders not merely dug in, how-ever, but at the highest state of readiness for an attack the start-time for which they knew, thanks to Ultra intelligence, to the day.

Over the course of two weeks, the German attacks led by tank masses 200 tanks strong drove mercilessly through the Soviet defenses. In places the penetrations reached more than 30 miles into the Soviet rear. Losses, how-ever, were horrific. Soviet anti-tank gunners, tanks, aircraft, and anti-tank "teams"—armed with Molotov cocktails and satchel charges—decimated the attackers. The northern pincer bogged down soonest—a Soviet relief at-tack launched on 12 July pretty much spelled the end of the attack in that sector. The southern pincer had greater success. Supported by the massive tank formations of the II SS Panzer Corps, this attack made rapid headway. As it reached the main defensive belts of the Soviet lines 20 to 30 miles in the rear, however, it bogged down. An attack by Fifth Guards Tank Army on 13 July, launched into the teeth of a renewed attack by the II SS Panzer Corps, effectively shut down the advance. Although fierce fighting continued for several days, by the third week of July *Citadel* had clearly failed.

As the attack against the Orel salient continued, a brief operational pause ensued in the south. Unlike its procedure in earlier operations, in this one *Stavka* determined to attack with prepared forces and took the time to redeploy and refit before moving to the counteroffensive. The battered Germans were only too pleased to accept the rest and, rather than reinforcing the now-threatened sector, instead drew forces away. Soviet attacks against the Mius River line drew some German troops there, the attack in the Orel sector drew others to the north, while the Anglo-American invasion of Sicily, launched on 10 July, caught and held Hitler's attention. Von Manstein was convinced that the Soviets must be as exhausted as his own troops and that the operational pause would be lengthy. He was soon disillusioned.

Operation *General Rumyantsev*, as the Belgorod-Kharkov operation was code-named, began on 3 August. Its planning and conduct reflected many lessons the Soviets had painfully learned in their preceding half-successes. Rather than frittering away operational maneuver forces in scattered groups in the enemy's rear, the Soviets concentrated two massive tank armies for the exploitation of a breakthrough to the northwest of Belgorod. These two armies, furthermore, were to operate along parallel axes of advance, swinging to the west of Kharkov and enveloping it. Those armies were strong enough and fast enough to beat off or crush any German attempt to stop them—there would be no Soviet mobile groups trapped and destroyed by German counterattacks this time.

Operation *General Rumyantsev* represented the fullest implementation of Soviet prewar operational art, modified by wartime experience, yet seen. Massive artillery preparation, punctuated by a pause and using irregular patterns of fire, confused the German defenders even as it disrupted their positions. As a result, the breakthrough of the German lines was achieved on the first day of operations, and the exploitation units were able to drive straight through the hole without becoming engaged in the penetration battle. The assault on the German front, moreover, was time-phased. Soviet attacks fell on different sectors of the German lines sequentially, forcing the Germans to shift reserves repeatedly and confusing the defenders about the main lines of the attack.

The power and organization of the exploitation forces, finally, was critical. During the envelopment of Kharkov, the Soviets encountered a full SS Panzer Corps composed of three SS Panzer divisions. In previous operations, a force of that size had sufficed to force the Soviet advance to a halt. In this one, although the SS Panzer Corps tied down significant Soviet forces, enough strength was left to the other mobile forces to complete the encirclement. One historian of this operation has noted, "The Belgorod-Khar'kov operation (and its sister operation at Orel) was the first 'modern' Soviet operation of the Great Patriotic War in terms of Soviet operational intent and the force structure they [*sic*] relied on to achieve their [*sic*] offensive aims." For the first time since the encirclement of Stalingrad, a Soviet offensive operation fully achieved its objectives at an acceptable cost.

The consequences of Operations *Citadel* and *General Rumyantsev* were devastating for the Germans. The forces they hurled at Kursk had represented the sum total of the reserves available to the Wehrmacht. The losses taken in that failed attack would never be replaced. What is more, the grand strategic situation began to turn dramatically away from Hitler. With the Allied landings on Sicily and then Italy, Mussolini's fall was only a matter of time. By August Italy was effectively out of the war, and the Germans were forced to scrape together the forces to hold their lines in that theater. Although it was clear that there would be no Allied attack on France in 1943, moreover, it was equally clear that an attack in 1944 was a distinct probability. And all the while, the Allied strategic bombing effort against Germany's cities and industries was intensifying. After their defeat at Kursk, it was clear that the Germans would not be able even to retake the strategic initiative on the Eastern Front, let alone launch a large-scale offensive operation in that theater. It was only a question of how long the expulsion of the Wehrmacht from Russia would take.

In August 1943, it did not look as if it would take very long. *Citadel* and *Rumyantsev,* together with the Orel operation, had ripped a gaping hole in the German lines, and once again Stalin ordered his armies into a full-scale pursuit. Between the end of August and the end of September, five Soviet fronts raced more than 100 miles from the line Taganrog-Kharkov-Sevsk to the Dnepr River. There, spurred on by the promise of awards and honors, Soviet units competed with each other to cross the river and continue the liberation of Ukraine. To the north, against the much less damaged Army Group Center, Soviet attacks had made less progress, although by the end of September, Smolensk and a good deal of Belorussia had been recaptured.

This successful Soviet drive revealed that the Soviet commanders had learned a number of critical lessons and made some important adjustments.

To begin with, the tables of organization for Soviet units had been reworked prior to the Battle of Kursk. Tank armies had received a homogenous establishment for the first time, and mechanized and armored units at all levels had increased in size and complexity. This change, made possible by the growing number of commanders experienced in maneuver war on a large scale, gave the Soviet forces much greater flexibility and staying power.

As the war progressed, the Soviets more and more began to deploy their forces in echelons, tactically, operationally, and even strategically. This development reflected, in part, the changing correlation of forces on the Eastern Front, whereby the Soviets could afford to place units in second echelons, but it also reflected a recognition by the Soviet commanders of the truths described by Soviet theorists. Even with the numerical superiority the Soviets attained on attack sectors, echelonment still required that attacks be made on more narrow sectors than previously. In the past, commanders had been reluctant to adopt such measures. By the time of the Belgorod-Kharkov operation, they had embraced them fully.

The Soviets had also learned the importance of sensing and responding to German preparations for counterattacks. Following the capture of Kiev on 6 November, Vatutin's forces raced westward along diverging axes. They did not suffer the fate of the forces exploiting the breakthrough in Operation *Little Saturn* because, on the one hand, they were much stronger and better coordinated, and, on the other, Vatutin wisely reined them in and went over to the defensive as the Germans counterattacked. The days when the Germans could count on the Soviets to overextend themselves and offer lucrative targets for armored stop-thrusts were gone.

By early 1944 the Germans came to feel the full horror of the multi-front war into which Hitler's foolishness had dragged them. Allied forces slowly but doggedly climbed up the Italian peninsula. The strategic bombing campaign was in high gear and had already demolished Cologne, Hamburg, and other German cities and industrial centers. The massive buildup in England made it clear that an invasion of France was almost certain to occur in that year. As a result, however desperately the German forces in Russia needed reinforcements and replacements, none were available. What is more, as the strategic bombing campaign eroded the Third Reich's ability to produce the machines and supplies essential to modern war, the Soviet war economy, safely out of reach of German bombers and tanks since early 1943, was producing equipment in unfathomable quantities.

Even so, the idea that the Soviets merely ran over their adversaries with an avalanche of manpower is false. At the beginning of 1944, the Soviets deployed 5.5 million soldiers to the Germans' 4.9 (including 700,000 allies) and 5,600 tanks to the Germans' 5,400. Their greatest superiority, surprisingly, was in the air, where 8,800 Soviet planes confronted 3,000 German aircraft. The numerical advantages were important, but they were not so great as to be decisive of themselves, particularly considering that the Germans intended only to stand on the defensive and that their ability to stand off much larger forces in that posture was well known. Yet within a year and a half the Red Army would launch a virtually uninterrupted series of shattering blows that would take them all the way to Berlin.

## Soviet Operational and Strategic Art to the End of the War

Part of the reason for the Soviet success lay not in operational, but in strategic art. In each operation from mid-1944 to the end of the war, the Red Army enjoyed enormous superiority over the Germans in the sectors under attack. Two factors, beyond general Soviet numerical superiority, made this possible: deception and operational sequencing. The Soviet emphasis on deception (*maskirovka*) is legendary, and the legends are well justified. Prior to the summer offensive of 1944, Soviet *maskirovka* convinced the Germans that the Red Army might attack in the north, against Finland and to relieve Leningrad, from the massive salient in the south into Galicia, in combination with American forces in a naval attack on Romania, and elsewhere—everywhere except where the attack actually came. So successful was this deception plan that when Soviet attacking forces concentrated in the vicinity of Vitebsk and Orsha, the Germans believed that that deployment was a feint to draw their attention from the real Soviet main effort to the south. When Operation *Bagration* began on 22 June 1944 (coincidentally three years to the day after the German invasion), therefore, Army Group Center was totally unprepared. Most of its forces were forward in defensive positions at the front, and it had no significant reserves and no significant mobile forces at all.

'The Soviet attack plan itself, moreover, was different in many important respects from those of previous Soviet offensive operations. Instead of creating two or three major breakthroughs and exploiting with mobile forces at depth, *Bagration* aimed literally to shatter the entire front of Army Group Center into more manageable pieces. Nor would the mobile forces themselves, furthermore, be expected to reduce the pockets they had created. The Soviet high command had learned to fear the pause in operations that ensues when the mobile forces have to stop to reduce a pocket, and now required the mobile forces to drive on, while second echelon combined arms forces reduced the pockets. The fact that the shattered German front presented many but smaller pockets also made the task of reducing them easier—the Soviets had learned the hard way at Stalingrad the drawbacks of seizing enormous groups of enemy forces.

*Bagration* was, perhaps, the most successful armored operation of the entire war. In a little over a month, Soviet forces advanced more than 500 kilometers and completely destroyed Army Group Center. When the attack began to bog down as reinforcements arrived from the Army Group North Ukraine (one of the remnants of Army Group South), the Soviets did not press their luck or open themselves up to counterattack. Instead, the forces involved in *Bagration* made a graceful transition to the defensive. That transition did not mark the end of the campaign season, however.

Instead, as *Bagration* was shut down, another enormous Soviet offensive began to the south on 20 August. The Jassy-Kishenev Operation took advantage of the fact that *Bagration* had drawn significant German armored reserves to the north by striking into the Balkans. By the end of September, Soviet forces had overrun Rumania and Bulgaria and were threatening Yugoslavia and Hungary. For the rest of the war the Soviets continued to shift the weight of their blows sequentially from north to south, forcing the Germans to shuttle their inadequate reserves and reinforcements hopelessly from one catastrophe to another. With the perfection of this strategic and operational art, the Soviets made the destruction of the Wehrmacht look almost easy.

## Conclusions

On one level the Great Patriotic War was a triumph of flexibility over rigidity. The Germans launched three massive armored attacks against Russia, and all were fundamentally the same in conception and execution. Armored spearheads crushed the initial Russian defensive positions and rolled into the Soviet rear, pressing forward indefinitely, without relief, but pausing to reduce massive pockets of encircled Red Army troops. Each time the objectives set for the attack were well beyond the capacity of the forces earmarked for it; each time the Germans came up short and presented the Red Army with the opportunity to launch a devastating counterattack. German operational technique on the Eastern Front improved only in the smallest ways, and the Germans learned virtually nothing from their victories or their defeats there.

The Soviets, on the contrary, continually developed their techniques and abilities. By mid-1943 Red Army operations were on a par with what had been conceived of in the 1930s. By 1944 they had surpassed their prewar doctrine both theoretically and practically. The formal program of reviewing all operations, successful or unsuccessful, and the agility with which the Red Army continually reinvented itself, were marks of the highest professionalism. The changes resulting from those reviews, far more than Soviet superiority, helped bring a rapid close to this devastating war.

The Great Patriotic War was a war of the entire Soviet people. When it commenced the Germans were convinced that the national minorities and even the Russians themselves would turn away from the regime that oppressed them and, if not join with the invaders, then at least refrain from too active a participation in the Soviet Union's defense. Stalin himself, it seems, shared this fear to some extent. But the German program was too brutal and too obviously aimed at subjecting the Slavic and non-Slavic peoples of the USSR to an even worse oppression to make the Nazis seem more attractive than the Bolsheviks. What is more, the traditional Russian determination to ward off the invader from the West proved greater than any revulsion against Stalin.

As a result, not only did young Soviet men and women work willingly and determinedly in Soviet factories and in the Red Army, but the strongest and most significant partisan movement in Europe sprang up rapidly behind German lines. The partisans performed a number of very important functions for the Red Army. They gathered and transmitted intelligence about German movements and attacked German lines of communication and depots. They were far from disorganized bands hiding in the woods. Many partisan groups were properly organized formations, supplied by Red Air Force airdrops, and sometimes even led by regular Red Army officers who had parachuted in to join them. Before almost every major operation on the territory of the Soviet Union, partisan bands were alerted and issued orders to support the attack.

Partisan support of Soviet attacks was extremely important. Both interwar theory and the practice of World War II had made it clear that disrupting the enemy's lines of communication deep in his rear during the attack was essential to success. The Germans rarely wasted much time before sending armored units racing to plug holes and launch local counterattacks to blunt Soviet (and Anglo-American) offensives. Soviet interwar doctrine had called for the disruption of these movements by air attacks on critical transportation nodes, but in practice the Red Air Force was rarely able to accomplish those missions. The critical importance of breaking through the initial German defensive positions as in the Belgorod-Kharkov operation, for instance, or the need to make up for the inability of artillery to keep pace with the attack in Operation *Bagration* tended to draw the Red Air Force into continual close air support missions at the expense of operational interdiction.

The partisans helped make good this deficiency. During the Belgorod-Kharkov campaign and Operation *Bagration,* for example, large partisan detachments were alerted well in advance and instructed to destroy main and branch rail lines, telegraph lines, and supply depots; in other words, to perform the basic functions of operational air interdiction. The partisans were by no means always successful, but their inclusion directly into Soviet operational planning represented a remarkably flexible adaptation to circumstances and played a very important role in the success of Soviet offensive operations.

The Great Patriotic War was the formative experience of the Red Army and the Soviet state. To this day, Russian military archives remain chary of releasing documents now more than 50 years old not merely because of bureaucratic inertia, but because the modern Russian army is so closely tied to its origins in 1941–45. Until the Soviet Union fell, the Great Patriotic War would remain the basic laboratory within which ideas could be tested—after all, the mammoth confrontation had seen virtually every kind of combat in virtually every kind of terrain and weather. Even more, the horrors and rigors of this war naturally burned themselves into the Russian collective consciousness. It may be that the generation of Russians that grows up without a Cold War will also finally cast aside the shadow of the Great Patriotic War, but, if so, it will be the first generation to do so. It will be many decades before this war ceases to be studied as a turning point in Russian and even world history.

## Sources and Further Reading

See Chapter 8 for suggestions for sources and further reading and research.

CHAPTER 10

# THE SOVIET AIR FORCE, 1917–1991

*Mark O'Neill*

THE AIR FORCE HOLDS A SPECIAL PLACE IN THE ANNALS of Soviet military history. Although overshadowed in sheer size by the ground forces, the Soviet Air Force, in addition to conducting its normal military tasks, advertised the regime's technological success and was a major element of Soviet foreign policy from the earliest days.

Throughout its history Russia has suffered an inferiority complex due to its technological backwardness compared to Western European nations. The exploits of Soviet airmen in war and peace served as announcements both to the Soviet people and to the outside world of the success of communism in transforming a feudalistic peasant society into one of the most technologically advanced nations on earth.

The ability to produce modern aircraft and train large numbers of proficient pilots is a mark of an advanced industrial society, and the USSR proved capable throughout much of its history of producing some of the best aircraft and pilots in the world. However, the cost of building and maintaining what became one of the largest flying arms in world history proved exceedingly high, both in monetary and human terms. Yet it is perhaps one of the most accurate stereotypes of Russian history: Nothing is gained without great suffering and surviving near disaster.

Soviet aviators and aircraft set new world records before and following The Great Patriotic War. They were the envy of their rivals and a source of fierce pride to Soviet citizens during the 1930s and again during the Cold

War. During the Great Patriotic War, the VVS (*Voyenno vozhdushniye sily*—Military air forces), its leadership still reeling from the purges, initially suffered the greatest defeat ever inflicted on any air force, but rebounded to help crush Nazi Germany. Afterward, the Soviet Union also sent its pilots and planes around the world to help advance foreign policy aims and support friendly states. Beginning in the mid-1920s and extending until the collapse of the USSR, Soviet combat aircraft, often flown by Soviet pilots, were the gold standard of military assistance to Communist regimes and nationalist movements in Eastern Europe, Asia, Africa, and the Caribbean.

## Origins of Soviet Air Power, 1909–28

Russian enthusiasm for powered flight began with a small number of aviation clubs that spread quickly among the upper levels of tsarist society. While one of the Wright brothers' aircraft flew over St. Petersburg in 1909, French builders quickly moved in on the Russian market. The Imperial Russian Navy purchased a French design in 1910 and began testing it at Sevastopol'. The Russian Army followed the next year by buying a Bleriot for the new flight school at Gatchina. Although there were a few factories in the major cities that built aircraft parts, Russian military aviation was dependent upon foreign sources for substantial elements of production.

In the area of aerodynamics Russian scientists began working independently in 1901 at the Kuchino laboratory. One of the most famous of those who utilized the wind tunnel and other facilities at Kuchino was Nikolai E. Zhukovskii. He later headed the Central Institute of Aero-Hydrodynamics, the leading aviation research institution in the USSR, and was known throughout the Soviet era as the "Father of Soviet Aviation." Those members of the aviation community who did not join the Bolshevik Revolution were expunged from the history of flight in the Soviet Union. One of these "lost" individuals was the aircraft designer Igor Sikorsky. His S-16 single-engine fighter and four-engine transport/bomber, the *Il'ia Muromets,* flew during World War I and demonstrated that Russia was not entirely dependent on foreigners for innovative aircraft design and construction. The *Il'ia Muromets* equipped the world's first long-range bombing squadron during the war.

Russian newspapers and aviation journals of the pre-revolutionary era covered the exploits of Russian pilots, the latest aviation theories, and the newest designs. Flying fever struck Imperial Russia with much the same intensity as it did the United States and Western Europe. The government, particularly the Grand Duke Alexander Mikhailovich, joined with private groups to sponsor air shows and races. Pilots such as V. M. Abramovich and P. N. Nesterov set new international flight records foreshadowing a long series of daring Soviet pilots and record-breaking flights. This initial phase of government support and public enthusiasm foreshadowed the Soviet celebration of the exploits of "Stalin's Falcons."

Prior to World War I, the Grand Duke's "Committee for Strengthening the Air Fleet," in conjunction with the major civilian flying club, nurtured Russian military aviation and oversaw training and aircraft procurement. By the beginning of 1914, the Russian air force had approximately 250 planes, not including the naval air arm. As was the case in most of the world's air arms, early Russian combat aircraft primarily flew reconnaissance and artillery spotting missions. Air-to-air battles and other independent tasks for aviation were rare in an army dominated by conservative commanders who doubted the combat-worthiness of the fragile stick and fabric flying machines. Aviation factories in Moscow and Petrograd grew as government contracts increased, but even with increased domestic production and innovative design, imported French aircraft still played a major role in the fledgling air force.

The defeat of the Russian Army on the battlefield and the end to the Romanov dynasty in the 1917 Revolution ushered in the era of Soviet aviation. Six months before the Bolsheviks seized power, an All-Russian Congress of civil and military aviation figures convened to plan the future of Russian aviation. This group called for a centralized effort to push Russia to the forefront of aviation technology to end the dependence on foreign supply. This nationalistic call for self-sufficiency found a resounding echo during the early international isolation of the Soviet era. In spite of the efforts of these early flight enthusiasts, however, World War I, revolution and civil war practically destroyed the basis for Soviet air power.

Lenin's government began rebuilding a new "Red Workers-Peasants Air Fleet" in 1918. During the Civil War, aircraft contributed in a limited way to battles on a number of fronts. One of those influenced during the period was the future commander of the VVS during the Great Patriotic War, Alexandr A. Novikov. He witnessed Semen Korf's squadron bombing and strafing the positions of the Kronstadt mutineers across the desolate frozen stretches of the Gulf of Finland. Serving as a member of Tukhachevskii's staff in charge of field reconnaissance, the future air marshal learned firsthand the impact of aerial reconnaissance and bombing on ground operations. Even as the air forces recovered from near annihilation, the new regime faced many of the same structural limitations that plagued the imperial government.

Technological weakness, particularly in engine production, could only be overcome by technology transfers from the West obtained either through licensing agreements or espionage.

Air power played a prominent role in the earliest attempts at Soviet foreign policy in both Europe and Asia. Following the Treaty of Rapallo in 1922, the Soviets agreed to allow Germany to conduct secret pilot training at Lipetsk. Although this was only one element of military and economic cooperation between the two pariah states, it did allow for limited technological and doctrinal transfers. In China, Soviet advisors helped organize Sun Yat-sen's Guomindang (GMD) along Bolshevik lines beginning in 1924. By July 1925 and following the deaths of Lenin and Sun, Victor P. Rogachev and about 1,000 other Soviet advisors were in Canton helping develop Jiang Jieshi's new aviation units. During this period, Stalin had the primary responsibility for Soviet policy toward China and, despite Jiang's coup against the Chinese Communist Party and its Soviet advisors, sent military equipment to aid the GMD on its Northern Expedition. Pragmatism replaced ideology in Sino-Soviet relations as Soviet pilots and aircraft, albeit in small numbers, flew air support for Jiang's troops, and Stalin ordered the Chinese Communist Party to subordinate itself to the GMD. This action not only set a precedent for Stalin's use of air power as a foreign policy tool, but also his overall pattern of subordinating the success of local Communist parties to the security concerns of the Soviet Union.

Despite the fact that Soviet pilots flew themselves into exhaustion supporting the GMD Army, Jiang Jieshi abandoned the united front strategy and began slaughtering Chinese communists. Sino-Soviet relations deteriorated to the point by 1929 that VVS pilots flew combat missions supporting the Special Far East Army under General V. K. Bliukher as it fought Chinese troops to retake the Chinese Eastern Railroad. Soviet security and economic concerns in the Soviet Far East worsened as the Japanese, having only withdrawn from Vladivostok in 1922, seized all of Manchuria in 1931.

The USSR reorganized its air forces to meet the international economic and military challenges it faced during the 1920s. By the end of the decade, the VVS had expanded to 24 squadrons and 40 aviation detachments and constituted about 10 percent of the Soviet armed forces. These formations were reorganized from units of mixed aircraft types to ones with only fighter, bomber, ground attack, and reconnaissance aircraft. The USSR still lagged behind Western Europe in its ability to build quality power plants and imported planes and motors from, among others, German, Dutch, and U.S. companies.

## Stalinist Aviation in the 1930s

Surviving the political fallout from his involvement in the disastrous support for the GMD, Stalin succeeded by 1928 in establishing a dictatorship that lasted until his death in 1953. Soviet aviation both suffered and benefited from Stalinism during the coming decades. Stalin's "Falcons" received the adoration of the Soviet people and greatly increased access to industrial resources beginning with the First Five-Year Plan. Soviet designers such as Andrei N. Tupolev and Nikolai N. Polikarpov began designing bombers and fighters that were rugged, reliable, and made from standardized parts. This simplified approach to military and civilian aircraft construction greatly increased the ease of maintenance, production, and logistical support.

In 1931 Iakov I. Alksnis took control of the VVS as it began its most explosive growth period. The Soviets built new factories to produce Wright Cyclone engines licensed from the United States and many aircraft types. From a modest figure of around 1,000 aircraft built in the first year of the Plan, production expanded to an average of 1,500 for the period. By the middle of the Second Five-Year Plan in 1936, production figures hit 8,000 per year and closed in on 12,000 by 1940. Not only did the VVS increase in quantity, but it also increased dramatically in quality. The I-15, I-16, and I-153 fighters and TB-3 and SB-2 bombers were among the best in the world for the time. By 1935 the USSR had the largest bomber force in the world, but VVS pilots soon discovered in Spain that they had lost their technological edge to the Luftwaffe.

Soviet pilots also made headlines throughout the world with feats such as Valerii P. Chkalov's daring rescue of a stranded icebreaker crew and his trans-Arctic flight. Chkalov and his crew received the first Hero of the Soviet Union medal for their bravery. Other pilots, male and female, set international distance and altitude records throughout the mid to late 1930s. The VVS provided propaganda for the regime at home as well. Flyovers of Red Square by massed formations spelling out the names of Lenin, Stalin, and the USSR entertained crowds and trumpeted the strength and success of the Stalinist dictatorship. As Lazar M. Kaganovich stated in 1938: "Our aviation is a child of Stalinist industrialization; flyers are our proved falcons, raised lovingly and with care by Stalin."

Soviet aviation once again served foreign policy goals during the Soviet intervention in the Spanish Civil War in 1936–38 and in China when nearly 1,000 planes and pilots went to the aid of Jiang Jieshi. In 1937 Japan opened its invasion of China with air superiority and a technological edge over the

GMD forces. Soviet fighters, bombers, and pilots again flew to the aid of Jiang's regime to help correct this imbalance. This intervention went a long way in helping the Chinese fight the Japanese to a standstill. The Japanese offensive bogged down as it reached further inland, forcing its turn to the north. In 1938 they struck at Soviet border positions near North Korea at Lake Khasan and the next year along the Mongolian border at Khalkhin-gol. At Khalkhin-gol both sides employed extensive ground and air forces. Eventually Georgii K. Zhukov took command of the Soviet forces that included a large VVS contingent led by a hero of the Spanish Civil War, Ia. V. Smushkevich. Soviet pilots gained control of the skies over the Mongolian battlefield and flew bombing and ground attack missions as part of the combined-arms attacks that crushed the Japanese Sixth Army. Soviet pilots claimed to have destroyed over 600 Japanese aircraft prior to the end of hostilities in August 1939.

The VVS did not display the same qualities against the puny obsolescent Finnish air force later the same year. During the Winter War, Soviet bomber squadrons suffered particularly heavy casualties at the hands of the heavily outnumbered Finns. The fighter force did not fair much better against a motley collection of Gloster Gladiator biplanes, Fokkers, and Brewster Buffaloes as the Finnish air force claimed between 700 to 900 enemy aircraft shot down. Soviet aircraft designs were showing their age as the 1930s came to a close. The newest model German Bf–109 fighters, Ju–87 dive bombers, and He–111 bombers had completely driven Soviet pilots from Spanish skies by 1939, and Finnish pilots revealed glaring flaws in both the machines and leadership of the VVS.

Stalin's loving care and close attention had its negative impact on the growth of his falcons and other branches of the military. The Great Purge era for the military began when the NKVD arrested Marshal Tukhashevskii in May 1937. The VVS took its turn the next year when Commander-in-Chief Alksnis followed Tukhashevskii to prison and execution. Many of the VVS' senior leaders were arrested including General Smushkevich, whose turn came following the Winter War debacle. Most military district air commanders were also arrested, as were significant numbers of pilots and other aircrew. The purge extended to aircraft designers, many of whom like Tupelov, were forced to work in prison design bureaus. Engineers and scientists at the research institutes, aviation industry leaders, and other members of the aviation community did not escape the attention of Stalin's secret police. These purges coincided with another massive Soviet military expansion to face the growing security threats in Europe and Asia.

## Barbarossa and the Resurrection of the VVS

The purges not only stripped the VVS of many of its most experienced leaders, it also demoralized and stifled innovation among the survivors. Soviet aviation woes grew in 1940 as the German Luftwaffe began regularly flying reconnaissance missions over Soviet territory. In the short breathing space afforded by the Molotov-Ribbentrop Pact of 1939, Stalin began replacing some of his more feckless cronies within the government with competent and decisive personalities. Marshal Semen K. Timoshenko replaced Kliment E. Voroshilov as defense minister, Zhukov became chief of the General Staff, and A. I. Shakurin replaced Kaganovich at the head of the Aviation Industry Commissariat.

Two years into the Third Five-Year Plan, defense spending increased exponentially and talented new designers set to work correcting the technological deficiencies so glaringly apparent in Spain and Finland. Aleksandr S. Yakovlev, Semen A. Lavochkin, Pavel O. Sukhoi, and the team of Artem I. Mikoian and Mikhail I. Gurievich helped counterbalance the Soviet focus on bomber construction by designing new fighter aircraft that defined the VVS until the end of the Cold War. Modern fighters such as the Yak–1, MiG-3, and LaGG-3 were just beginning to reach front-line Soviet units as yet another world war began.

When the Second World War erupted in September 1939, these designs still suffered serious flaws, were not available in quantity, and were piloted by inexperienced crews, but they were evidence that Soviet aviation was not moribund. Sergei V. Il'iushin's team produced the very effective Il–2 ground-attack aircraft. Known as the "Shturmovik," the Germans would later call it the "Concrete Bomber" or "The Black Death." It too was just coming into service in an early and more vulnerable version by 1940. The massive rearmament and expansion of the VVS had not yet succeeded in rebuilding the combat effectiveness of Soviet aviation when disaster struck.

On 22 June 1941, 3,500,000 German troops and their allies invaded the Soviet Union, beginning The Great Patriotic War, arguably the most destructive struggle in world history. As large as the VVS appeared on paper, it lacked the leadership, training, and equipment to fight the battle-tested Luftwaffe. The havoc wreaked on the VVS by Stalin's purges paled in comparison to the devastation that attended Operation *Barbarossa*. Thousands of Soviet aircraft were destroyed on the ground and in the air. By September, 7,500 planes were gone. As the Wehrmacht overran huge stretches of the western Soviet Union, many of the factories vital to the aviation industry were lost at least temporarily as they were evacuated beyond the Ural

Mountains—some were lost altogether. While the VVS lost much of its equipment, it simultaneously lost the capability of replacing it. By the winter of 1941, the VVS and the rest of the Soviet Union faced extinction as enemy forces closed in on Moscow, laid siege to Leningrad, and seized Kiev.

The VVS kept fighting despite its diminishing strength. Over 1,000 aircraft, most of them obsolete models such as the I-16, supported Zhukov's counteroffensive that pushed the Germans back from outside Moscow in December 1941. Only a trickle of replacement aircraft arrived from surviving factories as others were still being unpacked in the frozen expanses east of the Urals. Any military aid from Great Britain and the United States was still many months away, and Soviet losses continued to mount even with the success at Moscow. The desperate situation in the USSR demanded extraordinary measures, and, as a result, many young commanders who succeeded on the battlefield found themselves catapulted into higher command positions.

A. A. Novikov and Sergei I. Rudenko were two such air commanders operating around besieged Leningrad and against German troops cut off in the Demiansk pocket early in the war. In April 1942, Stalin promoted Novikov to overall command of the VVS while Rudenko, commander of the Sixteenth Air Army, became one of the best tactical air commanders of the entire war. His air army was created as the Germans closed in on Stalingrad in August 1942; fought during the successful Soviet counterattack from the Volga to the Don River during the winter of 1942–43; supported the Central Front at the pivotal Kursk battle in July–August 1943; spearheaded the destruction of Army Group Center during the Belorussian campaign in June 1944; and, reinforced to over 3,000 aircraft, led the final assault on Berlin in April 1945.

The successful combat path of Rudenko's Sixteenth Army traced the rebirth of the VVS as an air support weapon that flew a wide variety of missions to support Soviet fronts. Under Novikov's leadership the VVS developed into a formidable tactical air weapon whose greatest impact was felt directly over and just behind the battlefield. This development did not occur overnight, but began slowly with the aerial blockade of the German forces trapped at Stalingrad. This experience in a limited, albeit vital, theater improved Soviet ground-control intercept techniques that would be a mark of Soviet air defense forces until the very end. Soviet pilots learned to conduct ground attacks, formation flying in pairs and four-plane groups, and other necessary combat skills on the job around Stalingrad.

The VVS began to display its newfound capabilities in combat over the Kuban bridgehead in early 1943. It was here that the VVS first established air superiority over the Luftwaffe. There, some of the VVS' greatest aces, such as Aleksandr I. Pokryshkin, the Glinka brothers, and G. A. Rechkalov, who flew U.S. Lend-Lease P-39 Airacobras, began their careers and became mentors for a new generation of falcons. The Soviet pilots learned from their experiences fighting the Luftwaffe and developed new tactics or copied successful German maneuvers in order to increase their chances of survival and victory. Pokryshkin, eventually the second leading Allied ace of the war and a three-time winner of the Hero of the Soviet Union, preached the simple adage of "altitude, speed, maneuver and fire" for combat pilots. However, altitude was relative in the VVS, as most combat sorties were flown below 5,000 feet and often not much above 50 feet. These tactics paralleled aircraft design in that they both were very simple, durable, and easily reproduced throughout the VVS. The Soviets continued to lose large numbers of aircraft, but as their armies advanced many pilots were rescued and returned to combat, although many did not survive. Improving aircraft types, better tactics, and training helped the VVS prevail in the largest air battle on the Eastern Front to that point.

The growing combat capabilities of the VVS did not occur overnight. Soviet losses continued to be frightful in the bloody war of attrition, and pilot training—30 hours per pilot in *Stavka* Reserve formations—was always inadequate by Western European and U.S. standards. Communications remained rudimentary and plagued by technical difficulties, and combat losses of aircraft and crews were high throughout the war. German pilots continued to demonstrate considerable combat skill and often inflicted serious losses on Soviet bomber and fighter formations even as growing Soviet air power accelerated the attrition of German air and ground forces.

The eventual success of the VVS in the struggle against the Luftwaffe was not simply a case of quantity over quality. Changes in Soviet tactics, improved aircraft, and a growing cadre of experienced pilots enabled the VVS to fight its next battle incrementally better than the previous one. The Luftwaffe, particularly after 1943, had to divert fighter aircraft and pilots to the defense of the Reich and began to lose the ability to train qualified replacements. The VVS inflicted grievous losses on enemy transport, artillery positions, and supply movements, while disguising Soviet troop movements and extending the most effective battlefield weapon, the artillery, deep into the enemy's rear areas. The VVS contributed most to the USSR's success by supporting the Red Army's ground forces in the horrific slaughter on the Eastern Front.

Rudenko's Sixteenth Air Army, along with several others, helped halt the last great German summer offensive at Kursk and launched the counterattack that threw the Germans back three hundred kilometers across the Dnepr River. This same group destroyed large numbers of tanks, half-tracks, and trucks outside Bobruisk in June 1944. The Red Army and VVS were irrevocably winning the war of attrition on the land and in the air by the time the Western Allies landed in Normandy. The Allies' war effort aided the VVS' task as many Luftwaffe units were transferred to defend the Reich from U.S. and British bombers, and those that remained were bled white by the relentless attacks of growing swarms of Soviet fighters.

Lend-Lease equipment helped fill in vital gaps in Soviet production; however, the latest U.S. and British aircraft types were not sent to the USSR. The second and third generation of Yakovlev and Lavochkin fighters began to equal and exceed the performance of the Luftwaffe's Bf–109s and FW-190s. By the end of 1942, German aircraft faced the same obsolescence with which the VVS had entered the war. Improved Il–2s and fast twin-engine Pe–2 bombers forced German mechanized formations to devote more weapons to anti-aircraft defense and carefully camouflage their daylight movements. Even the tiny Po–2 biplanes contributed to the erosion of German combat effectiveness by flying night bombing raids designed to deprive the enemy of sleep and the comfort of open fires far in the rear.

Female pilots flew with the VVS in large numbers as fighter pilots, and as day and night bomber crews. Women staffed three entire air regiments and other women flew with male-dominated units. During the war, women, always a significant part of the Soviet workforce, made up the largest percentage of industrial workers and took over nearly all agricultural labor. Soviet society worked, fought, and died in unprecedented numbers to defeat Nazi Germany. In 1945, massed Soviet air power pulverized the Berlin defenses and supported the attack on Japanese forces in the Far East. The VVS conducted aerial resupply missions for Soviet tanks formations traveling through the Gobi Desert, parachute drops in hostile territory, and swept what was left of the Japanese air power from the skies over Northeast Asia.

The USSR lost approximately 27,000,000 people in this cataclysmic struggle. The VVS lost 46,100 aircraft of all types in combat and a total of 106,400 to all causes while flying 3,124,000 combat sorties during the war. Aircrew losses, while not insignificant, did not equal those suffered by the ground forces. The VVS, along with the rest of the Red Army, stood supreme from Eastern Europe to North Korea. Never had an air force suffered the devastation that the VVS had from the purges through *Barbarossa* and come back to vanquish all of its foes. The USSR had passed through the test of world war and triumphed despite hideous losses. The challenges of the coming Cold War would be of a different sort, and the USSR would ultimately fail that test.

# The VVS and the Cold War, 1945–91

The Soviet Union began the Cold War with the same problem that plagued the regime prior to *Barbarossa*. The numerically superior VVS was technologically well behind the United States and Great Britain. In order to compete with, or even hold its own against its erstwhile allies, the USSR needed to upgrade its air forces. Stalin was aware of his vulnerability, and the 1946–50 Five-Year Plan included a special focus on developing four new technologies: atomic weapons, rockets, jet engines, and radar. Stalin's regime got a head start on these developments by capturing a substantial portion of Nazi Germany's aircraft production facilities and reaping the scientific and engineering benefits of enemy research. In addition, the USSR seized three U.S. B-29s that had been forced down in the Soviet Far East and reverse-engineered them to produce the Tu–4 bomber in 1947. In both cases "borrowed" technology helped give Soviet aviation a boost into Cold War competition with the United States. The Soviets also purchased advanced Rolls-Royce Nene and Derwent centrifugal-flow engines from Great Britain to increase the performance of the swept-winged jet fighter that the MiG design team began producing in 1948.

Despite these acquisitions, the USSR still lagged behind U.S. and later NATO technology by a substantial margin. The USSR was still economically, physically, and demographically devastated from World War II and was driven by an overarching concern that a rearmed Germany and Japan would soon join the Western alliance. These security concerns were concretely expressed in 1947 when the Air Defense Forces (*Protivozhdushnie oborony strany*—PVO) was established as a separate service to defend against U.S. and Royal Air Force bomber attacks. Stalin's concerns with the internal and external security of the USSR should not be mistaken as a sign of passivity. While the anti-Communist hysteria that plagued the United States was a poorly focused overreaction, the Soviet regime was fully capable of making mischief.

The USSR stunned the world when it detonated its first atomic bomb in August 1949. With the Tu–4 available to deliver atomic weapons, the Soviets had broken the U.S. monopoly. This technological success was followed up by the announcement by Mao Zedong of the establishment of the People's Republic of China (PRC) in October of the same year. Although Mao and Stalin did not trust each other completely, they were forced to cooperate with each other in order to oppose U.S. power in the Pacific. Mao needed Soviet investment and expertise to rebuild a shattered China, and Stalin needed a strong PRC to defend the Soviet Far East. This new communist partnership, with all of its strengths and limitations, was soon tested during the Korean War.

As part of the 1950 Treaty of Friendship and Cooperation between the USSR and the PRC, the Soviet Union agreed to defend Chinese territory from attack. Stalin used this agreement to leverage Mao into supporting Kim Il-Sung's Korean People's Army as it retreated toward the Yalu River following the UN invasion at Inchon. While there is disagreement over how much air support Stalin promised Mao, the Soviets did begin flying air defense missions over the northwestern corner of Korea known as "MiG Alley." U.S. Air Force pilots were quite aware that there were Russians flying many of the advanced MiG-15 jet fighters defending the supply route from Manchuria and the hydroelectric facilities further up the Yalu, but the Soviet involvement was never officially acknowledged by either side until well into the 1990s. The Soviets also trained Chinese and North Korean pilots to fly the MiG-15, Tu–2 bomber, and Il–10 ground attack aircraft, thus creating the world's third largest air force (the Chinese People's Army Air Force) in a very short time.

Soviet pilots began flying missions in "MiG Alley" on 1 November 1950 and continued flying and fighting until the end of the war on 27 July 1953. Soviet MiG-15s and anti-aircraft guns helped keep supplies flowing to Chinese and North Korean field forces despite the best efforts of USAF and UN pilots to interdict the trucks and trains heading south from Manchuria. As the Soviet intervention in 1937 had given Jiang Jieshi's forces some respite from Japanese air superiority, so too had the Soviet pilots helped the communist cause during the Korean War. Although Stalin was loath to get directly and openly involved in any war outside the Soviet Union, the use of Soviet air defense fighters, pilots, advisors, radar, and AAA weapons proved an effective way to influence foreign policy without risking Soviet ground troops. After Stalin's death on 5 March 1953, those who inherited his power in the Kremlin made Soviet air power a vital part of the USSR's global strategy for the remainder of the Cold War.

## The Khrushchev Era, 1953–64

Nikita Khrushchev did not immediately seize power following Stalin's death, but by 1957 he had thwarted a coup attempt and took over control of the Soviet Union himself. Khrushchev wanted to reduce the size of Soviet conventional forces and expand Soviet influence in the Third World in order to put pressure on the United States and NATO. His strategy to reduce the size of the armed forces relied on building a strategic rocket fleet to challenge U.S. superiority while his Third World strategy included using Soviet air power to extend his influence.

The Soviets allowed China and India to license build the advanced MiG-21 jet interceptor. This Mach 2 aircraft was one of the best in the world for most of the 1960s. Soviet air defense systems and fighters, on occasion piloted by Soviet pilots, appeared in many of the world's hot spots. In addition to the PRC and India, Egypt, North Vietnam, and Cuba benefited from Khrushchev's "anti-imperialist" largesse. When the Soviet premier decided to deploy nuclear missiles to defend Fidel Castro's regime, he also threw in a regiment of MiG-21s, Il–28 bombers, surface-to-air missiles and Soviet pilots for good measure. The combination of disastrous economic policies at home and foolish foreign policy risks abroad helped mobilize opposition in the Kremlin, and Nikita S. Khrushchev "retired" to his dacha in 1964. He had begun the globalization of the Cold War highlighted by advanced Soviet technology that increased the fear of the USSR among its enemies and committed the new regime under Leonid Brezhnev to supporting a vast array of Third World clients while continuing to sustain a massive military force in Eastern Europe.

## The Brezhnev Era and Beyond, 1964–89

Khrushchev's aggressive global foreign policy, despite the setback in Cuba, proved too enticing for the new Soviet leadership to abandon. The USSR and PRC fell out as allies early in the 1960s and came to blows in a short border war in 1969, but the Soviets expanded their list of clients throughout the 1960s and 1970s. In 1970 Soviet pilots went into action against the Israeli air force in order to defend Egypt and demonstrate the superiority of Soviet weapons in Russian hands. These pilots fared little better than their Egyptian, Syrian, and Jordanian pupils in combat against the Israelis.

On the other hand, Soviet air defense systems, and perhaps a pilot or two as well, created heavy losses among USAF F-4s, F-105s, and U.S. Navy fighters bombing targets in North Vietnam until 1973. While there were many instances in which Soviet equipment came out second best to U.S. or Western European technology in skilled hands, there were many others in which Soviet MiGs gave a local African, Asian, or Latin American regime the prestige and power it needed to retain power or incur the wrath of the United States. The Soviet Air Force itself grew in size, strength, and capability at home and in Eastern Europe. Although Soviet technology tended to be slightly behind that of the United States and its allies, it still made the VVS a force to be reckoned with and justified increased defense spending by the late 1970s and into the 1980s.

The Cold War greatly accelerated in 1979 when the Soviet Union began its ill-fated involvement in Afghanistan. This 10-year conflict included the massive use of Soviet ground attack and bomber aircraft as well as Soviet ground troops. As the Vietnam War drained U.S. resources, resolve and combat capabilities in other theaters, so too did the Afghan War cripple the Soviet Union. Soviet pilots dropped tons of bombs and aerial mines, but with little effect on the ground fighting. Every target worth destroying was obliterated, but the Afghan resistance continued and strengthened. In 1986, the United States supplied Stinger anti-aircraft missiles to the *Mujahedin* and Soviet losses mounted as the accuracy of air attacks worsened. The USSR pulled out in 1989.

The USSR could not afford the military forces that were the very basis of its power and legitimacy. Throughout the 1980s Soviet power weakened and its ability to field effective weapons against a technologically advanced foe in NATO, resupply needy clients in Asia, the Middle East, and Latin America. and fight a bloody war of attrition in Afghanistan, began to fall apart. Finally it took its new leader, Mikhail Gorbachev, beginning in 1985, to acknowledge the truth and attempt to reform a system that was beyond salvation. The VVS and PVO, the pride of the Soviet military from nearly its inception, was no more capable of meaningful reform than the Soviet Army or Navy. Soviet Air Forces ended the Cold War and the Soviet era as a numerically massive force without the ability to operate effectively. The rot, economic, moral and political, had set in deep, and the largest air force in the world collapsed from its own weight and inefficiency.

## The End of the Soviet Union, 1991

The VVS, soon joined by the PVO as a separate service, grew from a force capable of only direct battlefield support of the Red Army to one of the largest and most diversified air forces in the world. Ironically, the cost of this expansion was one of the major factors that helped lead to the eventual economic and political collapse of the USSR. Between 1947 and 1991, the Soviets produced advanced jet fighters such as the MiG and Sukhoi that measured up to the very best in the world. Although its bomber force never equaled that of the United States, it did produce large numbers of heavy-lift transport planes and very long-range reconnaissance machines, as well as fighter-bombers that made Soviet air power an instrument of fear among NATO allies, admiration among communist countries, and respect in the Third World.

The Afghan War marked the last hurrah of Soviet air power. The inability of advanced aircraft and massive firepower to make a decisive impact in a long-term, low-intensity conflict certainly paralleled the U.S. Air Forces' experience in Korea and Vietnam. Unlike the United States, the USSR could not afford the sustained losses that the Afghan War inflicted on its armed forces. The huge expense of combat, coupled with the cost of trying to match the technological innovations of NATO and maintaining massive ground forces throughout the Soviet empire, accelerated the economic decline that began at least as far back as World War II. The USSR was born as a militarized state at the end of the Russian Civil War, and it died as a militarized state in the summer of 1991.

Since the fall of the USSR, the VVS and PVO have been drastically reduced. Pilot training, equipment procurement, repair, and maintenance budgets are close to zero. The new Russian air force has been blooded in two actions in Chechnya. In neither case, despite overwhelming superiority and a lack of serious aerial opposition, did the new VVS demonstrate anything other than mediocre operational capabilities. Another indication that the USSR was past its peak came also in 1991 when the Soviet-era air defense forces that Saddam Hussein's regime possessed did nothing to slow the massive air attacks on Baghdad or over the Iraqi army in Kuwait during the Gulf War. The Russian military in general is in complete disarray as draftees avoid service in huge numbers, and servicemen beg on the streets of Moscow and work as field hands in the countryside. As we begin the twenty-first century, Russia is again in crisis. Given the history of the last century, it would be best if the USSR's former enemies did as much as possible to prevent the return of a remilitarized Russian state to the world stage.

## Further Reading and Study

The end of the Soviet Union and the collapse of its military has provided new opportunities for research in Russian archives. Conversely, the end of the Cold War has also meant that research interest and funding have dried up dramatically. Many aspects of VVS history still await thorough study. To date there has been no complete operational history of the Soviet Air Force during the pre–World War II era. Von Hardesty's seminal work, *Red Phoenix: The Rise of Soviet Air Power 1941–1945* (Washington, D.C.: Smithsonian Institution Press, 1982) is still the best treatment of the VVS during the Great Patriotic War. Hardesty did not have access to much in the way of archival sources for his work, and a larger-scale operational and institutional history is still needed.

Robin Higham, John T. Greenwood, and Von Hardesty have also recently edited a volume entitled *Russian Aviation and Air Power in the Twentieth Century* (London: Frank Cass Publishers, 1998). This work is a much needed major revision of Higham and Jacob Kipp's *Soviet Aviation and Air Power: A Historical View* (Boulder, CO: Westview Press, 1977). Higham and Kipp's edited work served researchers well for many years, but *Russian Aviation and Air Power* is based on many newly available sources and is much more than just an update of *Soviet Aviation*. Other classic works such as Asher Lee's *The Soviet Air Force* (New York: John Day Company, 1962), Jean Alexander's *Russian Aircraft since 1940* (London: Putnam, 1975), Alexander Boyd's *The Soviet Air Force since 1918* (London: Macdonald and Jane's, 1977), and Kenneth Whiting's *Soviet Air Power* (Boulder, CO: Westview Press, 1985), while still required reading, are in serious need of similar reworking.

Mark O'Neill, "The Other Side of the Yalu: Soviet Pilots in the Korean War, 1950–1951" (Florida State University dissertation, 1996), addresses the Soviet involvement in that conflict and is currently under consideration for publication. The overall Cold War era has been addressed to a certain extent in Tony Mason, *Air Power: A Centennial Appraisal* (London: Brassey's International, 1994), and in Mark O'Neill, "Air Combat on the Periphery: The Soviet Air Force in Action during the Cold War," in Higham, Greenwood, and Hardesty, *Russian Aviation and Air Power*. William Odom, *The Collapse of the Soviet Military* (New Haven, CT: Yale University Press, 1998) includes coverage of the Soviet Air Force's role in the economic, social, and military collapse of the Soviet Union. Benjamin Lambeth does an admirable job of analyzing current Russian aviation's decline and remaining strengths in *Russia's Air Power in Crisis: A RAND Research Study* (Washington, D.C.: Smithsonian Institute Press, 1999). Despite the efforts of these fine historians and others not mentioned here, the history of Soviet aviation still has many gaps that need filling.

# CHAPTER 11

# THE RUSSIAN/SOVIET NAVY, 1900–1945

*Christopher C. Lovett*

## The Russian Navy on the Eve of the Russo-Japanese War

THE RUSSIAN NAVY, LIKE MOST NAVIES IN THE 1890S, was influenced by the writings of the American Alfred Thayer Mahan, who advocated a blue-water fleet of battleships. Mahan had a loyal following in Russia, particularly in Nikolai Klado, who had popularized many of his ideas. Following the conclusion of the Sino-Japanese War in 1894, St. Petersburg notified Tokyo that Russia was sending a squadron of first-class battleships to the region. This threat resulted in the cession of Port Arthur to Russia. At the same time, the Admiralty maintained a squadron in the Mediterranean.

The mission of the navy in the 1890s was to project power into areas deemed important for Russian security interests. By the dawn of the twentieth century, Imperial Russia ranked third among the naval powers with 20 battleships, 11 armored cruisers, 20 cruisers, 25 destroyers, torpedo boats, and an assortment of coastal defense vessels. At the same time mishaps were common in training exercises and in groundings in the shallow Baltic.

By the mid-1890s, the Russians began constructing ships in distinct classes. As a result, when the *Petropavlovsk, Poltava,* and *Sevastopol* entered service they were comparable to other foreign battleships of their day. With minimum armor protection and reaching speeds of 16.5 knots, they were armed with 4 12 inch guns and 12 6-inch guns. The *Peresvet, Pobeda,* and

*Osliabia* followed in the next larger generation, but lacked the firepower of the *Petropavlovsk*-class, with 10-inch rather than 12-inch guns. At the same time, the Admiralty turned to France and the United States to construct two modern warships—*Tsarevich* and *Retvizan*—each with the standard 4 12-inch and 12 6-inch guns and speeds of 18 knots. On the eve of the Russo-Japanese War (1904–05), another class entered the fleet, somewhat larger than the *Tsarevich* and *Retvizan* but in many ways quite similar—the Russian-built *Borodino, Orel, Slava, Alexandr III,* and *Kniaz Suvorov.*

So, the Admiralty's interest in torpedo boats diminished. In the waning decade of the nineteenth century, the Russians added approximately 20 torpedo-boat destroyers to the fleet. The most remarkable was the British-built *Sokol,* which reached a top speed of 30 knots during sea trials. Contemporaneously, the Russian Auxiliary Fleet, merchant supply vessels that could be pressed into service in wartime, diminished as they were not upgraded to meet modern fleet needs.

## Technology and Naval Bases in the Early Twentieth Century

Here two remarkable individuals deserve mention. One was an academician, A. A. Popov, who worked at the Torpedo School at Kronstadt and pioneered the use of radio beginning in 1897. His successes included transmitting a radio signal for a distance of 35 kilometers and using the radio to save Russian fishermen stranded on an ice floe in the Gulf of Finland. In spite of this, the Admiralty limited the use of radios during the Russo-Japanese War. Consequently, Russian communications were deficient and reflected the Russian refusal to utilize modern technology at sea, as demonstrated at Tsushima (1905).

The other person, Admiral S. O. Makarov, rose from humble peasant origins to become a principal naval designer and scientist in the late nineteenth century. He was responsible for the world's first icebreaker. The 8,000-ton *Yermak* made it possible to use the northern approach to Siberia during the summer. Makarov's other design was a new class of minelayers capable of carrying 300 mines and reaching speeds of 18 knots. These contributed to the initial Russian leadership in mine warfare.

But Russia lagged behind the other powers in modernizing shore installations; Vladivostok, the major naval base in the Pacific, had, by Western standards, only second-rate facilities. Russia had acquired Port Arthur and Darien from China following the Sino-Japanese War in 1895, and managed to improve both, but they were too far from Vladivostok for the Russians to support both ports logistically in time of war.

Sevastopol and Nikolaev were Russia's principal facilities in the Black Sea. The Admiralty provided modern fortifications to protect these bases, but only Nikolaev had up-to-date dockyards and sophisticated industrial plants to support the fleet, though older Sevastopol could still maintain the Black Sea Fleet in port.

The Baltic had the most bases available, starting with St. Petersburg, whose yards—Kronstadt, Baltic Works, New Admiralty, Izhora, Obukhov, and Galernyi Island—included various industrial plants and employed skilled well-paid workmen. Either because of industrial accidents or worker slowdowns, the construction rate of new vessels never reached the Admiralty's goal. With the approach of inclement weather, roofs were constructed over building slips to protect shipyard employees from the elements, but still construction was delayed by winter. Only with the introduction of icebreakers was the situation partially corrected. Besides St. Petersburg, the Baltic Fleet had bases at Helsinki, Revel, and Libau. The latter was particularly important since it was ice-free and served as a point of departure for vessels going to either the Mediterranean or the Pacific. With the changing geopolitical situation after the signing of the Franco-Russian Military Convention in 1892, Libau lost its appeal since it was only 50 miles from the German border. Revel, on the other hand, served as a motor torpedo-boat base in the years before World War I.

## Naval Personnel in the Late Tsarist Period

As noted in the companion volume, the most glaring weakness in the years before World War I was the quality of naval personnel. As a consequence the navy lacked the technical cadres essential to a modern navy, a problem that was only slightly improved in the Soviet navy.

Like those in the army, officers in the navy came from naval families or from the gentry. Cadets entered the navy at the age of 12 or 14 and went through a six-year training. To eliminate incompetents, a system of competitive examinations was used to evaluate officers for future promotion. Still, many officers tended to avoid sea duty and the Admiralty had to provide financial incentives to get them to accept such billets.

So the Russian navy never reached the proficiency of the other world naval powers. Poor performance during maneuvers, lack of funds for naval facilities, and minimal financial incentives to attract a higher quality of individual for naval service contributed to foreign observers noting that the Russian navy's strength was exaggerated. The obvious weakness of the Imperial Russian Navy was not evident during the Boxer Rebellion (1900), when the gunboats *Bobr, Giulik,* and *Koreets* gave a fairly good account of themselves by silencing the Chinese forts that protected Tientsin. This was, however, only the calm before the storm.

## The Russo-Japanese War

Very few Europeans understood Japan in 1904. For most Westerners, she was a rather new nation, recently emerging from a state of barbarism, inhabited by strange, short yellow people. Before taking the throne, Tsar Nicholas II had visited Japan during an Asian tour in 1890–91 and was not impressed by those "monkeys." It was clear to many people in Japan, however, that Russia posed a serious challenge to Japanese imperial ambitions in Korea, Northern China, and Manchuria as Chinese power declined. In 1901–02, the Russian government sought to expand commercial influence in Manchuria as a means to spur Russian industry, which found it very difficult to compete with European concerns on the Asian continent. Instead St. Petersburg looked upon Manchuria as a ready market. However, American and British interests regarded China as a client. In a future war with Russia, Tokyo needed support from the West or at least benevolent neutrality from London (achieved in 1902) and Washington. Negotiations began between St. Petersburg and Tokyo in 1901 and continued until late 1903, but all attempts to resolve the outstanding differences were fruitless.

The Japanese military advised the emperor in early February 1904 that it was imperative for Japan to attack the Russians prior to a declaration of war. Considering Japan's limited resources, Tokyo realized that the war had to be short. Japanese naval authorities estimated that the navy could handle the Russian Pacific Squadron, but could lose half of its surface strength in the process. On 5 February, Tokyo notified St. Petersburg that a prolongation of negotiations was pointless and severed diplomatic relations, leaving Japan the right to take appropriate action to defend her position in northern China.

The Russians were so confident that they could defeat the Japanese that Admiral V. E. Alekseev, the commander of naval and land forces at Port Arthur, had reported to St. Petersburg in 1903 that it was impossible for the Japanese to either defeat his squadron or land troops in or near Port Arthur. The Japanese Admiral Togo demonstrated how wrong Alekseev was. On the night of 8–9 February 1904, after avoiding the pickets, the Japanese conducted a sudden torpedo attack on the Russian squadron. Alekseev's two modern battleships—*Retvizan* and *Tsarevich*—and the cruiser *Pallada* were hit by torpedoes and had to be beached. When the Russians realized what had happened, it was too late to take corrective counteraction.

Following the Japanese surprise attack, the Russians brought the *Tsarevich* and *Pallada* into port and dispatched the minelayer *Yenisei P.1* to lay a minefield at Talien Bay, but the *Yenisei's* commander was inexperienced. Thinking that the *Yenisei* had been lost to Japanese destroyers, Alekseev dispatched the cruiser *Boyarin* to investigate. She too was lost.

Though Admiral Togo knew that the Russians lacked the dry-dock facilities to repair their damaged battleships, they had enough combatants to challenge the Japanese if they attempted a landing. So, Togo tried unsuccessfully to block the harbor's entrance by sinking five ships there on 23 February. In the meantime, the Russian naval commander at Port Arthur was replaced by the tsar's most competent naval officer, Admiral S. O. Makarov. He purged incompetent officers and gave command of the *Sevastopol* to Nicholas von Essen, who would become one of Russia's most distinguished naval commanders in World War I.

The Russian squadron at Port Arthur was doomed as Togo maintained a tight blockade near the base and managed to entice Makarov to do battle beyond the Russian minefield barrier that protected the approach to the port. Why Makarov took the bait will never be known, but when the Russians sought to reenter the harbor the Russian flagship, *Petropavlovsk*, struck a mine. Only eighty men survived the catastrophe; among the dead was Makarov.

In May, Togo declared a total blockade of Port Arthur and warned that all neutral vessels in the waters adjacent to the Liaotung Peninsula were at risk. Following Makarov's death Russian naval morale dropped. Captains refused to take their ships to sea and Russian troops held the navy in disdain. The most effective Russian naval weapon in and around Port Arthur were mines resulting in the damage to two Japanese battleships, the *Hatsuse* and the *Yashima,* on 14 May. After repeated orders from Alekseev his ships were refitted with the guns, which had been sent ashore for use against the invading Japanese army, and the new Admiral Witgeft ordered the squadron to sea on 23 June. Togo initially had hoped to intercept the Russian squadron as they left port. But before 1800 hours the Japanese had spotted the Russians, and by 1900 the two fleets were closing. Suddenly, Witgeft decided to return to port, fearing a night torpedo attack and another Russian defeat.

Both the tsar and the viceroy encouraged Witgeft to sortie again to relieve the Russian army. Witgeft held a council of war with his officers, who unanimously recommended that the squadron remain at Port Arthur until the Baltic Fleet arrived in October. So Witgeft delayed until he had no other alternative, since the squadron was now in range of Japanese field artillery. Then and only then did he comply with the tsar's and vicreroy's directives to close with Togo. Already the *Retvizan* had been hit by at least seven rounds, further reducing her speed. On 10 August, the squadron put to sea, led by the flagship *Tsarevich*, six battleships, four cruisers, eight destroyers, with a hospital ship astern. A damaged armored cruiser, the *Bayan,* and six destroyers remained in port. The two opposing forces were roughly equal, with Togo holding an advantage in destroyers and torpedo boats.

By noon, both fleets had commenced firing in the first major naval engagement of the post-ironclad era. The fighting was intermittent; at one point both fleets were within six thousand yards of each other, allowing the main batteries of the cruisers and the secondary batteries of the battleships to be brought to bear. Momentarily it looked as if Togo, then trailing, had been outwitted by Witgeft and that the Russians would escape to Vladivostok. But Togo increased speed to about 14 knots and closed. It appeared that a full-scale engagement would take place before nightfall, but Russian gunnery began to take its toll, according to a confidential report sent to the British Admiralty. Togo changed tactics; instead of attempting to block the Russian return to Port Arthur, he decided to intercept the Russians before they reached Vladivostok.

By late afternoon Togo was closing on the *Poltava,* which opened fire on the Japanese battleship *Mikasa* at about nine thousands yards. Soon the Russians were holding their own in this running gun battle. The possibility existed that Witgeft still might make his escape, but by then Togo had closed on the Russian van. At approximately 1745, the *Tsarevich* was hit by at least two Japanese shells, resulting in Witgeft's death. Pandemonium ensued; the *Tsarevich* was out of control. Togo used the deteriorating Russian situation to his advantage by closing to four thousands yards and raking the Russian ships with his main and secondary batteries. Admiral Ukhtomski took command and ordered the squadron to return to Port Arthur. Some Russian vessels broke contact and sought to make it to Vladivostok, but others sailed to British and German treaty ports in China and were interned.

Although the Russian squadron faced disaster at Port Arthur, Russian cruisers operating from Vladivostok had some success against the Japanese. In 1904, they seized British and German ships in and around the Strait of Tsushima. In one operation near Gensan from 23 April to 27 April, Russian cruisers overtook a Japanese troop transport. When the vessel refused to surrender, she was sunk with the loss of all hands. But the most remarkable achievement of the Russian cruisers was their triumphant bid to force the Tsugaru Strait and intercept vessels bound for Yokohama. This Russian Pacific cruise was so successful that the Japanese had to suspend departures for a few days in the summer of 1904, yet despite limited success, disaster befell the Russian cruiser squadron as it steamed out to meet the Port Arthur squadron at the Battle of Ulsan. There, the *Rurik* received the most serious damage and was lost. The *Gromoboi* and *Rossiya* attempted to shield the battered *Rurik,* but they too were damaged in the engagement, the *Rossiya* losing her main batteries.

## The Destruction of the Baltic Fleet
## and the Mutiny on the *Potemkin*

By late summer of 1904, the Russians had accumulated sufficient vessels to counter Japanese naval strength in the Far East. The heart of the squadron was the five battleships, four of which were comparable to the *Tsarevich,* including *Aleksandr III, Suvorov, Borodino,* and the *Orel.* Five modern cruisers, two of them fast light cruisers of the *Novik*-class, were in various states of readiness for the voyage as well.

Following the disaster at Port Arthur, the St. Petersburg press called for swift and decisive action to punish Japan. The decision to send the Baltic Fleet was not easy to implement. The voyage required coaling stations and friendly ports to repair the vessels along the way. A conference was held to determine the viability of the mission. The arguments against sending the Baltic Fleet to the Pacific were sound; opponents acknowledged that Port Arthur might fall (it did on 2 January 1905) well before the fleet arrived and the Pacific squadron could be destroyed, leaving the fleet to sail to Vladivostok through Japanese-dominated seas.

The commander of the task force, Vice Admiral Rozhestvensky, privately acknowledged his doubts about the enterprise yet maintained a belligerent posture to satisfy public opinion. Grand Duke Alexander Mikhailovich, who had participated in the decision, noted later in his autobiography that Rozhestvensky was "quasi-Nelsonic," that he stood no chance in a sea battle against Togo, but like many military figures in the early twentieth century, honor compelled him and Nicholas II to risk the Baltic Fleet on such a dubious venture.

Planning the voyage, the naval ministry had to locate the necessary coaling facilities and bases en route to support the Baltic Fleet. With the Russo-French alliance, St. Petersburg had hoped to rely on the French facilities in

Africa and the Far East. Paris, however, did not want to become involved in such a dubious undertaking when France's own strategic interests were in Alsace-Lorraine, and not in Manchuria. The French hid behind neutrality to avoid antagonizing St. Petersburg. The British adamantly opposed any neutral colliers refueling Rozhestvensky's ships. Only William II, the German emperor, who sought Russian favor, authorized the Hamburg-Amerika line to provide 340,000 tons of coal for the squadron during the expedition.

When the fleet departed Libau, it included five new and two older battleships, five cruisers and eight destroyers, the repair ship *Kamchatka,* and six supply ships. An additional complement from the Volunteer Fleet was to rendezvous later. Soon after leaving Libau, intelligence reports reached Rozhestvensky that Japanese patrol boats were operating in the North Sea, waiting for the opportunity to attack his squadron. In the confusion, after leaving Danish waters the repair ship *Kamchatka* opened fire on any merchantmen in her path. From the various messages sent to Rozhestvensky, he believed that the task force was under attack. In a brief ten-minute exchange, one British trawler from Hull was sunk, two others were damaged, and the Russian cruiser *Aurora* was hit as well. Still believing that Japanese patrol boats were in the vicinity, Rozhstvensky did not stop to rescue survivors. The international reaction was swift; the British called for a state of war with Russia over the Dogger Bank incident.

The squadron then proceeded to Spain and Tangiers, where the fleet split—the larger vessels went around the Cape of Good Hope while the smaller used the Suez Canal. They were to reassemble at Madagascar before continuing the journey into the Indian Ocean. Rozhestvensky, obsessed with the fuel question, ordered that each ship carry 50 percent more coal on deck than the bunkers could hold. Morale declined and a mutiny occurred on the *Navarin* near Crete, a harbinger of the future *Potemkin* incident. Training was haphazard, the crews grew bored, and officers appeared incapable of maneuvering their vessels in formation. During gunnery exercises, ammunition proved defective and the seaworthiness of the squadron came into question.

The St. Petersburg press continued calling for additional reinforcements for Rozhestvensky, but by then the Black Sea Fleet already had been cannibalized to meet initial requirements. Yet a third squadron was sent to the east via Suez and rendezvoused with the Baltic Fleet at Camranh Bay in French Indochina. In mid-May, following repeated Japanese protests, the Russians set sail for Vladivostok. The task force had reached Korean waters by the end of the month and hoped to slip past Japan during hours of darkness or in rain squalls, but the Japanese scouts spotted the squadron as it approached the Tsushima Strait and reported by wireless.

Togo had a cruiser follow the Russians and soon more Japanese cruisers arrived in support. By early afternoon, Togo had met Rozhestvensky's column and crossed his T, allowing Togo to fire his broadsides at the Russians while only the nearest Russian vessels could reply. Togo's move caused considerable confusion for the Russian gunners, who failed to score hits, according to British observers. Even when the Russians scored, few of their rounds exploded. In the gunnery exchange, the *Oslyabia* capsized after being hit several times near her waterline and the *Suvorov, Borodino,* and *Aleksandr III* suffered as well. Rozhestvensky was wounded and transferred command to Admiral R. I. Nebogatov. By nightfall, the Russian battleships were continuing to steam toward Vladivostok, but Togo's battle line barred the way, causing the *Aleksandr III* to capsize, followed by the *Borodino.* Only the withdrawal of Togo's battleships kept the *Orel* from the same fate.

Nebogatov ordered the remnants of the Baltic Fleet to Vladivostok. But following the withdrawal of Togo's battleships, Japanese torpedo craft conducted night attacks, which accounted for the loss of the *Navarin* and at least three other vessels. At first light, Nebogatov realized the gravity of the situation. Most of his destroyers had already fled for Vladivostok, while others sought a friendly shore on which to scuttle their vessels. Only the *Orel, Apraksin, Seniavin,* and the cruiser *Izumrud* continued to steam toward the remaining Russian base. At first Nebogatov did not grasp the full extent of the Russian calamity, but when he did, he cast naval tradition to the wind and decided to surrender by running up a white flag followed by the Japanese flag. The *Izumrud* refused to surrender and managed to break through the Japanese line, but once she ran out of fuel, her captain, fearing her capture by the Japanese, ordered her scuttled. Of all the vessels that comprised the Baltic Fleet in the Far East, only the *Almaz* and two destroyers reached Vladivostok. The *Aurora* was interned by the U.S. government in Manila.

Tsushima was one of the decisive battles of world history. The autocracy had to find scapegoats to explain the Russian defeat. Nebogatov was a handy target and was sentenced to death by a court-martial, but this was reduced to a short imprisonment. Other officers were cashiered or reduced in rank. Rozhestvensky, the most likely culprit, survived Japanese custody and remained silent until the 1930s. But if the loss of the Pacific and Baltic Fleets were not enough, in June 1905 the crew of the battleship *Potemkin* mutinied and sailed along the Black Sea coast bombarding Odessa before seeking asylum in Rumania. Not only was the tsar's ability to continue the war in doubt, but the fate of the regime was in question, as Russia experienced the revolutionary upheaval that followed in 1905.

## The Navy Between the Wars, 1905–14

The naval ministry had to rebuild the fleet as quickly as possible. Nicholas II, however, would not agree to any fundamental reforms that threatened the autocracy following the Revolution of 1905. Nor would the new Duma, the Russian parliament, fund either the army or the navy without a thorough debate of failures during the war with Japan. As a consequence, the Duma refused to provide credits for new naval vessels. Philosophical arguments also raged within the government about whether Russia needed a blue-water navy in light of its industrial inadequacies or whether Russia should only maintain a coastal defense force, centering around submarines and torpedo boats.

The blue-water navy was supported by Nikolai Klado, who voiced his concerns in *Morskoi sbornik,* the official naval journal. Klado argued that naval defense was more complicated because of the nature of naval weapons and changes in modern technology. He stressed that Russia's naval strategic planning had to take into account both the country's geographic position and the necessity to support the army.

Still, despite the writings of Klado and others, Nicholas II was in no great hurry to rebuild a blue-water navy, even after Petr Stolypin became premier and produced pro-government majorities in the Duma. A modest naval construction program was initiated in August 1909 when the Duma appropriated 1,125 million rubles, but in March 1910, the sum was reduced to 731 million. The bulk of the rebuilt navy would be concentrated in the Baltic, while torpedo vessels protected Russian interests in the Pacific and the White Sea. The Black Sea was another matter. The government approved modest increases—50 percent above the strength of other Black Sea naval powers—since the Turkish navy was even in more deplorable condition than the Russian fleet, this was not a very expensive proposition.

In 1913, the naval ministry agreed to a 15-year building program, at the heart of which was a marked decrease in construction delays for capital ships, cruisers, destroyers, and submarines. The majority of the new construction, as agreed, was to be deployed with the Baltic Fleet. If World War I and the Revolution had not interfered with the building schedules, by 1927 the navy would have included 27 battleships, 12 battle cruisers, 24 light cruisers, 108 destroyers, and 36 submarines.

Before World War I, the Russians had experimented with naval aircraft. At first, junior officers in both the army and the navy were their prime proponents. When the use of fixed-wing aircraft appeared impractical, the navy had used balloons, dirigibles, and kites for reconnaissance during the war with Japan. The naval ministry even planned on sending the *Rus',* a converted ocean liner for balloons and kites, with Nebogatov's squadron to the Pacific. The *Rus'*, however, proved so unseaworthy that she was left behind in Libau.

Russians made noticeable advances in aerodynamics in the decade before World War I. N. E. Zhukovskii did much of the pioneering work, including the construction of a wind tunnel for the testing of aircraft propellers and wings. Still, Russia lacked an indigenous aviation industry and bought engines from the French. Once the War and Naval Ministries realized the future of heavier-than-air craft, the government made a concerted effort to purchase these from foreign suppliers. When the Duma industrialists heard of this plan, they pressed the army and navy to use native industry to fill the orders. The Naval Ministry established flying schools, first at Kronstadt, and, somewhat later, at Sevastopol. All told, the navy had approximately 330 aircraft and 8 airships in 1914. Ten of the aircraft were Igor Sikorsky's behemoths, the *Ilia Muromets*, a plane that was capable of carrying either 16 passengers or a bomb load of half a ton, had a ceiling of 10,000 feet, and a cruising range of 80 miles, but lacked targets.

## The First World War

Many officers, particularly senior officers, lacked the qualifications to hold their posts before the outbreak of World War I. Promotions in the navy, long before Tsushima, were based on age rather than on merit. Compared with the army, the navy was viewed by many supporters of the old order as a bastion of privilege. But with the dawn of the twentieth century, the navy required a higher level of technological expertise, especially from members of the emerging Russian middle class. Consequently, friction was evident, sometimes on the same ship, especially with so many officers of non-Russian origin from the other 41 nationalities in the state. Native Russians sometimes looked at Baltic German and Finn-Swedish officers with disdain. (The remarkable exception was Admiral Nicholas Ottovich von Essen, the commander of the Baltic Fleet from 1908 to his death in 1915.)

The heart of the problem, even in the enlisted ranks, was the generational cultural divide that separated the classes. Former Soviet scholars constantly point to the working-class composition of the navy, particularly the Baltic Fleet, but it appears that only 25.4 percent of those sailors from 1914 to 1916 were from the proletariat, the majority coming from the peasantry and petty bourgeois. As the navy modernized, the Admiralty had to find recruits who could operate machinery, and in the process, had to raise reading levels drastically. Even then, the low pay, five-year enlistment, boredom, lack of adventure, and brutal punishments did little to quell the anger of sailors.

The situation was volatile in both the Baltic and Black Sea fleets according to foreign observers. In the Baltic Fleet, sailors were restive owing to the quality of the rations and the harsh treatment administered for slight infractions as late as 1912. Likewise, naval authorities were concerned about the situation at Sevastopol. The investigation into subversive activities onboard ship culminated in the arrest and trial of 142 men and the execution of 17 others. It is remarkable, given the state of Russian industrial development and the limited time for training, that the Russians had progressed as far as they had by the outbreak of the war in 1914.

When Franz Ferdinand was assassinated on 28 June 1914, the Baltic and Black Seas, the principal theaters of operations, had 10 pre-dreadnought battleships, 1 coastal-defense vessel, 6 armored cruisers, 6 protected cruisers, 25 destroyers, 72 torpedo boats, 12 gunboats, and 22 submarines. As for the Russian Far Eastern squadron, most of its vessels were considered obsolete.

On the outbreak of the war both the Germans and Russians assumed that the other nation had naval superiority in the Baltic, that unique closed sea, which could be entered only through the narrow strait between Denmark and Sweden. This was closed by German mines and so kept the British and French from entering the Baltic to aid the Russians. The Germans, on the other hand, could use the Kaiser Wilhelm Canal at Keil and move their naval forces between the North Sea and the Baltic at will. The only way for the Allies to aid the Russians was the northern route to Archangel and Murmansk, which was as hazardous in World War I as it would be during World War II. The climate also affected naval operations, particularly in the Gulfs of Finland, Bothnia, and Riga, which froze for a few months each year, hampering Russian naval operations through much of the conflict.

Before 1912, the Russians assumed that Sweden would align with Germany as a means of regaining Finland. As a consequence the Baltic Fleet was expected to block any Swedish landing that threatened Viborg—St. Petersburg—and the army was expected to delay any German advance into the Gulf of Finland. The Admiralty assumed that Libau and Helsingfors would be lost, whereas Sveaborg would serve as the fleet's forward base and Kronstadt as the main anchorage. The Russian plans were that the Baltic Fleet would maintain the close defense of the capital, reflecting the lessons learned following the Russian defeat in the Russo-Japanese War.

The situation changed when Admiral Essen assumed command of the fleet in 1909. He immediately improved training and re-energized the navy. He assumed that the Swedes would declare war but that the Germans would not use their main naval assets in the Baltic. With that, he advocated a more aggressive approach, including laying mines in anticipated German sea lanes. At first Essen's plans were rejected by the Admiralty, but by 1910 the Russians had adopted a contingency plan that foresaw laying mines along the Nargen-Porkkala-Udd line. Behind the mines, Essen proposed to contest any German advance and then withdraw to his fallback position near Gogland, and by 1912 still be covered by Russian coastal batteries along the Finnish coast. The Baltic Fleet could then use Revel as a main naval base, but until it was fully operational, Helsingfors would serve that purpose. Unfortunately, both Revel and Helsingfors could not provide docking facilities for major capital ships, forcing the Baltic Fleet to rely on Kronstadt, which was icebound during the winter months.

On the outbreak of war, 1 August 1914, Essen laid 2,124 mines, and extra mines were to follow, particularly near the Finnish coast. When Essen heard of anti-Russian demonstrations in Sweden, he had his chief of staff, Kolchak, prepare for a surprise attack on the Swedish naval forces assembled at Gotland. Essen, however, was blocked from carrying out his plans, since the Baltic Fleet fell under the operational control of the Russian Sixth Army, which had to keep Essen on a tight leash. Still, for the most part the war in the Baltic was fought from a distance, often behind mines and obstacles. Essen scored one of the most remarkable coups before his untimely death in 1915 when the German cruiser *Magdeburg* was run aground and the Russians recovered the German naval code books intact. These they passed on to the Royal Navy in London.

Essen was aggressive by his very nature and, on 27 August 1914, on a particularly dark night, conducted a raid against German shipping. The task force consisted of the armored cruisers *Rurik* and the *Pallada,* without additional escorts. Essen encountered no Germans, but his daring-do lifted the morale of his sailors. He wanted more aggressive actions and sought approval to use battleships in mining operations. Although he was willing to take risks, Essen discovered the same lessons the British had learned earlier concerning the U-boat menace when *U-26* sank the *Pallada* on 10 October.

The naval war in the Black Sea is often overlooked, but the transfer of the German cruisers *Breslau* and *Goeben* to the Turks was an instrumental factor in Constantinople's decision to enter the war (4 November 1914). Likewise, following the Treaty of Brest-Litovsk in March 1918, the Germans managed to seize elements of the Black Sea Fleet at Sevastopol. Those actions tended to distort what actually had happened in the Black Sea theater. In reality, the Russian fleet was the master of the region, and much more successful than the Baltic Fleet in World War I.

The Russian Stavka, the high command, was more concerned about the battering its armies were experiencing in the north and the possibility of a Turkish landing near Odessa, than in naval operations on the Black Sea. At first, the fleet conducted successful mining operations along likely Turkish or German naval approaches and had laid approximately 4,200 mines by the end of 1914. Soon the Russians were interdicting Turkish transports destined for the Caucasus. After one such mission, the *Goeben* and *Breslau* tried to ambush the Russian squadron as it returned to Sevastopol on 18 November. The Russian managed to hit the *Goeben,* but the *Evstafi* took four hits in the exchange. The lesson was clear. The Russians must maintain their squadron to equalize the speed and firepower from the *Goeben* and the *Breslau.* But the Russians had no dreadnoughts or long-range destroyers available to threaten the Bosphorus.

In 1915, the Black Sea Fleet continued to raid the Turkish coast and lay mines. At the same time, the Russians experimented with seaplane tenders—the *Amaz* and the *Imperator Nicholai I*—and battleships and destroyers to create an early carrier-based task force to strike the Turkish coast near the Bosphorus. While the battleships shelled lighthouses and the entrance to the Bosphorus, the seaplanes conducted aerial reconnaissance and sought targets of opportunity on 27 and 28 March 1915. When Allied troops landed at Gallipoli on 25 April, the Black Sea fleet supported the British and French with two battleships and three destroyers that bombarded Turkish forts located on the Black Sea coast, and returned on 2 May for a repeat raid. The situation changed when the Germans sent two submarines to the Bosphorus—*U-21* and *UB-8*—as the Russians could not then afford to risk the loss of their precious few warships in the region. However, the Admiralty did not realize that the Black Sea was never a principal theater for German submarines.

Later in 1916, the Black Sea Fleet was used to support the Russian army in the Caucasus, particularly in Lazistan, an area known for its difficult terrain and lack of an adequate road network. Here, Russian naval power could be used to sever the Turkish lines of communication from the port of Trebizond to Rize, since the road network was vulnerable to naval fire. To support the army, the Black Sea Fleet moved to the eastern shore, often operating from Batum. Likewise, Russian destroyers and the obsolete battleship *Rostislav* interdicted coastal steamers that were supporting the Turkish army in the region. As the Russians mounted an offensive, the Black Sea Fleet responded by escorting 22 troop transports from Odessa and Novorussisk to Rize for an advance on Trebizond on 5 April 1916. Protecting the convoy en route, the Black Sea Fleet employed the *Imperatritsa Maria,* 15 destroyers, 3 cruisers, 3 seaplane carriers, and additional torpedo boats. As the troops disembarked, seaplanes provided air cover. As the Russians anticipated a swift Turkish response, so the Black Sea Fleet continued to escort additional convoys to Rize.

The high point of Russian naval power in the Black Sea came in the second half of 1916, following Rumania's declaration of war, when Admiral Kolchak began to wage an aggressive mining campaign near the Bosphorus. At one point, the Russian submarine *Krab* sowed approximately 60 mines near the channel and additional minefields near the entrance to the Strait. On the eve of the Rumanian declaration of war on 27 August 1916, a Russian carrier task force appeared off Varna, and launched seven planes against the port, hoping to damage German submarines located there. Unfortunately, the rough seas hampered a concentrated air attack. As a result of the task forces' proximity to Varna, the Germans launched their own seaplanes against the task force without success.

For 1917, the Russians had planned an extensive naval campaign in the western Black Sea. The Admiralty wanted to conduct an amphibious operation near the Bosphorus, supported by naval aviation with from two to six seaplane carriers. The Russians refitted four captured Rumanian passenger liners—*Dakia, Imperator Trajan, Regele Carol I,* and *Rumyniya* into seaplane tenders, capable of maintaining four to seven seaplanes and used to conduct reconnaissance flights to discern potential locations for amphibious operations near Constanza in March 1917. During one mission, a damaged Russian seaplane landed at sea and captured a Turkish vessel. But the days of Russian naval dominance were coming to an end in the Black Sea, as political events in Russia following the March Revolution disrupted the war effort.

## The Revolution and After

After three years of war, the political and social situation in Russia was volatile. The people were ready for change following repeated military defeats, worker unrest, and the collapse of the social infrastructure. The Romanov dynasty had come to an inglorious death.

During the early days of the March Revolution military order came to an end, soldiers and sailors refused to obey their officers and attacked all symbols of authority. Consequently, discipline was nonexistent. The Petrograd Soviet, fearing the possibility of a conservative reaction from the officer corps, issued Order No.1 on 14 March, effectively curbing the authority of officers in the army and the navy. The sailors of the Baltic Fleet played an important role in the upheaval by disregarding orders, murdering the commander of the naval depot troops, and marching on the Winter Palace and Nikolaevsky stations.

The Provisional Government eventually, after repeated crises, found a democratic voice, Alexander Kerensky. Unfortunately, Kerensky was determined to continue the war and honor Russia's commitments to the Allies. In the meantime, the Bolsheviks mobilized the masses—soldiers, sailors, industrial workers, and peasants—under the able leadership of V. I. Lenin. Still, during the height of the political upheaval, most sailors had no clear political consciousness. The Bolshevik message slowly made inroads with Baltic Fleet sailors and, in time, sailors' committees were founded in all Baltic Sea naval bases. By the summer of 1917, the command authority of the Baltic Fleet reflected the general breakdown of order in Russia.

As morale declined and political agitation grew in the spring and summer of 1917, the Germans were preparing for a major offensive in Moon Sound, where they planned to land on the northern coast of Oesel Island on 29 September an amphibious force of 24,600 men, supported by over 300 ships. The object was to expand the German lines of communication, allowing the German army to resume the offensive toward Petrograd. Though some 12,000 troops opposed the Germans, they quickly disintegrated. Uncharacteristically, the Baltic Fleet sailors gave a good account of themselves during the fighting. Pavel Dybenko, one of the leading Bolsheviks in the fleet, recalled that when Admiral Razvozov, the fleet commander, appealed for support from the Second Congress of the Fleet, he got it. Historians may debate the impact of the naval engagement at Moon Sound, but the Germans were so leery of Russian mines that further naval offensive operations in the region came to a halt.

The sudden upsurge of élan in the fleet did not signify that the revolutionary fervor had ended. While the battle raged, sailors were entering a more radical stage. Lenin was concerned that Kerensky would make a deal with the Germans, allowing them to enter Petrograd. In Lenin's planning, the Baltic Fleet would play a key role in the coming coup d'etat. So sailors, with the soldiers and workers, were to seize the telegraph and telephone offices, bridges, and railroad stations, as well as other key points in Petrograd during the night of 7–8 November 1917. A few days before the uprising, the cruiser *Aurora,* manned by a radical crew, was stationed in the Nava. Earlier, when the *Aurora* had been outfitted with new engines and armaments, the ship's committee refused the order to go to Helsingfors for sea trials. Even when force was attempted to convince the *Aurora* to leave, the ship's committee kept the vessel at its anchorage. During the early hours of 5–6 November, the *Aurora* slowly made her way up the Nava to the Nikolaevsky Bridge before dropping anchor. Her appearance close to the Winter Palace made it clear that a final reckoning with the Provisional Government was at hand. Firing rounds at the Winter Palace signaled the end of the last democratic government in Russia until the collapse of the Gorbachev regime 74 years later.

The coming of the Bolshevik Revolution in October 1917 brought forth a general breakdown of order. Officers were attacked and sometimes lynched by their men. Numerous high-ranking officers left the service to be replaced by politically active junior officers or enlisted men. In naval aviation, however, the division was between officer pilots and mechanics. When the Bolsheviks required shock troops to restore the situation on various fronts during the Civil War (1918–20), these often came from the Baltic Fleet moving from one sector to another. Likewise, the remnants of the fleet challenged the British, who were operating in the Baltic to protect the newly independent Baltic states and insure a German withdrawal from the region.

With the conclusion of the long and bloody civil war, the Bolsheviks were not willing to tolerate any questioning of their authority, even from the zealots in the Baltic Fleet. The origins of the Kronstadt Mutiny (28 February–18 March 1921) can be traced to the rise of political discontent in Petrograd associated with war communism and the political repression exercised by the Bolsheviks. On 28 February, the sailors of the *Marat* (formerly the *Petropavlosk*) circulated a declaration calling for a secret ballot, releasing political prisoners, instituting free elections, and abolishing special privileges for the Bolshevik elite. In a general meeting of Baltic Fleet sailors at Kronstadt on 1 March, a complete reform program was introduced, effectively denouncing Lenin and the Party.

The regime could not tolerate this threat and ordered M. N. Tukhachevskii, the most able of all Red Army commanders, to crush the sailors. The assault came across the frozen waterway to Kronstadt on 7 March, but the first two assaults were repulsed by heavy machine-gun and artillery fire from the naval base. The final assault began on 17 March. The Red Army managed to secure a bridgehead. By the following day Kronstadt was in Tukhachevskii's hands. Those not killed or captured sought refuge in Finland. Reports reached the West that the captured were executed; the exact total may never be known.

The defeat ended any debt the regime had to the sailors, and raised serious questions within the Bolshevik inner circle of the value of a navy. Lenin at one point even thought of scuttling the warships and disbanding the sailors; only Leon Trotskii's intervention kept Lenin from implementing his program. However, the Kronstadt rebellion, combined with the protracted civil war, demonstrated the general state of the navy's decline, or, as the leading military pundit Mikhail Frunze noted, "In sum . . . we had no fleet."

## The Navy in the Twenties and Thirties

Following the Kronstadt Mutiny, Lenin made a tactical retreat from "socialism," and embarked on an ambitious program to recover from the economic devastation of the war and revolution, particularly in agriculture, where land under cultivation did not reach 1914 levels of production until 1928. The retail economy slowly recovered and a form of prosperity returned, but the Communist Party maintained its hold on power. The situation drastically changed following Lenin's death in January 1924, and a struggle ensued for Lenin's mantle between Josef Stalin and Leon Trotskii. Stalin, using his superior position as general secretary, ensured his ultimate victory over Trotskii and the other Old Bolsheviks by 1927, ushering in an age of five-year plans, superindustrialization, and bloody purges. But a question remained: How would this affect the future of the Red Navy?

In the early 1920s, the navy was in search of a mission. One voice came from Professor Boris B. Gervais, a leading theoretician from the Naval War College, who advocated a return to the old tsarist position of a Mahanian, command-of-the-sea strategy. Gervais realized that the Red Army would maintain Soviet security, and, in many ways, he acknowledged that predominance. Still, he felt that building a blue-water navy was necessary to protect the Soviet Union's sea lines of communication and as a means of defeating any possible enemy amphibious threat to the homeland. Gervais was such a partisan of battleships, as crucial for a fleet-in-being, that he overlooked the potential of modern aircraft carriers. One of Gervais's colleagues, Mikhail A. Petrov, proved to be more astute when it came to naval strategy, since he realized it would take time to develop a navy capable of implementing Gervais' Old School program.

By 1926–27, opponents of the Old School stressed that the Soviet Union could develop a navy of submarines, patrol boats, and destroyers and wage a naval version of guerrilla warfare on the high seas in order to ensure Soviet security. The proponents were the Young School, intellectual descendants of the French *jeune école* of the 1880s. It is difficult to fault Gervais and Petrov for maintaining the need for a blue-water fleet and advocating an expensive naval building program, since they closely monitored foreign naval trends. Both Gervais and Petrov, however, believed that the future of aircraft carriers in the Soviet navy rested as auxiliaries to battleships. The capability of building a fleet of modern warships during the formative years of the Soviet Union remained unlikely as a consequence of Soviet industrial development in the 1920s. But by 1927, when the political climate in Moscow had changed, Petrov shifted his position vis-à-vis aircraft carriers and stressed that they were the wave of the future; perhaps his mind was more attuned to reading the political winds than were those of many other naval theorists.

A vicious struggle took place between the Old School and the New School starting in 1928 and concluding with the defeat of the Old School in 1932. By the late 1930s there emerged a synthesis of the Old and Young Schools, which has been referred to as the Soviet School. The latter basically advocated an adjusted Old School approach of "command of the sea" to a "limited command of the sea" doctrine. This interpretation fit nicely with the emerging strategic planning of the Red Army by 1936, allowing the navy to support the army in the critical defense areas. The Soviet School took from the Young School the emphasis on submarines and aviation. Out of this came discussions of aircraft carriers in the pages of *Morskoi sbornik*. Although this was a philosophical debate, it did have important repercussions, since Admiral N. G. Kuznetzov recalled that the greatest shortcoming of naval development in the 1930s was not including aircraft carriers in the 1937 building program.

But the internal situation following Stalin's ascension to power was volatile, particularly after collectivization and the First Five-Year Plan (1928–33). Some people in Stalin's inner circle advocated moderation. Sergei Kirov, the Leningrad Party boss, was one such individual. Suddenly, Kirov was murdered near his office on 1 December 1934. His death allowed Stalin to move against all internal opposition. The Old Bolsheviks were the first victims of Stalin's purge of 1937. No one was spared, and no single branch of the armed forces was immune. In the navy, members of the Young School were the initial victims during the summer of 1937. Then the key command structure of the navy was rocked with the downfall of Admiral V. M. Orlov, the commander-in-chief of the navy, and all of the fleet admirals and Orlov's principal supporters by July 1938. Similar purges took place in the Baltic, Northern, Black Sea, and Pacific fleets as well as in the Caspian flotilla. The most noticeable exception to Stalin's purge was Admiral Viktorov of the Pacific Fleet. In many respects, the naval purge proportionally exceeded the purge in the Red Army and the Red Air Force.

The purges signified a change of direction for the navy as it appeared that Stalin could not accept the interpretation that the day of great surface combatants was over. In his heart, Stalin liked big things, often the bigger the better, and that included the navy. Stalin had his own vision of the navy, which required that it have its own command structure as well as a Soviet effort to renegotiate the 1930 Treaty of London, allowing the navy to construct or purchase two 16-inch-gun battleships. With an independent naval establishment, Soviet industry accelerated deliveries of destroyers, submarines, and cruisers. By 30 December 1937, the Naval Commissariat was reestablished for the first time since 1918.

## Soviet Readiness on the Eve of the Great Patriotic War

The Soviet emphasis on industrialization made it possible for the Kremlin to embark on a tangible naval buildup. Stalin would never accept Soviet naval inferiority and approved measures that reestablished a Soviet presence in the Pacific and the Black Sea. After ceasing to exist following the Civil War, the Black Sea Fleet was restored in 1930, followed by the Northern Fleet in 1932 and the Pacific Fleet a year later. All Soviet naval forces were understrength—Baltic, Black Sea, Northern, Pacific, Caspian, and Amur flotillas—all included destroyers, a few obsolete battleships and cruisers, torpedo boats, and submarines. Each fleet had an organic naval aviation arm, which in time would become one of the most effective weapons available to the navy during the coming war. Sailors able to operate the new machinery were impressed.

The execution of Admiral Orlov, and the reestablishment of an independent naval commissariat, brought to the forefront younger officers to replace those who had disappeared. The new chief of the Naval Commissariat was Admiral Kuzentsov. By 1938, the traditional naval ranks, abolished in 1918, had been re-instituted, including admiral and vice admiral. Kutzentsov, L. M. Geller, and I. S. Isakov were promoted to admiral, while vice-admiral appointments went to V. F. Tributs (Baltic Fleet) and I. S. Yumashev (Pacific Fleet). Corresponding with those command changes, Stalin authorized a comprehensive naval construction program with an emphasis on battleships, heavy cruisers, and submarines. An internal debate took place regarding the construction of aircraft carriers, at least on the scale of the U.S.S. *Ranger*. The Red Army objected and the ensuing threat from Germany altered Soviet naval plans. As war approached, the Kremlin revised proposed naval construction plans, particularly those for the construction of battleships and heavy cruisers. Soon, only vessels nearing completion were authorized, and the issue of aircraft carriers was left for the future.

By mid-March 1939, barely 20 years after the last war, Europe was on the verge of another great conflict. As Britain sought an ally she turned to Poland, not fully trusting the Kremlin, but she also made overtures to Moscow; however, Polish objections impeded any progress. Hitler gambled that he could reach an accord with Stalin before the Western democracies could ally with Moscow. Hitler was right. By late August, Stalin signaled Hitler that he would accept a resolution of all outstanding differences. With the signing of the Molotov-Ribbentrop Pact on 23 August 1939, World War II was inevitable. From the collapse of Poland (September 1939) and Hitler's attack on Norway (April 1940), Stalin sought to solidify his position in the Gulf of Finland and improve the defenses near Leningrad. After negotiations failed, the Soviets attacked Finland on 30 November 1939, without benefit of a declaration of war.

The Red Army did not distinguish itself against the Finns in the Winter War (30 November 1939–12 March 1940) but simply overwhelmed them at great cost. The Baltic Fleet conducted a blockade of the Finnish coast, cutting the link to Sweden as well as periodically shelling positions. In mid-December, the *Kirov* and supporting destroyers conducted a raid near Hango in which the *Kirov* was slightly damaged and one destroyer was lost. The Baltic Fleet followed up this raid with a second on 18 December at Koivisto with the old battleships *Oktiabrskaia Revolutsiia* and *Marat*. When the Soviets laid mines, the Finns promptly swept them before they wreaked havoc on Finnish shipping. By the time the war ended on 13 March 1940, the Baltic Fleet and fleet aviation had conducted limited raids on Finnish positions and had sunk at least four Finnish and one Swedish merchantmen. Although Stalin won the Winter War, he drove the Finns closer to the Germans.

## The Great Patriotic War

On the eve of the Russo-German War, the Soviets had a clear advantage in warships in the Baltic—2 obsolete battleships (the *Oktiabrskaia Revolutsiia* and *Marat*), 2 cruisers, 75 submarines, numerous torpedo boats, and 47 destroyers. More submarines, destroyers, and 4 cruisers were on the way in Soviet shipyards. The fleet's command structure was its most serious weakness. Even before the war, German naval officers who had served in World War I had limited regard for their Soviet counterparts.

Unlike the Red Army, the Red Navy was somewhat better prepared for the outbreak of war, particularly in the Baltic, since the Soviets had tracked German voyages to Finland. The Germans swiftly moved to restrict Soviet fleet movements by laying mines and linking them to existing Swedish minefields, which accounted for the high Soviet losses during the initial period of the conflict, especially in submarines and destroyers. The most serious threat to the Baltic Fleet was the Wehrmacht's advance upon the east coast, threatening one naval base after another. When Finnish troops landed in the Åland Islands, the Baltic Fleet put up virtually no resistance, despite the proximity of two Soviet battleships and six destroyers. Instead, the Soviet squadron sought refuge in Kronstadt, but on 22 September, the Luftwaffe sank the *Marat*. However, the waters in Kronstadt were so shallow that her turrets were still able to fire in defense of the naval base. Then the Wehrmacht laid siege to Leningrad for nearly 900 days (4 September 1941–January 1943), the fleet batteries provided fire support for the Red Army, and eighty thousand sailors of the fleet helped man the besieged city's defenses.

Before the war, as during World War I, the Turks were the only nation in the Black Sea region that could effectively challenge the Red fleet, but Istanbul remained neutral during the Russo-German War. Only Rumania, a German satellite, gave the Germans a base from which to mount a challenge. So Berlin sent four destroyers, three torpedo boats, and an assortment of gunboats via the Danube or by rail to be reassembled in Rumanian yards.

As in the Baltic, however, the Wehrmacht managed to seize Soviet naval bases from landward approaches without assistance from the Kriegsmarine or the Rumanians. One major objective was Odessa. S. G. Gorschkov, commanding the Soviet naval forces in the city, ably defended the port as well as organized the removal of unfinished naval vessels to safety. To harass the Rumanians, the Soviets conducted joint amphibious and airborne assaults on the Rumanian rear, delaying the Axis attacks on the city. After a 73-day siege, when the defense of the city was no longer feasible, Gorshkov ordered withdrawal.

After the capture of Odessa, the Germans ran convoys along the coast as they moved men and supplies forward to keep up with the advancing Wehrmacht. The Soviets countered by laying mines and organizing submarine and torpedo-boat strikes on unprotected convoys. Next the German advance threatened Sevastopol, which avoided capture during the first year of the war. Stavka realized its importance and kept the sea lines of communication open for the garrison, at the price of one cruiser, the *Chervonaia Ukraina,* and an assortment of smaller craft. Unlike the Russian experiences in the Crimean War and the Russo-Japanese War, the Soviets did not allow their major surface combatants to be cornered in port.

To ease the pressure on the naval base, the Soviets conducted their most impressive amphibious operation of the war. Taking advantage of the calm seas and moonless nights of 26–29 December 1941, the Soviets landed at ten points supported by a task force comprised of the cruisers *Krasny Krym, Komintern, Krazny Kavkaz,* destroyers, and MTBs. The Germans managed to reduced six of the Soviet bridgeheads. Although the Red Army could not expand their positions, the Soviets managed to delay the final German assault on Sevastopol. When it was impossible to resupply the garrison by ordinary means, the Soviets used submarines. Black Sea sailors and marines, the 20,000 men of the garrison, played a key role in the heroic defense. Many sailors and marines threw themselves at German tanks to stem the German advance. Still, Sevastopol fell on 1 July 1942, after a prolonged 250-day siege.

By the end of that month, the Germans had secured a hold on the Sea of Azov, but the Black Sea Fleet still conducted amphibious operations behind German lines to slow the German summer offensive. Soviet naval aviation, the most aggressive arm of the fleet, struck German and Axis targets, particularly during a raid on an Italian MTB base at Yalta that caused considerable damage. With American Lend-Lease aircraft, naval aviation continued to conduct a relentless series of attacks on the Germans. Although Russian pilots made crude bombing runs on German positions and lacked the aerial skill of their Western Allies, the deployment of mines tied up German naval assets. From late 1942 through 1944, naval aviation managed to gain mastery of the air from the Luftwaffe even before the Soviet victory at Stalingrad and became the most aggressive arm of the navy.

The Northern Fleet by 1936 consisted of three destroyers, three submarines, an aviation component, as well as an assortment of auxiliary vessels, including tankers and icebreakers. When Germany attacked Norway in the spring of 1940, the Germans saw an opportunity to use the Norwegian bases for future submarine operations in the North Atlantic to avoid the extensive North Sea mine barrage that impeded German submarines in World War I. When Hitler ordered the OKW to plan for an invasion of the Soviet Union, the facilities in northern Norway were to be used to sever the Soviet Union's link to the West, if and when war occurred. Following the German attack on 22 June 1941, both Winston Churchill and Franklin Roosevelt immediately offered military aid to Stalin. Three routes were open to the Allies to supply the Soviet Union— the Persian Gulf, the Pacific, and the northern route to the White Sea. There the Germans seized Petamo (Petsamo) in the initial attack in July, but were unable to take Murmansk.

The Northern Fleet's missions included fleet protection, sea interdiction, anti-submarine warfare, and support of the Red Army and Air Force. As the northern route became important to the war effort, the protection of Allied convoys from U-boats and the Luftwaffe reached critical importance. Most of the merchantmen were American, often under British Royal Navy control. The Northern Fleet was responsible for the protection of the convoys in Soviet waters but, during the first two years of the war, it was difficult for them to do this. The British consistently complained about Soviet escorts breaking down and failing to appear at the appropriate rendezvous times. But from 1943 increased Soviet strength, particularly airpower, led to diminished convoy losses as Northern Fleet aircraft and the Royal Air Force attacked German bases in northern Norway.

The fleet also conducted combined arms operations integrating submarines, MTBs, and aircraft against German convoys in the region, a strategy that the Soviet Navy would emulate in the 1970s and 1980s. A typical combined-arms mission occurred on 24 September 1944, when the submarine *S-56* notified Northern Fleet headquarters of the approach of a German convoy in the vicinity of Nordzal. Fleet headquarters sent a brigade of MTBs to the attack and ordered fleet aviation to conduct reconnaissance and to prepare a strike on the German vessels. All told 52 aircraft were involved in the attack—18 *Shturmoviks,* 14 fighters serving as light bombers, and 18 fighters as the combat air patrol (PVO). The *Shturmoviks* conducted the initial strike before the MTBs arrived on station. Then two naval aircraft made smoke to conceal the MTBs' approach, forcing two German vessels to run aground and so battering others that they had to be towed into port. Although the results would appear modest by Western standards, they allowed the navy to make the improvements necessary for the coming war with Japan.

During the early stages of World War II, Japanese moves in Asia worried Stalin, particularly as the Wehrmacht approached Moscow in late 1941. Were the Japanese going to strike in Siberia? Were they going to move against Great Britain and the United States? Stalin's intelligence indicated that Japan was going to move south, allowing the Soviets to transfer their crack Siberian troops eastward. Likewise, Soviet neutrality gave Tokyo the impression that Moscow could be a fair broker with the Americans in order to negotiate with Washington in the war's waning days.

Stalin astutely negotiated with the Anglo-Americans concerning the Soviet Union's entry into the Pacific War. According to the Yalta Agreements (7 February 1945), the Soviet Union would declare war on Japan 90 days after VE day, and in return Stalin would receive extensive concessions—annexation of Sakhalin Island, the Kurile Islands, port facilities in and occupation of Manchuria and Northern Korea—at minimal cost. From the end of the European war, the Soviets massed three fleets, the North Pacific flotilla, the Amur flotilla, and the Pacific Fleet to overwhelm the Japanese in Manchuria. The blow was the culmination of combined arms operational art developed by the Soviets during the war to crush an opponent during the initial period of hostilities. The Pacific Fleet command worked to correct the fleet's defects by reviewing procedures used by the other fleets during the war. Naval aviation was destined to play a greater role in the Pacific than it had in other theaters. Consequently, the Pacific Fleet had over 1,750 aircraft in its inventory, of which 1,495 were combat aircraft—665 fighters, 243 *Shturmoviks,* 164 bombers, 157 torpedo bombers, and 266 reconnaissance aircraft. Combined with the Ninth, Tenth, and Twelfth Air Armies, the Soviets had overwhelming air superiority over the Japanese by the outbreak of the conflict. Effectively using that advantage allowed the Soviets to suppress Japanese resistance.

The navy conducted crude yet effective amphibious operations in northern Korea at Rahin, Seichshin, Odaejin, and Wonsan. The Pacific Fleet for Operation August Storm had 2 *Kirov*-class cruisers (the *Kaganovich* and *Kalanin*), as well as 10 destroyers, and 78 submarines, and additional vessels such as destroyer escorts, subchasers, and minesweepers supplied by American Lend-Lease aid. The war officially started on 9 August and ended on 23 August 1945. The first Soviet amphibious operations began on 11 August. Landings were supported by either naval or aerial bombardment. If reconnaissance determined that the Japanese had evacuated the area, naval bombardment was omitted. Within a short time, the Soviets occupied all of southern Sakhalin Island and followed with similar operations in the Kuriles. In less than a month, the Soviets had overcome Japanese resistance, and, with the assistance of the navy, managed to regain areas that tsarist Russia had lost to the Japanese during the Russo-Japanese War.

## Conclusion

The Russian/Soviet Navy had come a long way from the debacle of the Russo-Japanese War of 1904–05. By 1945, it had overcome the initial German victories and developed an effective naval strategy based on submarines, motor torpedo boats, and naval aviation to such an extent that the Soviets managed to interdict German convoys in the Northern Sea, support the Red Army in the Baltic, interrupt German movements in the Black Sea, and overwhelm an already defeated Japan in August 1945.

With the revival of the Soviet economy in the postwar years, *Morskoi sbornik* reviewed the war and naval performance in the struggle against Nazi Germany as well as the record of the other naval powers in the conflict. From those musings and the desire to challenge the United States on the high seas, the modern Soviet Navy was born. A clear lesson its naval command drew from the historical record was the importance of naval aviation and thus they decided to take naval air to sea. The rebirth was about to begin when, in 1956, Nikita Sergeivich Khrushchev replaced Admiral Kuznetzov with Admiral G. S. Gorshkov, a naval officer who had learned the lessons of the past and had the desire to build a blue-water navy to challenge the enemies of the Soviet Union on the high seas.

## Further Research

Detailed histories of naval construction, of the recruitment and social life of the navies, and comparative studies with other navies would be helpful now that the Soviet-era archives are open.

## Sources and Further Reading

To understand the history of the Russian and Soviet navy it is important to begin with Donald W. Mitchell's older work, *A History of Russian and Soviet Sea Power* (New York: Macmillan, 1974) and Jacob W. Kipp's "The Navy and Combined Operations: A Century of Continuity and Change" (Ft. Leavenworth, KS: Soviet Army Studies Office, 1987). At the moment, a pressing need exists for both a popular and contemporary operational history of the Russian navy.

For additional information concerning the Russo-Japanese War, readers can turn to Ian Nish's *The Origins of the Russo-Japanese War* (New York: Longmans, 1985), Richard Hough's *The Fleet that Had to Die* (New York: Viking Press, 1958), R. M. Connaughton's *The War of the Rising Sun and Tumbling Bear: A Military History of the Russo-Japanese Conflict 1904–5* (New York: Routledge, 1988), J. N. Westwood's *Witness of Tsushima* (Tokyo: Sophia University, 1970), and *Russia Against Japan, 1904–05: A New Look at the Russo-Japanese War* (Albany: State University of New York Press, 1986). For a Soviet explanation of the conflict, see the edited work of I. I. Rostunov, *Istoriia Russko-Iaponskoi Voiny, 1904–1905 gg* (Moscow: Nauka, 1977) and David C. Evans and Mark R. Peattie in *Kaigun: Strategy, Tactics, and Technology in the Imperial Japanese Navy, 1887–1941* (Annapolis, MD: Naval Institute Press, 1997).

For the Revolution of 1905, see John Bushnell's *Mutiny amid Repression: Russian Soldiers in the Revolution of 1905–1906* (Bloomington, IN: University of Indiana Press, 1985), Richard Hough's gripping *The Potemkin Mutiny* (Annapolis, MD:

Naval Institute Press, 1996), and Paul G. Halpern's *A Naval History of World War I* (Annapolis, MD: Naval Institute Press, 1994) as well as Victoria Bonnell's *Roots of Rebellion: Workers' Politics and Organization in St. Petersburg and Moscow, 1900–1914* (Los Angeles: University of California Press, 1983).

For the Baltic Fleet, see Norman Saul's classic *Sailors in Revolt: The Russian Baltic Fleet in 1917* (Lawrence, KS: University Press of Kansas, 1978) and Allan K. Wildman's *The End of the Russian Imperial Army: The Old Army and the Soldier's Revolt (March–April 1917)* (Princeton, NJ: Princeton University Press, 2 vols., 1980) and *The End of the Russian Imperial Army: The Road to Soviet Power and Peace* (Princeton, NJ: Princeton University Press, 1987), John L. H. Keep's *The Russian Revolution: A Study in Mass Mobilization* (New York: Norton, 1976) and Paul Avrich in *Kronstadt 1921* (New York: Norton, 1970). See also Robert Herrick, *Soviet Naval Theory and Practice* (Newport, RI: Naval War College Press, 1988).

John Erickson's *The Soviet High Command: A Military-Political History, 1918–1941* (New York: St. Martin's Press, 1962) places the navy within the general parameters of the Soviet defense establishment; Robert Tucker's *Stalin as Revolutionary, 1879–1929: A Study in History and Personality* (New York: Norton, 2 vols., 1973) and *Stalin in Power: The Revolution from Above, 1929–1941* (New York: Norton, 1990), as well as General Dmitri Volkogonov's recent biography, *Stalin: Triumph and Tragedy* (New York: Grove Weidenfeld, 1988).

On the purges read Robert Conquest's *The Great Terror: A Reassessment* (New York: Oxford University Press, 1990) and Roy Medvedev's *Let History Judge: The Origins and Consequences of Stalinism* (New York: Columbia University Press, 1989), as well as Vitaly Rapoport and Yuri Alexeev, *High Treason: Essays on the History of the Red Army, 1918–1938* (Durham, NC: Duke University Press, 1985).

For the Soviet navy during the Great Patriotic War, in English, see V. I. Achakasov and N. B. Pavlovich's *Soviet Naval Operations in the Great Patriotic War 1941–1945* (Annapolis, MD: Naval Institute Press, 1981), Friedrich Ruge's *The Soviets as Naval Opponents* (Annapolis, MD: Naval Institute Press, 1979), and Jurgen Rohwer's *Chronology of the War at Sea 1939–1945* (New York: Arco Publishing Company, 1972).

For Soviet institutional histories of the navy during the war, see A. I. Achkasov's *Krasnamennyi baltiiskii flot v bitva za Leningrad, 1941–1944* (Moscow: Nayka, 1973), P. Bolgari's *Chernomorskii flot* (Moscow: Voenizdat, 1967), and S. E. Zakharov's *Tikhookeanskii flot* (Moscow: Voenizdat, 1966). On naval aviation see N. M. Lavrent'ev's *Aviatsia VMF v Velikoi Otechestvennoi Voine* (Moscow: Voenizdat, 1983) and P. N. Ivanov's *Kryl'ia nad morem* (Moscow: Voenizdat, 1973), as well as battle-damage assessments in Rohwer's *Chronology of the War at Sea*.

# PART II

# THE SOVIET ARMY AND NAVY
# IN THE COLD WAR AND BEYOND

# CHAPTER 12

# SOVIET/RUSSIAN STRATEGIC NUCLEAR FORCES, 1945–2000

*Steven J. Zaloga*

FROM THE BEGINNING OF THE NINETEENTH CENTURY TO THE END of World War II, the power of weapons went from the muzzle-loaded cannon, capable of firing a small high-explosive charge a few hundred yards, to the strategic bomber, capable of delivering a 30-kiloton atomic bomb several thousand miles. This revolution would continue in the Cold War years, as new technologies further extended the range and power of modern weapons. By the end of the 1960s, the range and lethality of these weapons peaked with the advent of intercontinental ballistic missiles and thermonuclear warheads. The strategic arms race of the 1960s led to the construction of enormous arsenals of Soviet and American nuclear weapons capable of genocidal levels of destruction. The superpowers were forced to confront the political and military utility of these weapons in the face of their disturbing destructive power. Both sides continued to develop and deploy new generations of weapons in the hopes of maintaining technologically plausible deterrence while at the same time engaging in arms control treaties in the hopes of limiting future arms races and decreasing the probability of nuclear war. The contradictory impulses of arms control and weapons modernization lay at the heart of many Cold War controversies.

# The Stalin Years, 1946–53

The Soviet Union had no significant atomic bomb program during World War II, and its long-range bomber force was almost non-existent. The need for such programs became evident following Hiroshima and Nagasaki in 1945. As a British diplomat in Moscow reported about the situation in 1945 "then plump came the atomic bomb. The balance which now seemed set and steady was rudely shaken. Russia was balked by the West when everything seemed to be within her grasp. The three hundred divisions [of the Red Army] were shorn of much their value." Josef Stalin ordered a crash program to respond to these revolutionary changes in the nature of military power. By possessing its own bomb, Stalin expected that the Soviet Union would be better able to resist any American or British pressure in the international arena, and to deter them from attacking the USSR. Besides the bomb itself, this also required the creation of weapons to deliver it at intercontinental ranges.

Continental powers like the Soviet Union and Germany traditionally were less interested in creating powerful long-range bomber forces during World War II than were maritime powers like the United States and Britain. As a result, there were no influential institutions in the Soviet Union with the experience or inclination to shape the early direction of its strategic nuclear efforts. Instead, Stalin formed three directorates that transcended normal party, military, and industrial organizations to ensure that the new programs were given the highest priority. The First Main Directorate of the Council of Ministers, under Vyacheslav Malyshev, was assigned the development of nuclear weapons; the Second Main Directorate, under Dmitriy Ustinov, the development of strategic offensive systems such as bombers and missiles; and the Third Main Directorate, under Colonel General V. M. Ryabikov, the development of strategic air defenses.

The Soviet atomic bomb program was based around a small group of physicists headed by Igor Kurchatov, who had been trying to convince the senior leadership of the feasibility of nuclear weapons since the first years of World War II. Little funding had been provided prior to Hiroshima, but the involvement of the Soviet secret police under Lavrentiy Beria led to an effective espionage program, which netted considerable detail about the American atomic bomb program. While Kurchatov's team worked on the bomb design, an extensive and costly program began to fuel the bomb. The prospecting, mining, and chemical processing of the uranium and plutonium for the early bombs was an enormous industrial undertaking that cost nearly 2 percent of the Soviet GNP and required the labor of hundreds of thousands of workers, many of them from the Gulag labor camps. Stalin insisted that the first Soviet bomb follow the stolen American design, and the resulting RDS-1 fission bomb was successfully detonated on 29 August 1949. It was followed by the detonation of an indigenous Soviet design, the RDS-2, on 24 September 1951.

At the time of the detonation of the first atomic bomb, the only method of nuclear weapons delivery was by long-range bomber. Soviet backwardness in heavy bomber design led Stalin to order the copy of the American B-29 Superfortress. A total of 847 were built under the designation Tupolev Tu–4 from 1947 to 1952, but they did not have the range to reach the continental United States even from forward bases in the Soviet Arctic. The Korean air battles in 1950–51 led to serious doubts about their survivability against modern jet fighters. This led Stalin to initiate a program to develop jet bombers for nuclear weapons delivery while at the same time authorizing an expensive strategic defense program to protect Moscow with new radar-directed missiles, guns, and fighters. Through Stalin's last years, the United States had the capability to launch large-scale air strikes on the Soviet Union with jet bombers based in the United States and Europe. The Soviet Union lacked this capability. A number of schemes were considered to circumvent this asymmetry such as basing medium-range bombers on the Arctic ice, or seizing forward bases in Greenland and Alaska using special submarines. Besides shortcomings in nuclear weapons delivery, shortages in fissionable material meant that series production of Soviet nuclear weapons did not begin until 1953–54. As a result, the Soviet Union had very little capability to conduct intercontinental nuclear strikes through the end of Stalin's reign in 1953.

# The Post-Stalin Interregnum, 1953–57

Stalin's death did not bring about any major changes in the Soviet strategic nuclear weapons program as senior party leaders focused on a succession struggle. To an important extent, this was a period when technology was the primary driver in strategic force decisions, with technological limitations largely dictating the shape and capabilities of the forces. These years saw the maturation of the nuclear weapons program started by Stalin and the completion of the "nuclear archipelago," a network of ten new cities, closed to the outside world, which served as the primary centers for the design and manufacture of nuclear weapons. The nuclear industry was run as a fiefdom by E. P. Slavskiy, and its annual budget was exceeded only by those of the Russian and Ukrainian republics.

By the mid-1950s, the first Soviet strategic bombers with intercontinental range began to enter service—the troubled Myasishchev 3M (Bison) jet bomber and the more successful Tupolev Tu–95M (Bear) turbo-prop bomber. There were still doubts about their survivability against modern air defenses, and so they were manufactured in smaller numbers than their American counterparts.

Although bombers had been viewed as the most likely basis for strategic offensive forces in the mid-1950s, they were not the only possibility. The second alternative was the missile. The Soviet Union had a program to examine missiles derived from the wartime German V-1 cruise missile and V-2 ballistic missile. Series production of the R-1, a copy of the German V-2, began in 1950, and was followed by improved types such as the R-2 (SS-2) and R-5 (SS-3). The R-5, the first indigenous Soviet design, was also the first Soviet missile armed with a nuclear warhead and was deployed in 1956. Its limited range of 750 miles meant that it was only suitable for use against targets in Europe. The Soviet program was a patient attempt to sequentially increase the range of missiles until a true intercontinental ballistic missile (ICBM) proved feasible. By 1954, Soviet engineers headed by Sergey Korolev concluded that the design of an intercontinental ballistic missile or cruise missile was feasible. This was made possible by the design of lighter nuclear weapons, and the development of the first thermonuclear weapons in 1953–54. Parallel programs were initiated—Korolev's R-7 intercontinental ballistic missile and Lavochkin's and Myasishchev's intercontinental cruise missiles. Korolev's team won the race, both against his Soviet competitors, and against American designers who were developing the Atlas ICBM. The first successful launch of the R-7 ICBM in August 1957 was followed shortly afterward by the launch of the first earth-orbiting satellite, the *Sputnik 1.*

The *Sputnik 1* was created on the initiative of the Soviet missile engineers and was originally viewed with indifference by the Kremlin and with outright hostility by the Soviet military. It had substantial and totally unanticipated consequences. In the United States, it created the false impression that the Soviet Union had raced ahead in strategic technology. The "missile gap" would be a major political issue in the United States over the next several years, and led to an accelerated U.S. missile program that ignited the strategic arms race of the 1960s. The world wide clamor and jubilation over *Sputnik,* and the consternation in the United States, profoundly impressed Nikita Khrushchev. Many observers saw the *Sputnik* launch as evidence of Soviet leadership in science and technology, a view that resonated among first-generation Soviet Communists who viewed the Soviet Union as the vanguard of the new century. The strong international reaction to *Sputnik* sparked Khrushchev's enthusiasm for missile weapons, and had a substantial effect on Soviet defense policy over the next decade. While *Sputnik* had the short-term effect of accelerating the strategic arms race, in the long term it initiated trends that would reduce the likelihood of nuclear war. By establishing the precedent that satellites could fly unhindered in space, *Sputnik* opened the door to reconnaissance satellites. The first American and Soviet spy satellites were launched into space in the early 1960s, and helped provide the first reliable information on the scope of opposing strategic weapons programs. This reduced the level of uncertainty for policymakers on both sides and helped paved the way for the first efforts at arms control.

## The Khrushchev Era, 1957–64

One of Khrushchev's central dilemmas was how to cut the Soviet defense budget to help stimulate the domestic economy, while at the same time retaining or expanding Soviet military might in the face of American power. Missiles offered a panacea. Khrushchev began to believe that missiles offered a more cost-effective alternative to conventional weapons. Anti-ship missiles were seen as an alternative to the gun-armed cruisers favored by Stalin, tactical ballistic missiles were an alternative to conventional artillery, anti-tank missiles would doom tanks, missile-armed fighters would doom strategic bombers, and so on. Khrushchev's missile mania was based on a naïve view of the nature of military revolutions. Yet because of the concentration of power in his hands by the end of the 1950s, Khrushchev was able to act. Due to the growth in Soviet GNP, Khrushchev was able to keep defense expenditures close to the levels of the late Stalin years, though they shrank as a fraction of the state budget. One of the immediate impacts of Khrushchev's missile mania was the reorientation of the Soviet defense research establishment. The shift in defense resources was startling. In 1958, missile procurement represented 460 million rubles, or 6.2 percent of weapons procurement. In 1965, it had increased more than tenfold to 4.1 billion rubles, and represented nearly 53 percent of total Soviet weapons procurement. Space expenditures saw similar rates of growth, increasing tenfold from 17.2 million rubles in 1957 to 179.8 million rubles in 1961.

The success of the R-7 ICBM led Khrushchev to cut back strategic bomber programs to a bare minimum. The Soviet Navy had been pressing for a role in the strategic forces, and had launched the world's first submarine ballistic missile, the R-11FM, in 1955. The Soviet Navy began deploying nuclear-armed cruise missiles and ballistic missiles on submarines in the late 1950s. The short range of early Soviet nuclear naval missiles meant that the submarines would have to run the gauntlet of NATO anti-submarine warfare forces to strike at the continental United States. Direct communication with the submarines once they went on patrol was almost impossible. While this was acceptable in wars of the past, the idea that submarines would be ordered to sea with a mission to carry out nuclear strikes against the U.S. several days hence with no assurance that they could be recalled or re-targeted, caused severe anxiety to the Soviet General Staff. The Soviet submarine force was relegated to a secondary or tertiary role, responsible for attacking ports and other coastal targets, but not being seriously considered a part of the main strategic strike force.

By the end of the 1950s, the future configuration of the Soviet strategic forces was beginning to take shape. The Soviet ballistic missile force was clearly the front-runner in the competition for the defense budget. The ICBMs were by no means mature weapon systems, but they promised the capability to strike targets in the United States in the face of any American defenses. In contrast, both the strategic bomber force and the submarine missile force had substantial tactical liabilities due to questions about their ability to carry out their mission reliably, their vulnerability to hostile defenses, and the difficulty of integrating them into a secure command and control system. Soviet attitudes toward the three force options were undoubtedly shaped by institutional biases. The Soviet Army held a predominant sway within the General Staff and had managed the early strategic missile programs. After some initial skepticism, the army was becoming comfortable with the missile as a long-range artillery weapon. In contrast, the General Staff was not enthusiastic about the Navy's role in the strategic mission, holding the Navy in contempt for its minimal role in the Great Patriotic War of 1941–45. The Soviet submarine force, the largest in the world at the outbreak of the war, had been bottled up by the Germans until the Soviet Army drove the Wehrmacht back beyond the Soviet borders in 1944. There was little confidence that the modern submarine would perform any better when faced by aggressive U.S. and NATO anti-submarine warfare forces. A similar attitude applied toward the Soviet Air Force's feeble Long Range Aviation force. Khrushchev offered the air force leadership a share of the strategic missile force in return for their support in conventional force cutbacks in the late 1950s. The leadership bungled the opportunity, and Khrushchev responded by cutting the air force structure anyway and converting several bomber divisions to missile divisions. In December 1959, Khrushchev ordered the formation of a new branch of the armed forces, the RVSN (Strategic Missile Force). He made it quite clear that he regarded the

RVSN as the primary branch of the Soviet armed forces, even over the established Ground Forces. While this annoyed the victors of Stalingrad, Kursk, and Berlin, the fact that the troops of the RVSN wore the khaki uniform of the Army and that its senior leadership was made up almost entirely of Ground Forces generals, lessened the insult.

Khrushchev's view on nuclear doctrine was not particularly complicated. He felt that even a modest force of 200 to 300 ICBMs would serve as an adequate deterrent to prevent the United States from initiating a full-scale nuclear attack. Early ICBMs were terribly expensive weapons systems due to the high cost of the associated launch complexes. So in order to achieve economic savings, Khrushchev was inclined to believe that a modest ICBM force would be enough. Most of the initial procurement for the new RVSN was for an intermediate-range ballistic missile (IRBM) force of R-12 (SS-4) and R-14 (SS-5) missiles targeted on Europe. Such an IRBM force could not entirely replace the Ground Forces, but it would provide a rationale for trimming back the army to a more economical level. While it may seem preposterous that the Kremlin had any fears about a NATO attack on the Soviet Union, for the war-scarred and ideologically blindered Soviet leaders of the Khrushchev years, such a threat was very real.

U.S. strategic nuclear forces of the Cold War years are often described as a triad: nearly equal land, air, and naval elements. In the Soviet case, a more appropriate analogy would be a tricycle. The land-based Strategic Missile Force was the predominant "big wheel," while the air force and naval elements were less important "little wheels."

## The Cuban Missile Crisis

In 1962, the United States enjoyed a clear lead over the Soviet Union in strategic forces even though public perceptions were otherwise. Neither side had a mature missile force, and the U.S. advantage clearly rested in its more mature and extensive strategic bomber force. The U.S. advantage was amplified by the momentum of its missile programs. The *Sputnik* shock, combined with the politicization of the "missile gap" controversy during the 1960 presidential election, assured steady funding for the U.S. ICBM and SLBM efforts. The U.S. aerospace industry was infinitely richer in resources than its Soviet counterpart. Even though the Soviet Union had been the first country with an ICBM and SLBM, the U.S. programs quickly raced ahead into deployment. The first Soviet naval missiles were primitive and were not adequate to create a real force structure. In contrast, the first U.S. SLBM, the Polaris, was a versatile and clever design that would serve for over a decade. Likewise, the American solid-fuel Minuteman ICBM proved to be the most successful missile design of the era, and is in service to this day in a modified form.

In spite of all of Khrushchev's bluster about the primacy of strategic missiles and his "missile rattling" diplomacy, the Soviet Union was badly falling behind in the nuclear arms race. The R-7 had proven to be a failure as an ICBM. It took much too long to launch, and its launch complex was too expensive and too complex to erect. The Soviet defense industry was being pushed by the Kremlin to field new strategic weapons to make up for the deficiencies of the pioneer R-7 design. The Yangel R-16 (SS-7) and Korolev R-9 (SS-8) ICBMs entered trials in the early 1960s. By the time that they were ready for deployment, the strategic program of the new Kennedy administration had become public. It consisted of an unexpectedly large deployment of a thousand solid-fuel Minuteman light ICBMs, a small number of heavy Titan ICBMs, and about 40 submarines armed with the Polaris SLBM. As worrisome as were the numbers of these missiles, they offered significant technological advantages over the new Soviet designs. In particular, the Minuteman was to be deployed in dispersed hardened silos while Soviet missiles were based in clustered, lightly protected launchers. Instead of the anticipated small ICBM forces that were favored by Khrushchev, it now appeared that the United States was racing ahead to a fundamentally new level of strategic weapons. The size of the new force suggested that they would not be aimed solely at major political and urban centers, but that they might be sufficient in number to be used against the weakly defended Soviet ICBM soft launchers, posing a preemptive "counterforce" threat.

It was presumed that the location of Soviet missile bases would remain secret when design began on the new missiles in the late 1950s. But by the early 1960s, they had become visible to the new reconnaissance satellites, and their obsolete basing mode made them vulnerable. In February 1962, Khrushchev and the military leadership had a major confrontation over his continued failure to deploy even a minimal strategic missile force. Khrushchev's "missile rattling" diplomacy was a major catalyst in the vigorous missile program of the Kennedy administration. Yet the new R-9 and R-16 missiles were significantly behind the U.S. designs in capability and survivability. As a result, the deployment program for the R-9 and R-16 was curtailed and in April 1962 a new second-generation ICBM program was initiated. These new missiles would not reach the deployment stage until the late 1960s. In an effort to redeem himself and to provide the Soviet Union with some short-term missile capability, Khrushchev conceived a bold idea. An inexpensive shortcut to remedy the strategic force imbalance would be to deploy several hundred intermediate range missiles on Cuba as an immediate counterweight to America's intercontinental advantages. While Khrushchev later argued that his primary motivation in the missile basing was to protect Castro's regime from U.S. invasion, this could have been accomplished by force deployments in Cuba other than long-range missiles. The Cuban crisis became the Cuban *missile* crisis due to the Soviet Union's own "missile gap."

The Cuban missile deployment was reckless, ill-conceived, and poorly managed. Khrushchev believed that the missiles could be surreptitiously deployed and he intended to hand the Kennedy administration a stunning fait accompli in November 1962. In fact, Soviet attempts at concealment were hopelessly inadequate and inept, and the missile sites were discovered long before they became functional, by U-2 reconnaissance aircraft. At the time of the crisis, the Soviet Union's missile force was substantially smaller than the American force: six launch pads for the R-7, two improvised launch pads for the unproven R-9A, and about a dozen interim launchers for the R-16. The Soviet bomber force was a fraction the size of the U.S. force. Faced with America's overwhelming strategic superiority, the Soviet Union was forced to back down. Khrushchev was obliged to remove the missiles, with a promise from Kennedy not to invade Cuba, and a minor concession on U.S. missiles in Turkey.

The Cuban Missile Crisis of 1962 had as profound an effect in Moscow as the *Sputnik* shock had on the White House in 1957. Soviet political and military leaders regarded the Cuban crisis as an unacceptable humiliation and it was one of the catalysts for the 1964 coup against Khrushchev. His heir apparent, Leonid Brezhnev, had been the Communist Party's chief overseer of the strategic weapons program, and an enthusiastic supporter of further Soviet efforts to overcome U.S. superiority in the strategic arms race. The Cuban Missile Crisis ended the debate within the Soviet military over the primacy of strategic nuclear weapons. More traditional leaders in some of the military branches had been slow to embrace the priority afforded the new Strategic Missile Force, in part due to the distaste they felt toward Khrushchev and his "hare-brained schemes." The Soviet humiliation in the crisis ended any resistance within the military to strategic missile weapons once and for all, making clear the centrality of such weapons in contemporary Great Power confrontations. The future basis for Soviet military power would be parity or superiority in strategic nuclear arms.

Soviet military doctrine in the Khrushchev years was established by Marshal V. D. Sokolovskiy's seminal work, *Voyennaya Strategiya* (Military Strategy). Given the significant technological limitations of the time, idealized doctrine presented few real guidelines for the essential tactical decisions of nuclear warfighting such as strike initiation and targeting. Furthermore,

Soviet nuclear doctrine was constrained by obvious U.S. superiority in the means to deliver nuclear strikes against the USSR versus the likely Soviet response through most of this period.

An underlying theme in Soviet war planning during the Khrushchev years was the concept of the "initial period of war." This had particular resonance in Soviet military thinking of this period due to the catastrophic lessons of recent Russian wars. Both the 1905 Russo-Japanese War and the 1941 Soviet-German War had begun with a surprise strike by the opposing forces and the devastating consequences of the German assault in 1941 had an enduring effect on nuclear war planning. Three basic options existed for an initial period of strategic nuclear war: preemption, launch-on-warning, or launch-on-attack. Soviet military planners through much of the 1960s were inclined toward preemption, a surprise attack on the enemy's strategic forces, if for no other reason than the historical example presented by the 1941 invasion. To allow the enemy to strike first was to invite destruction. Launch-on-warning became favored in the 1970s, once the Soviet Union had deployed an adequate network of ballistic missile early warning radars. Launch-on-attack held no attraction, since U.S. superiority in strategic nuclear weapons would mean that most if not all of the Soviet strategic forces would be destroyed before they could launch a retaliatory blow. Although cultural and doctrinal factors led to a preemptive warfighting doctrine, this policy was not without its severe shortcomings. Soviet strategic forces in the Khrushchev years did not have a high probability of eliminating the U.S. nuclear strategic forces without triggering a devastating counterstrike. This was due to the larger size and greater sophistication of U.S. strategic forces, inherent shortcomings in the reliability of Soviet strategic forces (especially the bomber and submarine forces), and intelligence shortcomings regarding targeting, poststrike assessment and follow-on strikes. While the Soviet strategic forces may have preferred the preemptive strike policy in the early 1960s, it was inherently untenable due to the catastrophic results that the execution of such a mission was likely to have on the USSR. As a result, there were severe contradictions between the established Kremlin doctrine of no-first-use, the military's predilection for preemptive strike, and the limited technical capabilities of the Strategic Missile Force.

## The Race for Parity 1965–73

The second generation strategic missiles were still in development at the time of Khrushchev's ouster in 1964. In the wake of the Cuban humiliation, the senior Soviet military leadership demanded that the Soviet Union reach parity with the United States in strategic missiles. The late 1960s saw the most intense buildup of the Soviet missile forces during the entire Cold War, and during this period, the Strategic Missile Forces consumed a larger share of the Soviet defense budget than at any other time. The intended size of the force was based largely on the size of the U.S. forces, more for its symbolic numerical equivalence than any notion of counterforce or any formal doctrinal requirement.

The heavy Yangel R-36 (SS-9) was adopted as a counterpart of the U.S. Titan while the light and inexpensive Chelomey UR-100 (SS-11), like the U.S. Minuteman, fleshed out the force. The new Navaga (Yankee) submarine armed with the R-27 (SS N-6) gave the Soviet Navy a weapon system comparable to the U.S. submarine deployed Polaris nearly a decade earlier. Improvements in strategic command and control including the new Dnestr missile warning radars began to make a launch-on-warning doctrine possible. The Soviet Union and the United States reached rough numerical parity in the late 1960s and early 1970s at a time when the United States was embroiled in the Vietnam War. As the Soviet Union reached rough numerical parity, this ended the first phase of the arms race. The second phase was to reach a "deeper parity" with the United States, in the sense of matching or surpassing not only its intercontinental power, but its regional power projection around the Soviet frontier as well.

The goal of deeper strategic parity seemed far more obtainable to the Kremlin in the early 1970s than at any time since the beginning of the Cold War. The Vietnam War had a detrimental impact on U.S. strategic weapons programs, draining them of funding during the war itself and undermining efforts to modernize the force. From the Soviet perspective, the "correlation of forces" in the early 1970s finally seemed to be moving in the Soviet Union's favor.

Although the Soviet Union and the United States had begun strategic arms limitations in the Kennedy years such as the Partial Test Ban Treaty, no serious discussion to control the delivery systems took place until January 1969, when the USSR was finally reaching parity. The Kremlin's goals in strategic arms control talks were to end the uncertainty in the strategic arms race, to rationalize and stabilize the strategic balance, and to secure the advantages that the Soviet Union had acquired in certain areas. The arms control process was favored by the top party leadership including General Secretary Brezhnev, Foreign Minister Andrei Gromyko, and the party secretary on national defense, Dmitri Ustinov. It was vigorously opposed by the military headed by Marshal Grechko, who viewed the whole process as an elaborate deception by the United States to win unilateral advantages. In spite of military resistance, two arms control agreements were reached in May 1972, the SALT I and ABM (Anti-Ballistic Missile) Treaties. The ABM treaty was conceivable mainly due to the failure of the Soviet ABM effort and worries over the potential of the U.S. ABM effort. Although the treaties were not viewed with enthusiasm by the military leaders in the Soviet Union, they were palatable because of the success of the Strategic Missile Forces in reaching parity with the United States in strategic nuclear arms.

## Beyond Parity, 1973–85

By the end of the 1960s, there was a broad consensus on the desirability of strategic force modernization, but there was no consensus on the details of the program. Development of the third generation of ICBMs began in 1968 prior to the beginning of the arms control effort. From the offensive perspective, the advent of integrated circuits promised much more precise guidance systems that were no longer hard-wired against a single target, but could be reprogrammed for other targets, thereby increasing force flexibility. This was an important consideration due to the rise of the Chinese threat, and the need to have a more flexible force that could be targeted at either the United States or China. Soviet doctrine for the use of strategic nuclear forces was not particularly refined at the time and certainly not detailed enough to provide any firm guidelines for the next generation of weapons. Soviet research institutes had begun to use computer modeling and other techniques to help determine the tactics of nuclear war and the requirements for future weapons in a manner that paralleled U.S. efforts a decade earlier. The conclusions of these studies were resisted by Grechko and the Ministry of Defense, which regarded them as an usurpation of military prerogatives by contemptible civilian analysts. The matter came to a head in 1968 when attempts were made to define the requirements for the third generation of ICBMs. This bitter controversy, called the "Small Civil War," was the most intense debate on Soviet strategic force options during the postwar period. The greatest controversy centered around a replacement for the UR-100 (SS-11), which made up the bulk of the force.

Based on their interpretation of Soviet deterrence doctrine and the need to have an assured capability to respond to an American preemptive strike, Soviet research institutes argued that the next generation would require innovations such as much harder silos, computer-based flight controls for greater terminal accuracy, and the introduction of MIRV (multiple independently targetable re-entry vehicles) warheads. In contrast, the Soviet military leadership preferred a launch-on-warning capability, and from this perspective, the institutes' positions devoted too much attention to the defensive aspects of force modernization such as silo hardening. The military proposed that instead of hardening the silos, the fields be protected by a territorial ABM system. The "Small Civil War" was not simply about weapons acquisition. Underlying the debate was the resistance of the military to involvement by the Party and civilian specialists in shaping defense options. From the standpoint of Party officials and the more forward-looking elements of the military industry, the debate underscored the inability of the poorly educated military leadership to foresee the dynamic nature of state military policy and military technology. Contrary to the widespread impression in the West, the Soviet military leadership was often resistant to technological innovation, since the officers were overwhelmed by the difficulties in continually introducing new weapon systems into a force structure based on poorly trained conscripts. The industry and its related institutes tended to play a more active role in technological innovation, in part because it served their institutional interests, and in part because they did have a deeper appreciation of the dynamics of technological change.

A State Defense Council meeting chaired by Brezhnev was held near Yalta in July 1969 to reach a final decision on the controversy, but could not reach a consensus. In the end, Brezhnev simply approved a little of everything: shallow modernization of some of the UR-100 sites with the evolutionary UR-100K, and deep modernization of the remaining UR-100 systems with a mix of the new Chelomey UR-100N (SS-19) and Yangel MR-UR-100 (SS-17). The heavy R-36 (SS-9) was replaced by a modernized evolution, the R-36M (SS-18). The third generation of Soviet ICBMs were deployed from 1975 to 1981. In the wake of the Small Civil War, the management of military innovation was reorganized to prevent future deadlocks. Rather than rely on the outdated straight-jacket of the five-year plan, the new policy of programmed planning introduced a three-phase approach. The research institutes prepared a 15-year scientific research study, which laid out the likely threat as well as new technological potential. A ten-year plan proposed specific engineering development efforts that should be pursued to respond to this forecasted threat. The resulting five-year plans ensured that the programs progressed smoothly through the industrial phase, coordinating the manufacture and deployment of the new weapons. This new method was introduced into the next round of five-year plans in the 1976–80 cycle.

In parallel to the development and deployment of the third generation of ICBMs, during the early 1970s the Soviet Union embarked on an ambitious modernization and expansion of the other two legs of its strategic nuclear forces—the submarine missile force and the strategic bomber force. While neither component challenged the primacy of the land-based RVSN force, changes in technology enabled both to assume a more important position in Soviet nuclear force planning. In the case of submarines, significant SLBM range extensions permitted the newer classes of submarines and their missiles to operate closer to Soviet home waters, enabling them to limit their vulnerability to NATO anti-submarine forces. In the case of bombers, the advent of long-range cruise missiles removed the need to penetrate U.S. air defenses since the missiles could be launched from stand-off range. These programs did not follow in precise parallel to the third generation missile deployments, and reached the deployment stage later.

The Soviet effort in strategic force modernization in the 1970s was more vigorous than that in the United States, and the Soviet Union finally began to surpass the United States in terms of the numbers of missiles and warheads. ICBM modernization in the United States had been limited to the deployment of the modified Minuteman III ICBM with a triple MIRV warhead in 1970. Strategic force modernization in the United States had concentrated more heavily on the submarine leg of the triad, with the deployment of the Poseidon C-3 SLBM with its 10-warhead MIRV beginning in 1973. Attempts to modernize the U.S. Strategic Air Command were limited to ALCM cruise missile deployments on the old B-52 bomber, as the Carter administration canceled the supersonic Rockwell B-1A bomber. The former technological dominance of the U.S. strategic force was heavily eroded. While the U.S. forces continued to enjoy many narrow technological advantages, especially in the new MIRVs, the Soviet forces began to enjoy overall advantages due to the sheer size and power of the land-based force. The short-term U.S. advantage in MIRVs was illusory since the larger Soviet missiles permitted the RVSN to field improved variants with their own MIRV technology, exceeding the U.S. MIRV count by a large margin as the third generation deployment progressed. The Soviet ICBM force began exceeding the U.S. force in the number of warheads in 1975, and within a decade was three times greater in number. In addition, the third generation missiles enjoyed a substantial increase in accuracy, which some U.S. analysts argued put U.S. ICBM silos at serious risk. The rapid increase in Soviet MIRV warheads toward the end of the 1970s undermined the balance that was supposed to be achieved by SALT I. Furthermore, U.S. concern about the growing accuracy of Soviet ICBMs when used in a counterforce role against U.S. missile silos created the impression of a "window of vulnerability" to U.S. critics of American arms control and strategic weapons policy.

The Soviet Navy exceeded the U.S. Navy in total number of SLBMs in 1972–73, though the U.S. Navy maintained a substantial edge in the number of warheads at sea, especially once the U.S. Navy began deploying MIRVs in the early 1970s. In addition, American submarine silencing ensured a higher degree of survivability in the U.S. submarine force compared to the Soviet submarine force, especially in the context of the vigorous U.S. Navy anti-submarine warfare capabilities. The only area of clear American superiority was in the intercontinental bomber force, where the United States continued to enjoy advantages both in the number of aircraft and the number of deliverable weapons.

To arms control advocates in the United States, these developments further reinforced the need for the SALT 2 treaty and more explicit restrictions to tame further growth. To U.S. arms control critics, the Soviet third generation improvements represented clear evidence of the futility of arms control in the face of Soviet determination to win strategic superiority. In spite of the success of the Soviet Union in reaching parity with the U.S., the Soviet Union still did not have the capability to launch a preemptive strike against the U.S. strategic forces that would eliminate U.S. retaliatory capability. While the Soviet Union continued to rely on land-based ICBM forces, the American force structure was turning increasingly toward the naval SLBM force. Even if the U.S. ICBM force was becoming more vulnerable to Soviet counterforce capabilities, the SLBM force remained essentially invulnerable to any new Soviet ASW advances. Furthermore, the U.S. SLBM force remained the most worrisome element of the American force to Soviet strategic planners due to the continued shortcomings of Soviet strategic command and control. American SLBMs could be launched closer to the Soviet Union than ICBMs, thereby reducing their flight time to under 15 minutes, too little time for the Soviet command and control system to fully activate their own forces. The potential of the U.S. submarine force was a major factor in the development of the fourth generation of Soviet ICBMs in the 1980s.

## To the Brink of Collapse 1985–91

Development of the fourth generation of Soviet ICBMs began in 1976. From the technological standpoint, continuing advances in electronics and computers promised continued payoff in accuracy. Also, Soviet solid fuel propulsion technology was approaching the point where it was becoming feasible to build a new generation of missiles around solid rocket engines with the associated advantages in readiness and maintenance. Finally, Soviet missiles had a finite certification life, and so there was a built-in institutional tendency to field a new generation roughly every decade. From a threat standpoint, the requirements for the fourth generation were to shorten the time between initial warning and launch, and to further enhance the survivability of the force. This was predicated on improvements in the U.S. force, in particular, the development of counterforce capability in the U.S. SLBM force such as the new Trident missile. The RVSN concluded that by the year 2000, the U.S. ICBM and SLBM force would triple its counterforce capability and increase its soft-target destruction capabilities by one-and-a-half times. In addition, the new Reagan administration began to reinvigorate the dormant strategic defense program, an unanticipated wild card that disrupted the fourth-generation effort.

The potential vulnerability of Soviet ICBMs could not be entirely addressed by silo hardening. The obvious solution to this dilemma was missile mobility. Doubting the reliability of command and control over the Soviet submarine force, and its vulnerability to American anti-submarine warfare forces, the Soviet General Staff favored some form of land-mobile missile to enhance retaliatory force survivability. This led to two programs, the rail- and road-mobile Molodets/Tselina–2 (SS-24) and the road-mobile Topol (SS-25). Land mobility was not practical for very large missiles like the modernized Voevoda (SS-18), and arguably, its primary role was a preemptive counter-force mission. While the fourth generation missile systems would provide important enhancements to force survivability, the decapitation threat remained. Work on a unique system to avert this problem, code-named Perimetr, began in the early 1970s. The Perimetr, sometimes nicknamed "the Doomsday Machine," was a method to launch automatically a significant fraction of the ICBM force in the event of the decapitation of the national command authority. It had a role akin to the U.S. EC-135C airborne launch control system aircraft.

Modernization of the SLBM force continued in parallel to the development of the fourth generation of ICBMs. The Akula (Typhoon) missile submarine program was so delayed by technical problems that it was not fielded in significant numbers until the mid-1980s. Indeed, the costs of the program led to a parallel liquid-fuel missile program, the R-29RM (SS N-23), which armed the cheaper Delfin (Delta IV) class of submarines. After years of controversy and false starts, the Soviet air force began to acquire a new strategic bomber, the Tu–160 (Blackjack).

# Further Arms Control Efforts

One of the consequences of the SALT I talks was that it placed a premium on all missiles dubbed "strategic" by the United States. While the RVSN controlled strategic missiles of both continental and intercontinental range, the U.S. arms control initiatives were concerned only with the intercontinental missiles. The UR-100 (SS-11) was targeted at both intercontinental (U.S.) targets, and at intermediate range targets in Europe, China, and Japan. The SALT I treaty had the unintended consequence of pushing the USSR into a much more substantial expansion of its intermediate range missile force. By adding shorter range missiles to take over targets previously assigned to the UR-100, the RVSN could free up all of its ICBMs for targeting against the United States. This decision was further reinforced by the deteriorating relations between Moscow and Beijing. This coincided with a Kremlin pledge to reach "deeper parity" with the United States to encourage the military to support the SALT I arms control effort. The resulting modernization of regional nuclear force included the new Pioner (SS-20) intermediate range missile, which began to replace the outdated R-12 (SS-4) and R-14 (SS-5) IRBMs starting in 1976, and the new Tu–22M (Backfire) bomber to replace obsolete types.

The substantial modernization of Soviet regional strategic systems in the 1970s and early 1980s led to unintended political and military repercussions. The excessive scale of deployments of the Pioner led to NATO decisions to enhance their own theater nuclear forces including the deployment of the new Pershing II ballistic missile and GLCM cruise missile, leading to yet another political confrontation in Europe. The Pershing II ballistic missile, based in Germany, had the range to reach targets deep inside the Soviet Union, and its terminal guidance system combined with a tactical earth penetrator warhead suggested that its mission could be to decapitate the Soviet national command authority through destruction of its command bunkers in the Moscow area. The Soviet political leadership had not anticipated the vociferous criticism of the Pioner deployment in Western Europe, and the General Staff was seriously dismayed by the problems posed by the Pershing II.

By the mid-1980s, the Gorbachev administration reconsidered the issue as part of their rethinking of Soviet security policy. In view of the wide scope of political and military problems posed by the Pioner deployment, Gorbachev signed the Intermediate Nuclear Forces Treaty (INF) in 1987, which eliminated the U.S. Pershing II, U.S. GLCM, Soviet SS-20, and other weapons in this category. While the Soviet military eventually acquiesced to the need for the INF Treaty, there was considerable controversy within the RVSN in the wake of this decision related to its future force structure. The Politburo and the General Staff were inclined to disband all 14 RVSN missile divisions formerly equipped with the INF missiles both as a matter of economy and as prudent foreign relations gesture. However, the RVSN staff urged the disbanding of only five of the most obsolete divisions. In April 1988, a decision was reached with General Staff support to add a further 135 Topol (SS-25) mobile launchers to the Topols already planned to be deployed, allowing 4 more former INF divisions to remain in the force structure.

In the strategic arena, the deployment of the fourth generation of ICBMs that had been started under Brezhnev finally came to fruition under Gorbachev. Their deployment came at a time of intense debate between the political and military leadership regarding the future of the strategic force structure in relation to arms control agreements with the United States, especially the potential impact of the deployment of the Strategic Defense Initiative (SDI) by the United States. By 1987, the military position had coalesced around three force options for the year 2000, dependent on the fate of SDI: a force similar to the existing size but with more modern missiles; a force without the heavy MIRVed missiles so objectionable to Washington; or a force configured to counter SDI through a combination of new ICBM designs and a Soviet space-based defense system called Fon–2. Ultimately, none of these options proved tenable as the United States and USSR traded off concessions to win an arms control agreement. The final START-I treaty, signed on 31 July 1991, envisioned major cuts in the Soviet heavy missile and MIRV force, with an aim toward creating a force less well suited to a preemptive counterforce strike. The former head of the RVSN estimated that the changes inherent in the START-I treaty would decrease the counterforce capability of the Russian forces by 8 times, decrease the overall counterforce capability of all Russian strategic forces by 2.2 times and cut the retaliatory capabilities of the force by 1.5 times.

## Soviet Becomes Russian: 1991–2000

The collapse of the Soviet Union in December 1991 affected the RVSN more profoundly than any other branch of the Soviet armed forces. As in the case of the other combat arms, the RVSN lost a significant fraction of its forces to the newly independent republics. More important, it suffered major setbacks in terms of its industrial base, its command and control facilities, as well as its testing facilities.

The largest and most important development and production center for Soviet ICBMs at Dnepropetrovsk, the new solid rocket engine plant at Pavlograd, and the main plant for inertial guidance systems in Kharkov were now on Ukrainian soil. There were losses in other republics such as the Baikonur test range in Kazakhstan, but nothing to compare to the massive hemorrhage of development and manufacturing capability in Ukraine. Russia was left with only one ICBM design bureau, compared to three bureaus at the peak in the early 1970s. The loss of these facilities affected not only future production possibilities, but also the maintenance of the existing ICBM force. Due to these factors and the drastic decline in the Russian defense budget, by March 1997 about half of the ICBMs in Russian service were beyond their certified life. The situation with SLBMs was not as bleak, as the only SLBM design center in Miass remained in Russia, as did the two production plants at Zlatoust and Krasnoyarsk–26. In addition, the main inertial guidance system manufacturer for SLBMs remained in Russia. The main Soviet heavy bomber design bureau was also in Russia, as was the main bomber plant in Kazan.

The loss of the republics on the periphery of the Soviet Union stripped away many of the key early warning radars of the strategic command and control network, leaving gaping holes in the early warning network. This could be partly remedied by more reliance on early warning satellites, but budget shortfalls in the 1990s led to the attrition of the space-based network as well.

The loss of former Soviet military bases to the newly independent republics had a serious effect on the Soviet ICBM force. Russia lost control of nearly a quarter of the ICBM force including some of the most recent fourth generation systems. Belarus inherited two new Topol (SS-25) road-mobile ICBM bases. Kazakstan controlled two major SS-18 ICBM bases with a total of 104 silos, and Ukraine controlled a further two SS-19 bases and one of the new SS-24 silo bases, totaling a further 176 launchers. The Russian SLBM force remained intact, since the force was based entirely in Russian waters with the Northern Fleet in the fjords near Arkhangelsk, and with the Pacific Fleet. The losses of the Air Force bomber fleet were the most serious of any leg of the triad, due to the loss of many Tu–95MS bombers to Ukraine and Kazakhstan, and the loss of the only serving regiment of the new Tu–160 bomber in Ukraine. Russia retained control of 101 heavy bombers, many obsolete, while Ukraine and Kazakhstan retained 75 heavy bombers, including most of the modern aircraft. For a short time, there was concern that both Ukraine and Kazakstan would retain their strategic nuclear forces. However, Russia made clear that it would not assist in maintaining these forces, and that they would wither on the vine due to a lack of maintenance capability in the newly independent republics. With U.S. pressure as well, they all de-nuclearized.

A fifth generation of ICBMs entered development in the Soviet Union in the late 1980s in the concluding years of the Gorbachev administration. The main development effort was the Topol-M (SS-27) ICBM, an evolutionary upgrade to the existing Topol (SS-25). This missile is well suited to the conditions of the yet-unratified START-2 agreement and is planned to be the center of the Russian strategic force in the next century. The first missile was deployed in a silo launcher in December 1998. The collapse of Russian state funding has put this missile considerably behind schedule. The Russian Navy's program is in turmoil due to the cancellation of the new 3M91 Bark (SS-NX-26) after a string of test failures. This forced the start of a new SLBM program code-named Bulava in 1999. The decay of the existing missile submarine fleet and the delay in developing a new missile raises serious questions about the viability of the Russian Navy's strategic force early in the 21st century.

The Russian air force continues to be the weakest partner in the strategic triad. Plans for a new long-range bomber collapsed due to lack of funding by 1998, but a new stealth cruise missile, the Kh–101, has continued in development for any upgraded bombers.

By 1997, the Strategic Missile Force was down to 112,000 troops, about 10 percent of the total Russian armed forces, and it accounted for 5 to 6 percent of the defense budget. This was less than half the size of the RVSN at its peak strength during the Soviet period. It retains a disproportionate share of Russia's strategic nuclear missions in spite of the cutbacks, being responsible for about 90 percent of the strategic missions even though it possessed only about 60 percent of the missile and warheads of the total strategic nuclear force.

The rise of nationalist sentiment in the Russian Duma led to strong resistance to the START-2 arms control treaty, which was grudgingly ratified in 2000. Russia's strategic nuclear forces will decline over the next decade in both size and efficiency due to the industrial problems associated with the Soviet collapse and Russia's harsh economic decline. Although the Russian Ministry of Defense has asserted that the strategic programs will receive the top priority of all of its procurement program, none of its programs have received even the minimum acceptable level of funding in recent years. Starved of funds, and entangled in the contradictions between the superpower pretensions of Russian nationalists and the painful realities of Russia's faltering industries, the strategic nuclear forces will decay in an uncontrolled and unpredictable fashion.

## Further Research

The flood of Russian-language material on this subject that has become available since 1991 has not been widely exploited in scholarly studies. The development of nuclear bombs and the nuclear industry have seen the most attention, but the development of the delivery systems has been neglected. An account of the evolution of Soviet command and control of the strategic forces is badly needed. The study of the role and evolution of space-based systems in the operation of Russian strategic forces would also be useful. Traditional accounts have ignored the role played by the aerospace industry in defense decision making, which makes this a particularly fruitful area for future research. The difficulties of absorbing complicated high technology weapon systems into an armed force based on conscripts is also a topic in need of serious investigation. A new assessment of the interplay between the RVSN, Navy, and Air Force over their role in strategic missions may eventually be possible. Finally, the new Russian material could be used in conjunction with declassified CIA National Intelligence Estimates to compare U.S. perceptions of Soviet strategic weapons programs with Soviet plans and intentions.

## Sources and Further Reading

Details of the development of Soviet strategic nuclear weapons and the evolution of the associated force structure were closely guarded secrets through the Cold War. As a result, these aspects of the subject are most weakly covered in available English-language literature. Standard accounts such as Robert Berman and J. C. Baker's study for the Brookings Institution, *Soviet Strategic Forces: Requirements and Responses* (1982), and the NRDC's *Soviet Nuclear Weapons* (T. B. Cochran et al., 1989), were based on limited U.S. intelligence material and are out of date. The author's book on this subject (*Target America: The Soviet Union and the Strategic Arms Race 1945–64*, 1993) provides coverage through the end of the Khrushchev years and will be followed by a more comprehensive study for the Smithsonian Institution.

Although some Russian archives have been sporadically opened since 1991, the material released to date has been concentrated mostly in the early Cold War years, and most of this topic still remains out of bounds. The most accessible source in this regards is the extensive effort by the Cold War International History Project at the Woodrow Wilson International Center for Scholars in Washington, D.C. There has been a wealth of new material on this subject from Russian authors, of which the most comprehensive is Pavel Podvig's 1998 overview *Strategicheskoe yadernoe vooruzhenie Rossii (Russia's Strategic Nuclear Armaments)* and official histories such as *Raketniy shchit otechestva (The Fatherland's Rocket Shield)* published by the RVSN in 1999. Another useful source has been the increasing number of Russian memoirs by former participants in these programs, and limited-circulation histories of the major design bureaus and institutes. However, most of the new Russian material is difficult to find in the United States. An embarrassingly thin selection of formerly classified U.S. intelligence reports is becoming available through the CIA's half-hearted declassification effort. The collection of the National Security Archives at George Washington University in Washington, D.C. is extremely helpful in this respect, and much of the material is available in microfiche collections, which are available at some university libraries. While this material provides an intriguing glimpse of U.S. perceptions of the Soviet strategic forces, it is not very useful in understanding actual Soviet plans and motivations. The early development of the Soviet A-bomb has been covered in David Holloway's landmark study *Stalin and the Bomb* (1994), and the nuclear industrial infrastructure in the NRDC's *Making the Russian Bomb: From Stalin to Yeltsin* (Thomas Cochran, et al., 1995). The development of Soviet strategic bombers is covered in considerable detail in both Russian and English; the history of the missile submarines less so. Missile development has been the most poorly covered though new Russian studies are beginning to close the gap, such as A. V. Karpenko's *Otchestvennye strategicheskie raketnye kompleksy: spravochnik* (*The Fatherland's Strategic Rocket Complexes: A Guide*) and Mikhail Pervov's *Raketnye kompleksy RVSN, (The Rocket Complexes of the RVSN)*, both published in 1999.

Since military doctrine was more openly discussed than technology or force structure, there is an extensive literature in English on this subject, such as the writings of Raymond Garthoff. Likewise, there is an extensive literature on arms control, though little is from the Russian perspective except for A. Saveleyev and N. Detinov's study, "The Big Five: Arms Control Decision Making in the Soviet Union." There has been pioneering work on the vital issue of strategic command and control in several books by Bruce Blair.

# CHAPTER 13

# THE COLD WAR ON
# THE GROUND, 1945–1981

*Mark O'Neill*

AS THE TWENTY-FIRST CENTURY BEGINS, YET ANOTHER RUSSIAN politician stakes his political future on the success of the nation's armed forces in a struggle against a non-Russian foe. As it searches to define its new role nationally and internationally, the Russian military faces an expanding NATO and a resumption of the war in Chechnya with a nearly non-existent budget and greatly reduced force levels. Once the most feared and respected Cold War military machine, the Russian Army today is hard-pressed to reclaim a small fragment of its former empire. It also faces the prospect of watching impotently as NATO follows the 1997 absorption of the Soviet Union's former *cordon sanitaire* in Poland, Hungary, and the Czech Republic with the inclusion of the Baltic states of Lithuania, Latvia, and Estonia. The status of the Soviet Army during the Cold War, particularly in East-Central Europe, as a pillar of the USSR's political regime, economic system, and foreign policy is difficult to perceive in today's walking shadow.

The army has been a defining institution of Russian nationalism among the elite levels of society, since the earliest foundations of the Muscovite state and the origins of a Russian empire. The organic social and political relationship between tsar and army began under the Mongol yoke and developed over centuries; nor did the collapse of the Romanov dynasty in 1917 signal the end of the army's pivotal role in both shaping the national identity of the new Bolshevik elites and carving out a Soviet empire. Although the Red Army had been critical to Bolshevik success in the

October Revolution and the subsequent civil war, Lenin warned of the possibility of a military dictatorship in Russia in 1917, and Leon Trotskii accused Stalin of Bonapartism 20 years later in *The Revolution Betrayed.* Stalin's autocracy, itself an extension of Lenin's "dictatorship of the proletariat" led by the Bolsheviks, was patterned on the crisis leadership of the Civil War era's "war communism," in which aggressive enemies from without and within made a large army and internal repression necessary.

The Soviet empire reached its global peak in the period from 1945 to 1979, and the end for the USSR began with the 1979 invasion of Afghanistan and the Soviet reaction to the 1981 Polish Crisis. It was difficult at the time to detect the seeds of eventual collapse in a military superpower that was at its Cold War peak in size, political influence, and international notoriety. The escalating cost of superpower status, coupled with Mikhail Gorbachev's attempts at systemic reform, eventually led to the end of the empire in 1991. Understanding the role of Soviet ground forces in this process is critical to our conception of the history of the Soviet Union, the Cold War, and the late twentieth century.

The Soviet Army was an instrument of Soviet internal and external security, of foreign policy in occupied countries and many Third World political movements, and an object of intense civic pride within the USSR stemming from the Great Patriotic War and fear of its opponents. Although the Communist Party of the Soviet Union (CPSU), like the tsarist regime before it, relied on military force to maintain its dominant position within the USSR, the connection was often troubled as the party leadership sought to maintain its control over this vital social, political, and economic institution. The CPSU's relationship with and use of the Soviet Army varied from 1945 to 1981 as Soviet leadership transitioned from Stalin's unquestioned authority, penchant for blood purges, and overriding concern for security; to Nikita Khrushchev's international brinkmanship, attempts to slash military force levels, and other "hare-brained schemes"; and, finally, with nearly two decades of economic stagnation, détente, and increased military spending under Leonid Brezhnev.

Although Khrushchev and Brezhnev did not use terror to maintain control over the military as Stalin had, both committed Soviet ground forces into action, or withheld them, as it suited their particular foreign policy or internal security goals. Throughout the Cold War the CPSU, the military, and the Soviet economy remained tightly knit as the party and KGB dominated the officer corps and the upper echelons of economic decision-making. The Soviet military, particularly its senior officer corps who were all party members, was not a wholly passive player in the Cold War. It is by examining the emerging details of the Soviet Army's involvement in the development of the Soviet empire after 1945 that historians can begin to acquire a more accurate picture of the past half-century.

## Stalin and the Early Cold War, 1945–53

The victory of the Red Army in the Great Patriotic War heralded the USSR's arrival on the world stage as a major military power. This victory not only served to legitimize Stalin's regime in the eyes of many Russians and foreign Communists, but it also expanded Soviet domination into East-Central Europe. The Red Army, albeit under the tight rein of the CPSU and under close scrutiny of its vast security apparatus, provided the USSR with political and economic leverage in postwar Europe unequaled in Russian history. The August 1945 victory over the Japanese Army in Manchuria provided similar opportunities and challenges for the Soviet Union in Northeastern Asia.

The Great Patriotic War on the one hand left Soviet troops in control of much of East-Central Europe and on the other shattered the Soviet Union economically and demographically. Soviet military strength was tempered by the reality that its army had suffered incredibly high casualties, exhibited low morale, and was in the process of a large-scale demobilization. The war destroyed the economic infrastructure of the European Soviet Union, killed tens of millions of workers, and permanently restricted the trajectory of its economic recovery. The Red Army had rounded up many of the roughly six and a half million soldiers who crushed the Wehrmacht as it marched toward Berlin through Poland, Czechoslovakia, Hungary, Bulgaria, Romania, and Eastern Germany and pressed them into service to sustain the combat power of the Red Army as its casualty rate skyrocketed. The horrific nature of warfare on the Eastern Front was magnified by the rape, robbery, and murder directed at the local civilian population spread as this often undisciplined and desensitized force moved into enemy cities.

Immediately following the war, the Soviet Army helped institute social, political, and economic reforms in the occupied countries by confiscating and redistributing land as part of a program to abolish "feudalism." The military also distributed food and other supplies to the shattered populations in occupied Eastern Europe. The ambiguity of the Red Army's presence as liberator and oppressor complicated the positions of the pro-Moscow regimes that eventually came to power. While the threat that such an army intended to, or had the capacity to, invade the rest of Europe was overrated by the Truman administration, the Soviet Army was the symbol and instrument of Stalin's policies in postwar Europe. By 1948 force levels for the army fell to just under three million soldiers, and about eight hundred thousand of these were involved in occupation duties, fighting anti-Soviet guerrilla forces, and implementing the policies of the USSR. With both the Soviet and U.S. armies rapidly demobilizing, the Cold War did not begin to take on a militarized aspect until 1949.

In Central and East Asia, Stalin tried to secure an advantageous Soviet position without unduly antagonizing the United States and Great Britain. He backed down from his attempts to intimidate Turkey over Black Sea access, and withdrew his troops from northern Iran in 1947 to avoid conflict with his erstwhile allies. Soviet units occupying Manchuria did not openly interfere with U.S. troops supporting Jiang Jieshi's forces in the former Japanese colony; they did however secretly turn over captured weapons to Mao Zedong's Chinese Communist forces. At the very end of the fighting with Japan, Stalin halted the Red Army's advance into Korea at the request of the United States; leaving that country artificially divided along the 38th Parallel. Soviet military units withdrew from North Korea shortly before U.S. forces left South Korea in 1948, but military advisers remained behind to continue building Kim Il Sung's military power.

Within the Soviet Union, practical and ideological concerns blended in Stalin's suspicion of the military's potential as a political rival to the CPSU. The Great Patriotic War had replaced the manufactured enemies of the state that precipitated the purges of the 1930s with a very real and lethal invader. The war also forced Stalin to rely on professional military officers, rather than just the NKVD and other security organs, for the very survival of the regime. Stalin did not revert to blood purges on the same scale as those of the late 1930s to reassert his control over the military; however, he did order Beria's security apparatus to arrest Marshal of Aviation Aleksandr Novikov and other officers. Novikov's forced confession that Marshal Georgii Zhukov planned a military coup, along with other "testimony" extracted by Beria, gave the Soviet dictator the evidence he wanted to compromise the three-time Hero of the Soviet Union.

In June 1946, after ordering Zhukov home from Berlin to assume command of Soviet Ground Forces as deputy defense minister, Stalin convened the Supreme Military Council to confront Zhukov. Most of the Soviet Union's leading generals and politicians were present at the meeting where Stalin demoted Zhukov to command the Odessa Military District. The message was unmistakable—there would be no challenge to Stalin's authority and the Soviet Union's greatest military hero would live as an example of the CPSU's dominance. While Stalin treated the military elite with a somewhat greater level of respect than he had during the late 1930s, tens of thousands of freed Soviet prisoners of war were transferred from Nazi concentration camps, where millions of their comrades had perished, to the tender mercies of the Soviet gulag system. There can be no doubt that the Soviet military, despite its massive sacrifice in winning the Great Patriotic War, was a fully subordinate tool of Stalin's foreign policy only a year after the victory.

The international nature of the Cold War changed dramatically after the United States announced its Marshall Plan in late 1947. Stalin's hopes of gaining U.S. monetary support to rebuild the devastated Soviet economy, already flagging the year before, finally disappeared and along with it any reason, in the Soviet dictator's worldview, not to look unilaterally to the military and economic security of the USSR. Although the Soviet economy had not recovered sufficiently to allow for an expansion of the army, Stalin began to use the military forces at his disposal to exert direct political control over Poland, Hungary, and East Germany. The USSR could not afford, economically or politically, a massive military presence in every occupied area, but employed a generally reactive policy in its foreign relations. In each case the goals of security and economic recovery were measured against the risks of internal resistance and U.S. and Western European reaction. Soviet policy in Czechoslovakia is one example of Stalin's flexibility, a flexibility based as much on economic weakness as military strength, in Eastern Europe.

The Czech government allowed the USSR to extract uranium ore and ceded Ruthenia even as the Red Army prepared to leave the country at the end of the war. When Czech Communists seized power in the 1948 coup, Soviet military units were outside of Czechoslovakia, although they were near enough had they been needed. Stalin's comparative leniency in this case can be explained by the fact that the Czech government voluntarily made geographic and economic concessions to the USSR and did not sit astride the vital communication artery for the Group of Soviet Forces in Germany. Another indication of Soviet priorities during the initial postwar period was the 531 military advisers assigned to the Czechoslovakian People's Army and the 16,396 deployed with the Polish People's Army. The Communist government in East Germany was particularly dependent on the Group of Forces Germany for its political power, while Romania proceeded with comparatively little overt interference although its forces had joined Germany in invading the USSR in 1941. Stalin's inability to remove Tito and assert control over Yugoslavia during the postwar period is further evidence of the geographic and economic constraints limiting Soviet foreign policy.

The Soviet military presence, while not uniform in each country, was crucial as Stalin negotiated trade treaties that heavily favored the USSR. The army was only the most visible element of Soviet influence in these areas. The political leadership in Moscow remained in close contact with the communist parties in Eastern Europe, and the same security organs that kept a close watch on Soviet society were at work in all parts of the empire. This use of military leverage by the Soviet Union in order to gain its economic and security goals defined its imperial identity and underlined the importance of Soviet ground forces in shaping relations throughout the region. The forces of empire did not always succeed, however, as Stalin's failed attempt to use military pressure to crush Tito in Yugoslavia demonstrated. But it was the desire to use military coercion to oust the Western allies from Berlin that truly set the stage for a militarization of the Cold War.

The Berlin Blockade from 1948 to 1949 was the first of many Cold War crises centered in the former German capital. East Germany was the geopolitical lynchpin of the Soviet defensive zone in East-Central Europe; divided Berlin was its strategic center. Berlin symbolized the sacrifice and achievement of the Red Army during World War II, but it was also a dangerous island of U.S. and Western European influence in the Soviet empire. The Soviet Union's military policies toward the rest of Eastern Europe hinged on the issue of access to and control of Berlin and later of the German Democratic Republic (GDR).

When the United States and Great Britain moved to create a separate government in West Germany, Stalin decided that an East German state should have a capital city without Western influence. By closing off ground access to the city, the Soviet dictator hoped to force his erstwhile allies out of Berlin. The political will, technological superiority, and economic strength the Berlin airlift embodied not only kept the Soviets out of West Berlin, it also pointed out the technological deficiencies of the USSR's ground forces. When President Truman stationed B-29s in Great Britain, albeit not atomic-capable versions, the message was unmistakable, and Stalin was not ready to escalate the crisis to a ground war. He was motivated to rebuild his own armed forces, use brutal repression to install Communist regimes throughout Soviet-controlled Eastern Europe, and to encourage the reconstitution of national armies in his East European client states.

Both sides of the Cold War used the Berlin Crisis to justify increased military spending and greatly heightened tensions. Many observers in Washington and London interpreted the Berlin Blockade and the subsequent Stalinization of Eastern Europe as obvious signs of Soviet aggression and as preludes to a possible attack on Western Europe. In Moscow the focus was on the vulnerability of the Soviet position in Eastern Europe, particularly the comparative economic weakness of the USSR, and its failures to implement its policies. While the situation in Europe was not developing the way Stalin hoped, events in China provided an opportunity to challenge the United States without having to engage Soviet ground forces directly.

In 1949, following the creation of the Federal Republic of Germany, the German Democratic Republic, and the North Atlantic Treaty Organization, the USSR detonated its first atomic bomb and Mao Zedong's forces created the People's Republic of China (PRC). The institutionalization of a divided Germany and the creation of an anti-Soviet military pact were evidence of Stalin's failed policies in Europe, but the situation in the Far East offered an opportunity to counterbalance U.S. success in Japan and Europe. The USSR did not have the economic or military resources to defend its massive Pacific coastline, let alone challenge U.S. naval superiority in the region. A communist China, if properly allied with the USSR, could provide an effective challenge to the United States and security against the possibility of a remilitarized Japan.

Following the invasion of Manchuria in 1945, Stalin signed a treaty with Jiang Jieshi's Guomindang government giving the Soviets control of Outer Mongolia, Xinjiang, and the Chinese Eastern Railroad through Manchuria to the ports of Dairen and Port Arthur. While this treaty could not have increased Mao's confidence in his Russian comrades, he desperately needed economic and military aid. By denouncing Tito, arresting U.S. diplomats as spies, and announcing that he was ready to "lean to one side," he cast his lot with the Soviet Union and against the United States. The Treaty of Friendship and Cooperation was signed between the USSR and the PRC in February 1950, and not long after, Soviet pilots and antiaircraft gunners began defending Chinese coastal cities against Guomindang air attacks. The Soviet agreement with China helped create a third superpower and spread Cold War competition into East Asia, but it did not ensure cooperation and continued friendship between the communist powers.

Stalin's attempt to redress the problems he helped create in Europe led him to commit one of the most dangerous missteps of the Cold War. Kim Il Sung had been petitioning the Soviet leader for permission to reunify the Korean peninsula for some time. Kim was finally granted permission to attack the South on the condition that he first get Mao's permission. The Chinese Communists were preparing for their final offensives against Jiang Jieshi's forces in Taiwan and Tibet and perhaps agreed with Kim that U.S. intervention was unlikely. Soviet military advisers under the command of Lt. General V. N. Razuvaev helped the North Koreans plan and train for the attack, but withdrew from the front lines before 25 June 1950. The USSR supplied Kim's forces with T-34/85 tanks, artillery, aircraft, and ammunition, but it was Mao's release of 66,000 ethnic Korean veterans of his People's Liberation Army to join the attack that provided a dramatic boost to the combat effectiveness of the North Korean People's Army (NKPA).

When Truman did order U.S. armed forces to South Korea and the Seventh Fleet into the Straits of Formosa, the Korean War quickly evolved from a localized civil war into a global hot war. When UN forces under General Douglas MacArthur pushed the NKPA back across the 38th Parallel, the Chinese threatened to intervene militarily in the conflict. Stalin and Mao discussed this intervention well before the Inchon operation, and the Chinese Thirteenth Army was in position on the Yalu by August 1950. Mao insisted on Soviet air support as the price for sending the Chinese People's Volunteers into Korea. Stalin provided air cover for General Peng Duhai's troops in Manchuria, but the ill feelings generated by these negotiations created a climate of distrust between the USSR and the PRC that eventually led to a Sino-Soviet split by 1960.

The Soviet Union did send air defense units equipped with advanced MiG-15 jets, radar, and anti-aircraft guns to defend the railroad bridge across the Yalu River between Antung and Sinuiju and the hydroelectric facilities further up the river at the Suiho reservoir. These units fought U.S. and UN pilots in the northwestern corner of Korea known as "MiG Alley" from 1 November 1950 until the armistice on 27 July 1953. Large numbers of Soviet military advisers worked with the North Korean high command throughout the war, and Razuvaev eventually replaced Terentii Shtykov as Soviet ambassador to North Korea. Although Soviet anti-aircraft gunners and their radar-guided searchlight units did move into North Korea, Soviet soldiers did not join the ground war, and the MiG-15 pilots were not deployed south of the Yalu. The Chinese People's Volunteers served as the proxy forces for the Soviet Union in East Asia.

The Korean War dramatically changed the pattern of global military involvement for much of the rest of the Cold War. The USSR and the U.S. began spending more on their armed forces and increased force levels in Europe and at home. The Soviet Union stunned the U.S. by deploying advanced jet fighters, radar systems, its own A-bomb and the Tu–4, a reverse-engineered copy of the U.S. B-29, to deliver the bomb. Not only had they ended the U.S. atomic monopoly, but also the MiG-15 coupled with intercept radar threatened to halt U.S. bombers before they could hit Soviet cities. The Soviet Air Force and the nuclear arms race is covered in other chapters.

## Khrushchev and the Globalization of the Cold War, 1953–1964

Stalin's death on 5 March 1953 not only helped bring an end to the Korean War, but also set the stage for a political struggle for control of the Kremlin that helped accelerate the return of the Soviet army leadership back into national prominence. A month before he died, Stalin recalled Zhukov to Moscow most likely in preparation for another round of purges. In 1949 the Soviet dictator had appointed Vasilii I. Chuikov, the defender of Stalingrad and one of the few army officers actually promoted during the postwar crackdown, commander-in-chief of Soviet Occupation Forces and chief of the Soviet Military Administration in Germany. At the same time, Konstantin K. Rokossovskii, one of the USSR's best combat leaders, became both minister of defense and a member of the Polish Politburo. These military leaders in Poland and East Germany illustrated the direct role Moscow assumed in controlling East-Central Europe as Cold War tensions increased.

While Stalin lived there was little chance that any military or political leader would challenge the *vozhd'*. Once the Generalissimus passed from the scene, Lavrentii Beria, the head of the Ministry of Internal Affairs, made the first move into the power vacuum. Although Beria had been in charge of the NKVD and headed up the Soviet atomic project, he had been made a Marshal of the Soviet Union following the war to add an aura of legitimacy to one of Stalin's most bestial henchmen. Beria's short reign as the most powerful of the triumvirate that included Georgii M. Malenkov and Nikita S. Khrushchev crumbled when worker protests got out of hand in Berlin during the summer of 1953, and the Soviet Army moved to crush the strikes.

Following this most public of failures, Khrushchev enlisted the aid of the Soviet Army's Russian leadership to arrest, try, and execute Beria. Zhukov led the group that actually arrested the Minister of Internal Affairs inside the Kremlin, and Ivan S. Konev, Zhukov's erstwhile rival, headed the military tribunal that sentenced Beria to death. Khrushchev departed from Stalin's model by staking his political future on an alliance with the military elites. Perhaps his wartime experiences, particularly with the veterans of the Stalingrad campaign, gave him more reason to trust these generals. It is just as likely that Khrushchev had no other option when faced with Beria's personal army of Interior Ministry troops. Whatever the motivation, a new era for the military opened as Khrushchev began his ascent to supreme power in the USSR.

Beria's defeat and the suppression of the Berlin uprising were just the opening acts for the newly empowered military leaders. The importance of the Soviet Army as a tool of Soviet control in East-Central Europe and thus as a pillar of Cold War policy became institutionalized with the creation of the Warsaw Treaty Organization (WTO) in 1955. While the establishment of national armies and the reinstitution of conscription in East-Central Europe was part of the militarization of the Cold War, these new armies could serve as a focal point for anti-Soviet nationalism. For most of its existence the WTO served primarily to control any national ambitions among the member states. It also served to justify the presence of Soviet troops in East Germany, Poland, Hungary, and Romania.

The Soviet professional military elites, albeit still under surveillance of the security apparatus and as members of the CPSU, also began to participate more openly in decision making at the highest levels. Marshal Zhukov, after receiving his fourth Hero of the Soviet Union award in 1955, began to reform the military to bring it into line with developing science and technology. The next year, following Khrushchev's famous "Secret Speech" denouncing many of Stalin's crimes, the military had to assist the political leadership in dealing with crises in Poland and Hungary. Zhukov, as a member of the Presidium of the CPSU's Central Committee, played a leading role in the decisions not to intervene in Poland but to invade Hungary.

Zhukov flew with Khrushchev to meet with the Polish leadership, after ordering Rokossovskii to begin moving tanks and troops toward Warsaw, and tried to bully the Poles into quelling the worker strikes in Poznan. The Poles did not back down in the face of Soviet threats, but did work to reassure the Soviets that they would not leave the WTO, and that they would resist any Soviet military moves. The Hungarian case was much different, as Imre Nagy's government tried to chart its own foreign policy course and called for the ouster of Soviet troops. Only Anastas I. Mikoian opposed sending troops into Budapest, and in the end the rest of the Presidium overrode his concern. In November 1956, Marshal Konev, as commander-in-chief of WTO Forces, crushed the Hungarian Revolution and in the process destroyed any legitimacy the WTO had as a cooperative alliance.

Zhukov used his influence in the Soviet military to ensure that Khrushchev defeated the attempted 1957 coup by the "Anti-Party" group. This was Zhukov's last action as a major political figure. Four months later Khrushchev accused the USSR's greatest military hero of "Bonapartism" and forced him into an early retirement. Konev, Zhukov's rival and a very popular and politically reliable leader, became Khrushchev's champion in the military and presented evidence of Zhukov's failures during the Great Patriotic War. Marshal Rodion Ia. Malinovskii replaced Zhukov as defense minister and one of the most important figures for the future modernization of the Soviet Army, Matvei V. Zakharov, became commander-in-chief of Soviet Forces in Germany.

Khrushchev had succeeded in defeating Zhukov and getting the army back under some semblance of political control, but he had not crushed the military or its leadership. The successful Sputnik launch in 1957, coupled with a lagging economy and the new Soviet premier's desire to make his mark as an international politician, led to the most serious clash between the political leadership and the Soviet Army since the Great Purges of the 1930s. Khrushchev severely reduced the size and capability of Soviet ground forces in order to increase economic investment and to build a defense strategy based on nuclear missiles. As the Soviet military dropped from a postwar peak of 5.8 million men in 1955 to 3.6 million in 1960, tens of thousands of officers, mostly CPSU members, were released from the army without jobs, proper housing, or pay. Konev, Rokossovskii, Malinovskii, Zakharov, and other military leaders protested and many "retired" to display their dismay and displeasure. Khrushchev tried to shift the cost for defending East-Central Europe to the WTO members so as to build the USSR's Strategic Rocket Forces.

Marshal Zakharov took major steps to whip the East German Army into battle readiness and continue Zhukov's plan to mechanize the Soviet Army and upgrade its artillery with tactical missile units. After his tour of duty in East Germany, Zakharov successfully countered Khrushchev's attempt to destroy the General Staff Academy and thus the foundation of the professional General Staff officers in 1960. By 1961 the reductions had degraded morale to the point that Soviet troops involved in the Berlin Crisis were not combat ready and many attempted to defect. Konev was called out of retirement to strengthen Soviet morale while the Berlin Wall went up in the late summer. Khrushchev's aggressive foreign policy of confronting the United States, berating his erstwhile Chinese allies, and supplying advanced weapons and infrastructure to many Third World clients did not prove conducive to reducing military budgets. Khrushchev also used the army to suppress worker protests in Novocherkassk in 1962. The near disaster and humiliation of the Cuban Missile Crisis was the "hare-brained" foreign policy scheme that helped lead to Khrushchev's ouster by Brezhnev's clique in 1964.

## The Brezhnev Era, 1964–1982

Despite being one of the primary objects of Khrushchev's scorn and attempts at downsizing, the Soviet Army did not play a direct role in his forced retirement. Brezhnev, with the support of the KGB, led the CPSU through nearly two decades in which the USSR reached its peak of Cold War military might, but began to stagnate economically and politically. The Soviet Union competed against the United States in a global arms race by building a massive ICBM fleet that Khrushchev had only dreamt of and sending Soviet military advisors and weapons into conflicts in Asia, the Middle East, and Africa. This massive military might was built, at least in part, to disguise the crumbling Soviet economy and in an attempt to provide some political legitimacy to the Kremlin leadership.

Soviet concern with its defensive zone in East-Central Europe did not change with the arrival of the new leadership. In fact the "Brezhnev Doctrine" stated unequivocally that the USSR would intervene militarily if necessary to support socialist governments. This policy faced its greatest test in 1968 when the USSR again ordered Soviet and WTO forces into action. By crushing Anton Dubcek's "Prague Spring" reforms, Brezhnev showed that the WTO was still primarily an instrument of Soviet control. Despite massive increases in Soviet weaponry and frequent joint training exercises, most WTO armies had little loyalty to the USSR and their combat value was highly suspect unless they were faced with a foreign invader. The following year Soviet ground and air forces fought a series of skirmishes against the Chinese People's Army along the southeastern Sino-Soviet border. With U.S. forces in Vietnam at their peak and the USSR crushing Czechoslovak reform and fighting the other communist superpower, the world in the late 1960s was indeed a dangerous place.

After surviving Khrushchev's attempts to destroy the General Staff, Zakharov redefined its role and that of the Ground Forces in general for the 1960s and 1970s. The General Staff took control of armaments policy, military aid to the Third World, and developing military doctrine. General Staff officers, such as Lt. General Nikolai Ogarkov, played pivotal roles in the SALT (Strategic Arms Limitations Talks) I and II negotiations with the United States in the 1970s and administered and monitored much of the foreign aid that went to 30 Third World countries. Soviet officers served and suffered casualties in Egypt, Vietnam, Syria, Angola, Mozambique, and Ethiopia. These advisors helped staff the command and control, air defenses, artillery, military intelligence, communications, and engineering units in their client countries. With the United States arming one side of the Third World and the Soviets the other, the number and ferocity of "brushfire wars" increased throughout the world in the 1970s. This was one of the most dangerous, destabilizing, and intractable elements of the Cold War that lingers on today.

Zakharov helped spearhead technological change in Soviet Ground Forces in line with Zhukov's reforms from 1955 to 1957. Soviet troop strength grew again to 5.3 million by 1985 and these troops were increasingly armed with large quantities of tanks, armored personnel carriers, tactical missiles, and artillery. The cost of building and maintaining this massive international force began to destroy the Soviet economy by the 1970s. The military also had a dramatic impact on Soviet society particularly among the rapidly expanding officer corps. By 1978 roughly 25 percent of the military was made up of literate, well-trained officers whose ability to cope with modern technology was much higher than that of the average recruit. The lack of professional non-commissioned officers, the poor educational quality of recruits, racism against non-Slavs, alcoholism, corruption, and the impact of environmental pollution on the health of recruits were all elements that served to degrade the quality of the Soviet military even as its size increased. The problems of the army were a reflection of the society from which it was drawn.

Brezhnev's regime could not separate itself economically or politically from its military image at home or abroad. The political reliance on the trappings of military power was grotesquely reflected in Brezhnev being awarded Hero of the Soviet Union medals in 1966, 1976, 1978 and 1981, and being made a Marshal of the Soviet Union as well. Brezhnev's role in the Great Patriotic War was officially elevated to absurd levels throughout this period. The difference between civilian and military production in the Soviet economy was nearly impossible to discern. There were military officers in GOSPLAN (State Planning Agency), the Academy of Sciences, and the ministries for coal, steel, chemicals, and transportation, just to name a few. The military was the major consumer of the best the Soviet economy could produce. When the United States began to deploy more advanced weapons systems in Europe in the mid-1970s, the USSR became less and less capable of coping with the challenge, but was even less capable of political or economic reform.

The end of the Brezhnev era, and the beginning of the end for the USSR, began with the invasion of Afghanistan in late 1979 (see chapter 15). The Soviet Army was fighting a large-scale war for the first time since 1945. This war only increased the pressure on the Soviet economy, raised the stakes for Soviet foreign policy, and eventually stirred social resistance within the USSR before it ended in 1989. More important for the Soviet empire was the Polish Crisis of 1980–81. Polish labor unrest once again threatened to topple the Communist regime, but, despite its apparent massive military strength, the Soviet Union could only threaten but not carry out a military intervention. The Soviet Army could do nothing to ensure the success of the

Polish military coup. In Poland, one of the areas of greatest defensive concern for the USSR, the most powerful land army in Europe, and perhaps the world, proved impotent. Although it would be another seven years following Brezhnev's death in 1982, before the collapse of the USSR, the cracks in the Soviet empire in Europe were already showing.

## Conclusions

It was as much a shock as it was a relief that one of the greatest military empires in human history came to an end without using its massive conventional and nuclear arsenal. There was, and still is, much violence associated with the breakup of the Soviet Union, but there was no World War III and it appears ever less likely that such a clash will occur between the United States and Russia. That is not to say that the passing of the Cold War and the USSR did not leave the world with enough hot spots and leftover weaponry to cause anxiety. Unfortunately, peace is still too elusive and wars still too common to yet put military historians out of work. The study of the military, economic, and political dynamic of the Soviet state still serves a purpose for those trying to make sense of conflicts in many areas of the world.

## Further Research

Now that there is a definable end to the Soviet Union, we can begin to fill many of the blank spots that are still left in recent history. Much of this chapter was gleaned from bits and pieces of many sources. There is not, as yet, a definitive history of the Soviet Army for the Cold War period. While the Afghan War has received a substantial amount of attention, there is still a need for operational histories based on archival research of the Soviet attacks on Budapest and Prague and for more work on Soviet military involvement in Africa, Latin America, and the Middle East. Vojtech Mastny is working on a history of the WTO that should help flesh out the details of that critical organization and its function in supporting a Soviet empire in East-Central Europe. The political involvement of military officers in decision-making in the Presidium and the Politburo throughout the Cold War is only now coming to light as Soviet-era archives slowly begin to open. William Odom has contributed an excellent analysis of the economic and social impact of the Soviet Army at the end, but his kind of treatment still needs to be extended back to 1945. The history of the Soviet Army during the Cold War is truly a global history and will require scholars from all areas of the world to paint a complete picture of this era. For Russian/Soviet historians, the challenge is to define the nature of the society, economy, and political structure that rose to such prominence in the second half of the twentieth century but now, as it has so often in its troubled past, struggles just to survive.

## Sources and Recommended Readings

In addition to the following volumes, the Woodrow Wilson Center's Cold War International History Project *Bulletin* is indispensable for any research into the Cold War era. Christian Ostermann, Mark Kramer, Hope Harrison, L. W. Gluchowski, Jim Hershberg, Kathryn Weathersby, Chen Jian, Odd Arne Westad, Ilya Gaiduk and Shu Guang Zhang are among the scholars who have contributed to this remarkable project.

Jonathan R. Adelman ed. *Communist Armies in Politics* (Boulder, CO: Westview Press, 1982)

Jeno Gyorkei & Miklos Horvath, eds. *Soviet Military Intervention in Hungary 1956* (Budapest: Central European University Press, 1999)

Dale Herspring. *Russia Civil-Military Relations* (Bloomington, IN: Indiana University Press, 1996)

Wilfried Loth. *Stalin's Unwanted Child: The Soviet Union, the German Question and the Founding of the GDR* [Robert Hogg, trans.] (New York: St. Martin's Press, Inc., 1998)

Vojtech Mastny. *The Cold War and Soviet Insecurity: The Stalin Years* (NY: Oxford University Press, 1996)

Jaromir Navratil, ed. *The Prague Spring 1968* (Budapest: Central European University Press, 1998)

William E Odom. *The Collapse of the Soviet Military* (New Haven, CT: Yale University Press, 1998)

Roger R. Reese. *The Soviet Military: A History of the Soviet Army, 1917–1991* (NY: Routledge, 1999)

Vlad Zubok and Constantine Pleshakov. *Inside the Kremlin's Cold War: From Stalin to Khrushchev* (Cambridge, MA: Harvard University Press, 1996)

CHAPTER 14

# THE SOVIET COLD WAR NAVY

*Christopher C. Lovett*

## The Navy after the Great Patriotic War

THE SOVIET UNION WAS IN DIRE STRAITS FOLLOWING the conclusion of the Great Patriotic War. The economy was in shambles, human losses were nearly incalculable, agriculture was disrupted, basic industry needed to retool, and numerous ports were destroyed. It would appear that the navy would not be held in high esteem; however, Stalin, as always, basked in the glory of Soviet arms, including the navy. Official propaganda informed the public that the Soviet Union was a genuine naval power. Stalin engaged in the charade and delighted in the naval triumphs at Leningrad, Sevastopol, and in the Caucasus and the Pacific. The record was exaggerated in order to bolster naval morale and to support the necessity of naval expansion in a hostile and threatening postwar world.

Yet the fact remained that the Soviet navy was ill-used during the war. Instead of employing their surface combatants to sever Germany's sea lines of communications, the navy had become the handmaiden to the army. Still, in 1946 the navy's prime mission remained to protect the state by expanding the naval frontier far from Soviet shores. Thus, the Old-School strategic plan, developed in the period immediately before the outbreak of World War II, remained in force. It will never be known whether Stalin would have authorized the construction of a navy capable of effectively challenging the Anglo-Americans on the high seas. If that was his desire, it would have necessitated building aircraft carriers, a point that many Soviet naval experts clearly realized at the time.

Following the end of the war, Stalin was limited in his ability to construct a balanced fleet by the effort to restore the Soviet economy. As Soviet naval officers realized, only naval aviation and submarines had played a distinguished role in the war. Such a realization forced the Kremlin to improve the navy in the early Cold War, at a time when the Soviet Union confronted its greatest threat. From Stalin's perspective, the United States was the threat, particularly as the U.S. Navy extended its might into the Mediterranean. Stalin recognized the USSR's inferiority and vulnerability to the anti-Communist Truman Doctrine (12 March 1947) and the possibility of atomic strikes by American B-29s in an armed conflict. With those dangers in mind, Stalin had to review Soviet naval strategy to fit into the new paradigm of the postwar world.

With the emergence of only two superpowers from 1945, the geopolitical factors in which the USSR lived changed dramatically. It faced an opponent who had won the anti-submarine war in the Atlantic and the submarine and carrier war in the Pacific.

Moreover the United States had, it seemed, usable atomic bombs, and the means of delivery. Mother Russia now found the seas were both the highways for USN carrier task forces and the by-ways under the ice in which by the 1960s nuclear-powered ballistic missile submarines could hide. As the ranges of both missiles and jet bombers increased, so the vulnerable Soviets had to push their defenses further out to cover salt water, from whence attacks could be launched. No longer could Russia hide behind space.

One mission was clear. The navy had to provide the state with a credible defense against any possible seaborne attack. In the future, additional missions included force projection, sea denial, and anti-ship taskings in the struggle with the West. Although Soviet naval authorities privately discussed the importance of aircraft carriers, the Soviet Navy would not be taken seriously by the traditional naval powers until their construction. In the meanwhile, shore-based naval aviation filled the void. In the 1950s, reports had reached the West that 150 MiG-15s had been constructed with arresting gear, possibly to be used as carrier-capable aircraft. Still, Western intelligence was insufficient to produce a viable picture of Soviet naval intentions at the time.

Of course, no carriers were constructed or were under construction in the 1950s. Instead, the navy continued to rely on shore-based aviation as its principal weapon to defend the state from foreign naval threats. The reliance on land-based air denied the Kremlin the opportunity to develop an "active defense"; instead, the navy continued to be subservient to the army. During the Cold War era, however, naval aviation played an important yet overlooked role in the Korean conflict, 1950–53.

# The Immediate Postwar Era, 1945–55

In the ten-year period from the mid-1940s through the mid-1950s, advances in technology and nuclear weapons development greatly altered the war at sea. As the Soviet Union established her new defensive position in Eastern Europe, her maritime frontiers remained exposed. In both the Baltic and Black Seas, the Kremlin did not have a naval component worthy of the name, whereas her potential adversaries were well-established sea powers. From the Kremlin's perspective, an amphibious invasion was not only possible, but highly probable. Consequently, the navy had to be reconstructed as quickly as possible with an emphasis on air power and submarines.

The Soviets learned quickly, especially from captured German experts and German warships, including U-boats, that were incorporated into the Soviet Navy. With the completion of previously ordered vessels after July 1945, the overall readiness of the fleet continued unabated. The navy experimented with improved models of submarines already on the drawing boards. Using the German method of submarine construction, building submarines in sections and then welding them together, the Soviets managed to increase production. In 1950, the Soviets used this technique to good effect in their *Whisky* class modeled after the German Type XXI design. It was smaller, however, but capable of reaching submerged speeds of 15 knots. While the *Whisky* class could not favorably compare with the U.S. Navy's *Tang*, the Soviets managed to produce 240 boats between 1951 and 1957. By this time, Soviet designers were already preparing the next generation of submarines, the *Zulu* class, a larger and longer-range submarine than the *Whiskys*. But there was another issue of concern for the Soviet Navy in the early 1950s.

# The Korean War, 1950–53

The Kremlin found it impossible to build aircraft carriers owing to the fragile state of the Soviet economy. Instead, the Soviet Navy relied once more on shore-based aviation. Immediately before the outbreak of the Korean War, the naval air arm underwent modernization as jet models—MiG-9 and the Yak–15—were introduced in 1946. Shortly, more advanced designs including the La–15, Yak–23, Su–9, MiG-15, and MiG-17 displaced the MiG-9 and Yak–15. Over time, the MiG-15 became the workhorse for both the air force and the Soviet Navy. Soon jet designs phased out the older models that had remained in the naval inventory since World War II. Naval aviation became the premier arm of the surface navy since Soviet surface forces lacked the punch necessary to deal a crippling blow to either the U.S. Navy or the Royal Navy, and the *Whisky*s had limited range.

Since the Cold War, Western analysts and historians have debated the role of the Soviet Union in the Korean War. In the long and protracted history of the Cold War, it was only in Korea that pilots from the Soviet Union and United States confronted each other in aerial combat. Sometime between November 1950 and January 1951, a regiment from the Air Defense Forces (PVO) was sent to the Korean theater. A majority of the aircraft came from the 303rd Air Defense Division. To confuse American intelligence, the Soviets painted the planes with Chinese markings and stationed them in northwest China within easy air distance of the front.

The Soviets consolidated their aviation assets into the 64th Air Defense Corps. Roughly 72,000 men served in Korea during the war, with the peak level reaching nearly 26,000 men in 1952. Lieutenant General G. A. Lobov was the Soviet commander, following his arrival in Vladivostok. While there, Admiral N. G. Kuznetsov told him that he could not rely upon the naval version of the MiG-15, since the United States probably would retaliate by attacking Soviet facilities. Despite those concerns, Kuznetsov did his utmost to provide the pilots and even the MiG-15s that Lobov needed. The introduction of the MiG-15 forced the United States to send F-86 Sabres to Korea in order to nullify the Communists in the air. The Soviets naturally exaggerated their successes—the Kremlin claimed to have shot down 1,300 aircraft while only losing 200 pilots. The actual number of aircraft shot down was much lower, and Soviet losses much greater; perhaps as many as 420 Soviet pilots were lost in the conflict.

Stalin's death in 1953 allowed for an orderly termination of the conflict and also a change in fortunes for the navy. By the conclusion of the action, naval aviation, for instance, stood at approximately 4,000 planes all told, including nearly 2,000 fighters. As the political situation changed, and N. S. Khrushchev consolidated his authority, he reversed much of Stalin's influence over the armed forces. Khrushchev believed that the navy was outdated, in light of the military-technological revolution, particularly in an age of missiles and jets, and he didn't think that Admiral Kuznetsov, who had followed the purges, was capable of leading the navy during the period of reorganization. If not Kuznetsov, then who should command Soviet naval forces at that critical time?

## The Navy in the Age of Khrushchev

When Khrushchev came to power, a major change in naval policy was in the offing. Unlike Stalin, he was not committed to a blue-water navy. So in the summer of 1955, Khrushchev circulated a memorandum from Admiral Kuznetsov concerning future naval construction within the Central Committee and arranged for a formal discussion of the issue in the Presidium. According to Khrushchev, he had invited select military figures to attend, including Kuznetsov and Bulganin, Khrushchev's ally and minister of defense. Kuznetsov's proposals staggered the Party leadership; the meeting concluded without reaching a clear decision, but Kuzentsov realized the fate of the navy hinged on the outcome.

Kuznetsov could neither accept nor tolerate Khrushchev's attitude toward the fleet and, according to Khrushchev's account, shouted, "How long do I have to tolerate such an attitude toward my navy?" Not long after, after nearly 20 years as commander in chief, Kuznetsov found himself relieved and demoted. Why did Kuznetsov fall? The answer is simple: it was a direct result of his unrelenting desire to establish a balanced fleet and his unwavering challenge to the new collective leadership. Khrushchev's decision to dismiss Kuznetsov could have marked a possible return to a neo–Young School strategy. Instead, Khrushchev turned to a staunch comrade and Party loyalist, Admiral S. G. Gorshkov, a former flotilla commander and postwar commander of the Black Sea Fleet.

With Gorshkov, Khrushchev thought he had found a commander who was solely committed to the new weapons systems produced by the revolution in military technology. In Khrushchev's view, the era of battleships and cruisers was long over; he believed the new age belonged to surface-to-surface missiles and nuclear-powered submarines. It seemed that the idea of creating a balanced fleet, at least for the moment, was over. The new weapons that altered war at sea were sea-launched cruise missiles (SLCMs) and nuclear weapons, according to Khrushchev. Gorshkov even hinted that these new weapons might mark the end of the surface fleet. Over time, Gorshkov managed to modify Khrushchev's plans, but first he adopted Khrushchev's missile development program. By appearing to be a "team player," Gorshkov was able to circumvent Khrushchev's original objectives. Even as early as 1958, Gorshkov managed to declare that the Soviet Union was a major naval power and that the navy deserved missions and materials reflecting the new reality.

But from the start, Gorshkov reinforced the presumption that he was a loyal Khrushchev supporter by reducing the size of the surface fleet by 300 mostly obsolete ships and reducing the size of the naval air arm by half. More important, Gorshkov had demonstrated incredible political savvy, necessary in the byzantine world of Kremlin politics, skills that he fine-tuned during the early Khrushchev years. Still, although Admiral Gorshkov was willing to follow Khrushchev's lead, he realized that there was a pressing need to modernize the fleet. One of his major achievements was to use his political talents to keep at least 14 *Sverdlov* class cruisers from the budget ax. At the same time, probably in 1957, Gorshkov started the modernization process with the *Krupny* class missile destroyers, a design started well before Gorshkov's rise to prominence, but identical to the *Tallin* class that appeared in 1954.

It appears that the *Krupny* class was an effort to compensate for the appearance of the new USS *Forrestal* class carriers then entering American service. If that was the Kremlin's intention, the effort failed, since the associated radars could engage only single targets and needed air cover to survive in a combat environment. Eight *Krupnys* reached the fleet between 1959 and 1961. The *Kildin* class experienced similar shortcomings and were the last destroyers armed with surface-to-surface missiles until 1971.

Initially, the Kremlin theorized that the aircraft carriers had lost their primacy, even though American strike carriers were the greatest danger to the Soviet Union. This assumption reflected Khrushchev's own views that aircraft carriers were obsolete, in many cases as obsolete as battleships. This was for public consumption, however; the naval establishment often discussed merits of aircraft carriers in *Morskoi sbornik* (the Naval Digest). Unfortunately, the journal was closed to Westerners during the critical years of the Cold War. Only following the collapse of the Soviet Union and the end of the Cold War have scholars had the opportunity to realize the extent of those discussions in the navy's inner circles.

Most information concerning Soviet carrier decisions came from Nicholas Shadrin, a former Soviet destroyer commander who defected to the West in 1959. According to Shadrin, the Soviet military—army, navy, and defense experts—evaluated the issues throughly in light of recent technological advances. Still, Admiral Gorshkov concluded that the main striking forces of the Soviet Navy should revolve around the surface fleet, submarines, and aviation. Why then, did the Soviets fail to move in the direction of aircraft carriers? According to Shadrin's account, the decision was made in an atmosphere that seriously downplayed the importance of surface combatants. Yet at the same time, Shadrin stressed that this did not mean the total condemnation of such warships. It would appear that Shadrin was hedging his bets concerning the future course of Soviet naval construction.

With Khrushchev's guidance concerning modern technology, the Soviet Navy moved further away from carrier development and placed greater reliance on land-based air power and submarines to counter American naval predominance. By arming surface ships and submarines with cruise missiles, the Soviets were not particularly disturbed by the lack of aircraft carriers in their inventory. For Khrushchev, a reliance on new weapon systems was much more cost-effective than embarking on an exorbitant naval construction program.

## Aviation and Submarines in the Khrushchev Era

Before the introduction of anti-ship missiles (ASM) into the naval inventory, aircraft remained the prime nuclear delivery system for the navy. During this period, the missions for Soviet Naval Aviation included strikes against ports and embarkation facilities, as well as anti-ship and anti-submarine roles. The naval air arm expanded to reflect those assignments and by the mid-1950s numbered over 90,000 men and over 4,000 aircraft. Then suddenly, naval aviation experienced a major reorganization. The navy lost most of its fighters to the National Air Defense Units (PVO Strany). In return, fleet aviation received the IL-28 Beagle light bomber to be used in the navy's expanded anti-submarine (ASW) duties. Still, the losses were staggering; aviation strength was reduced from 4,000 aircraft to a mere 800.

The "*Whisky* Twin Cylinders" were the first Soviet submarines to be outfitted with cruise missiles. Each *Whisky* class had two SSN-3 launchers on deck, and were followed by the "*Whisky* Long Bin," another *Whisky* variant, but with four launchers located in the fin section. It would appear that the new *Juliet* class, which first entered service in 1962, was designed for such a missile configuration, with two SSN-3 launchers forward and two aft. The Soviets were reacting to the USS *Enterprise,* the first nuclear-powered aircraft carrier, which entered service in 1958. The *Enterprise* had a speed of 35 knots, equal to the other non-nuclear aircraft carriers in the U.S. Navy, but combined with the USS *Long Beach* and USS *Bainbridge,* the *Enterprise* could serve as a strike force of incredible range that could easily threaten the entire Soviet Union. However, reacting to American upgrades of aircraft carriers and submarines set the development pattern for most future Soviet naval designs.

The diesel-powered boats of the *Whisky* and *Juliet* classes were no match for the new carriers entering the American inventory. With those threats in mind, the Soviets responded with the nuclear-powered *Echo I* class submarines, which resembled the *November* class, but were armed with cruise missiles. Clearly, they were direct responses to the new American challenge. *Echo I* boats had the endurance but not the speed to confront the *Enterprise* and the other American nuclear-powered attack carriers. By 1963, the *Echo IIs* had replaced the earlier models, and with new hull designs and power plants, could easily threaten Western surface forces. But whereas the SSN-3 had a range of 300 miles, Soviet submarines could only launch when surfaced, further reducing their stealth qualities.

So the Soviets had to upgrade their submarine arm in order to combat the U.S. Navy in a future conflict, especially if the Americans continued to upgraded their strike carriers. As a response, the Soviets launched the *Charlies* in 1967. This class had an improved speed of nearly 30 knots and a better power plant, but more important, the new SSN-7, like the USN *Polaris,* could be launched while submerged. Both the *Echo* and *Charlie* classes combined torpedoes and ASMs, guaranteed to inflict damage on any potential Soviet adversary. After evaluating the Soviet answer to the emerging American carrier threat, the Kremlin had acted with speed and practicality.

## The Period of Forward Deployment

The 1960s marked a further shift in the official Soviet position toward aircraft carriers. By the 1960s, the U.S. Navy had begun to deploy first the Polaris SLBM (submarine launched ballistic missiles) system and subsequently improved SLBM systems, a far more serious threat than the Kremlin had encountered from strike carriers. With the growing prestige of the Soviet Union, aircraft carriers could render a valuable service improving security to the Soviet Union as well as in power projection, long a trademark of the United States. While new warships were still in Soviet shipyards, however, Khrushchev embarked on an adventurous confrontation with the United States during the Cuban missile crisis in October 1962. As a result of that perceived Soviet humiliation, a new era for the Soviet Navy was about to unfold.

It is safe to assume that the period between 1957 and 1964 marked the age of the Soviet Union's limited navy. During that era, the importance of the navy declined proportionally in comparison to the strategic rocket forces in Khrushchev's eyes. Consequently, some individuals within the Soviet naval community realized that the absence of strong surface forces and naval air assets limited Soviet options against all potential adversaries. According to Khrushchev's calculations, a future war would be either a total nuclear exchange or a surrender by one side or the other. The Soviet Union and its navy lacked a non-nuclear option when facing the likelihood of a low intensity conflict. The only remedy was to develop a balanced fleet.

Immediately before Khrushchev's removal, Soviet naval experts waged an effective campaign that challenged the perception of aircraft carriers in general nuclear war. Naval officers claimed that carriers were vulnerable to enemy attack and hence not a viable weapons system for the navy. Instead, they opted for increased development of submarines. Marshal V. D. Sokolovskii concurred and wondered if aircraft carriers were the answer, for the Soviet Union had to oppose the perceived growing belligerency of the United States.

When the Kremlin made the decision to embark on the construction of the 17,500-ton *Moskva* in 1957–58, the navy had the opportunity to witness the relative ease in which the U.S. Navy supported amphibious operations in Lebanon during the Lebanese crisis in 1958 and the effectiveness of carriers during the American naval blockade of Cuba during the Cuban missile crisis. Likewise the final decisions to go forward with the *Moskva*-class came when the USN's *George Washington*–class SSBN and Polaris systems went on line in the 1960s, forcing the Soviet Navy to formulate an effective and comprehensive anti-submarine capability to counter the new threat from American SLBMs.

Naval authorities have debated the issue of carriers since the 1930s in *Morskoi sbornik,* and in 1963 similar arguments appeared in *Voenno-istoricheskii Zhurnal,* traditionally an army publication. An article titled "Anglo-American Aviation in the Battle with German U-boats in World War II" noted the importance of escort carriers in defeating the Germans during the Battle of the Atlantic, and drew parallels to the current threat raised by the United States. In the author's words, only the technology had changed; the threat remained the same.

The *Moskva* allowed the Soviets to extend their anti-submarine (ASW) capabilities further out to sea and enabled the navy to conduct ASW surveillance in the Arctic region as well. The chief weakness of the *Moskva* became evident when the Americans introduced the *Poseidon*-class SSBNs and missile system. Now the *Poseidon*'s range (2,500 miles) was expanded even further, forcing the Soviets to extend the range of their naval defensive zone. The *Moskva*-class did not have the capability to handle this challenge with 15 or 20 *Hormone* ASW helicopters. Soviet authorities realized those shortcomings. Consequently, only two *Moskva*-class carriers were constructed— the *Moskva* and her sister, the *Leningrad.*

As the threat from American SSBNs accelerated, Soviet naval aviation gained in stature. The Soviets realized that carriers could become a major weapon in anti-submarine operations as well as in combined-arms missions with Soviet submarines. Soviet commentators argued for the development of a task-specific carrier to counter the escalating SSBN menace. The final decision to construct a conventional carrier rested with the realization that the Soviet Navy could not control the sea, if it could not control the air. Thus, the period of forward deployment, extending the Soviet naval defensive perimeter to a range of 1,500 nautical miles from Moscow, was conceived. The defensive zone was extended by an additional 1,000 nautical miles in

1967–68, and it was anticipated that this move would curtail all potential threats from carrier strike forces and first generation American SSBNs. The Kremlin may have hoped that a ten-year period would be sufficient to develop a number of future options to the Polaris threat. Unfortunately, such expectations were unduly optimistic.

The difficulty in covering such a wide expanse of ocean eventually forced the Soviets to rethink their naval construction patterns. It would appear that even before the *Moskva* underwent sea trials, the navy leadership decided to design a new, much larger carrier. At one swoop, Gorshkov pressed for a true, multipurpose nuclear-powered carrier, which would displace approximately 80,000 tons and support an air component of 70 VTOL aircraft. The objective was to provide the aircraft carrier with a fighter, early warning, and attack component, very similar to an American carrier that the Soviets witnessed in operation during the Vietnam War. What happened? Marshal Grechko, minister of defense, died and his replacement, Marshal Ustinov, did not support Grechko's plan. Instead, a compromise was reached and the new design was considerably less ambitious. The new carrier was reduced to about 39,000 tons, with approximately half the air wing. In the new *Kiev* class Soviet designers incorporated much from the *Moskva* and improved the ship's command and control capabilities in order to turn the new carrier into a command center for future task forces. The *Kiev* would have a complement of 36 helicopters and VTOL aircraft, double that of the *Moskva*.

Unlike the earlier carriers, the *Kiev* was capable of not only anti-submarine missions, but also anti-anti-submarine assignments (AASW). In such a capacity, the *Kiev* could overwhelm an opponent's ASW forces and ensure the survivability of Soviet submarines at sea. The Soviets had assumed that the Yak 36/38 Forger fighters would be able to overcome the U.S. Navy's P-3 Orion and any other of its variations, since those aircraft had no air-to-air defense ability. Admiral Gorshkov realized that one of the key failures of the *Kriegsmarine* during the Second World War was the inability to coordinate their missions with the Luftwaffe. Gorshkov may have believed that the *Kiev,* and possibly her replacements, could secure a safe passage through the Greenland-Iceland-UK gap during wartime.

## The Carrier Debate and the Future of the Soviet Navy

The *Kiev* and her sister ships allowed the naval air arm, still primarily land-based, to play multiple roles for the navy, from supporting amphibious

**Table 14.1 Soviet Aircraft Carriers, 1964–95**

| Name | Builder | Laid Down | Launched | Displacement | Class |
|------|---------|-----------|----------|--------------|-------|
| Moskva | Nikolayev | 1962 | 1964 | 18,000 tons | Moskva |
| Leningrad | Nikolayev | 1964 | 1966 | 18,000 tons | Moskva |
| Kiev | Nikolayev | 1970 | 1972 | 36,000 tons | Kiev |
| Minsk | Nikolayev | 1972 | 1975 | 36,000 tons | Kiev |
| Novorossiysk | Nikolayev | 1975 | 1978 | 36,000 tons | Kiev |
| Groshkov (ex-Baku) | Nikolayev | 1978 | 1982 | 36,000 tons | Kiev |
| Kuznetsov (ex-Tbilisi, and Leonid Brezhnev) | Nikolayev, Ukraine | 1983 | 1985 | 65,500 tons | Kuznetsov |
| Varyag (ex-Riga) | Nikolayev | 1985 | 1988 | 65,500 tons | Kuznetsov |

*Sources:* Norman Polmar, *Guide to the Soviet Navy,* 4th ed. Annapolis: Naval Institute Press, 1986; Captain Richard Sharpe, RN, *Jane's Fighting Ships, 1995–1996,* 98th ed. London: Jane's, 1995; Robin J Lee, *A Brief Look at Russian Aircraft Carrier Development,* 1996 at http://www.webcom.com/~amraam/rcar.html

operations, providing PVO for ships at sea, and conducting sea denial far from Soviet shores. With her extensive armaments, the *Kiev* caused serious concern in NATO. This would be especially true when a new class of Soviet cruisers entered service. Those warships, the *Kirov*-class, were nuclear-powered battle cruisers and were the largest surface combatants built since World War II. The 36,000-ton *Kirov,* laid down in 1973 and launched in 1977, was armed with an assortment of anti-ship and anti-submarine missile systems and associated early warning radars and *Hormone* ASW helicopters. Combined with the *Kiev,* the Soviets would have a command of the sea combination that was capable of area control for the first time in Soviet history.

By 1971, the Soviets had realized that the primary danger to their SSBN bastions came from USN nuclear-powered attack submarines (SSNs). Combined with nuclear-powered strike carriers, they could overwhelm Soviet ASW defenses and seriously threaten, if not degrade, the Soviet Union's nuclear defenses. The Kremlin came to realize that American carrier-based aircraft could quickly gain air mastery and hence achieve sea denial for Soviet naval forces. Therefore, the Soviets had to embark on a comparable sea-based air program. As concerns mounted, discussions took place among Soviet naval experts concerning the construction of aircraft carriers, even though the Soviets came up with a varied nomenclature to describe such ships. The submariners continued to advocate the strengths of submarines, while questioning the value of carriers.

New technology kept outpacing Soviet capabilities just as it had in past naval construction programs. With the commissioning of the *Kiev* in 1975, the Kremlin had expected to counter the American challenge posed by the *Poseidon*-class SSBNs, especially when the *Kiev* was capable of launching and recovering both VTOL aircraft and helicopters. The Americans then countered with the third-generation *Ohio*-class SSBNs and *Trident* SLBM systems, forcing the Soviets once again to funnel scarce resources into naval construction. This time the Soviets were determined to build a true mid-size nuclear-powered attack carrier (CVN) of their own.

Admiral Gorshkov conducted an internal reexamination of the naval art and the future role of aircraft carriers in an ongoing debate in *Morskoi sbornik,* begun in 1979, when Soviet naval officers raised legitimate questions concerning the navy's mission, naval construction, and more importantly of a balanced fleet. At the heart of the issue lay the naval art, the theory and practice of conducting naval operations at sea on tactical, operational, and strategic levels. Naval art did not occur in a void, but in collaboration with the other armed services. According to Gorshkov, if the navy sought to be victorious in wartime, the principles of naval art had to be mastered in peacetime. From Gorshkov's study of Soviet naval operations in the Second World War, only naval aviation and submarines played a significant part in the refinement of Soviet naval theory.

Soon, Admiral K. A. Stalbo, a leading Soviet naval theorist, argued for aircraft carriers by noting the increasing emphasis that carriers played in world politics following the Second World War. What is remarkable is Stalbo's sudden conversion to carriers; it reflected a remarkable shift from his earlier position. Now aircraft carriers provided the Soviet Union with presence and suasion to such a level that the admiral wrote of a new age of carrier diplomacy. Stalbo did not rest there. He went further by arguing that aircraft carriers could even render viable the possibility of achieving hegemony in regions of the world deemed vital to Soviet interests as well as defending SLOC (sea lines of communication) and SSBN bastions.

The centerpiece of Stalbo's contention involved the realization that the Soviet Union had to develop a comparable carrier platform with the West to fulfill the navy's mission. In this regard, Stalbo stressed the need to build a 50,000-ton, mid-size carrier, which was more economical than building another, less cost-effective *Kiev*. The admiral, speaking more like a Pentagon spokesperson, remarked that the mid-size carrier could handle more aircraft at a fraction of the overall cost. He seriously doubted whether the position of carriers would wane in the future and actually stressed that the role of carriers would expand over time.

Stalbo's article rocked the Soviet naval establishment, for it challenged the Soviet perception of cruise missiles, ICBMs, and submarines in future naval conflicts. Whereas Stalbo argued for the carrier's place within a balanced fleet, others, most notably Rear Admiral A. Pushkin, led the charge for submarines. To prove his point, Pushkin reexamined submarine operations during the Second World War. In the first of a series of articles, Pushkin reviewed the course of the submarine war in the Pacific, particularly submarine operations against aircraft carriers. Pushkin challenged Stalbo's central thesis that carriers played the predominant role in the conflict. The old submariner did not stop there; he went further by claiming that Stalbo overlooked the obvious vulnerability of carriers to submarine attack.

Pushkin kept up his barrage in other articles analyzing both German and Japanese submarine forces in the war. The message was clear: modern submarines pose a very serious threat to aircraft carriers. With the emergence of new technologies that enhanced radios and sonars, submerged attacks would be more effective than they were in the last war. Pushkin grudgingly had to acknowledge that mounting an effective submarine war against an aggressive and comprehensive ASW defense would be costly, particularly with the reliance upon shore-based aviation combined with an organic ASW capability.

Pushkin went even further by seeking allies in the other services to oppose Stalbo by pointing to Stalbo's failure to acknowledge the Eastern Front's predominant role in the Great Patriotic War, an issue that was not lost on aging veterans. Likewise, Pushkin would not accept Stalbo's assumption that the carrier was on an equal footing with the submarine. In his defense, Pushkin quoted Gorshkov's opinion in *Sea Power of the State,* in which he claimed that surface ships had lost their former place to naval aviation and submarines.

Still, Stalbo's critics failed to silence the vice admiral, who called for a comprehensive review of Soviet naval doctrine to take into account the technological advances made since the Second World War. Stalbo made his case in a two-part article in *Morskoi sbornik* in 1981, where he addressed the Soviet Union's need for a balanced fleet. His reinterpretation of the command of the sea further contributed to a new and more savage wave of criticism, particularly his proposal for a new, 50,000-ton mid-size carrier. Stalbo argued that the new carrier should be placed on an equal footing with other branches of the Soviet Navy—including submarines, surface forces, and land-based aviation. The extent of the debate and the intensity of the opposition surprised not only Stalbo, but also his main supporter, Admiral Gorshkov.

The next wave of criticism came from Rear Admiral G. Kostev, who was the commanding officer of the naval faculty at the Lenin Political-Military Academy. Kostev's position as an academic gave considerable weight to the anti-Stalbo forces that emerged during the course of the carrier controversy. The most serious charge Kostev leveled against Stalbo was that the admiral was attempting to draft a new and completely independent naval doctrine, totally alien to the Soviet military tradition. Kostev argued that it was impossible to separate the navy from the general defense capability of the Soviet Union, which now became the central weakness in Stalbo's argument.

Although Kostev and his allies had always acknowledged the importance of combined arms operations in naval theory as it had occurred in the Second World War, another of Stalbo's opponents, Captain First Rank B. Makeev, maintained that naval blockades could be especially effective by using various arms of the navy, such as nuclear-powered submarines, land-based and sea-based aviation, and other surface combatants. Makeev's discussion went so far as to even avoid the term "aircraft carrier"; he referred to them as "aircraft carrying surface ships." Makeev represented naval officers, particularly submariners, who were threatened by carriers and carrier-based aviation.

The ensuing debate among flag officers and their surrogates soon attracted the attention of American analysts, who concluded that Gorshkov could be in political trouble. The perceived threat came from Admiral V. N. Chernavin, a young and up-and-coming submariner. When Chernavin entered the fray his attacks had serious political overtones, since he had commanded the Northern Fleet, and currently was the navy's chief-of-staff. Chernavin's leading complaint against Stalbo concerned his near total disregard for a unified theory.

The magnitude and breadth of the reaction to Stalbo created the impression, not totally mistaken, that a major change within the navy was in the offing. The change in command did occur, but it happened later rather than sooner, at least later than most analysts thought at the time. By the mid-1980s, the up-and-coming leaders in the Kremlin power structure realized that there was a need for younger men to implement the Soviet Union's future naval policy. It is fair to say that Gorshkov, the architect of the modern Soviet Navy, retained his position following the debates, but his fate clearly was sealed by the shifting political climate in the Kremlin. Even as the carrier debates were coming to an end, a small local conflict in the South Atlantic, the Falklands, demonstrated to the naval leadership the value of carriers in a future conflict at sea.

## The Retirement of Admiral Gorshkov

Gorshkov's ultimate retirement resulted from a variety of factors that originated in the early 1980s, the least of which was his advanced age. In 1956, when he became comander-in-chief of the navy, he was already 46 and by early 1985 he was already 75. The logical heir to Gorshkov's post was Chernavin, an ambitious officer, the first deputy chief of staff of the navy, and a key player in the carrier debate. The post is significant, since there is a tendency to promote the first deputy to the next higher post, commander-in-chief. But if Chernavin was to be promoted, a number of more senior candidates for the billet, such as N. I. Smirnov, would have to be bypassed. Smirnov, for instance, had held the same post since 1974, but his advancing years kept him from being considered as a candidate. Chernavin's elevation sent a clear signal not only to the navy, but also to the rest of the Soviet military, that the new leader, Mikhail S. Gorbachev, wanted his own team to direct the defense establishment.

The reasons for Gorshkov's retirement were complex. Clearly, the carrier debates were damaging to the admiral's position. Also, it appeared that some personalities in the Kremlin apparently believed that Gorshkov was unable to cope with the complex nature of modern technology and appreciate the potential that it offered. Likewise, the changing political winds in Moscow may have demanded a shuffle in the naval command. Yuri Andropov, one of Gorbachev's early supporters, had little faith in Gorshkov because of his past record of political independence as well as his advocacy of controversial weapons programs. But probably the most egregious complaint about Gorshkov concerned the fear of a "cult of personality" that surrounded the admiral; a similar charge was used against Marshal Zhukov in the 1950s, following the death of Stalin.

To the United States and NATO, the Soviet Navy as envisaged by Admiral Gorshkov faced a challenge that defied both Hitler and the Kaiser; to maintain an effective submarine blockade of the North Atlantic shipping lanes. To accomplish that mission, the navy continued to expand and modernize, particularly the submarine branch on which so much depended. By the mid-1980s the Soviet Union had the largest submarine force the world had seen since the Second World War. At that time, the Soviet Union had a submarine inventory three times larger than its American counterpart, yet the Soviets continued to build yet more submarines. Western intelligence sources reported to Washington that the Soviets had up to seven different submarine classes in production. No other major power went to such lengths to produce submarines as the Soviet Union. American intelligence analysts believed that the Soviets could build up to 20 nuclear submarines a year, if Soviet suppliers could maintain their ambitious construction schedule. Still, many analysts in the West feared that improved Soviet submarines were in the design pipeline. As the navy expanded so did the defense budget. By all accounts, especially by Kremlin watchers, Gorshkov was one of the best connected military figures still in service, an element that Gorbachev was not unlikely to miss. Not only was Gorshkov associated with the old guard, according to the youthful Gorbachev, he was the old guard.

By the mid-1980s, the continued expansion of the navy was well beyond what the new Kremlin could afford. The particular timing of Gorshkov's retirement, combined with the launching of the new 65,000-ton carrier, *Tbilisi,* raised questions in Western capitals about that very issue. But in many ways, Gorshkov's retirement reflected the sudden move toward younger men in key positions in both the navy and the army. Chernavin's elevation to commander-in-chief did not mean a shift in naval priorities. Instead, Chernavin continued to follow the Gorshkov legacy to a point, at the same time placating his sponsor, Mikhail Gorbachev. This required a major shift from open-ocean maritime offensive operations to anti-SLOC mis-

Table 14.2  Soviet Construction, 1981–85

| Shipyard | Class | Lead Vessel Completed |
|----------|-------|----------------------|
| Severodvinsk | SSBN Typhoon | 1983 |
|  | SSBN Delta IV | 1985 |
|  | SSGN Oscar | 1981 |
|  | SSN Mike | 1985 |
| Komsonmolsk | SSN Akula | 1985 |
|  | SS Kilo | 1982 |
| Gor'kiy | SSN Sierra | 1982 |
|  | SS Kilo |  |
| Admiralty (Leningrad) | SSN Sierra |  |
| Sudommekh (Admiralty) | SS Kilo |  |

*Source:* Norman Polmar, *Guide to the Soviet Navy,* 4th ed. Annapolis: Naval Institute Press, 1986, 109.

sions. The new naval doctrine reduced the need for costly and expensive port facilities in Vietnam and operations in the Pacific, for example.

## Gorbachev's Navy and the Collapse of the Soviet Union

One component of this shift in naval development was the emphasis placed upon Gorbachev's domestic program of perestroika. Chernavin had reported to Gorbachev that the previous assumption that the use of submarines alone could defeat the West had collapsed. In time, Western analysts observed that Soviet out-of-area operations were reduced by 6 percent per annum during the years between 1986 and 1989. Those sudden reductions probably were used to offset the economic shortfalls in the Five-Year Plan from 1986 to 1990. Still, many analysts in NATO countries continued to play it safe and assumed that the Soviet Navy would continue to seek foreign bases at the very time when the facilities were being closed. It was nearly incomprehensible that Gorbachev would seek a serious reduction in armaments.

Those changes came precisely at the time when the Soviets had realized their long-held dream of developing a true carrier capability. With the construction of the *Tbilisi* or the *Leonid Brezhnev* (it went by many different names), the Soviets had to find a way to skirt the 1936 Montreux Convention, which restricted the movement of carriers through the Turkish Straits. In order to avoid the diplomatic stipulations of the Montreux agreements, the Soviets notified the Turks that the *Tbilisi* was a heavy aircraft carrying cruiser, in other words, an improved *Kiev*. Finally the Soviets could take to sea the best of their aviation inventory—MiG-29 Fulcrums, Su–25 Frog-foots, Su–27 Flankers, and Su–24 Fencers. But this development occurred precisely when Gorbachev realized that the economy had to be both modernized and reformed. The Cold War and the expensive military and naval procurement programs placed a considerable strain on the Soviet economy. Ever since 1979, the Soviet economy had grown slowly and had faced the likelihood of negative economic growth by 1980. This startling evidence forced the Kremlin to meet that threat and the new challenge of the Reagan administration's massive arms buildup.

Georgi Arbatov, an influential Soviet insider, noted that although Brezhnev argued with the military at times, the generals and admirals still managed to get most of what they wanted in the late 1970s and early 1980s, but he was worried even more about the impact it would have on the nation. Arbatov and his colleagues at the Institute of the U.S. and Canada in Moscow believed that by building carriers, the Soviet Union was falling into a U.S. trap, since the Soviet Union would be playing into American strengths. Soviet policy "wonks," like their American counterparts, questioned the wisdom of building another aircraft carrier.

Gorbachev's economic and political reforms alienated many officials in the bureaucracy and the military, who longed for a return of the order and discipline of the Brezhnev era. The reduction of tensions with the United States and the desire to reduce the military budget drove some military officers to ally themselves with the Party and the security services. The objective was to topple Gorbachev. If Gorbachev was to remain in power, he had to return to traditional Communist orthodoxy. Unfortunately, many Western observers were blind to what was about to happen. They overlooked the loss of prestige and status within the officer corps, the military defeat in Afghanistan, and the deteriorating economy, and failed to predict the coup. Conservative elements in the army and the KGB played on those fears, particularly with the breakup of the Soviet Union. Soon, National Bolshevik and protofascist organizations emerged, some with the active support of the KGB.

In the months leading to the 19–21 August 1991 putsch, the navy, like the other services, faced cutbacks in appropriations, which were reflected in the Thirteenth Five-Year Plan, which began in 1991. All told, the navy would lose 26 submarines, an air regiment, a naval infantry unit, and 45 surface vessels. Western analysts reported that most of those assets were obsolete and, in time, that the cuts would eventually increase the overall effectiveness of the navy. But more dangerous was the disintegration of the

Soviet Union, which would mean the loss of bases in the Baltic and the Black Sea, and raised serious questions concerning the fate of the Black Sea Fleet itself.

The history of the August 1991 coup has been told elsewhere, but it is important to remember that the air force, strategic rocket forces, and the navy did not take part in the conspiracy to topple Gorbachev. Chernavin may have been aware of the plotters' intentions, but his name does not appear on the Declaration of the Committee for the State of Emergency (GKChP). Instead, Admiral Chernavin, General Yuri Maksimov, and Marshal Shaposhnikov opposed the putschists. Shaposhnikov undoubtedly played the most important role, since he had the forces at hand to use against the GKChP. On one hand, he arranged for the transportation of airborne troops to the Kremlin to arrest the ringleaders, and on the other hand, he warned the GKChP not to attack the White House. If they did, he was prepared to order his bombers to conduct an air strike on the Kremlin.

When the coup collapsed, there were repercussions in the navy. Chernavin had emerged from the crisis as a supporter of the government. The commander of the Black Sea Fleet, Admiral Mikhail N. Khrongopulo, had gambled that the coup would succeed; he was relieved. Admiral Vitalii P. Ivanov, who in the past questioned Gorbachev's reforms in the Baltic States, walked a fine line with the Baltic Fleet. Although he lost his command in the aftermath, he remained on active duty by becoming the commandant of the Kuznetsov Naval Academy. Both commanders of the North and Pacific Fleets retained their commands, even though the local Soviet had its doubts concerning the loyalty of Admiral Gennadi A. Khvatov, since he placed the Pacific Fleet on a heightened state of readiness. Following a special session of the local Soviet, Khvatov was exonerated, yet the damage was done. The coup and subsequent collapse of the Soviet Union further weakened the Soviet Navy to the point of no longer posing a threat to NATO or the West.

Over time, the once feared Soviet Navy slowly rusted away in port. One authority wondered how many vessels, particularly how many aircraft carriers, were up for sale. The decommissioning started in 1992 when the *Ulyanovsk, Minsk,* and *Leningrad* were sent to the breakers. The *Novorossiysk* followed a year later; the *Kiev* lasted until 1994. Rumors persisted that the *Varyag* could be sold and converted into a floating hotel, but it is virtually certain that construction will never be finished. The fate of the *Gorshkov* has led to the most conjecture. Reports reached the press on a weekly basis that the *Gorshkov* was either to be sold or leased to India, which finally bought it in October 2000. But the Russian governments of Boris Yeltsin and, currently, Vladimir Putin are less interested in carriers than their Soviet predecessors. Showing the flag has reached a more critical stage, evidenced when the *Kuznetsov* was sent to the Adriatic during the recent Bosnian crisis, representing a true blue-water navy. The Soviet Navy had come full circle, from the mutinies and decay that the navy experienced in 1918 until today, when the navy has become a luxury that the new Kremlin leadership has found difficult, if not impossible, to maintain.

## Other Activities

Although this final naval chapter has laid the emphasis upon the struggle for naval policy and its reflection in the creation of major warships, it must not be forgotten that in the Cold War, Soviet naval forces played confrontational games in the Mediterranean and the Atlantic and ultimately in the Indian Ocean with USN task forces, as did Soviet submarines with their USN rivals and ASW forces, but also that the Soviet Navy sent a vast array of intelligence snoopers to sea to gather intelligence, even sometimes penetrating Scandinavian waters to trigger defensive reactions so as to glean more "gen."

## Suggestions for Further Research

An institutional history of the Soviet Navy during the Cold War.
A biography of S. G. Gorshkov.
A review of Soviet military education.
An oral history of Soviet naval commanders in the Cold War era, particularly submariners and aircraft carrier officers.
The development of Soviet submarine forces and antisubmarine doctrine since 1945.
The training of Soviet sailors and the increase of deviant behavior, i.e., alcoholism, desertion, and violence in the navy.
The politicalization of the naval officer corps and the role of the naval command in the August Coup.

## Bibliography

To understand the Cold War, see Norman Friedman's recent book, *Fifty Year War: Conflict and Strategy in the Cold War* (Annapolis: Naval Institute Press, 2000) and Robert Herrick's *Soviet Naval Strategy: Fifty Years of Theory and Practice* (Naval Institute Press, 1968) and *Soviet Naval Theory and Policy* (Naval War College, 1988). For information concerning the Soviet position, see S. G. Gorshkov's *The Sea Power of the State* (Annapolis: Naval Institute Press, 1976) or the Russian version, *Morskoai mosch' gosudarstva* (Moscow: Voenizdat, 1976). Jurgen Rohwer and Mikhail Monakov have examined the previously closed Soviet archives and created a vivid picture of Stalin's impact on the Soviet Navy from construction programs and the purges, through the World War II and the early Cold War in *Stalin's Ocean-Going Fleet: Soviet Naval Strategy and Shipbuilding Programs, 1935–1953* (London: Frank Cass, 2001).

For early infighting in the post–Stalinist era, see the second volume of Khrushchev's memoirs, *Khrushchev Remembers* (Boston: Little, Brown, 1974), particularly Khrushchev's emphasis on technology; M. G. Saunders, ed., *The Soviet Navy* (New York: Praeger, 1958) has useful articles that allow readers to see how the West perceived the Soviet Navy in the early Cold War.

For Soviet involvement in the Korean War, see Oleg Sarin and Lev Dvoretsky, *Alien Wars: The Soviet Union's Aggressions Against the World 1919–1989* (Novato: Presidio Press, 1996) and Yefim Gordon and Vladimir Rigmant, *MiG-15: Design, Development, and Korean War Combat History* (Osceola, WI: Motorbooks International, 1993).

For Soviet naval developments in the postwar era, see Michael MccGwire, Ken Booth, and John McDonnell, eds., *Soviet Naval Policy: Objectives and Constraints* (New York: Praeger, 1973) and Michael MccGwire and John McDonnell, eds., *Soviet Naval Influence: Domestic and Foreign Dimensions* (New York: Praeger, 1977); Norman Polmar's *Soviet Naval Developments* (Baltimore: Nautical and Aviation, 1979), *Soviet Naval Power: Challenge for the 1970s* (London: MacDonalds and Janes, 1974), and *Guide to the Soviet Navy*, 4th ed. (Naval Institute Press, 1986) are all helpful; Bryan Raft and Geoffrey Till, *The Sea in Soviet Strategy*, 2nd ed. (Annapolis, MD: Naval Institute Press, 1989) provide differing interpretations by Western analysts to offer a balanced account of the evolution of the Soviet Cold War Navy. Finally, John E, Moore's *The Soviet Navy Today* (New York: Stein and Day, 1977) is a history and a guide to the evolution of the Soviet Navy through the 1970s and is beneficial for the general public.

For a general overview of the Soviet military, see Harriet Fast Scott and William F. Scott, *The Armed Forces of the USSR*, 3rd ed. (Boulder: Westview Press, 1984) is an influential source for everyone in the field. Bruce and Susan Watson, *The Soviet Navy: Strengths and Liabilities* (Boulder: Westview Press, 1986) and *The Soviet Naval Threat to Europe; Military and Political Dimensions* (Boulder, CO: Westview Press, 1989), bring together a respected team of scholars, including Milvan Vego and Jurgen Rohwer, to analyze the threat of Soviet naval expansion to the West as well as examining training and other issues important for scholars.

For studies concerning the growth of the Soviet Navy, including aviation, submarines, and aircraft carriers, see *The Soviet Armed Forces Review Annual, Proceedings*, or various editions of *Janes*. For Soviet Naval Aviation, see Jacob W. Kipp, "Soviet Naval Aviation," found in McGwire and McDonnell's *Soviet Naval Influence: Domestic and Foreign Dimensions*, as well as *Soviet Aviation and Air Power: A Historical View* (Boulder: Westview Press, 1977), edited by Robin Higham and Jacob W. Kipp.

For issues relating to carriers and the carrier debates, see Jacob W. Kipp and Christopher C. Lovett, "Soviet Naval Aviation," in *Soviet Armed Forces Annual* (Gulf Breeze, FL: Academic International Press, 1983) edited by David Jones. For the fall of Gorshkov, see Robert Suggs, "Silently, In Darkness and Fog"(*Proceedings,* April 1983: 41–48). For carriers in general, readers should examine Charles C. Peterson, "Aircraft Carrier Development in Soviet Naval Theory" in *Naval War College Review* (January/February 1984) and Oles Smolansky, "Soviet Policy Toward Aircraft Carriers" in *Soviet Naval Influence* (New York: Praeger, 1977). Likewise, no study of the Soviet Navy would be possible without reading Michael McGwire. His works are numerous and cover a wide range of important topics of interest to scholars such as "Soviet Naval Power" in Paul Murphy's *Naval Power in Soviet Policy* (Washington: Government Printing Office, 1978) and "Soviet Naval Doctrine and Strategy" in Derek Leebaert's *Soviet Military Thinking* (Boston: Allen and Unwin, 1981).

For special studies concerning Soviet naval operations in the Pacific and the Indian Ocean, see Derek da Cunha's *Soviet Naval Power in the Pacific* (Boulder: Lynne Rienner Publishers, 1990) and Geoffrey Jukes, *The Indian Ocean in Soviet Naval Policy* (London: International Institute for Strategic Studies, 1972).

For Soviet submarine violations of Swedish territorial waters, see Milton Leitenberg, *Soviet Submarine Operations in Swedish Waters 1980–1986* (New York: Praeger, 1987) and demonstrates the level of risk taking Moscow was willing to take in order to defend the homeland. For an analysis of the Soviet appraisal of the Falklands War, see Jacob W. Kipp, *Naval Art and the Prism of Contemporaneity: Soviet Naval Officers and the Lessons of the Falklands Conflict* (College Station, TX: Center for Strategic Technology, 1983).

For the August Coup and the economic conditions that set the stage for the putsch, see John Dunlop, *The Rise and Fall of the Soviet Empire* (Princeton: Princeton University Press, 1993); John Matlock, *Autopsy on an Empire* (New York: Random House, 1995); and William Odem, *The Collapse of the Soviet Military* (New Haven: Yale University Press, 1998), who examines how the economic reforms, the end of the Cold War, and the internal political disintegration had upon the navy and the armed forces in general.

CHAPTER 15

# THE SOVIET-AFGHAN WAR

*Scott McMichael*

THE SOVIET INVASION OF AFGHANISTAN IN DECEMBER 1979 appeared to many at that time as a sign of mounting Soviet strength, perhaps even as a milestone in a shift in the relative balance of power between the United States and the USSR. In contrast to this well-executed military operation extending Soviet power toward the Indian Ocean, the United States seemed to be beset with stagnation, having suffered the successive failures of Vietnam, *Mayaguez,* the fall of the Shah of Iran with the imprisonment in Tehran a year later of 52 American hostages, and the subsequent disastrous rescue attempt in the Iranian desert. Senior officers within the United States and NATO defense establishments warned about an extended "window of vulnerability," during which it was feared that the Soviet Union would retain a significant conventional advantage in Europe.

It all turned out largely to be an illusion; the facts may have been correct, but the projections were all wrong. Although some predicted that Afghanistan had the potential to become the Soviet Vietnam, no one foresaw the degree to which the Soviet military would be humbled during the nearly decade-long Soviet-Afghan War, nor how that ill-fated venture, during the Gorbachev era of glasnost', would come to reveal the rotten core of the Soviet military and contribute to the ultimate demise of the USSR itself.

The Soviet-Afghan War can be divided into four primary phases: the invasion and initial occupation; the occupation during which the Soviets strengthened their forces in country and developed a long-term military strategy; and the employment of specialized light counter-insurgency forces against the Afghan *mujahedin,* and ending in the withdrawal of Soviet forces.

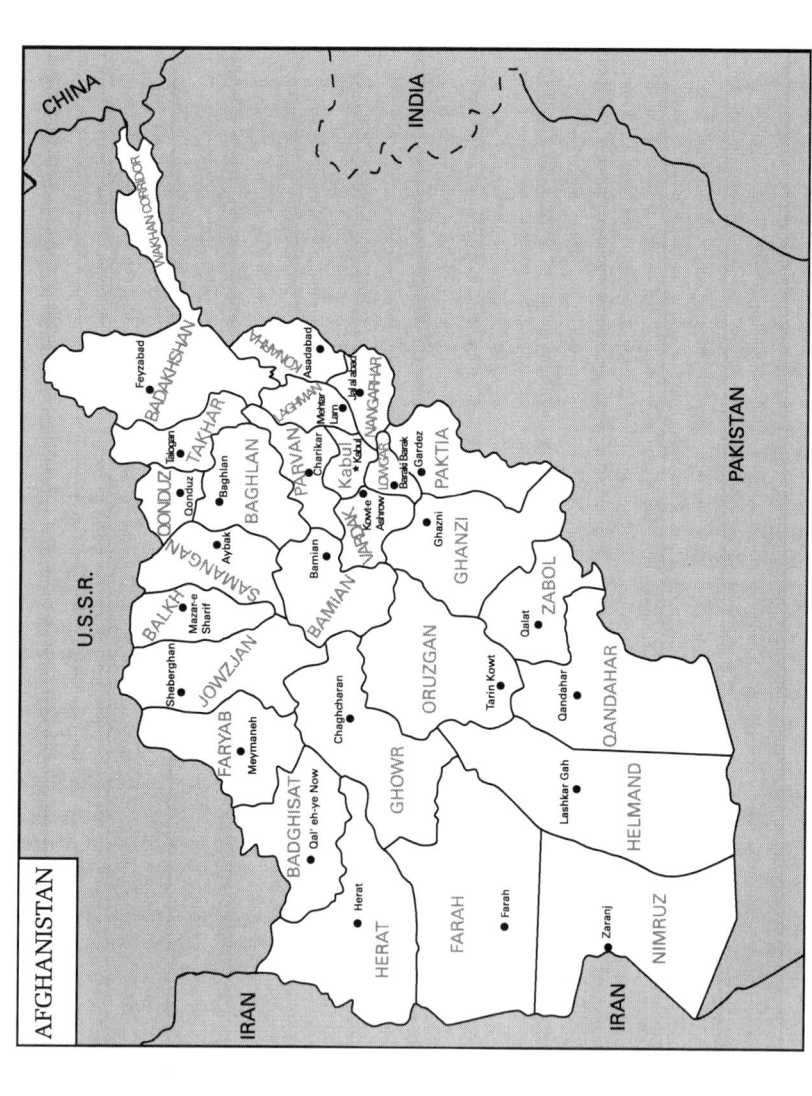

## Phase 1—Invasion and Initial Occupation

### The Decision to Intervene

The Soviet decision to intervene in Afghanistan was taken under the "Brezhnev Doctrine," i.e., the declarative policy of the USSR that it possessed the right and duty to intervene in neighboring countries if and when an existing socialist regime was threatened. The Soviet client regime established under Nur M. Taraki in April 1978, the Democratic Republic of Afghanistan (DRA), had never achieved a satisfactory level of stability, with conditions worsening further after Taraki's execution by his successor, Hafizullah Amin, in September 1979. The Soviet Politboro probably concluded shortly after the Amin coup that the only certain way to preserve the regime was through force of arms.

Military preparations and planning had begun earlier, based in part on reports from the Soviet military and political advisors in country. In April 1979, Army General A. A. Yepishev, chief of the Main Political Administration, led a visit by a general officer team to inspect conditions, which resulted in an immediate expansion of military aid. Four months later, Army General I. Pavlovski, commander-in-chief, Soviet Ground Forces, made a similar visit with 50–60 officers from the Main Staff of the Ground Forces. At about the same time (September 1979), several divisions in the Central Asian military district began to mobilize, followed in November-December by similar activity in the Turkestan military district, as well as the repositioning of aircraft and the establishment of logistical stockpiles near the Soviet border. The nature, scope, and timing of these preparations suggest that the Pavlovskii visit was intended both to inform, perhaps also to confirm, the invasion decision and to help finalize invasion planning.

How culpable was the Soviet military for a decision that ultimately came to be openly castigated by such Soviet Politboro members as Shevardnadze and Gorbachev? Naturally, the generals themselves—Marshal Ogarkov (Chief of the General Staff), his deputies Army Generals S. A. Akhromeev and V. Varennikov, and others—uniformly claimed that their advice *not* to intervene was ignored. Although the true story may never be known, given the deaths of many of the key players, it is reasonable to assume that the strength of the warnings by the Soviet High Command was not sufficient to deter Brezhnev and his inner circle. It is equally clear, as will become evident below, that the Soviet High Command failed in many ways to assess the magnitude and difficulty of the challenges that lay ahead, despite the advantages that were provided by the significant military presence they enjoyed in the country prior to the invasion.

## The Invasion

Invasion planning focused foremost on establishing military control of the capital, Kabul, in late Dember 1979, accompanied by an investment of urban centers and airbases located along the main highway arc that encircled the entire country. Pre-invasion measures in early December included pre-positioning a regiment of airborne troops at the Kabul (civilian) and Bagram (military) airbases and taking some creative, deceptive actions to neutralize Democratic Republic of Afghanistan (DRA) Army forces in key areas. The torch was lit on Christmas Eve with an airlanding assault at Kabul and Bagram airports. Within a few days, Soviet troops invested the capital city while a special strike force of *Spetsnaz* killed President Amin in the Darulaman Palace. Babrak Karmal assumed his place.

Simultaneously, five Soviet motorized rifle divisions (MRD) advanced from the north. The 357th and 66th MRDs moved from Kushka on the border to occupy Herat, Shindand, Farah, and Kandahar, while the 360th drove from Termez through Mazar-I-Sharif toward the Salang Pass to complete an eventual ground link-up in Kabul, establishing a key logistics lifeline. A third invasion axis, followed by the 201st and 16th MRDs, led to the occupation of key cities in Konduz, Badakhsan, and Baghlan provinces. As the in-country operational headquarters, 40th Army HQ moved down from Termez and located itself in Kabul under General Yu. Tukharinov, replaced shortly thereafter by General Lieutenant V. Mikhailov.

The DRA Army put up a good fight in Kabul, Herat, Jalalabad, and Kandahar, but the ill-trained, faction-ridden indigenous forces proved no match for the superior, better-equipped Soviet MRDs, which were solidly supported by airpower.

By the end of January 1980, the Limited Contingent of Soviet Forces in Afghanistan (LCSFA) numbered over 50,000. Initial objectives had been achieved, providing working control of Kabul, key centers, garrisons, airbases, and the highway arc. By any measure, the Soviet invasion and initial occupation of the country must be considered a resounding success. Harder tasks lay ahead, however—the elimination of insurgency, the stabilization of the country, and the institutionalization of the socialist regime—tasks that would prove beyond the will and means of the USSR to achieve.

## Phase 2—Soviet Occupation from 1980 to 1982

## The Initial Strategy

The Soviet goals for Afghanistan—propping up and perpetuating the client regime—depended on the accomplishment of several key major political and military objectives:

- The People's Democratic Party of Afghanistan (PDPA) had to be transformed into an effective and legitimate ruling party.
- The population, widely non-supportive heretofore of the PDPA and its socialist programs, had to be won over or at least subdued into passive acceptance.
- The armed forces of the DRA had to be built up into an effective force capable of defending the regime.
- The resistance had to be eliminated.

Initially, Soviet estimates postulated that the LCSFA would have to remain in place for no more than two years, although a long-term military and political presence would certainly be required. The military component of the strategy described above rested upon five main pillars:

- The LCSFA would provide a base of stability by establishing garrisons along the major transport routes and in the key locations previously cited.
- Freed from garrison responsibilities, the DRA Army would engage the *mujahedin* in their dispersed bases throughout the countryside.
- The 40th Army would support DRA Army operations logistically and with air, artillery, and intelligence support.
- Overall, Soviet forces would avoid contact with the local population while directing operations against the insurgents.
- Once the insurgency had been eliminated or neutralized and DRA forces appropriately strengthened, the LCSFA would withdraw.

The strategy proved untenable almost from its inception, largely because the Soviets grossly underestimated the strength of the resistance and the willingness of the Afghan people to join or support them and overestimated the feasibility of transforming the DRA Armed Forces into an effective force. Beginning in March 1980, the LCSFA was compelled to move out of its garrisons to respond to *mujahedin* incursions in what evolved rapidly into a continuous series of anti-guerrilla operations. By the summer of 1980, the Soviet command realized that additional forces were required. From 1980 to 1982, the 40th Army slowly grew in size and reorganized to meet the peculiar conditions of an operational environment that had little relevance to Soviet ideology, doctrine, training, or force structure.

Restructuring the force included several core elements. First, the soldiers of Central Asian ethnicity, who comprised much of the personnel in the invading divisions, were replaced by others less likely to fraternize with the locals. In addition, separate units and subunits not needed for this unconventional campaign—air defense, missile, heavy artillery, and certain tank-heavy formations—were sent back. More significantly, the forces and the command structure were decentralized to simplify the conduct of operations that had to be carried out on a regional basis. The Soviet command also established independent regiments and brigades, as well as division task forces, because they were also more suited to the prosecution of a war that would be fought largely in terms of small, disconnected battles (instead of the large campaigns that would have characterized war in Europe). The number of aircraft increased sharply, particularly with respect to helicopters, again, largely in the form of independent air regiments and squadrons allocated to provide support on a regional basis. Overall, force strength increased to approximately 110,000–120,000 by mid-1982, a level that was maintained throughout the rest of the war.

During this period, Soviet operations focused on the conduct of periodic conventional offensives carried out on a divisional or brigade scale against rebel strongholds. In general, the offensives were conducted sequentially on a regional basis (as opposed to simultaneous operations in multiple regions) because of constraints with respect to logistics, force strengths, and availability of air support. Requiring several weeks of preparation, the operations typically involved 6,000–12,000 personnel (although larger operations were not unknown), supported by hundreds of aircraft. DRA formations always participated and often assumed the more vulnerable or exposed tasks.

These operations rarely, if ever, achieved surprise, because of the very visible preparations and the effective intelligence network that supported and informed the *mujahedin*. Once launched, the operations were quite predictable in tempo and pattern. Following an extended air bombardment of several days, Soviet mechanized (motorized rifle and tank heavy) formations moved along major routes toward the objective area, with maneuver by the armored forces restricted to main valley floors and side-valleys. Generally, insurgent forces withdrew and avoided contact. Eventually the rugged, compartmented terrain naturally separated the advancing forces into smaller elements, inhibiting their mutual support, limiting the effects of organic weapons, and making them more vulnerable to attack. Soviet MR infantry commanders consistently demonstrated tactical rigidity and inflexibility, proving slow to adapt as conditions changed, and prone to ambush and surprise by the lighter, more agile rebels as they moved deeper into the mountains.

Although these offensives usually gained temporary control of the objective area, they produced no lasting effects since the Soviets were unable to sustain a long-term presence because of logistical shortfalls. In addition, they rarely dealt a heavy blow to the *mujahedin*. When the Soviet units eventually returned to garrison, the *mujahedin* quickly reestablished their own control and presence, methodically driving out any outposts that might have been left behind.

As time went on, Soviet planners introduced some effective innovations, particularly improvements in reconnaissance and the insertion of light forces on high ground along the axis of advance to enhance security, preempt the enemy's occupation of key terrain, and block their retreat. Nevertheless, the overall effectiveness of these operations remained quite low, constituting, at best, temporary set-backs for the insurgents. The finest example of the latter point is the conduct of operations into the Panjshir Valley, a key area located north of Kabul near the Salang Pass and ground approaches to the capital city. One of the strongest *mujahedin* strongholds, the valley was subject to at least ten major offensives like that described above. Nevertheless, it remained under the near continuous control of the *mujahedin* during the long war, despite its proximity to Kabul.

Overall, Soviet reliance on conventional, mechanized operations applied the wrong kinds of forces, tactics, doctrine, and materiel for this austere, mountainous, non-guerrilla environment. As astute students of warfare, the Soviet command knew that change was necessary if they hoped to succeed.

## Phase 3—The Counterinsurgency Strategy

By the end of three years of war, the LCSFA had made little progress toward the achievement of its objectives. Although fragmented, ill-equipped, and prone to internecine warfare, the *mujahedin* had increased in strength and proficiency, consistently maintaining control of 75–90 percent of Afghan territory. In contrast, the DRA Armed Forces remained inefficient and even untrustworthy, while the Karmal regime had fundamentally failed to build substantial popular support. Although faced with a military stalemate, the Soviet Union was unwilling to apply the much larger troop strengths—perhaps 500,000—that would have been required to achieve victory.

Recognizing that time ultimately favored the resistance, the Soviet command shifted its emphasis to a comprehensive and brutal counterinsurgency (CI) strategy aimed both at the *mujahedin* and the population that supported them. In addition to a revision in military operations, the CI strategy included four other core components.

*Politically*, the Soviets continued their futile efforts to strengthen the puppet regime and its political arm, the PDPA. Judging Karmal a failure and an obstacle to success, he was replaced in 1986 by Ahmedzai Najibullah, former chief of the Afghan Secret Police.

*Ideologically*, the Soviets carried out comprehensive and traditional agitation-propaganda programs, with special emphasis on "sovietizing" the national educational curriculum and sending thousands of Afghan youth to the USSR for indoctrination, training, and reintroduction as future cadres.

On the *social front*, the strategy aimed at dissolving traditional Afghan society and remaking it into a socialist ideal. This program sought particularly to undermine the influence and authority of the religious hierarchy and land-owning elites that comprised the prewar social pillars.

Most brutal and destructive of all, however, was the program of *economic warfare* carried out throughout the entire country. Aimed at depriving the *mujahedin* of their popular support by driving off the population through the systematic destruction of the rural economy, which sustained both the insurgents and the villagers, this economic war depended heavily on military support. Bombers, artillery, rockets, anti-personnel mines, and chemical munitions were all used to bombard villages, destroy agricultural infrastructure, burn crops, contaminate food stocks and water, and kill livestock. By 1987, these ruthless policies had produced hundreds of empty villages, thousands of ruined fields and irrigation canals, and 5,000,000 internal and external refugees—slightly less than one-third of the prewar population of Afghanistan.

The military component of the CI strategy included two major subelements. First, recognizing that the LCSFA and its DRA allies lacked the power and resources to establish control throughout the country, the Soviets devoted more effort to strengthening their hold on Afghanistan's major cities, provincial capitals, economic centers, transportation arteries, and key facilities. They reinforced airbases and urban garrisons, established logistics centers, and created a system of outposts, strongpoints, and small unit garrisons to control the highways, secure unit movements, and extend control further into the countryside. These measures led to the evolution of three distinct kinds of operations carried out by the MR force:

*The Highway War.* Geography and austere infrastructure dictated that the logistical lifelines for the LCSFA and DRA depend on the main highway arc and its major arteries. Much of the highway system ran through territory dominated by the *mujahedin*. Naturally, the road system became one of the primary battlegrounds during the war, given the opportunities for guerrilla attack presented by the hundreds of daily convoys. Exploiting intelligence and positional advantage, the *mujahedin* exhibited sound planning, creativity, and effectiveness in the use of mines and ambushes. So challenging and dangerous were convoy operations, that the Soviet command routinely awarded decorations for every 20 successful negotiations of the gauntlet and drivers painted symbols on their vehicle doors like fighter aces.

*Defense of Fixed Sites.* Despite the energy and resources devoted to strengthening its fixed air and ground operating bases with extensive defense works and overlapping security rings in depth, fixed site defense still demanded heavy efforts. The *mujahedin* carefully planned and coordinated their attacks, combining deception with precise knowledge obtained from informants. Penetrating security checkpoints proved to be no major obstacle, particularly at night. The rebels frequently staged artillery and mortar attacks, laid mines and booby traps, and sabotaged equipment. In general, airbase security functioned better than sites located within cities where refugee populations provided food, shelter, and support to the insurgents.

*Outpost and Garrison Defense.* Just as the ubiquitous convoys drew the insurgents like bees to nectar, so did the many outposts and small garrisons present an irresistible set of immobile targets. Established in defensible terrain, their size varied up to battalion and regimental level, but normally fell between a reinforced platoon and several platoons. Outposts performed many functions, including the protection of the road net, providing secure rest stops for convoys, dispatching reaction forces to ambushed convoys, blocking approaches into important areas, guarding border routes, and interrupting rebel movements. In many cases, they were isolated, too distant from each other to provide mutual support unless artillery was present. *Mujahedin* attacks conformed generally to the broad patterns cited just above, featuring solid intelligence, artillery and mortar fire, night attacks, multi-directional assault (where possible), and infiltration. Although the isolation generated significant psychological pressure, Soviet MR forces defended these positions vigorously. When successful, the *mujahedin* plundered the facilities, using them as a supply source for food, equipment, weapons, and ammunition.

*The Counterinsurgency Force.*    Second, the 40th Army devised a new approach to direct operations against the *mujahedin*. Through a professional and accurate examination of their experiences, Soviet leaders concluded that the Afghan fighting environment presented a set of challenges unsuited to the MR force and beyond their capability to adapt. To be more precise, the operating environment required the LCSFA to fight a light infantry war. Instead of large conventional operations, tactical success demanded focused, decentralized operations by small, well-trained, combined arms elements acting independently at night, on foot, in complex terrain, in *mujahedin* territory. Because the MR force proved unable to rise to these challenges, even after years of combat experience, the Soviets withdrew them from direct operations except with respect to the large, periodic offensives. In their place, the command developed and employed a direct-action CI force composed of airborne, airmobile/air assault, special reconnaissance, and *Spetsnaz* units, to wit, the best elite units within the Soviet Armed Forces. Distributed regionally, the size of the force ranged from 18,000 to 23,000, roughly 20 percent of the LCSFA, with airborne troops providing the largest share.

CI forces conducted a variety of ground and heliborne (*desant*) operations, usually platoon to company size, beginning with support to the large offensives described earlier. In this role, CI forces were normally inserted by helicopter into numerous positions from which they could support the advance of MR units, preempt ambushes, and occupy blocking positions to seal off the objective area, the latter being a tactic called *blokirovaniye*. They also carried out large and small raids on important known and suspected enemy camps, supported by ground-attack fixed-wing aircraft and attack helicopters. A third specialty of the CI force, ambushes, focused on arms caravans, border crossing areas, trails, and water points used by the *mujahedin*. Finally, the CI force also conducted combat and long-range reconnaissance, calling for strikes by aircraft, attack helicopters, or stand-by air assault units as appropriate. Units tailored their composition for each of the operations mentioned above, often incorporating engineer, mortar, artillery observer, and automatic grenade launcher detachments to improve versatility, ground mobility, and firepower. On the whole, the *desantniki* (or *raidoviki,* as they were called by the rebels), carried out these operations with considerable expertise, earning the respect and fear of their enemies.

Combining the CI force with the helicopter proved to be the edge that the Soviet command needed to push the insurgency toward defeat. Airmobile capability provided an extraordinary advantage with respect to responsiveness, mobility, lethality, and surprise. Furthermore, the fieldcraft and hardiness of the CI forces presented the rebels with a level of tactical skill far above that of the MR infantry, a level that approached their own mountain light infantry expertise. Although the *mujahedin* developed new routines and tactics, they initially proved extremely vulnerable to the heliborne raiders. The most debilitating rebel weakness was the lack of effective anti-aircraft weapons, particularly against the armored Mi–24 (Hind) attack helicopter. As a result, Soviet and DRA forces were able to employ their strong rotary-wing forces for ground support and *desant* operations with relative impunity during most of the war.

Concomitant with the widening use and growing proficiency of the CI force, Soviet conduct of large offensives also improved gradually. In addition to the advantages provided by airmobile CI elements with respect to security, reconnaissance, and restrictions on *mujahedin* movement, the offensives were aided by better cooperation between Soviet and DRA units, improved intelligence, participation of KHAD (Afghan internal police) and regular police units (*Sarandoy*), and the use of simultaneous advances from more than one direction. The introduction of new weapon systems like the SU-25 Frogfoot ground attack aircraft, the AGS-17 automatic grenade launcher, the Vasilek 82-mm mortar, and the BMP-2 armored personnel carrier enabled Soviet forces to engage rebel forces more effectively.

## Phase 4—Turning Point

Given the increasing effectiveness of its conventional and CI operations, the Soviet command sharply stepped up military pressure from 1985 to 1986 in an effort to break the back of the insurgency. The number and scope of operations intensified. Repositioning of forces, movement of arms caravans, and border infiltration became increasingly difficult for the *mujahedin*. Rebel losses climbed; some strongholds that had proved impregnable in the past fell to Soviet offensives. The balance appeared to be shifting decisively. The *mujahedin* managed to hang on, but their fate clearly was in doubt for the first time.

Help finally arrived in the form of advanced air defense weapons. In the summer of 1986, the *mujahedin* began to receive Oerlikon 20-mm automatic anti-aircraft cannon and British-made *Blowpipe* shoulder-fired missiles. Shortly thereafter, the United States authorized the supply of *Stingers*, providing thereby the world's most effective man-portable missile threat against low-flying aircraft.

The appearance of these advanced systems had an immediate, dramatic effect on the battlefield, leading to a very steep rise in Soviet air losses in a short period of time. Soviet *desant* operations suddenly involved considerable risk. Air support to ground attack became difficult and dangerous. Although tactics changed, becoming less effective in their impact, losses continued at an unacceptable rate, perhaps as high as 500 aircraft a year after 1986. Ultimately, air operations had to be curtailed significantly. Both DRA and Soviet pilots assumed decidedly defensive orientations. By and large, DRA air forces refused to expose themselves to the deadly missiles and became wholly ineffective.

As the Soviet command dialed back its air operations, the *mujahedin* grew bolder. The pressure released, the insurgency rebounded in strength quickly and resumed a steady pace of attack against Soviet and regime forces.

If 1986 was the year of crisis for the *mujahedin,* 1987 was the year of decision for the USSR. Having failed to crush the resistance, the Soviet High Command realized that victory was now out of reach and would remain out of reach as long as the *mujahedin* possessed an effective air defense capability against Soviet air and airmobile operations.

Coupled with a number of pressing external factors—the worsening of the economy, the unrelenting opposition of the Reagan administration, highly sympathetic international reaction to the plight of Afghan refugees, and the growth of public concern within the USSR itself regarding the loss of its young men—the Gorbachev regime concluded that the war had to end. It had become a bleeding ulcer for which termination through a negotiated, humiliating withdrawal provided the only way out in 1988.

## Assessment

Despite a favorable strategic position and overwhelming advantages in materiel and technology, the Soviet Armed Forces achieved no better than a military stalemate against the poorly equipped, disunited, but fiercely resistant *mujahedin.* Although it is a statement of the obvious to assert that military failure is the result of a flawed strategy, in the case of the Soviet-Afghan War, it must be noted that the Soviet strategy was flawed across the board, i.e., in terms of ends, ways, and means, including execution.

The Soviet political leadership incorrectly expected that the stunning blow of the invasion coupled with a short-term military occupation would be sufficient to cow the insurgency into submission and establish the political and military stability needed for the strengthening of the Karmal regime. In short, they fell far short in their forecast of the complexity and difficulty of achieving their strategic objectives. Consistent with the point above, both the Soviet political and military leaders misjudged the strength and resilience of the *mujahedin*. In this regard, the Soviet High Command undoubtedly suffered from a severe *ideological blind-spot,* to wit, that socialist regimes do not fight counterinsurgency wars. The Soviet military initiated the war with no doctrine for CI warfare and only gradually recognized the unique requirements of a war that their ideology consigned exclusively to capitalist states.

Perhaps most surprisingly, the Soviets sharply overestimated the capabilities of their own forces. They entered a theater of war with forces that were unsuited for its requirements in terms of doctrine, structure, training, and equipment. Despite years of combat experience in country, the motorized rifle infantry proved unable to adapt and impervious to efforts to improve beyond a rudimentary level of cookbook warfare. With the exception of the CI force, the Soviet officer corps demonstrated an alarmingly low level of proficiency, especially when compared to Western armies. Despite these crippling deficiencies and the clearly ineffective use of MR forces, the 40th Army persisted in its largely conventional approach to an unconventional battleground. In addition, the Soviet command never overcame its logistical difficulties nor did it apply a sufficient force level to extend its control and achieve decision.

The war also illuminated some deep flaws within the Soviet military culture, the first among these being the quality of Soviet military leadership. Official military journals within the USSR itself noted significant shortcomings in tactical leadership, citing in particular the need for improvements in initiative and creative action under fire. However, Soviet leaders and the Armed Forces as an institution also failed their soldiers with respect to troop welfare and moral leadership. Three brief examples will illustrate the point.

First, life in the barracks and in the compound introduced its own threats to soldiers beyond that of the *mujahedin*. *Dedovshchina,* the unofficial and sometimes brutal system of seniority in the Soviet Army through which the older soldiers exercise power over the more junior recruits, was transplanted into Afghanistan through the LCSFA. Physical beatings apparently were common. Tormenting by the older soldiers occasionally drove their victims to desert, attack their comrades and officers, or commit suicide. Drug use was also widespread, financed at times by the sale of weapons, ammunition, and other military supplies.

Second, medical support in Afghanistan was notoriously poor. The medical structure was inadequate in both personnel and facilities. Preventive medicine, both in terms of training as well as in medical supply, fell far short of operational requirements. Infectious diseases were rampant, approaching the level of epidemics in some units and regions. Losses to disease and non-battle causes exceeded those of combat. Many soldiers finished their service and returned home alive, but with their health ruined. Both during and after the war, the failure of the Soviet military command to protect the health of its soldiers developed into a major scandal, politicizing many of the Afghan veterans—the *Afgantsii*—as well as their parents.

Most damning of all, Soviet commanders also tolerated and perpetrated isolated and systematic atrocities against the Afghan rebels, prisoners, and the civilian population. Although not well-publicized during the war by the international press, the scope of this criminal action—murder, rape, plunder, torture, and more—was comprehensive and prolonged, a devastating indictment of Soviet military leadership.

Public knowledge of the true state of affairs in Afghanistan and in the Armed Forces as a whole led to a startling reversal in attitudes about military service at home. Once widely considered a sacred duty, by the end of the war military service was viewed by most Soviet young men as something to be avoided by any means possible.

Finally, the Soviet-Afghan War demonstrated that the Soviet military, as an institution, was extraordinarily resistant to change. Despite the clear indications that the backbone of the army, the MR force, and its officer corps were severely hampered by tactical rigidity, lack of imagination, and an embedded absence of initiative—all flaws that could have had a major negative impact on Soviet operations in Europe—no efforts were taken during the war years to investigate or institute sweeping reforms. Despite clear indications that the Soviet training methods failed consistently to prepare their forces for war, no significant improvements to training programs were introduced. Similarly, Russian operations in Chechnya in 1994 and, to a lesser extent, in 1999, exhibited many of the same fundamental deficiencies that had characterized operations in Afghanistan, most notably the prosecution of an unconventional war in an unconventional environment with conventional forces and conventional methods.

## Conclusion

Overall, the Soviet-Afghan War constitutes an ugly stain on the glory that was achieved by the Red Army during the Great Patriotic War and heralded for decades thereafter. Looking back now, more than ten years since its conclusion, it is possible to view the war as a near perfect parallel to the USSR itself in its last decade of existence. Seemingly invincible in late 1979, both the state and the army appeared destined to rise further in power, the former at the peak of its superpower status, the latter its irresistible agent for action and influence. Over the next decade, however, the endemic flaws of the Soviet military machine, its leadership, and its institutional culture reaped gross failure in the mountains, deserts, and byways of Afghanistan. Similarly, the Soviet political entity, having passed its high point, finally withered under the weight of its inherent inconsistencies and deep-rooted seeds of failure. Although the army's humiliating performance in Afghanistan cannot be characterized as the proximate cause, it certainly was one of the factors that accelerated the demise of the Soviet Union.

## Further Research

Comparative studies of the Soviet experience in Afghanistan with that of the British could prove useful as could comparisons with other similar colonial ventures.

## Sources and Further Reading

The single best source of information and analysis on the conduct of military operations during the Soviet-Afghan War is the author's own *Stumbling Bear. Soviet Military Performance in Afghanistan* (London: Brassey's UK, 1991). Based primarily on an exhaustive analysis of Russian-language Soviet military journals, this book provides a unique, comprehensive analysis of Soviet objectives, doctrine, tactics, and force structure. In addition to a balanced account of operations by both the motorized rifle infantry formations and the counterinsurgency force, it includes chapters on the organization and operations of the *mujahedin,* the air war, combat support, logistics, training, and equipment testing.

Mark Urban's *War in Afghanistan* (London: Macmillan Press, 1988), Bruce J. Amstutz' *Afghanistan. The First Five Years of Soviet Occupation* (Washington, D.C.: National Defense University Press, 1986) and Joseph J. Collins, *The Soviet Invasion of Afghanistan* (Lexington, MA: Lexington Books, 1986) provide useful overviews and perspectives on the war at different stages during its occurrence.

Army General I. Ye. Shavrov's book, *Lokal'niye Voiny. Istoriya i Sovremennost'* (*Local Wars. History and Modern Times*) (Moscow: Voyenizdat, 1981) is the definitive exposition of Soviet understanding of the sources and conduct of local wars, such as the Soviet-Afghan War.

Regarding journals and other periodicals, the single best source within the Soviet military press on the Soviet experience in Afghanistan is *Voennyi Vestnik* (*Military Herald*), which published both veiled and explicit commentary and analysis on the war from 1983 through the 1990s. In addition, the Soviet Army newspaper *Krasnaya Zvezda* (*Red Star*) and *Voennyo-istoricheskii Zhurnal* (*Military History Journal*) are helpful sources regarding Soviet reporting of the war, including some occasional operational analyses. The *Monthly Bulletins* of the Afghan Information Center, University Town, Peshawar, Pakistan, ran from 1982 through the withdrawal of Soviet forces in February 1989, providing detailed, anecdotal reporting on the war, but strictly from the Afghan viewpoint. Similarly, *Asian Survey* published annual reports on the war from 1980 to 1988, providing a summary and evaluation of developments year-by-year. Finally, during the course of the war *Jane's Defence Weekly* published an eclectic, yet comprehensive and useful, collection of focused reports, many from eye-witness observers.

# CHAPTER 16

# THE SOVIET ARMY IN CIVIL DISTURBANCES, 1988–1991

## *Stephen Blank*

UNDER TSARISM AND SOVIET RULE, RUSSIA'S RULERS have long employed the armed forces to quell domestic insurgency and unrest. The Russian army was and remains very ambivalent about internal security operations, however. In 1905 the army almost broke down and in 1917 and 1991 actually did break down under the prospect of such activity. Foreign observers who analyzed the Soviet collapse therefore celebrated the armed forces' divided loyalties and especially their politicization that precluded their use against the Soviet people during the KGB- and army-launched coup of August 1991 against Mikhail Gorbachev's reforms.

That coup itself was the climax of earlier cases of internal use of the army against ethnopolitical unrest in Tbilisi, Baku, and Vilnius and the use of police provocations against Russia's democrats in 1989–91. The collapse of the August coup opened the way to the end of the Soviet Union, but in retrospect we can also see that the preceding "counter-insurgency operations" together with the coup opened the way to further use of the Russian army as an instrument of domestic political strife in Moscow in 1993, Chechnya in 1994–96, and again in 1999—in Chechnya. Today the armed forces' politicization appears in a different, more sinister light as recurrent internal wars have characterized the past decade of Russian military history. Even before the August coup some of these trends were visible and led some analysts to predict future domestic wars in the former Soviet Union.

Effective civilian control of the armed forces (including the Army, MVD, KGB, etc.) is not just a sine qua non of democracy, but also of a stable state. Too few analysts of Russia's supposedly democratic transformation have grasped this point and many altogether omit this issue from their assessment of Russian democracy's evolution. Such incomplete analysis misrepresents and overlooks many of the more unpleasant and inconvenient realities of the last decade regarding the armed forces' role and place in Russia. A careful examination of the post-1989 record suggests that military politicization in Russia represents the political decay of the institutions of civilian controls and of the armed forces themselves, as well as a profound and lasting obstacle to Russia's democratization, if not its survival as a state. Even as democratization grew within the military, the accompanying politicization was sowing the seeds of an opposing reaction against military democratization.

The revolutionary crisis of 1989–91 had not peaked when the August coup occurred. To borrow Marxist-Leninist terms describing earlier periods in Russian history, this revolutionary crisis appeared as a profound crisis of all the Soviet elites, not just the armed forces, and manifested itself both as a struggle to reform the Soviet system and to gain power over that transformation. But whereas the awakening of formerly repressed sectors of the Soviet population undoubtedly represented, at least in part, democratic or democratizing processes, the politicization of the various armed forces unleashed trends and temptations among them and their civilian leaders of a rather different order. Precisely because of the armed forces' functional role as experts in the legitimate use of armed force, the struggle over their role in Soviet affairs and their actual deployments were essential aspects of the key issue in any revolution, namely the struggle for power.

This politicization had a dual aspect. On the one hand, serving military officers now participated in uniform in public debates in Soviet or rival elected institutions. Thus many officers developed a taste for playing an active political role. Second, military politicization generated a continuing process of force restructuring to cope with the broader revolutionary crisis of the state and the revolutionary and ethnic struggles for power. Therefore the armed forces increasingly came under pressure to restructure and become a force used mainly for domestic purposes. They thereby experienced and participated in the splintering of that monopoly of force into many institutions even while performing their original mission of defending the state against external threats. Simultaneously ethnic, politicized, and irregular forces were forming to advance nationalist agendas against the unity of the state and the armed forces' hitherto sacred mission. All of these processes represented visible signs of decay in the armed forces and a harbinger, in the long term, not necessarily of democratization, but of a failing state. A decade after the Soviet collapse, Yeltsin's, and now, Putin's Russia still could not organize a functioning regular state that could enforce a state's legitimate and basic prerogatives or provide any regular basis for the development, formulation, and implementation of military policy. Even civil peace has proved elusive.

There are many related symptoms of this failure in regard to defense policy. The absence of any reliable, lawful, accountable system for formulating and implementing defense policy is one key element in this process. Second is the multiplication of agencies having statutory rights to bear arms and conduct quasi-military operations within Russia, another development with roots in this period. Third is the fact that the Russian Army's main missions in this decade have uniformly been domestic, making it primarily a force for internal war.

The development of the political struggle within and around the armed forces has been ably covered by Western historians, notably William Odom and Robert Barylski, and by the memoirs of such generals as Evgenii Shaposhnikov and Alexander Lebed. Much less attention, however, has been paid to the destructive parallel tendency to convert the military into forces optimized or intended for domestic counter-insurgency roles.

## The Creation of an Internal Army

The creation and configuration of forces deployed for those contingencies, their missions of quelling unrest and of rapidly neutralizing the enemy's command, control, communications, and its capacity to resist, and the process by which these mission-specific forces were organized can be traced back to the invasion of Afghanistan and subsequent operations there. The armed forces' post-1989 interventions against national and reform movements were the missions for which they were created. The Baltic operations of January 1991 showed that Soviet armed forces—including KGB and MVD forces—were increasingly organized and deployed for domestic counterinsurgency missions. In the Baltic operations elite *Spetsnaz* (specially designated forces; in Russian, *Voiska Spetsial'nogo Naznacheniya*), and airborne troops—precisely those forces that distinguished themselves by their performance in Afghanistan—took the lead.

Moscow reorganized these forces to perform both internal security missions and low intensity conflicts from their original sources in the Army or KGB, or MVD, according to its traditional practice of tailoring force packages to missions. Lessons from Afghanistan, particularly those relevant to the initial invasion of Kabul and the political tasks of dividing ethnic groups among themselves, were used to shape these forces' composition, missions, operational art, and strategy. Their operational structure also conformed to the later organization of Soviet forces in Afghanistan. Finally, the Baltic operations followed a strategic operational plan called Operation Metel' (Winter Storm), involving the use of combined KGB, MVD, and Army forces. It was first employed during Kazakhstan's protests in December 1986 and steadily refined thereafter.

These new force packages represented significant innovations for Soviet military-political leaders since their missions and even the names for them were new and often foreign. The gap between the U.S. terms—low intensity conflict (LIC) and counterinsurgency—and the Soviet term—local war— highlighted the enduring differences between the two militaries. The Soviets considered low intensity conflict and counterinsurgency to be Western concepts for sub-categories of what they call local war, and showed little readiness to examine unconventional war scenarios since 1945 despite their own extensive counterinsurgency and partisan warfare experience. Instead, Soviet examination of local wars in the Third World or Europe, such as the Spanish Civil War, focused exclusively on conventional scenarios and provided no operational-strategic lessons for conducting anti-guerilla wars.

These conceptual lacunas in Soviet thinking existed as well in official dictionaries and encyclopedias. The last *Soviet English-Russian Military Dictionary* had no Russian equivalent for "Local War," "Low Intensity Conflict," or "Unconventional War." And for the term "Guerrilla," the definition is either "partisan (soldier)" or a "diversionary-Desant [airborne or *Spetsnaz* in common parlance] force applying partisan tactics." The *1988 Dictionary of Military Terms* also omitted LIC and defined Local War as "a war, distinct from a world war, embracing relatively few states and a limited geographical area. Local war often appears due to the guilt of imperialistic states." This definition followed the *1986 Military-Encyclopedic Dictionary*'s description of the term. This dictionary also defined counterinsurgency activities or operations (*Protivopovstancheskie Deistviya*) as a purely imperialist series of punitive police, military, and subversive operations taken against the national liberation movements. Even reformers admitted that because such local wars still retained political utility, Moscow could become involved in those wars. But they and conservatives alike recoiled from admitting that Moscow could play an openly counterrevolutionary or counterinsurgency role in these smaller wars. Thus, Moscow lacked adequate situation-specific doctrine, strategy, and operational art for scenarios in which it was the counterinsurgent force.

## Soviet Acceptance of Low Intensity Conflict: The Link between Forces and Doctrine

Continuing crises after 1988 led some to suggest introducing the LIC concept into Soviet military planning and learning from the U.S. example. Sergei Ignat'ev cited the U.S. development and upgrading of highly mobile "light" general purpose and special forces during the 1980s. Citing the U.S. intervention in Panama in 1989–90, he favorably commented on the specialization of units with reference to their mission.

> [G]round forces alone have within them Ranger battalions (rescue and sabotage actions, military operations in urban conditions), battalions for psychological operations, groups of "civil administration," etc. Also, the use of special operating forces is closely linked up with operational plans of general-purpose forces. (Sergei Ignat'iev, "Low-Intensity Conflicts and Military Reform in the Soviet Union," *APN Military Herald*, no. 2, 1990, pp. 8–11.)

Ignat'ev recommended that Moscow develop analogous forces particularly since military, KGB, and Interior (MVD) troops were used within various Soviet republics to mount peacekeeping operations, form civil administration agencies, evacuate refugees, rescue hostages, and lift blockades. Therefore, specialized professional forces must exist within the regular armed forces' framework. Their missions and operations should also be "agreed and closely linked with general operational tasks of the armed forces in ensuring reliable defense of the country."

That Soviet leaders clearly took Ignat'ev's article seriously is evident from the fact that subsequent changes followed his recommendations to coordinate the armed forces' internal and external missions and forces. Moscow specialized certain units, making KGB, MVD, and Ministry of Defense (MoD) forces "interoperable" for internal security and conventional missions. The combination of KGB border troops, MVD forces, and *Spetsnaz* formations (which existed within KGB, MVD, and all the regular armed forces) created an increasingly fungible force available to commanders at the theater level or below to accomplish strategic, operational, and tactical missions. The mission's nature, not the force's name, now defined both these forces' composition and their "special" designation.

The combination of new Soviet forces, missions, and planning requirements at all levels for a doctrine and strategy for their use and for surprise and *maskirovka* (deception) at all levels signaled the creation of a Soviet equivalent to the U.S. Rapid Deployment Force. This force could be rapidly mobilized from ostensibly non-military (militia or paramilitary) forces for assignments at home or abroad. It was composed either of airborne divisions, airmobile Motorized Rifle Divisions, or elements from either group, heliborne Air Assault Brigades, and/or the Airborne Troops.

The creation of such a force structure, and the related command, control, and communication ($C^3$) reforms, suggest that a prior operational plan did exist—in this case, Operation *Metel*—and required integrated, fungible forces. By creating these "fungible" and flexible forces for low, middle, or high intensity missions and counterinsurgency, Moscow could use its most professional and ethnically and politically reliable forces. These units also belonged to the General Staff and would therefore be less likely to have morale problems in internal security work. They saved Moscow from having to rely upon conscripted forces whose quality and reliability was increasingly dubious.

## The Components of the New Forces

These new force structures included forces from the Airborne Troops (VDV) under regular military control and those seconded to either the KGB or the MVD. Motorized Rifle Divisions, or forces under regular command, also were reconstituted for such purposes, as were various *Spetsnaz* forces in the Army, Navy, MVD, KGB, and Soviet Naval Infantry forces who received parachute training. All these units evidently functioned under the operational command of the front or theater commander who was directly under the *Stavka* VGK (the Supreme High Command) and its superior organ, Gorbachev's newly created Security Council.

The *Spetsnaz* and Airborne forces, like the MVD and KGB Border Troops, had substantial combat training and experience dating back to counterinsurgency operations since the Civil War. Now they underwent substantial reorganization and deployment. For example, in 1988, *Spetsnaz* forces were established within the MVD to conduct anti-terrorist, anti-criminal, and counterinsurgency operations. In the regular armed forces during peacetime each Military District was assigned a *Spetsnaz* brigade, which could be used by Front Headquarters only with the concurrence of General Headquarters. After 1986, army-level *Spetsnaz* units were placed under Army Headquarters, a change designed to give armies more independence and very likely a reflection of Afghan experience that illustrated the utility of decentralized and flexible command and control.

The MVD also created specially designated forces, often consisting of Afghan veterans, to deal with crime, drug running, rioting, inter-ethnic strife, and counterinsurgency operations. These forces were in some sense distinct from the MVD *Spetsnaz* forces. Thus KGB, MVD, and regular armed forces were restructured to expand the number of trained and experienced units who could be tasked for "special" missions and act as *Spetsnaz* forces. By 1991, then, the term *Spetsnaz* was no longer confined to the forces previously identified by Western observers. Indeed, the original Airborne battalions in the 1930s, like the original heliborne forces in the 1960s, were identified as *Spetsnaz*, which indicates that what was special was their mission, not their designation within the military structure. Thus, the term *Spetsnaz* became mission-specific and the principle of mission tailored forces continued.

This process of force restructuring to meet domestic contingencies became a planned operation. Its consequences became visible in the Baltics, with the dispatch of troops to a total of seven republics, and the decree of 29 December 1990 (not announced until 26 January 1991) that gave the military nationwide police missions and powers. This force restructuring was accompanied by an orchestrated threat assessment that was publicly disseminated to create a pretext for military intervention. There also was an accompanying *maskirovka* plan comprising: deception; psychological warfare to keep the targets off balance; alternating threats with ultimatums and apparent invitations to negotiate; and disinformation for foreign and domestic audiences regarding both the dispatch of troops to the Baltics and the issuance of orders to use force.

We can trace force restructuring within the following forces in detail: MVD Internal Troops, KGB Border Troops, the Airborne troops, Naval Infantry, and those forces previously known to be or identified as being *Spetsnaz*. Soviet planning for its multi-purpose rapid deployment force began no later than mid-1990 and was clearly a response to the uprisings in Tbilisi and Baku. In those instances ethnic mobilization stimulated massive anti-Moscow demonstrations and led Moscow to authorize the use of force against the demonstrators. In both cases it is now clear that the Politburo and Gorbachev refused to accept responsibility for their actions. This unfortunate precedent created a well-known "Tbilisi syndrome" and undermined the officer corps and the soldiers' belief in the legitimacy or viability of their political leadership. In Baku the KGB even played a large role in deliberately inciting nationalist reformers into excesses that could justify the use of force against them. The government's failure here as later in the Baltics and Moscow only bred more military disillusionment and politicization paralleling that of the restive minorities and reformers in Moscow.

# Preparing for Operation Metel'

The development of MVD, KGB, and railroad troops for domestic and/or foreign contingencies showed the military leaderships' planning for domestic contingencies. The December 1990 appointment of General Boris Gromov to the post of deputy minister of the MVD stimulated rumors that regular army divisions were being transferred to the MVD. Second, Gorbachev's new Soviet Security Council can be seen as an attempt to unify command of all available armed forces at the highest single centralized level. Third, the appointment of the commander of the Airborne Troops, Colonel General Vladislav Achalov, a passionate Russian nationalist, as deputy defense minister in the summer of 1990, can also be seen as facilitating those troops' use for internal security missions with the MVD and KGB. Finally, MVD efforts to transfer control over MVD troops from the republics to Moscow fits in with efforts to place all forces for any contingency under Gorbachev's centralized control and certainly foretold the August 1991 coup. The troops most readily used to quell internal unrest were the same ones that led the invasion and that were most useful in Afghanistan: Airborne forces, heliborne troops, and *Spetsnaz.*

In each branch of the MVD, KGB, Airborne, and heliborne units, forces capable of conducting internal and external security operations were developed. MVD forces' modernization accelerated in the wake of rising crime and inter-ethnic unrest. The commander of the MVD Internal Troops, MVD Colonel General Yuri Shatalin, created so-called Operational Designation Units (*Operativnoe Naznachenie,* or OPNAZ). The largest one was the Dzerzhinskii MVD Motorized Rifle Division in Moscow that still guards key government facilities. After 1988, it was fragmented to deal with many domestic crises, but rising inter-ethnic violence during 1988–90 led Moscow to increase the OPNAZ's numbers and quality in order to professionalize them. A second MVD "special force" was the MVD *Spetsnaz,* which numbered "several companies." A third force, subordinated to republican authorities, was the anti-riot forces, known as the OMON (*Otryad Militsii Osobogo Naznacheniya,* or Special Purpose Militia Detachments). They were also known as the Black Berets. Finally, anti-terrorist forces were formed within the MVD, but it is hard to distinguish them from the MVD *Spetsnaz.* The KGB also created an anti-terrorist force as well, whose active combat element would be deployed alongside that of the MVD. Its personnel could be recruited from other sources such as the Border Troops and the KGB forces assigned to protect key party leaders and offices, not to mention more shadowy KGB departments.

The MVD forces were already spending 70–80 percent of their time policing inter-ethnic conflicts and could not fully cope with criminal actions, such as drug trafficking. Soviet media reports increasingly cited the presence of forces answering to the OMON description for use against criminal activities. These troops were heavily staffed from former Airborne, Naval Infantry, and MVD *Spetsnaz* elements. Since the KGB had traditionally handled smuggling and cross-border infiltration issues, formation of such units expanded coordination between the KGB and MVD. In any case, the KGB had thoroughly penetrated and reorganized the MVD since Leonid Brezhnev's death, when Yuri Andropov's men took it over.

Soviet counternarcotics efforts also provided a possible template for using these forces. Those missions were concentrated along the USSR's southern borders in Central Asia, an area of concern to the central leadership for ethno-religious reasons as well. Frequent press reports alleged cross-border religious infiltration from Afghanistan, sometimes in conjunction with drug smuggling. So one threat provided good reason for expanding the border forces to fight the other threat as well. Other anti-drug forces included Special Sections (*Osobye Otdely*) of KGB Counterintelligence that were present in troops down to tactical levels, and were charged with preventing subversive activities among them. At least some spokesmen for these forces tied anti-drug operations to ethnic unrest in the Transcaucasus. Finally, helicopter forces were also used in anti-drug operations. Military participation in counternarcotics roles could also eventually involve the heavier use of aviation components, military counterintelligence (KGB *Osobye Otdely* elements), intelligence-gathering resources of the General Staff's Main Intelligence Directorate (GRU), lower-level military intelligence reconnaissance units, and ground maneuver or special operations (military *Spetsnaz*) forces.

The rising tide of ethnic unrest placed additional severe burdens on the MVD as a whole and its internal *Spetsnaz* forces in particular, as well as on the regular army and KGB forces. In 1990 in Moldova, Gorbachev gave the republic until 1 January 1991 to rescind its independence or else he would send in troops; the republic backed down. Later that month, he sent Soviet troops into the Baltics. In talks with Defense Minister Dmitrii Yazov, Finnish Defense Minister Elizabeth Rehn had earlier voiced traditional Finnish concerns about troop movements to the Baltics.

> I was interested in possible material and troops, especially if their numbers are increasing in areas close to Finland. I received very unambiguous replies that if there is an increase, then there will be reductions at the same

time, so that the number would remain unchanged. It is a question of special troops, which would possibly be increased, but at the same time other troops will be withdrawn. ("Finland's Rehn on Military Talks with Yazov," *FBIS-SOV,* December 10, 1990, p. 74.)

Thus the Afghan experience acquired by *Spetsnaz* and Airborne troops (the first to be sent to domestic hot spots) was adapted for use at home. Also, these forces were configured to combine maximum force and rapid mobility to enter and seal off trouble spots quickly. Martial law or coup scenarios in the USSR were such a distinct possibility that operations similar to the Afghan invasion or Jaruzelski's 1981 coup in Poland were other alternatives. The Soviet coup in Lithuania and Latvia in January 1991 was an almost textbook example of such a strategic operation, duplicating those in Kabul and Warsaw, and Prague in 1968. In the Baltic case, troops were reportedly inserted into the cities and key areas from elite units, apparently paratroopers (VDV). The MVD and regular army forces were also involved in seizing key political and $C^3I$ installations, in carrying out the bloody crackdowns in Vilnius and Riga, and in installing the "Committees of National Salvation" that ostensibly invited them into Lithuania and Latvia.

Accounts of the coups in Vilnius and Riga and of the dispatch of troops to six other republics to keep them in line make it impossible to state to whom these troops belonged operationally. Nevertheless, it is clear that by mid-1990, the stage was set for a possible deployment of MVD, KGB, *Spetsnaz,* VDV, and regular troops, as called for in Operation *Metel's* plans. Even more compelling are Yazov's admission to the Finnish defense minister about special troops, Soviet efforts to remove some of their forces from the purview of the CFE treaty, and Gorbachev's assumption of dictatorial powers in November 1990. These moves, taken together, strongly suggest the prior development of an operational-strategic plan for Operation *Metel'* to meet national unrest with force. The plan apparently coincided with Gorbachev's virtual dictatorship to restore or preserve imperial unity and with the first moves to implement a General Staff agenda having profoundly negative implications for democratization and Soviet international policy.

## Changes in MoD Forces

The restructuring of regular MoD forces in late 1990 illustrated this trend and plan. Several Western analysts charged that since about March 1990, the General Staff had gained control of the dimensions of military policy, including threat assessment. The General Staff's objectives and concerns emerged in developments involving force structure. For example, prior to the conclusion of the CFE talks, the USSR shifted almost 20,000 tanks, 15,000 armored personnel vehicles (APVs), and 25,000 guns to behind the Urals. In other actions more relevant to the local operations in the Baltics, Moscow broke the treaty. Specifically, the Soviets converted three Motorized Rifle Divisions (MRD) into Naval Infantry divisions (which were not counted under CFE provisions), transferred three Airborne divisions of the VDV to the KGB, and transferred three more MRDs to the MVD, both groups of forces (KGB and MVD) also being outside the CFE treaty.

Although the three Naval Infantry divisions were assigned to "coastal defense," they could also participate in coastal landings from stationing points that happened to be proximate to areas of nationalist unrest: Moldavia, Georgia, and Lithuania. These divisions had an exceedingly heavy armored complement indicating contingency planning beyond mere coastal defense. In his interview with Rehn, Yazov mentioned Special Troops in the Baltic Military District. It is unclear if these really were *Spetsnaz* forces or if forces sent into the Baltic from the VDV and the Army were so designated in planning documents. Lastly, Moscow also stripped the Airborne divisions returning from Europe of their BMDs (*Boevaya Mashina Desantnaya,* or Infantry Fighting Vehicles) and gave them to the VVMVD instead. They thus gained a capability to fulfill operational requirements for an airborne landing that also included maneuver from the landing zone to strike at key targets in the enemy rear. Moscow also set up an independent battalion of anti-sabotage forces for the strategic missile troops (RSVN) to guard nuclear missile sites against the threat of sabotage or terrorist attacks as a sign of its fear. They were largely created from the airborne assault forces (presumably airborne troops and air assault or heliborne forces of the army. Their mission was to fight terrorism and to participate in anti-terrorist operations with the VVMVD and the current domestic counterintelligence forces, the FSB. In 1990 that would have meant the KGB's forces. These troops' existence remained secret until November 1999.

These developments materially enhanced the MVD and KGB forces, the latter being the real control over the former's ultimate disposition. Indeed, both the MVD and KGB substantially increased their forces in 1989 and 1990. These developments also gave the Soviet High Command a reliable Russian striking force to replace the local MVD forces and perhaps some KGB troops in the republics, who failed to suppress unrest. The episodes of nationalist unrest seriously undermined Kremlin trust in the local police who had local sympathies and were subordinate to these republics and led Georgia,

Azerbaijan, Armenia, Moldova, and the Baltic republics to set up their own national police, intelligence, and paramilitary formations in late 1990. This generated enormous alarm within the central leadership, for a people's capacity to defend itself was, according to some analysts, the major catalyst for panicking Moscow into intervention in the Soviet bloc.

## Changes in MVD and KGB Forces

The shakeup of the MVD in December 1990 can also be seen in this context of operational planning. Gorbachev fired MVD head Vadim Bakatin, replacing him with a former KGB chief in Latvia, Boris Pugo, and naming General Boris Gromov as Pugo's deputy. These moves assured maximum coordination with the KGB and the readiness of MVD forces to conduct counterinsurgency operations. Bakatin was almost certainly fired because he would not interfere with the republics' MVDs while Pugo and Gromov did so. Gromov's appointment also ensured a military chain of command for the operation while removing the stigma of conducting internal security operations from the regular forces.

Similar moves within the KGB showed that it was covertly building up its overall striking powers. First, there is the evidence of KGB incitement in Azerbaijan in 1989–90. Indeed, the local Second Secretary of the Communist Party, a former KGB man who had specialized in fomenting inter-ethnic strife in Afghanistan, apparently led the incitement of Azeri nationalism against Moscow. Here and elsewhere KGB forces (not only military forces, but agents, too) stood on the sidelines during inter-ethnic unrest or violence, either egging it on or doing nothing until the violence reached a high point.

Another example of increased KGB striking power is evident in the account of the September 1990 maneuvers of Airborne troops jointly commanded by the KGB and the Army. Airborne and Air Assault forces were mobilized secretly and armed to the standard of operations in Afghanistan. They were secretly airlifted to undisclosed locations and placed under KGB authority. Formerly, they had belonged to the Supreme High Command, not the KGB. Thus the KGB, for the first time since Beria, assumed operational command of conventional MOD forces, and elite units at that. Although Airborne troops had formerly been used to quell rioting, at that time there were no such disturbances. Evidently the operation was either a rehearsal for a coup, or fed the conservatives' rabid fears of a "coup" by reformists against the government because the Airborne forces were issued live ammunition and flak jackets.

The KGB's role became even more sinister as it intensified planning for the August coup. The *Dresdener Morgenpost* reported that forces returning from former East German territory—including motorized battalions and construction units—along with other forces in the Moscow Military District, then came under KGB command, another enhancement of KGB power even beyond Beria's day. Draft legislation on the KGB, which it contrived to write to protect itself, gave it control over the Border, Signals, Construction, and Special troops—an unprecedented range of forces. Added to its effective control of the MVD, this put the KGB in an equally unprecedented position in the Security Council. The KGB used this expanded authority to allege connections between domestic and foreign "enemies," to call for Soviet citizens to spy on each other, to suggest a return to terror, and to win the right to oversee the entire economy's operations.

Gorbachev's Security Council became the nerve center of the military campaign against reformers and nationalists. It tied together in a single organization, the MVD, KGB, and regular military forces in a structure operating directly under Gorbachev's exclusive control that could move forces from agency to agency. It is not accidental that its creation opened the way for the Army and MVD to call for increased budgets and authority. Pugo claimed that the draft Union Treaty of 1990, which spelled out the constitutional rights of the center and republics, gave the MVD too little power. The MVD, he contended, should go beyond merely coordinating the struggle against crime. Another MVD officer called for a round-the-clock Security Council Staff to operate in every raion, oblast', and republic with a plenipotentiary power to act under Gorbachev's direction. He complained that in prior cases of national unrest, inadequate coordination occurred between the KGB, MVD, and regular military forces that operated independently, often in parallel, without liaison. He argued that the Council's staff also needed specially trained subunits armed and equipped for emergency operations.

> These troops, let us call them "security troops" or "national guard," could be formed on the basis of units of the internal and border troops, the KGB, civil defense formations, and a number of existing rescue structures. ("MVD Officer on Future USSR Security Council," *FBIS-SOV,* December 11, 1990, pp. 12–14.)

Other articles on the Security Council stressed its coordinating role, warning that the army might have to act on its own if coordination from the top was not forthcoming.

## Consequences of the New Force Structure

All these moves were part of the creation of a rapid deployment force for domestic contingencies that was equally capable of low-intensity or conventional operations. It comprised several hundred thousand men, airborne capabilities for them, heavy Infantry Fighting Vehicles (the BMD), a new command center merging them for operational purposes when necessary, and their systematic exclusion from any outside scrutiny or verification by the Soviet legislature or the CFE process.

This sequence of covert organization and force deployment had occurred on several occasions: in Prague in 1968, in Poland in 1981 with Polish troops from the regular and security police, and in Afghanistan in 1979. In each case Moscow also orchestrated a deception plan to surprise audiences who might resist. But in 1989–91 there was an ongoing though increasingly unbelievable attempt to pretend that the central government did not order the forcible seizure of buildings and the use of violence against unarmed protesters. Indeed, Admiral Vitalii Ivanov, commander of the Baltic Fleet, admitted that even he could not introduce martial law in the smallest garrison; only Gorbachev could do so. Viktor Tomkus, a Lithuanian deputy who participated in the investigation into the Tbilisi massacre of 1989, said that this inquiry showed that military orders to employ paratroopers in action could come only from Yazov or Gorbachev. As numerous Soviet accounts before and after 1991 indicate, only Gorbachev could launch a coup. And indeed, his statements to U.S. Ambassador Jack Matlock that he did not have control over the armed forces in Vilnius in January 1991 and continuing evasiveness concerning his role there and in Tbilisi did not and do not ring true.

But whether these forces were originally VDV, Soviet Naval Infantry, Motorized Rifle Divisions, MVD Internal Troops, or KGB forces, their training and equipment increasingly lent itself to deployment by land, sea, or air to either domestic or foreign hot spots to conduct tactical, operational, and/or strategic missions. These forces came closer than previous ones to realizing the tighter linkage of force and mobility needed for operations within the constraints of that time and could thus serve as the equivalent of a rapid deployment or counterinsurgency force and have a dual capability for either task.

In late 1990 and early 1991, the Soviet press, particularly the military media, identified several concurrent threats to order and security that were used to justify the Baltic coup and subsequent similar efforts in other republics. These threats included:

- Crime, often associated with nationalist separatism;
- Nationalist separatism in its own right, increasingly associated with incitement to violence against or harassment of military personnel and their families;
- Violations of minority rights in those republics, especially the Russian minority whose organized political components had been outspoken advocates of chauvinist policies;
- Threats of violence against other minorities increasingly aided or condoned by local governing and police agencies;
- The formation of domestic police, military, and paramilitary formations;
- Draft evasion and local collusion in this evasion; and
- Frequent direct charges that link nationalist movements with foreign subversion by the "special services" of foreign countries.

These particular threat assessments all had a long lineage in Soviet politics and had served as well at home as they have abroad in 1956, 1968, 1979, and 1981. Nonetheless these articles betrayed real fears apart from their use to justify military action. Foreign observers clearly noted that the authorities were "haunted" by what might happen in Central Asia if cross-border raids led to a replacement of existing MVD troops with Uzbek and Tajik forces. The Afghan situation is particularly interesting in this context. One Soviet commentator, lamenting Moscow's connivance in ending Afghanistan's former neutrality, candidly stated that the existing Afghan regime was Moscow's sole guarantee that its southern borders would remain free of cross-border efforts to rouse Soviet Muslims, a judgment seconded by foreign observers.

## Military Control of the Agenda, Operation Metel', and the Baltics

By mid-1990, the High Command found itself in limbo, since the new legislation on Gorbachev's Presidential Council made it unclear who commanded the armed forces: the president, the Presidential Council, the Defense Council, or the Legislature. The military then clearly demanded (and received) the reintroduction of one-man rule in the form of the newly empowered Presidency and the Security Council. This structure could have shielded the military from public scrutiny and control and allowed the military to continue to control the agenda of doctrinal and force reform. In a

January 1991 interview, Marshal Sergei Akhromeev laid out many of the military's preferences: the military opposed republican formations, viewed the United States and NATO as abiding threats, could not endorse an all-volunteer army and thus must enforce the draft laws, and would support introducing martial law "only to prevent an armed confrontation." Akhromeev also stated the driving force behind the military's efforts to gain control of its agenda: "it is the armed forces that ensure stability and permit the president to carry on his normal activities." ("A Soldier's Soldier Speaks Out," *Newsweek,* January 21, 1991, p. 40)

As party control over the armed forces ebbed, the military moved to assert control over its domain and constrain Gorbachev to remain within the boundaries of previous policies, that gave it a privileged position across a wide range of military, political, and economic issues. This perhaps also explains the rise in KGB control over key Moscow military district forces. As Gorbachev veered toward the anti-reform agenda in 1990, he may have tried to balance the two key components of the right wing, the army and the KGB. Two major elements of this agenda were the empire's integrity and silencing the media that criticized the military, as Akhromeev made clear in an ominous speech on 14 November 1990. The military made silencing its critics a high priority, and Gorbachev supported it by moving to squelch *glasnost'* and muzzle the Soviet media immediately after sending troops to Lithuania and Latvia. The KGB's similar agenda was equally ominous. To save imperial unity and military ascendancy, Soviet military-political leaders felt compelled to impose Afghan lessons at home. The innovations in force structure and the strategy of domestic repression to which they resorted threatened civil war. The strategy of coercion against the Baltic states after mid-1990 combined elements of an increasingly refined operational plan for Operation *Metel'* as a campaign in this civil war.

First Gorbachev sought to blockade Lithuania. Following the start of the blockade and diplomatic ploys, which continued unabated through 1990, came the reorganization both of Soviet force structures and of command and control for the operation. In the spring of 1990, Chief of the General Staff Mikhail Moiseyev lauded the introduction of the presidency as an instrument of centralized power favorable to Soviet military development because it streamlined the system of control over the defense forces, thereby making it easier to reform them. The old Defense Council had been abolished and its responsibilities transferred to the new Presidential Council. In wartime, that Council would change into the State Committee for Defense, the World War II Supreme command body, which would be led by Gorbachev. His powers included the ability to declare an emergency that entailed "temporary presidential rule," enabling him to overrule any local decision, such as secession from the USSR. Moiseyev specifically suggested giving Gorbachev virtually total powers over the drafting, deployment, and use of all military forces including the right to oversee implementation of military legislation, a process that would nullify legislative control over the military.

Second, the integration of the the MVD, KGB, and Army also intensified beginning in mid-1990. Paragraph 17 of the new law on national security placed the KGB in charge of coordinating all other military and paramilitary forces' internal security operations. The KGB set up a special Sixth Directorate in the MVD toward this end. In September 1990, as preparation for the subsequent coup, it was decided—in Bakatin's absence—to place the MVD OMON's Black Beret forces of Riga under the MVD command rather than under the republic. This decision meant that in the January 1991 events, those troops were effectively under Pugo, Gromov, and KGB Chief Vladimir Kryuchkov, and at the service of the Latvian Communist Party and its shadow "Committee of National Salvation."

The MVD's OPNAZ forces were doubled in size and were placed under Gromov's authority and command. Expansion of these forces and the MVD's Black Berets on a national scale coincided with the expansion of the KGB's internal security force, following the attachment of the 103rd Guards Vitebsk Division to the KGB Border Troops and the subordination of the MVD's OPNAZ and OMON forces to the All-Union MVD in Moscow, not the republics. These measures firmed up the $C^3$ for Soviet forces to operate as the leaders combined political orchestration of threats with economic warfare and diplomacy to keep Baltic negotiators off balance. Yet at the crucial moment Gorbachev (to his credit) refused to unleash a true civil war and restrained his forces. Why he did so remains uncertain. Perhaps Gorbachev was reluctant to face the domestic and international uproar that would then result, or perhaps he feared becoming hostage to the military.

Nevertheless civil war contingencies were planned for some time, almost two years. Several of the laws pertaining to states of emergency and the powers of the KGB and MVD were put through in 1989, setting the stage for the augmentation of KGB and MVD powers. A KGB defector, Vladimir Grigoriev, who worked for the KGB in Leningrad and the Baltic for 12 years, told a Swedish reporter that the planning for the January coups in the Baltic began in 1989. Grigoriev reported, "Two years ago I received information from a highly placed KGB officer in Tallinn, who said that Perestroika was to be used by the KGB as camouflage to advance KGB positions in the West, and also to prepare a change in the entire policy, in our case in the Baltics. This change could come as soon as 2 or 3 years time, that is, during 1990 or 1991." ("KGB Defector: Baltic Operations Preplanned," *FBIS-SOV,* January 23, 1991, p. 88.) Grigoriev's job was to infiltrate those groups. He also contended that the reason for deploying the General Staff's *Spetsnaz,* MVD Black Berets, and KGB Special Units in the Baltics was that they were directly under Presidential and General Staff control, while the readiness of the regular forces to carry out this mission was doubtful. This confirmed the power of the Tbilisi syndrome and the troops' politicization.

Furthermore, Petras Jonaitis, a senior officer at the First Section of the Lithuanian KGB, stated that Moscow had ordered a plan for future mass action in Lithuania in September 1989, that combined action by the local and Belorussian-based KGB and military forces and that was rehearsed in minute detail. The plan was approved by the head of the Lithuanian KGB. And shock troops, which could not be assigned without Kryuchkov's approval, were sent into Lithuania in April 1990. By far the most damning piece of evidence was a report published on 29 January 1991 by *Nezavisimaya Gazeta* containing a report by Politburo and Secretariat member O. Shenin of his August 1990 trip to Lithuania. As part of his report, Shenin advocated the following:

- an all-union propaganda campaign to blacken the Lithuanian independence struggle;
- attempts to provoke a Polish-Lithuanian rupture;
- acceleration of work to force through a new Union treaty;
- an emphasis on the issue of Lithuania violating the military draft laws;
- reaffirmation of all-union property rights over important political organizations and enterprises in Lithuania in order to create a pretext for stationing guards there;
- Communist Party intervention on behalf of the "healthy forces" of Lithuania; and
- making a KGB military detachment from the republic KGB part of the Lithuanian Party.

Clearly the most insidious element of his report was its Paragraph 7, which called for the CPSU State and Legal Department, which supposedly oversees the KGB as well, to employ Communists in legal, police, and judicial positions to execute criminal and administrative, i.e., closed trial, prosecution of nationalist and "anti-Soviet political formations, deserters, and extremists." Therefore it was necessary to coordinate the USSR Procuracy, MVD, KGB, and Supreme Court. The decree was secretly ratified on 29 August by Vladimir Ivashko, the number two man and Gorbachev's deputy in the All-Union Party. It is most unlikely that Gorbachev had not seen the decree before then. Events so closely followed Shenin's script that it is inconceivable that this was not part of the ultimate plan for the coup in the Baltics.

Events in the Army were also moving toward a showdown. On 3 September 1990 Gorbachev transferred control over the Main Political Administration of the Army and Navy from the Communist Party to the state. On 15 November, a CPSU Secretariat resolution called for strengthening Army-Party links. Ignoring the September decree, the Secretariat ordered the MPA to develop new means of patriotic indoctrination of soldiers in the spirit of Marxism-Leninism. This resolution came from a Central Committee commission on military policy, comprised of the highest Party officials on military affairs. It was also at this time that the topmost military and MOD commands urged Gorbachev to act immediately against republican "anti-military tendencies." Finally, at its 16 November meeting, the Politburo discussed measures to stabilize the country's condition, with particular reference to Lithuania.

Subsequently, military-political collusion at the local level also became apparent. Colonel Viktor Alksnis, head of the right-wing parliamentary faction, *Soyuz*, stated that the leaders of the National Salvation Committees in the Baltic told him they did everything Gorbachev wanted them to do to create a "dual power" situation there and precipitate a political crisis to justify military intervention. Other Soviet sources confirmed that central KGB and MVD personnel directed these committees' local leaders to incite the troops to action. Propaganda charging the restoration of prewar bourgeois "fascist" military and political organizations was a prominent part of such incitement to action.

After the initial coup, on 18 January 1991, a new Control Commission for the Party organization in the armed forces was set up to coordinate its actions with all the other military, paramilitary, and law-enforcement organs in the country. On 31 January, another commission to coordinate all law-enforcement agencies was established under Yu. V. Golik, just five days after the publication of a predated decree calling for joint military-police patrols in urban areas, ostensibly aimed at fighting crime. Finally, it was revealed that the forces that spearheaded the actual assault into Vilnius were the troops of the Vitebsk Division, now seconded from the Airborne Forces to the KGB. The Vitebsk Division and members of the elite Seventh Directorate of the KGB had previously been used in the violent suppression of disorders in Tbilisi and Baku, and in the invasion of Afghanistan and the assassination of its head of state in 1979.

## Conclusions

Obviously a broader agenda and political situation was at stake in connection with the domestic operations of 1989–91. Clearly political control of the armed forces through the Military-Political Administration of the Party had to be replaced. With the advent of a multi-party system, the MPA was replaced and taken out of the Communist Party's structure. The MPA and control over personnel assignments passed into the hands of the military administrations of the KGB, MVD, and MOD. The Central Committee and its *nomenklatura* left the picture and, formally speaking, the military and KGB escaped Party control. As Amy Knight explained,

> In the past the CPSU Secretariat, staffed with *apparatchiki* who were sympathetic to the KGB, determined KGB appointments and monitored the KGB budget and operations on behalf of the Politburo. Now that body has apparently relinquished this function, in formal terms at least. But the much hoped for parliamentary control over the KGB has not been established in the party's place and neither Gorbachev nor his colleagues seem anxious to see this happen. (Amy Knight, "The Future of the KGB," *Problems of Communism,* vol. XXXIX, no. 6 (November–December 1990), p. 31)

No single legislative or even executive body now controlled the armed forces, MVD, and the KGB. Accordingly high military spending, police administration of the economy, controls on *glasnost',* and the retention of the empire provided an agenda around which these forces could and did coalesce but could not be sustained. Only the person of the president, Gorbachev or Yeltsin, could exercise control, and since then we have had a government of men, not of laws, with visible results.

The military trends described here were not a recipe for stability though they did foster the multiple militaries' politicization; quite the opposite. In place of democratization, the Soviet Union fell and Russia restored a personalized quasi-tsarist structure of personalized and non-institutionalized (or irregular) forms of government. Gorbachev raised the specter of Lebanonization of the USSR if unrest and secession continued. However, by their own actions, Gorbachev, Yeltsin, and the military made that prospect all the more likely.

In the past decade, the Red Army has frequently been called into action to quell ethnic unrest and suppress dissent. The earlier episodes were warnings to Gorbachev and the military, but just as the coups of 1991 were a warning to the West so too are the domestic wars since then, particularly the current Chechen war. Today nobody can believe or pretend that the army and the people are one. Today the Russian Army's main operational mission, rhetoric aside, remains domestic counterinsurgency and preservation of its immunity from accountability. Thus Russia will continue to be militarily uncompetitive in the world. Nor can Russia support its current army. Finally, continuation of the present structure will lead to greater economic prostration without ensuring external security. By completing the cycle of using the Red Army for counterinsurgency first in Afghanistan and now at home, Gorbachev, Yeltsin and their generals brought the USSR and now Russia to a paradox and an impasse. The paradox is that the single greatest threat to Russian and European security is the present organization of Russia's government and armed forces. By acting forcefully within the USSR at Gorbachev's command, the military and KGB in 1991 crossed a Rubicon and successfully politicized themselves. They cannot now revert to their formerly more hidden status in the political game. When Caesar crossed the Rubicon he knowingly wagered on civil war. Gorbachev, Kryuchkov, Yeltsin, and their generals made a similar gamble. But Russia's domestic wars cannot and will not usher in a Russian Augustan age; rather they herald a new time of troubles for an already devastated country.

## Sources and Further Reading

This chapter relied heavily on an extensive selection of articles drawn from the contemporary press, both Soviet and American. The following lists only the major works likely to be of most immediate value to the student of this period.

Alekseeva, Ludmilla. "Unrest in the Soviet Union." *Washington Quarterly,* vol. XIII, no. 1 (Winter 1990), pp. 63–77.

Azrael, Jeremy R. *The KGB in Kremlin Politics.* Santa Monica, CA: RAND Corporation, 1989.

Azrael, Jeremy. *Restructuring and the Polarization of Soviet Politics.* Santa Monica, CA: RAND Corporation, 1990.

Barylski, Robert V. *The Soldier in Russian Politics: Duty, Dictatorship and Democracy under Gorbachev and Yeltsin.* New Brunswick NJ: Transaction Publishers, 1998.

Blank, Stephen. "Gorbachev's Agenda and the Next Administration." *Comparative Strategy,* vol. VIII, no. 4 (1989), pp. 117–136.

Blank, Stephen. "Gorbachev's Constitutional Coup." Unpublished Paper.

Blank, Stephen. "Winter Storm in the Baltic: The Soviet Armed Forces and Domestic Security." Susan L. Clark Ed., *Soviet Military Power in a Changing World.* Boulder, CO: Westview Press, 1991.

Blank, Stephen. "State and Armed Forces in Russia: Toward an African Scenario." Anthony James Joes, Ed., *Saving Democracies: U.S. Intervention in Threatened Democratic States.* Westport, CT: Praeger Publishers, 1999, pp. 167–196.

Brown, Archie. "Russia and Democratization." *Problems of Post-Communism,* XLVI, No. 5, September–October, 1999, pp. 3–13.

Burgess Collins, Major William H., III, Ed. *Inside Spetsnaz: Soviet Special Operations. A Critical Analysis.* Novato, CA: Presidio Press, 1990.

Cable, Larry. "Soviet Low-Intensity Operations and NATO." Paper presented to the SOMS Conference, 1987.

Covington, Stephen. "NATO and Soviet Security Reform." *Washington Quarterly,* vol. XIV, no. 1 (Winter 1991), pp. 39–50.

Dunlop, John B. *The Rise of Russia and the Fall of the Soviet Empire.* Princeton, NJ: Princeton University, 1993.

Dziak, John J. *Chekisty: A History of the KGB,* Lexington, MA: Lexington Books, 1988.

Fuller, William C. *Civil-Military Conflict in Imperial Russia, 1881–1914.* Princeton NJ: Princeton University Press, 1985.

Fuller, William C., Jr. *The Internal Troops of the MVD SSR,* College Station, TX: Center for Strategic Technology, Texas A&M University, 1983.

Galeotti, Mark. "Soviet Paramilitaries—Security Forces in the Throes of Change." *Jane's Soviet Intelligence Review,* August 1990.

Holcomb, Major James F., Jr., USA. *Soviet Special Operations: The Legacy of the Great Patriotic War,* Ft. Leavenworth, KS: Soviet Army Studies Office, 1987.

Hough, Jerry F. "Gorbachev's Endgame: Positioning for Radical Reform." *World Policy Journal,* vol. VII, no. 4 (Fall 1990), pp. 639–672.

Isby, David. *Ten Million Bayonets: Inside the Armies of the Soviet Union.* London and New York: Arms and Armour Press, 1988.

Jones, Christopher. *Soviet Influence in Eastern Europe: Political Autonomy and the Warsaw Pact,* New York: Praeger, 1981.

Lebed, Aleksandr'. *Za Derzhavu Obidno.* Moscow: Moskovskaya Pravda, 1995.

MacDonald, David McLauren. *United Government and Foreign Policy in Russia, 1900–1914.* Cambridge, MA: Harvard University Press, 1992.

Matlock, Jack F., Jr. *Autopsy on an Empire.* New York: Random House, 1995, pp. 455–456

Meyer, Stephen C. "How the Threat (and the Coup) Collapsed: The Politicization of the Soviet Military. *International Security,* XVI, NO. 3, winter, 1991–1992, pp. 5–38.

Meyer, Stephen C. "The Military." Robert Legvold and Timothy Colton, Eds., *After the Soviet Union: From Empire to Nations.* New York: W.W. Norton & Co. Inc., 1992, pp. 113–145.

Murphy, David E. "Operation 'Ring': the Black Berets in Azerbaijan." *Journal of Soviet Military Studies*, V, No. 1, March, 1992, pp. 50–66.

Odom, William E. "The Soviet Military in Transition." *Problems of Communism*, XXXIX, No. 3, 1990, pp. 51–71.

Odom, William E. *The Collapse of the Soviet Military*. New Haven, CT: Yale University Press, 1998.

Proektor, Danill. "Politics, Clausewitz, and Victory in a Nuclear War." *International Affairs*, no. 5, 1988.

Reitz, James T. "The Soviet Security Troops—The Kremlin's Other Armies." *Soviet Armed Forces Annual, Volume 6*. Gulf Breeze, FL: Academic International Press, 1982, pp. 279–327.

Shaposhnikov, Yevgenii. *Vybor*, 2nd Revised and Expanded Edition. Moscow: Nezavisimoye Izdatel'stvo PIK, 1995.

Taranovski, Theodore. "Institutions, Political Culture and Foreign Policy in Late Imperial Russia. " Catherine Evtuhov, Boris Gasparov, Alexander Ospovat, Mark Von Hagen, Eds. *Kazan, Moscow, St. Petersburg: Multiple Faces of the Russian Empire*. Moscow: O.G.I., 1997, pp. 53–69.

Turbiville, Graham H., Jr. "Restructuring the Soviet Ground Forces: Reduction-Mobilization-Force Generation." *Military Review*, December 1989, pp. 17–30.

Yasmann, Victor. "Mastering an Identity Crisis." *Report on the USSR*, January 4, 1991.

Zaionchkovskii, P.A. *Krisis Samoderzhaviia na Rubezhe 1870–1880 Godov*. Moscow: Izdatel'stvo MGU, 1964.

# CHAPTER 17

# THE MILITARY AND THE STATE

## Contemporary Russia in Historical Perspective

*William E. Odom*

THE RUSSIAN MILITARY HAS ALWAYS OCCUPIED A CENTRAL PLACE in the Russian state, never more so than in the Soviet period. In post-Soviet Russia, that place is changing. Precisely what new role it will have is far from clear, but Russia's senior officers are products of the Soviet military, not at all disposed to accept the kind of systemic military reform essential for liberal political and economic development in Russia, reform that would remove the military from its traditional place in the Russian polity. The influence of historical legacies remains strong, but the forces of change are also powerful, leaving the outcome uncertain.

This contemporary struggle is about far more than military reform. To expose its deeper meaning, we must review its historical context and place the Russian case in the comparative context of Western civil-military developments. The most important of these were (a) the change in the military's role from being virtually synonymous with the state to being an important but lesser part of the state, and (b) the modern professionalization of the officer corps. Against this background, the implications of what has occurred with the new Russian military in the 1990s will be much clearer.

## The Military as Synonymous with the State

From early times—certainly from the late fifteenth century when Muscovy displaced Mongol rule—the Russian military has been essentially identical with the state. The tsar always considered himself the state's first soldier, and women rulers were no exception. The persistence of this view was evident when Nicholas II abdicated in 1917. He addressed his decision to the commander of the army, ignoring the Provisional Government, which had demanded that he step down. In the Soviet period, the new Red Army quickly regained this traditional preeminence. As a revolutionary party committed to completing the world socialist revolution, the Bolsheviks assumed, following Karl Marx, that the property-owning classes would not give up without a fight. That meant an inevitable military showdown between the international working class and the capitalist-imperialist classes. Accordingly, the Soviet economic system was designed to insure that the Red Army (Soviet Armed Forces after WW II) enjoyed the kind of priority it needed as the military force to win this revolutionary showdown throughout the world. The Communist Party of the Soviet Union was, as Philip Selznick has described it, "a combat political organization." He emphasized the unique nature of this kind of party, and in some ways it was, but the new regime it constructed also retained some historical continuities from the Russian Empire.

The political primacy of the military in European states generally declined throughout the nineteenth century and became exceptional in the twentieth century. True, Hitler's Nazi regime in Germany put the military in a central place because his party depended on war to achieve its goals as much as the Bolshevik regime did in Russia, but the Nazi regime lasted only about a dozen years. One can also argue that the German and Austrian empires in 1914 had a lot in common with the Russian Empire. In all three the military enjoyed a special status with the nobility populating the officer corps and the emperors assuming military rank. True again, but these regimes were destroyed by the end of World War I. Yet the comparison is illuminating because it raises the long-standing question: Is Russia a European state or something very different?

In his study of the origins and nature of European states during the last millennium, Charles Tilly puts war at the center of his explanation. "[O]ver the long run, far more than other activities, war and preparation for war produced the major components of European states." In order to expand, or at least to survive, rulers needed armed forces. To build them, they had to "concentrate" both "capital" and "means" of "coercion" (to use Tilly's terms), but as their circumstances varied, so too did the mix of these resources that they achieved. This explains the different paths they followed, some depending more on an early "concentration of coercion," some resorting more to an early "concentration of capital." Tilly includes Russia as a European state, one that marked the most extreme path of first concentrating means of coercion and having great difficulty in concentrating capital. (The Dutch Republic and the Italian city states took the extreme opposite path, achieving capital concentration first.)

Brian Downing offers an overlapping explanation. Revolutionary changes in military technology made modern militaries increasingly more expensive. To afford them, kings centralized political institutions and revenue-collecting powers, breaking down the old feudal order in Europe. Countries that failed to centralize, like Poland, perished. The resulting absolutist state, however, did not last in most cases, eventually giving way to liberal political development, first in Britain, then in France, and later in Central, Northern, and to a lesser degree in Southern Europe. Downing explains the sequence of the appearance of liberal democracies as determined by the degree to which feudal institutions were fully or partially destroyed. Because they involved strong limits on the monarch, they carried the seeds of modern European Liberalism. Thus in England, where feudal institutions were least fully destroyed, their residual forms and traditions facilitated the earlier transition to a constitutional order. The farther east one goes in Europe, however, the more fully destroyed were feudal institutions, and, according to Downing, this explains the later arrival of liberal regimes in central Europe.

Russia, of course, never had the key institutions of West European feudalism. No Russian ruler recognized any inalienable rights on the part of the nobility or church. The tsar was answerable only to God for his patrimony, i.e., all the land that constituted Russia and the Russian Empire. While the *boyarstvo* and the later *dvoryanstvo* had some features common to feudal nobilities in Europe, the most important one they did not have was rights, especially ownership of land, which the king could not rightfully abridge. As Donald Ostrowski has recently demonstrated, the Muscovite princes took most of their secular statecraft from the Mongols, including the idea that " . . . all the land belonged to the ruler." This had not been true for boyars in Kievan Rus, but in Moscow it became an enduring principle down to the end of the empire. It was never true of the major states of Western Europe. Thus Russia stands as an exception, and this fact has had dramatic consequences for Russia's efforts to achieve a "concentration of capital," in Tilly's phrase.

Without inviolable and stable private property rights, modern capitalism simply cannot operate effectively. Whether it concerned the basis of peasant ownership of land or the right to create a "limited liability" corporation, the tsar's persistent refusal to grant stable private property rights severely limited Russia's industrialization, which had become critical for maintaining modern military power. As several chapters in this volume demonstrate, although Russia (and the Soviet Union) concentrated "coercion" rather effectively, it was consistently behind on concentrating "capital," and when it began to catch up in the mid-twentieth century, it had become irreconcilably hostile to the very economic institutions that make "capital" concentration yield the most effective results.

Not all historians, of course, agree that Russia was on a course apart from, and not just behind, Europe. Martin Malia has recently argued that Russia was following the European pattern, only lagging by about 50 years. Catherine the Great's granting of the Charter of the Nobility (1785), in Malia's judgment, put the Russian nobility on the same footing as the nobility of the ancien regime in France, and Alexander II's Great Reforms of the 1860s were equivalent to the Prussian reforms of 1807–12. Such a reading of the Charter of the Nobility is not uniformly accepted. While it declared that no nobleman could be deprived of his honor, life, property, and title of nobility without a trial by his peers, it allowed no countrywide organization of the nobility and greatly limited the provinces where such organization was permitted on a purely local basis. Nor did it give the nobility unqualified rights to buy and sell land and serfs. The nobility certainly acquired the de facto power to do so by the nineteenth century, but it was never made a legal right.

Comparing Alexander II's reforms with those of Prussia does not make Malia's case any more convincing. As Barrington Moore, Jr., has argued, the Prussian experience combined the survival of the conservative elites in the countryside, engaged in agriculture based on serf labor, with the industrialization of the country. This path led to modern dictatorship in Germany, Russia, and Japan, not to the liberal democratic outcomes in Britain, France, and North America. It is true that Alexander's Great Reforms were propelling Russia onto a new course through changes in local government, the introduction of Western law, and major changes in the military, but the forces of reaction were never fundamentally overcome before the collapse of the regime in 1917.

A new social, political, and economic articulation from below, beginning with the Renaissance and foremost in towns and cities, grew up in Western Europe and was spreading into Central Europe by the early nineteenth century. These changes between the state and the society were accompanied by fundamental changes in the military, namely, new technology, professionalization, and depoliticization. While Brian Downing has dealt with the political implications of changing technology, Samuel Huntington has best described the latter two developments in his construction of a theory of modern civil-military relations. Although his critics have insisted that military professionalism antedates the nineteenth century, his account of the specialization of modern military establishments in Europe is difficult to dispute.

Modern industrial states, not only in Europe but also in North America and East Asia, have experienced two major institutional changes that Russia evaded. First, they allowed a huge private sector economy to emerge, regulated but neither owned nor directed by the state. Second, they differentiated their military and political classes, setting their officer corps apart as professional corporations devoted mainly to achieving competence in waging modern warfare in order to provide security for the society and the state. These developments proceeded unevenly from country to country, but they enjoyed only modest progress in Russia in the last 50 years of its existence. Instead, the traditional fusion of political, military, and economic roles in the imperial state persisted, albeit deformed, but nonetheless able to prevent Russia from moving onto the path of military development followed by Britain, France, Germany, and, to a lesser degree, Austria.

When the Soviet regime is viewed in this comparative perspective, one sees it not as a revolutionary break with the Russian past but rather as a throwback to pre-1861, to a regime predominantly devoting its economy to accumulation of military power, an economy fueled mainly by serf labor in the agricultural sector and wholly state-owned and directed in the industrial sector.

For the last two centuries, therefore, as the role of the military in Europe and America acquired its modern specialized place within the state and society, Russia maintained its military as virtually synonymous with the imperial state, fully synonymous with the Communist Party-state in the Soviet period. Such a qualitatively different historical development explains the unique character of civil-military relations in Russia in modern times. What Western Europe achieved in civil-military relations in a century and a half, Russia is now faced with trying to achieve in a few years—that is, if Russia is to have a liberal democratic regime.

Changing civil-military relations in contemporary Russia, it should now be clear, involves a great deal more than Russia's uniformed military, its notions of professionalism, and so on. For example, the Russian officer corps could accept democratic ideals without any appreciable impact on the process of change. Until economic and political institutions are fundamentally altered, officers' ideals will not make much difference. How Russia works out the role for its military today and in the near future, therefore, will remain a revealing indicator of the character of the political regime. If the military again becomes synonymous with the state, then the forces of continuity will have prevailed. If it is to follow the Western pattern, Russia will have to reduce the military's role "synonymous with the state" to "guarantor" of the state's and society's security, a critical but much reduced place in the political system.

## The Military as the Guarantor of the Society's Security

The Soviet military could only meet two of Huntington's three criteria for a modern professional military. First, it was expert in the management of violence, not always at the highest levels, as for example in the Russo-Finnish War in 1939–40 and in the first two years of the war with Hitler's Germany, but it achieved an impressive level of expertise by 1945, and, during the postwar period, its force development and weapons and other materiel development were a serious challenge to NATO's militaries. Second, its officer corps enjoyed a corporate identity marked by uniforms, ranks, and many measures of alleged personal professional competence. Things were ambiguous in this regard in the military's connection to the Communist Party. About 95 percent of all officers were Communist Party members. No significant advancement in a military career was possible for an officer without a spotless party record. The last Soviet minister of defense, Marshal Yevgenii Shaposhnikov, complains in his memoirs of the party's Central Committee department of administrative organs meddling in selection of senior commanders in the Soviet air forces. Merely a call from the Central Committee, perhaps from a low-ranking functionary, was enough to block an appointment of an officer judged by all the top air force commanders to be the most competent candidate. Still, most of the officer corps, especially among the ground forces, remained party loyalists as the Soviet Union was collapsing in 1989–91. They became hesitant only when the survival of the regime began to come into question, as it did during the crisis of 18–21 August 1991, when the Emergency Committee temporarily incarcerated Mikhail Gorbachev, the party's general secretary. Still, we can say that the military enjoyed a corporate identity even if we place the officer corps as a subset of the Communist Party.

Huntington's third criterion is that a profession must have an ethic, and for the military this is the security of the society of a country. The Soviet military did not really meet this standard. Its ethical obligation was to the victory of the international working-class revolution, not to the Russian or Soviet society. Karl Marx, of course, would object to the notion of "ethical" as applicable to working-class institutions. His "scientific" viewpoint relegated such "subjective" terms to the bourgeois superstructures of capitalist states and disavowed the very idea of bourgeois notions of morality and ethics. The Red Army's role in repressing peasant rebels, the Kronstadt sailors' uprising, and many other social movements before World War II make it difficult to describe it as morally dedicated to the security of Soviet society. Its role in imposing collectivization on the peasantry is yet another example. Its use after World War II in occasionally putting down social disorders involved considerable bloodletting, and its use against other "socialist countries" such as Hungary and Czechoslovakia is difficult to classify as "ethical" in Huntington's sense of the term for the modern military professional.

Having discarded its Marxist-Leninist ideology, Russia today has taken the first imperative step toward making its military a modern professional organization. The implications are important to underscore. The Soviet Union was a multi-national state that denied "political" content to the nations within its borders. Moreover, its dedication to world revolution and working-class internationalism removed the nation state from its political categories and reduced it to a cultural category. In reality, of course, several "nations" within the Soviet Union had latent political content, and with Gorbachev's weakening of the Soviet military and introduction of *glasnost*, it became active content, producing the strong centrifugal political forces that Boris Yeltsin would use to unseat Gorbachev in the late fall of 1991.

Off-loading the largest national republics and ethnic groups with the breakup of the Soviet Union, Yeltsin created an objectively new context for the Russian military. True, over 20 national republics are still component within the Russian Federation, but Chechnya is the only one where Russian military forces have been used to keep it from seceding. In principle, therefore, after 1992 Russia has been in an objective condition that allows for a fundamentally new role for its military, the role of a "professional" military in Huntington's theory of civil-military relations. That has never been the case before in either Russian or Soviet military history. The prospects for a civil society with a market economy are better than before, even if they still are not all that promising. And the same is true for a state that regulates rather than runs the economy and for a military whose role is only to guarantee the security of the society.

Favorable prospects, however, do not ensure such an outcome, and the 1990s demonstrated that it will not be easy to achieve. In the past it was impossible; today it is possible but far from easy. Let us review the major outlines of the reform efforts as a basis for subsequent judgments and speculations about the prospects.

## The Russian Military Reform Struggle

Military reform, as Mikhail Gorbachev recognized in the beginning of his *perestroika* policy, was imperative for economic reform, but he did not realize that it would unhinge the Soviet Union. Deep cuts in Soviet military forces were indeed carried through, and most Soviet forces were withdrawn from the former Warsaw Pact countries during *perestroika*, but the basic Soviet military system survived into the new regime of the Russian Federation. Initially most of the Soviet officer corps and probably President Boris Yeltsin and his aides believed that the new Commonwealth of Independent States would retain the unified armed forces, or, as some officers said, the only thing that would change would be the sign on the Ministry of Defense building. A great deal more change has actually occurred since that time, but its directions remain cloudy. Let us consider a set of key policy areas that mark these directions.

### Foreign policy

Fundamental change in the role of the Russian military today depends on Russia's shifting from its long-standing expansionist foreign policy to one in support of the status quo. Having lost a large part of its former colonial areas—the former union republics—Russia is in a new position, different from any since Peter the Great's time. But is it reconciled to its new borders? At times, it seems so. At others, it seems not. Although Yeltsin appeared quite at ease with breaking up the Soviet Union and putting Russia on a non-imperial path, precisely what kind of new Russia he sought was never clear.

Since 1992, of course, Russia has tried to play the role of a major power within the community of Western liberal democracies. Within the Commonwealth of Independent States, however, it has pursued mixed and contradictory policies, some inspired by a strong desire to re-imperialize the former Soviet republics, others making re-imperialization impossible in the near term. Moscow has kept its intelligence and military organizations as deeply involved in Kazakhstan, Kyrgyzstan, Tajikistan, Armenia, Georgia, Azerbaijan, and Moldova as possible. The civil war in Tajikistan has allowed Russia to pose as a peacekeeper there while in fact its troops are more concerned with keeping a pro-Russian regime in power than in peace. Russian military influence in the other Central Asian republics is much reduced, but links through officer training and arms sales and supply remain significant channels of access. The Taliban successes in Afghanistan and fears of Muslim radical forces in Uzbekistan and Kyrgyzstan caused both regimes to soften their anti-Russian orientations in 1999.

In the southern Caucasus, Russia has backed the separatists in Abkhazia against Shevardnadze's Georgian regime, and it has used its traditionally strong ties to Armenia to keep the conflict in Nagorno-Karabakh from being settled. Furthermore, several attempts against the lives of President Shevardnadze and Azeribaijan's President Haidar Aliyev have been attributed to Russian intelligence operatives. In Moldova, Russia keeps military forces in the Transdniester region, using the Russian minority there to prevent it from being integrated into the new Moldovan Republic. In Ukraine, Russia has caused problems over the Black Sea Fleet and Ukrainian control of Crimea and alternatively pursued threatening and conciliatory diplomacy toward Kiev. In the Baltic republics, Moscow formally acknowledges their sovereignty but periodically makes threats and stirs up quarrels between the local ethnic groups and Russians still living there. The result has been the maintenance of a high degree of insecurity in all three republics, but especially so in Latvia, which has the largest Russian population as a percentage of the total.

In marked contrast to these assertive actions, Russian economic policies, beginning with the exclusion of the Central Asian states from the ruble-zone in the fall of 1993, have undercut the binding linkages between the CIS countries and Russia. Other linkages persist, however, especially in the energy sector and in some of the old heavy industry and military-industrial sectors.

For much of the 1990s, Russia has taken an ambivalent approach to its "near abroad" (its name for the former Soviet republics). Thus the question of whether Moscow truly accepts the "commonwealth" or merely wants it as a cover for reestablishing the Russian Empire is still open. And the Russian elites themselves seemed deeply split on the question—the economic reformers and more liberal-inclined political groups opposing re-imperialization, the military, the intelligence services, and several political parties favoring it. Vladimir Putin's coming to power, however, marks a swing toward imperial assertiveness.

In its dealings with NATO and the West, Russia has moved from an initial period of cooperation to one of tensions and hurt feelings. This has been conspicuous in Russia's reactions to NATO's enlargement and in its connivance with the Serb government against NATO in the spring of 1999. In the Far East, Russia has swung from radical improvements in its relations with China, South Korea, and Japan to stalemates with South Korea and Japan coupled with ambivalence toward North Korea, and continued cooperation with China. If there is a single theme in Russian foreign policy toward its "far abroad," it is a demand for a multipolar world in opposition to American unipolar hegemony. The leaders of China and France have endorsed this theme in principle but done little to advance it in practice.

## Military doctrine

Ever since the break up of the Soviet Union, the residual Russian military has been pushing for a formally adopted statement of a new military doctrine. The General Staff produced a draft in May 1992, but it was never endorsed officially by President Yeltsin. After the crisis with the parliament in October 1993, Yeltsin apparently decided that is was time to oblige the military and issued a decree on 2 November 1993 promulgating a version revised by the Russian Security Council. While this document acknowledged that Russia faced no military threat from the West, it revealed a contempt for the independence of the CIS states, introduced a nuclear weapons employment policy that was threatening in the cases of some non-nuclear states, and demanded that the military be restored to its proper place in society and in priority of claim on the state budget.

The ensuing six years left the military deeply frustrated with this document mainly because its budget demands were never fully met. But as the war resumed in Chechnya in the fall and winter of 1999–2000, not only did military spending begin to increase, but the new prime minister and acting president, Vladimir Putin, also signed a national security concept document that was to provide the basis for a new official military doctrine. A draft of the new military doctrine has also been published, and presumably it will be signed as well.

Neither the concept nor the military doctrine is significantly out of line with the formal military doctrine of November 1993, although they put more emphasis on creating a strong Russian state and first-use of nuclear weapons. One new thing, however, is the formalization of the "multipolarity" principle of Russian foreign policy. As the military doctrine declares, "the Russian Federation assumes that social progress, stability and international security can be secured only within the framework of the mulitpolar world and assists its creation in every way possible." This means, of course, that today's de facto U.S. global hegemony is a threat to progress, stability, and peace. In a word, the generals have once again, as they did in the Cold

War, defined the United States as the enemy, providing them with a justification for larger and larger budgets.

Whether these new documents portend the budgetary relief the Russian military desires is an open question. President Yeltsin's habit was to allow a fairly large budget authorization by the State Duma, then to disburse about half of authorized amount in the course of the budget year. All the while there was much talk in the State Duma and the government about more money for the military. Changes in this pattern began in 1999. NATO's air war against Serbia prompted fears and outrage at the state of the Russian military's weaponry and readiness throughout the spring, and when Moscow began preparing its campaign against the Chechens in the fall, defense spending began to increase. By the spring of 2000, the military budget was reported to be 5.3 percent of GDP while the "socio-economic" area received only 3.7 percent, a sign of changing priorities.

## Command, Control, and Force Structure Arrangements

At the very top, the Russian president has the "security council" to help him deal with military affairs that transcend issues manageable within the Ministry of Defense alone. This organization, created in 1992, looks somewhat like the Soviet Defense Council. It has been used at times, ignored at other times, and expanded in its staff (a group of commissions that oversees sets of ministries). A defense council was also created in 1998, probably as a device to help Yeltsin fire the defense minister, but it has not been very active.

The Ministry of Defense looks much the same as the Soviet ministry, only smaller, and the General Staff still holds its key position, exercising operational control of all the forces. Yet the spread of this control has been reduced, no longer including the border troops, the internal troops, KGB troops, and other military formations, as was the case for the Soviet General Staff. Much of the reason for this change is concern about the political behavior of the military with the dissolution of the old Communist Party and KGB structures within the Soviet military. Those military formations taken away from the Russian General Staff's operational control (as distinct from direct command and organizational lines) were placed under the direct control of President Yeltsin after the crisis with the parliament in October 1993. Frightened about the lack of the military's responsiveness, Yeltsin created a set of separate militaries, all beholden only to him, creating a de facto "praetorian" military arrangement.

The military districts have been retained although consolidated from 14 in 1991 to 8 in 1999 and reduced in the sizes of their staffs. Command structures within the operational forces have also been reduced and consolidated, but not without bitter rivalries and protests.

The Russian military's force structure differs from the Soviet military's mainly in the great reductions in the quantity of forces and commands that have taken place. From over 200 divisions, the ground forces have shrunk to a score or more. The navy has lost most of its two small fleets—in the Baltic Sea and in the Black Sea—and its large fleets in the Pacific Ocean and the Barents Sea have deteriorated dramatically. The air forces have also shrunk, and support for training and maintenance of aircraft has plummeted to the point where only a small fraction of pilots can maintain more than a modicum of flying competence. At the same time, the old air defense forces, composed of a huge inventory of surface-to-air missiles and also interceptor aircraft, have been merged with the air forces. The strategic rocket forces have deteriorated, suffered cuts, but also received a few brand new TOPOL-M missiles, beginning in early 1999.

Upon replacing Yeltsin, Vladimir Putin initiated a few changes aimed at returning to a more Soviet-like military. Specifically, the KGB "special sections" were restored to the military, and Putin himself praised the military and linked it to its Soviet past. Whether these steps were mere political expedients to secure the generals' support in the election for the presidency, or whether they portend the direction of state-building and political management Putin intends to pursue is not yet clear.

During Pavel Grachev's tenure as minister of defense, he repeatedly promised major "military reforms," but failed to deliver. His successor, General Igor Rodionov, was no more successful, spending most of his effort calling for more money to implement his reforms. Marshal Igor Sergeev, former commander of the rocket forces and defense minister after Rodionov, undertook the most sweeping reform effort, but even it was hardly "systemic."

It involved consolidation of several regional commands, causing loud complaining from generals who lost out in the process. It actually achieved the merging of the air defense forces into the air forces, eliminating one of the five branches of service. Its scheme for an independent strategic nuclear forces command, combining naval, air, and rocket forces under one headquarters with its own operational staff not subordinated to the General Staff of the armed forces, provoked stubborn opposition from the conventional forces. General Kvashnin, chief of the General Staff and a ground forces officer, was the effective leader of this opposition, and as the war in Chechnya resumed in the fall of 1999, Kvashnin's faction was still successfully blocking Sergeev's independent nuclear command.

Such a new organization not only meant that the General Staff would lose its traditional operational management of strategic nuclear forces, but it also reflected a shift in funding priority to favor the nuclear forces at the expense of the conventional forces. That procurement funds were flowing for the new TOPOL-M intercontinental ballistic missile while procurement for conventional forces was virtually nil reflected the allocation realities that Kvashnin and his supporters so strongly opposed. This episode was merely one in a series of such struggles that has blocked systemic reform since 1992. Yet it did have a modest impact, eliminating one branch of service and bringing procurement and command and control into line with the new doctrinal emphasis on nuclear deterrence as compensation for the overall weakness of the Russian military.

## Manpower policy

The Soviet Armed Forces were over 5 million strong in 1985. The breakup of the Soviet Union left the Russian Federation with roughly 2.5 million personnel under arms. The continuing disintegration of the ground forces and cuts in the naval, air, and rocket forces took this level down to 1.5 million by 1995 and, by 1999, the figure was about 1 million. Given the severe problems with draft evasion, the actual level is probably significantly below 1 million.

The key to manpower policy reform is a massive reduction, especially of high-ranking officers, but also of conscripts. Reforming a large force is far more costly and difficult than cutting the size to 100–200,000 and then instituting reforms. The senior military, however, has resisted not only such deep cuts but also radical changes such as an all-volunteer force. A small portion of the enlisted ranks are now filled with so-called contract soldiers, volunteers who sign a contract for a given number of years; but the larger part of the enlisted ranks is still composed of conscripts.

The problems in manpower are difficult to summarize briefly, but they are rooted in two key areas. First, the senior officers are irretrievably socialized in the old Soviet military culture, one that simply is not suited to a modern, high-technology armed forces. World War II produced a new generation of reasonably competent officers, and for a decade or more after the war, the Soviet military thrived on their competence. Time and corruption, however, began to take a toll, and by the 1980s, age, corruption, and stagnation marked most of the general officer ranks and also much of the field grade officer corps.

Second, the conscription system, as designed by the 1967 military service law, produced four cohorts of conscripts on active duty at any one time.

After a few years, the senior cohort began to take charge of life in the barracks and to introduce a system of hazing for the most junior cohort. Lacking a professional NCO corps, the enlisted ranks soon fell under the domination of this hazing system, in which each senior soldier had at least one junior soldier as his slave. Beatings, homosexual rapes, serious injuries, and deaths became notoriously common. The system of selecting a few recruits in each cohort to become NCOs simply could not compete for authority with the hazing system.

The junior officers were caught between the corrupt senior officers and the hazing system among the enlisted soldiers. Most of them hated the hazing system but could not stop it; at the same time, they feared their senior officers and detested their corruption, especially the widespread use of conscripts as slave labor, which generals rented out to construction firms or collective farms or anyone who would pay. To abandon the conscription system, as was frequently proposed during Gorbachev's *perestroika* years, was to take this money-making resource of free labor away from the generals. Thus they strongly resisted such change.

Both of these disorders have remained extremely serious problems for the Russian military. They cannot be cured short of a radical purge of the senior officers, the creation of a professional NCO corps, and a decade or more of time to grow up a new generation of officers in a radically different personnel system.

Such abuse of the ordinary soldier, of course, is not new in either the Imperial Russian Army or the Red Army. Life has never had much value in the eyes of military leaders in Russia. Thus manpower policy reform is up against weighty historical traditions as well as parochial interests in the present senior officer corps. How little has changed was evident in both the wars in Chechnya. Not only were the troops poorly trained and fed, but medical support was often inadequate, and dead soldiers' bodies were left in open fields for their next of kin to visit and retrieve or to be left and dumped into mass graves. That such practices undercut the popularity of the military in the minds of most Russian citizens should not be surprising.

## Military industries

The "burden of Soviet defense" as a percentage of the gross national income was considerably disputed during the Cold War decades, but since the collapse of the Soviet Union, the deluge of evidence on the degree of militarization of the command economy has been overwhelming. Even the highest Western estimates were below the mark. Reform of the Russian economy, of course, depends significantly on closing down most of the old Soviet military industrial sector, but so does military reform. As long as the huge military-industrial sector's lobby has significant influence, it will impede both economic and military reform.

During Gorbachev's last years, the hope for military-industrial reform was so-called military conversion, that is, shifting this sector to civilian production. As Western defense industrial experts have long known, in most cases, conversion simply does not make economic sense. Closing down military firms and building new ones is far more profitable. "Military conversion" in Russia has had a mixed life, mostly unsuccessful, and now more or less ended. Less is known about what has really happened to the military sector than to other parts of the economy, but large parts of its capacity have just been allowed to stand idle.

At the same time, it seems that selected parts of the military industries have been protected and sustained, and by the 1990s, they were showing recovery. No longer holding the priority on the state budget that it enjoyed in the past, it has secured sufficient fiscal support to salvage a part of the old Soviet military industries with their sector management system. Moreover, they have expanded foreign military arms sales over the 1996–2000 period. Procurement by the Russian Defense Ministry, however, has been extremely modest—in the tens of ICBMs and only a few score of conventional weapons such as armored vehicles, tanks, and aircraft.

In sum, one cannot say that the military industrial sector has been reformed. Far from it. The size has dropped dramatically, but the same old system remains, involving a state-owned sector and traditional management techniques. Moreover, Marshal Sergeev's emphasis on strategic nuclear forces has helped the ICBM builders in the military industries, and they have no doubt backed his plans for a separate strategic nuclear forces command. President Putin's promises of greater procurement funds may not materialize as he faces the economic realities for the whole economy, but his rhetoric encourages all those old military industrialists who oppose market reforms for their sector.

## The failure of reform

While great change, mostly decay, has occurred in the Russian military, it has not produced truly systemic reform. Moreover, it is not at all clear that most Russian political leaders want such reform. And incentives for it begin to disappear as Russian policy toward the CIS becomes more assertive. Such a policy virtually precludes genuine military reform in Russia.

## The Military Politics of Kosovo and Chechnya

The first war in Chechnya, because it involved a humiliating defeat for the Russian military, was a possible stimulus for liberal reforms in the view of the Russian human rights leader Sergei Kovalev. He rightly pointed to examples in the nineteenth and early twentieth centuries. In 1999–2000, as the second war raged in Chechnya with Russian forces obliterating the capital city, Grozny, and killing civilians (both Russians and Chechens as well as civilians of other ethnic distinctions) on a scale Kovalev described as "near genocide," he confessed that he was "cruelly mistaken" about the liberalizing impact of the first war. This time he noted the opposite effect, describing how Putin used the war cynically in his struggle to capture the presidency.

The impact on Russian politics, to be sure, extends far beyond the role of the military. Censorship of the media, anti-Chechen hysteria in the population at large, stirred up by bombings of apartment houses in Moscow (which some suspect were organized by the Russian security services), and the surprising consensus among most of the Russian intelligentsia in favor of the genocidal military campaign in Chechnya—all of these things are included. To distinguish analytically the role of the senior military, let us set aside those things and trace the events that began during NATO's war against Serbia over Kosovo in the spring of 1999.

President Yeltsin reportedly asked the Russian security council in late April why NATO was no longer frightened of Russia. If this actually occurred, one can imagine the defense minister and the chief of the General Staff exploiting the occasion to offer Yeltsin a way to make NATO show more regard for Russia. The United States insisted on including Russia in a search for a settlement although Russia clearly had voiced no interest in seeing NATO achieve its aims in Kosovo. The Russian military at once began conspiring with Milosevic, and the result was the swift move of Russian forces from Bosnia through Serbia to the airport in Prishtina in Kosovo—completely surprising Washington and European capitals. The rest of the Russian military's scheme, however, was blocked. Transport aircraft were loaded and ready to fly Russian forces into Serbia, or even Prishtina, but Western diplomatic efforts prompted Hungary, Romania, and Bulgaria to deny overflight rights. Had this not occurred and had the small Russian force at Prishtina airport been reinforced, the Russian military could have essentially seized the northern part of Kosovo as its zone and provided Milosevic with this base within Kosovo. Alternatively, this region could have been detached from NATO's Kosovo and given to Milosevic to administer.

The Russian generals failed to carry through the entire scheme, but what they did win was a place for Russian troops in Kosovo, providing Moscow a lever for trouble-making. It seems fair to suppose that this outcome considerably increased the political influence of the generals in top political circles in Moscow. They had made NATO take note of Russia. Within a month or two, preparations for the war in Chechnya were in progress, and Prime Minister Putin was making highly threatening noises toward Azerbaijan and Georgia. By November, Putin was promising increases in defense spending, and soon the war was ablaze, not only causing vast human atrocities in Chechnya but also frightening the leaders of Georgia and Azerbaijan.

Other actions show that Putin seemed to have a larger agenda, aimed at resubordinating several of the CIS countries to Moscow. The Moldovan Foreign Ministry issued statements in January expressing concern over Russia's evasion of its commitment to withdraw its troops from the Transdniester by 2002. Russia began tightening up its hold on the CIS air defense system. It formalized its free use of a military base in Armenia in March. In Central Asia, as Uzbekistan began aggressive action against Islamic groups operating from Kyrgyzstan into Uzbekistan, the Kyrgyz government turned to the Russian military for help. Ever since the breakup of the Soviet Union, of course, the Russian military has been ensconced in Tajikistan, participating at times in its civil war. As Turkmenistan has realized that it will not soon have pipelines for exporting gas that do not go through Russian territory, it has become more deferential to Moscow. Even Uzbekistan, the Central Asian regime with the most potential for holding on to its independence, as it gets into trouble with Islamic political groups is likely to fall back on Moscow at some point.

With the long-standing offer from Belarus for a union with Russia, with Armenia trapped into dependence on Russia for support against Azerbaijan and Turkey, with the Russian military ensconced in the Abkhazian province of Georgia, and with an intimidating victory over the Chechens, Moscow now has real prospects for forcing these states into closer and formal political obedience to Russia. The military link in these connections, of course, is crucial, not least because the wars in Kosovo and Chechnya seemed to have given this development surprisingly strong momentum.

## The Prospects

It is too early to forecast a clear outcome to this tendency toward Russian reimperialization of large parts of the former Soviet Union and to the setback for liberal political developments in Russia proper. Although it looked likely to occur in the mid-1990s, it did not. With Yeltsin's departure from power, however, and in light of the manipulative pattern Putin has used to take power, the situation in 2000 is considerably different from 1994–96. Perhaps the biggest change is that hopes both in Russia and in the West for a truly liberal political development in Russia have declined. And the broad public sense of disillusionment and resentment is stronger. What the second war in Chechnya has shown is how easily both the public and the intelligentsia can be turned against liberal norms for dealing with citizens of the federation, how easily strong public support for "near genocide" is whipped up.

If this political trend continues, the Russian military is likely to retain much of its more traditional place as near synonymous with the state. The budgetary implications are not good for the economy, and they are downright perverse for market reforms. The old Soviet statist economy could allocate to the military quite arbitrarily. In the new Russia, military funding has been opposed by competitive lobbies in the parliament, especially the collective farm bureaucracy and proponents of social welfare, but that changed somewhat during 1999–2000 as the military budget received significant increases.

Although the Russian military seems headed back to a more traditional place in the political system, we cannot be sure. But we can be sure that if it goes back, the resulting political and economic system will be weak and ineffective. It may remain stable for decades, but it cannot yield the kind of scientific and technology base required for a truly modern military or a vibrant economy. The choices are stark: *either* maintenance of tradition combined with economic and political stagnation, *or* a political, military, and economic transformation and the promise of prosperity.

The sharpness of this dilemma today is new in Russian and Soviet history. Russia managed to achieve considerable modernization of its economy and military in the nineteenth century without abandoning empire and the dominant role of its military. Under the Bolsheviks, the Russian Empire once again experienced a distorted kind of rapid modernization that greatly enhanced its military power but with the most anti-liberal regime in history. Today it is difficult to see how a resurgence of more modern Russian military power can occur without a truly liberal economic transformation, which will inevitably bring a political transformation. Putin and his allies can postpone liberal reform in Russia, but that will also postpone the economic modernization essential for modern military and political power. Russia can resist Westernization, but the price is now permanent Third World status.

## Further Research

As the archives open and the Russian economy becomes more transparent, detailed studies of the Soviet economy and industry need to be used to make comparisons with what has occurred since 1989.

The downsizing of the armed forces due to all causes needs study and merits comparison with the losses of empire in France, Britain, and the United States after 1945, and with the older empires after 1917–19. It also would be instructive to compare the current era of military change with those of 1919–25 and the 1950s and 1960s.

Recruiting and conscription, the role and place of NCOs in the Army and in society, and of the officer corps before, during, and after retirement all merit attention.

## Sources and Further Reading

Cooper, Julian. "The future role of the Russian defence industry," in *Security Dilemmas in Russia and Eurasia,* eds. Roy Allison and Christopher Bluth. London: The Royal Institute of International Affairs, 1998, pp. 94–120.

Dick, Charles. "The Military Doctrine of the Russian Federation." *The Journal of Slavic Military Studies* 7 (No. 3, 1994): 481–506.

Downing, Brian M. *The Military Revolution and Political Change: Origins of Democracy and Autocracy in Early Modern Europe.* Princeton, NJ: Princeton University Press, 1992.

FitzGerald, Mary C. "Russia's New Military Doctrine." The RUSI Journal, October 1992, pp. 40–49.

Florinsky, Michael. *Russia: An Interpretation,* Vol. I. New York: Macmillan, 1953.

Gaddy, Clifford G. *The Price of the Past: Russia's Struggle with the Legacy of a Militarized Economy.* Washington, DC: The Brookings Institution, 1996.

Huntington, Samuel P. *The Soldier and the State.* Cambridge, MA: Harvard University Press, 1957.

Jones, Ellen and James H. Brusstar. "Moscow's Emerging Security Decisionmaking System." *The Journal of Slavic Military Studies* 6 (No. 3, September 1993): 345–74.

Kaiser, Robert G. and David Hoffman. "Russia Had Bigger Plan in Kosovo; U.S. Thwarted a Larger, Secret Troop Deployment." *The Washington Post,* June 25, 1999, p. A01.

Kovalev, Sergei. "Putin's War." *The New York Review of Books,* February 10, 2000.

Kovalev, Sergei. "Russia After Chechnya." *The New York Review of Books,* July 17, 1997.

Malia, Martin. *Russia Under Western Eyes.* Cambridge, MA: Harvard University Press, 1999.

Moore, Barrington, Jr. *The Social Origins of Dictatorship and Democracy.* Boston: Beacon Press, 1966.

Odom, William E. *The Collapse of the Soviet Military.* New Haven: Yale University Press, 1998.

Odom, William E. and Robert Dujarric. *Commonwealth or Empire? Russia, Central Asia, and the Transcaucasus.* Indianapolis, IN: Hudson Institute, 1995.

Ostrowski, Donald. *Muscovy and the Mongols: Cross-cultural Influences on the Steppe Frontier, 1304–1589.* New York: Cambridge University Press, 1999.

Owen, Thomas C. *The Corporation Under Russian Law 1800–1917: A Study in Tsarist Economic Policy.* New York: Cambridge University Press, 1991.

Selznick, Philip. *The Organizational Weapon: A Study of Bolshevik Strategy and Tactics.* Glencoe, IL: The Free Press, 1960.

Shaposhnikov, Yevgenii. *Vybor,* 2d rev. and expanded ed. Moscow: Nezavisimoe izdatel'stvo PIK, 1995.

Shlapentokh, Vladimir. "The Strange Transfer of Power in Russia: The Unanswered Questions." Unpublished Manuscript, March 2000. It was written for the Office of Net Assessments, Office of the Secretary of Defense, the Pentagon.

Tilly, Charles. *Coercion, Capital, and European States, AD 990–1992.* Oxford, UK: Blackwell, 1992.

*Voennaya mysl,* May 1992 and November 1993. Both issues of the journal of the General Staff are entirely devoted to drafts and discussions of a military doctrine for the Russian Federation.

Yeltsin, Boris N. *The Struggle for Russia.* New York: Random House, 1994.

# INDEX

Printed in Great Britain
by Amazon